THE ART OF LOVE

THE ART OF LOVE

BIMILLENNIAL ESSAYS ON OVID'S ARS AMATORIA AND REMEDIA AMORIS

Edited by

ROY GIBSON, STEVEN GREEN AND
ALISON SHARROCK

OXFORD
UNIVERSITY PRESS

OXFORD
UNIVERSITY PRESS

Great Clarendon Street, Oxford ox2 6DP
Oxford University Press is a department of the University of Oxford.
It furthers the University's objective of excellence in research, scholarship,
and education by publishing worldwide in

Oxford New York

Auckland Cape Town Dar es Salaam Hong Kong Karachi
Kuala Lumpur Madrid Melbourne Mexico City Nairobi
New Delhi Shanghai Taipei Toronto

With offices in

Argentina Austria Brazil Chile Czech Republic France Greece
Guatemala Hungary Italy Japan Poland Portugal Singapore
South Korea Switzerland Thailand Turkey Ukraine Vietnam

Oxford is a registered trade mark of Oxford University Press
in the UK and in certain other countries

Published in the United States
by Oxford University Press Inc., New York

© Oxford University Press 2006

The moral rights of the authors have been asserted
Database right Oxford University Press (maker)

First published 2006

All rights reserved. No part of this publication may be reproduced,
stored in a retrieval system, or transmitted, in any form or by any means,
without the prior permission in writing of Oxford University Press,
or as expressly permitted by law, or under terms agreed with the appropriate
reprographics rights organization. Enquiries concerning reproduction
outside the scope of the above should be sent to the Rights Department,
Oxford University Press, at the address above

You must not circulate this book in any other binding or cover
and you must impose the same condition on any acquirer

British Library Cataloguing in Publication Data
Data available

Library of Congress Cataloging in Publication Data
Data available

Typeset by SPI Publisher Services, Pondicherry, India
Printed in Great Britain
on acid-free paper by
Biddles Ltd., King's Lynn, Norfolk

ISBN 0–19–927777–X   978–0–19–927777–3

Preface

Sets of rules and precepts on love and relationships retain the capacity to offend. An American bestseller of the 1990s by Ellen Fein and Sherrie Schneider—*The Rules: Time-Tested Secrets for Capturing the Heart of Mr Right*—dedicated to marrying off its female readers to suitable prospects, might appear to have little obvious connection with the poem that Augustus found guilty of teaching 'foul adultery' (*Tr.* 2. 212). But, in *Hypocrisy and the Politics of Politeness: Manners and Morals from Locke to Austen*, Jenny Davidson devotes a coda ('Politeness and its Costs') to taking issue with *The Rules* on grounds that may seem familiar to readers of Ovid's *Ars Amatoria*:[1]

The advice for women who want husbands that is given in the notorious bestseller *The Rules* is relentlessly pragmatic.... The book puts forward a practical thesis about the payoffs of delayed gratification and self-restraint in the form of 'simple working sets of behaviors and reactions': concealing one's feelings and withholding sex with the goal of receiving a marriage proposal.... The pragmatism of Fein and Schneider's language, and its relentless orientation towards a single goal, suggests a patently self-interested brand of self-control whose extension into other social arenas would be quite sinister.

We can perhaps grasp or relive something of the shock of the *Ars Amatoria* by taking on board the open hostility expressed here towards the very notion of pragmatic advice on 'love', learned behaviours, and concealment of feelings, and the evident anxiety expressed about the leakage of the principles of *The Rules* into cognate areas. But self-interest in matters of love is not all that worries Davidson. She goes on to argue that 'The authors of *The Rules* articulate many of our culture's most disturbing assumptions about women... that women are more manipulative and cynical than men, that they are deeply hypocritical, indeed that all women's relationships with men are colored by levels of self-interest and

---

[1] J. Davidson, *Hypocrisy and the Politics of Politeness: Manners and Morals from Locke to Austen* (Cambridge, 2004), 176–7.

opportunism that are matched only by those of the men who hope to trade guarantees of financial support for the promise of sex.'[2] Again, readers of the *Ars* and *Remedia* will find much that is familiar here, although they may also be struck by the way in which Ovid undermines this common and ancient calumny against women, by presenting his aspiring male lover as precisely the kind of self-interested, manipulative cynic who is well matched by his tricksy partner—as perhaps Davidson hints also in her (Ovidian) sting-in-the-tail.

Do a modern self-help manual and a scholarly work on the eighteenth century novel have anything to do with an ancient didactic poem? Is 'love' universal or culturally specific? Why—or rather how—do we read Ovid's *Ars Amatoria* and *Remedia Amoris* in the 21st century? What sort of poems are they?

It was to address these and other questions that a conference was held in September 2002, funded by the British Academy and the University of Manchester, which provided the genesis for this volume of essays. Magic numbers gave an excuse for a party: the purpose of the conference was to celebrate the bimillennium of Ovid's erotodidactic cycle of poems, traditionally assumed to have been brought to completion around AD 2. The aim of the present volume, which offers a mixture of revised papers from the conference and other specially commissioned pieces, is to galvanize current—and to stimulate new—research on the *Ars Amatoria* and *Remedia Amoris*.

It is conventional in a preface to a book on Ovid to claim that one's particular bit of Ovid has been uniquely neglected in recent decades, and to look mournfully towards a past golden age (often many hundreds of years ago) when it allegedly enjoyed a rather different status amongst readers of the poet. We are unable to claim any overwhelming contemporary neglect (or truly convincing past golden age) for these poems. On the other hand, as Steve Green points out in the introductory chapter, the rate of production of scholarship on the *Ars* and *Remedia* remains rather slow, at least in the Anglophone world. If our volume acts in any way as a stimulant to new research, it is our hope that critics will be encouraged to look at all four books of Ovid's erotodidactic cycle. Historically—again at least in the Anglophone world—critics have tended to concentrate on the first book of the *Ars*

---

[2] Davidson, op. cit., 177.

Amatoria. This is in part a testament to the excellence of Adrian Hollis's Oxford commentary on that book, perhaps testimony also to the perceived difficulty of tackling the other books of the *Ars* without a modern commentary or study. But it is also symptomatic of a reading practice in approaches to Ovid that shies away from his strategies of repetition, and conversely latches on to any available pegs of contemporary reference.

Three of the contributors to the current volume have provided the means for extending studies of the work beyond the first book of the *Ars*. Alison Sharrock's 1994 monograph on the second book of the poem was joined in 1997 by Markus Janka's detailed commentary on the same book. Roy Gibson's commentary on the third book of the *Ars* appeared just six months after the Manchester conference, in early 2003. Together these works contribute to 'joining the dots' between *Ars* 1 and the *Remedia*—the latter a work which possesses its own more or less independent critical tradition, having attracted five commentaries in just three decades (Geisler 1969, Henderson 1979, Lucke 1982, Lazzarini 1986, Pinotti 1988). Many of the contributions to the present volume take advantage of this new state of affairs, and roam freely across the whole of the *Ars* and *Remedia* or adopt a holistic perspective on the books of this cycle.

The contributors between them also offer a series of perspectives on the issues that have dominated scholarship on the *Ars* in recent decades. Questions of genre, intertextuality, narratology, and reception bulk large, as inevitably do Augustus and the historical and social contexts for the poem. One question that continues to fascinate is that of the nature of 'love' in the *Ars* and *Remedia*: are the poems predicated on behaviouralism or emotionalism? Can Ovid actually teach us anything, say anything to us about the way we relate as lovers? As readers? Following Steve Green's introductory survey of recent scholarship on the *Ars* and *Remedia* and some sample issues thrown up by this literature, we have arranged the chapters into four categories: Poetics, Erotics, Politics, and Reception. These divisions are somewhat artificial—some chapters straddle several categories—but nevertheless they provide a critically convenient place to start, by alluding to the main areas that have been at issue in Ovidian erotodidactic scholarship.

One final aim of the present volume (and its original conference) is to bring together the important cultural or national traditions—German, Italian, Anglophone (British, Irish, and American)—of scholarship on the *Ars* and *Remedia* that have so far existed largely in isolation. In particular, it is our aim to introduce to an Anglophone readership the Italian tradition of scholarship on the *Ars*, which perhaps has not so far received its proper critical due in the English-speaking world. That Italian tradition is represented in this volume by Alessandro Barchiesi, Sergio Casali, Mario Labate, and Gianpiero Rosati. Whether or not the love preached by Ovid is specific to a particular culture, our responses to its vehicle are undoubtedly enhanced by the sharing, and the difference, of these intellectual traditions.

The editors would like to thank Jim McKeown and Stephen Hinds, both of whom helped to make the original conference in Manchester a success, and Roberto Chiappiniello for translating the papers of Mario Labate and Gianpiero Rosati. The support of the British Academy and the University of Manchester is gratefully acknowledged. Finally, we would like to offer sincere thanks to Hilary O'Shea and all those at OUP who worked with our manuscript, especially Sylvie Jaffrey, Catherine Macduff, Dorothy McCarthy, Kathleen McLaughlin, and Jenny Wagstaffe.

R.K.G.
S.J.G.
A.R.S.

Manchester
September 2006

Contents

List of Contributors   xi

1. Lessons in Love: Fifty Years of Scholarship on the *Ars Amatoria* and *Remedia Amoris*   1
   Steven J. Green

PART I: POETICS

2. Love in Parentheses: Digression and Narrative Hierarchy in Ovid's Erotodidactic Poems   23
   Alison Sharrock
3. Staging the Reader Response: Ovid and His 'Contemporary Audience' in *Ars* and *Remedia*   40
   Niklas Holzberg
4. *Vixisset Phyllis, si me foret usa magistro*: Erotodidaxis and Intertextuality   54
   Duncan F. Kennedy

PART II: EROTICS

5. In Ovid with Bed (*Ars* 2 and 3)   77
   John Henderson
6. Women on Top: Livia and Andromache   96
   Alessandro Barchiesi
7. Ovid, Augustus, and the Politics of Moderation in *Ars Amatoria* 3   121
   Roy K. Gibson
8. The Art of *Remedia Amoris*: Unlearning to Love?   143
   Gianpiero Rosati
9. *Lethaeus Amor*: The Art of Forgetting   166
   Philip Hardie

PART III: POLITICS

10. Erotic Aetiology: Romulus, Augustus, and the Rape of the Sabine Women — 193
    Mario Labate
11. The Art of Making Oneself Hated: Rethinking (Anti-)Augustanism in Ovid's *Ars Amatoria* — 216
    Sergio Casali
12. *Ars Amatoria Romana*: Ovid on Love as a Cultural Construct — 235
    Katharina Volk
13. Ovid's Evolution — 252
    Molly Myerowitz Levine

PART IV: RECEPTION

14. *Paelignus, puto, dixerat poeta* (Mart. 2. 41. 2): Martial's Intertextual Dialogue with Ovid's Erotodidactic Poems — 279
    Markus Janka
15. Sex Education: Ovidian Erotodidactic in the Classroom — 298
    Ralph Hexter
16. Ovid in Defeat? On the reception of Ovid's *Ars Amatoria* and *Remedia Amoris* — 318
    Genevieve Liveley

Appendix: Timeline (Genevieve Liveley) — 338
References — 341
Indexes — 361

List of Contributors

ALESSANDRO BARCHIESI is Professor of Latin Literature at the University of Siena at Arezzo.

SERGIO CASALI is Associate Professor of Latin Literature at the University of Rome 'Tor Vergata'.

ROY GIBSON is Professor of Latin at the University of Manchester.

STEVEN GREEN is Lecturer in Classics at the University of Leeds.

PHILIP HARDIE Formerly Corpus Christi Professor of the Latin Language and Literature in the University of Oxford, is a Senior Research Fellow at Trinity College, Cambridge.

JOHN HENDERSON is Professor of Classics, University of Cambridge and Fellow of King's College.

RALPH HEXTER is Professor of Classics and Comparative Literature and President at Hampshire College in Amherst, Massachusetts.

MARKUS JANKA is *Privatdozent* of Classics at the University of Regensburg.

DUNCAN KENNEDY is Professor of Latin Literature and the Theory of Criticism at the University of Bristol.

MARIO LABATE is Professor of Latin Literature at the University of Florence.

MOLLY MYEROWITZ LEVINE is Professor of Classics at Howard University.

GENEVIEVE LIVELEY is Lecturer in Classics at the University of Bristol.

NIKLAS HOLZBERG is Professor of Classics at the University of Munich.

GIANPIERO ROSATI is Professor of Latin Literature at the University of Udine.

ALISON SHARROCK is Professor of Classics at the University of Manchester.

KATHARINA VOLK is Assistant Professor of Classics at Columbia University.

1

Lessons in Love: Fifty Years of Scholarship on the *Ars Amatoria* and *Remedia Amoris*

Steven J. Green

It is a critical topos to acknowledge that Ovid has enjoyed a resurgence of scholarly interest in the past twenty-five years. Among the modes of Ovidian scholarship receiving particular attention or development in this period have been the dynamics of genre, and Ovid's own acute generic self-consciousness; the complex intertextual dialogues created between Ovid and other writers, and indeed between Ovid's own works; Ovid's often subtle negotiation with the sociopolitical Augustan context in which he is writing; and feminist readings of Ovid's text. Though these developments are evidently fruitful for the study of all Ovid's poetry, it is quite noticeable that they have so far yielded particular benefits for the understanding and appreciation of *Heroides*, *Fasti*, and, above all, *Metamorphoses*.[1] By contrast, *Ars Amatoria* and *Remedia Amoris* have suffered relative neglect, especially by Anglophone scholars: at the current rate, a new monograph on the *Ars* can be expected to appear only once every ten years.[2]

---

[1] For the dominance of *Metamorphoses* and *Fasti* in recent Ovidian scholarship, see the review article of Myers (1999), and the strong bias towards the *Metamorphoses* in the *Aetas Ovidiana* conference held in Dublin in 2002.

[2] Before Gibson's (2003a) extensive commentary on *Ars* 3, the last major publications in English were Sharrock (1994a) and Myerowitz (1985). German scholarship has been slightly more active during this time period: Steudel (1992); Janka (1997); and Wildberger (1998). Compare this with the bibliography for *Metamorphoses* and *Fasti*, which enjoys new books on an almost yearly basis.

The present volume represents the first collection of essays devoted exclusively to Ovid's erotodidactic corpus to appear in English.[3] In order to set its contributions in context, the following pages offer a brief review—illustrative rather than comprehensive—of scholarship on *Ars Amatoria* and *Remedia* in the last fifty years, adopting a thematic and (broadly) chronological approach.[4]

1. DATING AND STRUCTURE

Despite our apparent familiarity with the details of Ovid's career, no supposed fact from the great Augustan trickster can be taken at face value without questions of its poetic purpose. Two different theories on the dating of Ovid's erotodidactic poems have been advanced over the past fifty years. It is a curious fact that, in outlining the structure for *Ars* (1. 35–40), Ovid makes no reference to his intention to instruct women: this intention is only revealed in the final (jolting) couplet of *Ars* 2 (745–6). Many readers have gone along with the poem's façade, and supposed that Ovid's poetic production occurred in two stages: *Ars* 1 and 2 were conceived together; these were then followed some years later, either separately or as part of a second edition of all the books, by *Ars* 3 and *Remedia*. All this occurred, it is

---

[3] A small collection of largely German papers on *Ars Amatoria* and *Remedia Amoris* appeared over thirty years ago edited by Zinn (1970). It is somewhat ironic that its most influential paper—by Little (in Zinn (1970: 64–105))—worked mainly to revitalize the issue of genre in subsequent scholarship on *Metamorphoses* and *Fasti*.

[4] For a survey of scholarship on *Ars* in the 1990s, see also Ariemma (2001). I do not deal below with contributions to the modern textual criticism of the poems. I merely point out here the immense boost that study of *Ars* and *Remedia* received with the publication in 1961 of Kenney's authoritative Oxford Latin Text. A second edition appeared in 1994 (corrected in 1995), incorporating the readings of one manuscript—the *Hamiltonensis*—which had until 1965 been wrongly classified as a fourteenth- rather than eleventh-century production (see, briefly, Gibson (2003*a*: 43–5)). Other major editions of the poems to appear in recent decades include those by Lenz (1969) and Ramírez de Verger (2003). As for commentaries on *Ars*, there are two single-volume editions on all three books, by Brandt (1902) (still useful) and Pianezzola, Baldo, and Cristante (1991). There are now also substantial commentaries on each of the books of the erotodidactic corpus: Hollis (1977) for *Ars* 1; Janka (1997) for *Ars* 2; Gibson (2003*a*) for *Ars* 3; and Henderson (1979), Lucke (1982) and Pinotti (1988) for *Remedia*.

generally agreed, between the years 2 BC and AD 2.[5] However, some recent scholarship has rightly advised against too literal a view of Ovid's (possibly tactical) silence in the poem's preface. For example, Sharrock (1994*a*: 18–20) suggests that Ovid early on obscures any hint of his coming instruction to women, so as to keep his male addressees on side at the beginning of the poem; the poet's *volte-face* is revealed to them only at the last possible moment.[6] Consequently, a consensus is growing that *Ars* 1–3 and *Remedia* were conceived as a whole (playfully mirroring the four-book structure of Vergil's didactic poem)—a view apparently strengthened by the consistent verbal and thematic links between the four books.[7]

The intrigue surrounding the last two verses of *Ars* 2 receives fresh examination in this volume in the contrasting readings of John Henderson and Niklas Holzberg. While Henderson argues that the 'surprise' of a third book has, in fact, been subtly telegraphed by Ovid's assertions in *Ars* 1–2 of the need for parity between the sexes and for the male to be vanquished, Holzberg maintains that the last couplet of *Ars* 2 is indeed a surprise, but one in keeping with Ovid's didactic strategies and the staging of reader response found elsewhere in Ovid and other poets.

2. GENRE AND LITERARY INFLUENCE

Critical attention has long been centred on the innovative 'crossing' of genres at work in Ovid's erotodidactic poems and on the range of literary influences that are visible in the text. A great deal of work has

[5] For the history of the debate, see now Watson (2002: 141), Gibson (2003*a*: 37–9). There have been some notable cases put forward for a radically different dating of Ovid's output. Syme (1978: 13–20) argues that the first edition of *Ars* may go as far back as 9 BC. Murgia (1986) argues on stylistic grounds for a date for *Ars* 3 of c.AD 8, i.e. subsequent to the composition of the first seven books of *Metamorphoses*; for criticism of Murgia's methodology, however, see Gibson (2003*a*: 39–43).

[6] See also Holzberg (1997: 111–12) (= (2002*c*: 103)), who, noting Ovid's assumption that both men and women will be readers of *Ars* 1 and 2, reads the 'silence' of Book 1 as a joke.

[7] For verbal and thematic links between *Ars* and *Remedia*, and the coherence of the four-book structure, see especially Küppers (1981: 2530–41); Wildberger (1998: 343–7).

been done on highlighting the poems' didactic qualities, by means both of recognized features of the didactic genre and of pointed (if ironic) allusion to generic predecessors, but it has been equally clear that there is nothing straightforward about the generic status of the poems.

Kenney (1958) noted the ways in which the poems observe generic 'norms' in their systematic use of introductory and transitional formulae typical of serious didactic; Gibson (1997) studied imperatival expressions in the *Ars* in the context of conventional usage of such expressions by other instructional texts in both verse and prose; Durling (1958) drew attention to the (colourful) poetic persona of the didactic teacher; and many have commented on Ovid's varied use of mythological digressions and *exempla*, a key component of ancient didactic.[8] Fresh observations on the vitality and innovation of Ovid's didactic project have been made recently by Volk (2002: 157–95), who highlighted Ovid's novel status as practitioner of the art he teaches—he is lover as well as teacher and poet—and his conscious strategy of forging 'simultaneity' between the progress of the poems and the stages of his teaching. The poems also establish affiliation to didactic poetry by pointed allusion to poems in the genre, although the sentiments of Ovid's predecessors are often recast to serve the ironic and incongruous function of 'proving' a point in the philosophy of love. Leach (1964) illustrated Ovid's debt to Vergil's *Georgics*; Sommariva (1980) and Shulman (1981) shed light on Ovid's use of Lucretius; and Hollis (1973: 89–93) and especially Steudel (1992) produced evidence of much wider and complex appropriation of generic predecessors both Greek and Roman.

But the fact that Ovid has chosen the elegiac metre (novel in extant didactic) for these poems highlights a generic mixing with love elegy, which, as Küppers (1981: 2509–30) has demonstrated, is reinforced by the interplay with the erotodidactic tradition carried by characters such as Priapus and the *lena* from Roman love elegy. By a brilliant sleight of hand, which slips deceptively between apparent autobiography and literary device, Ovid regularly draws on his amatory

---

[8] For the mythological digressions, see Section 6 below. For the varied functions of shorter, mythological *exempla*, see Watson (1983); Davisson (1996); Jones (1997: 50–9).

'experiences' from the *Amores*, adapting these emotionally turbulent encounters to the more serious purpose of rational directives to students.[9]

Other important, though perhaps less obvious influences have also been analysed. Labate (1984: 121–74) emphasized the conceptual similarities between Ovid's instructions and socio-philosophical treatises such as Cicero's *De Officiis*.[10] Gibson (2003a: 13–19), drawing on the work of earlier critics, attempted to trace the history of erotodidaxis back to early Socratic traditions and, in focusing on Book 3, detected the influences of the 'anti-cosmetic tradition' (2003a: 21–5). The richness of the various sophisticated traditions behind Ovid's love teaching, thus far detected, suggests that further work in this area may produce rewards.

3. THE SEARCH FOR THE SERIOUS MESSAGE IN *ARS*

With the affiliation of *Ars* to (and parody of) the didactic genre acknowledged and documented, scholars started to question whether such parody, along with other forms of Ovidian humour, were a purely literary game—as had been implicitly assumed previously—or a means of saying something more serious.[11] From the 1970s onwards, scholarship on the poem took on a sterner aspect, as critics set out to find a 'serious' or more deeply 'controversial' message behind the laughter: no longer assumed to be simply a repository of splendid jokes, the poems began to be probed for implicit commentary on Roman love and Augustan politics.

Amor, Cultus, and Ovidian Sincerity

The *Ars* claims to offer a cultural service to its readers: it will teach us how to love. But critics have rightly asked what exactly 'love' (*amor*) is

---

[9] See e.g. Dalzell (1996: 138–46). Sharrock (2002) alludes to the way in which Ovid refuses to let us know how 'seriously' to take his poetic and erotic personae.
[10] See Section 3 below.
[11] The issue is not unconnected with wider debates on the seriousness of messages in didactic poetry, on which see Heath (1985).

in the poem, in what sense it is teachable, and ultimately, whether there is any sense in which Ovid might be acting sincerely and seriously in his erotic advice. Fyler (1971) articulated what everyone has always known—that there is a serious problem in Ovid's love teaching, the inherent paradox of controlling the uncontrollable. He argued that *amor* is an irrational passion, and that the poet's attempt to bring it under a rational framework works only by trivializing the passion and reducing it to the level of an emotionless stratagem. On a more general level, he argued that *Ars*, therefore, could be seen as a serious anti-classical treatment of art and experience, in that it offered 'a sceptical examination of the limitations of genre as an ordering principle' (1971: 196). If it had become impossible for Ovid to be serious about love, then he could at least be serious about art.

A more optimistic view of Ovid's cultural aims in *Ars* was advanced a few years later by Solodow (1977). Solodow argued that, by comparing the life of the lover to that of the soldier, farmer, orator, and philosopher, Ovid seeks to raise the status of the lover and the (love-)poet to the plane of more traditionally respectable 'career paths': Ovid simultaneously plays with the didactic tradition and seeks to ennoble the lover, to attain dignity and authority for both himself and his subject. By means of his mock-solemn tone, which can be taken either as a joke or serious comment, Ovid allows us to entertain the notion of the lover as a 'cultural ideal'. The lover is presented first and foremost as a deceiver—of others and indeed himself—in love, the game of illusions. This deception is seen as a form of art, and the lover consequently as an artist: both the lover and the poet himself are thus included within this cultural ideal. Along the same lines, but with a more specific focus, Stroh (1979a) demonstrated the ways in which Ovid equates the skills of the lover and the orator: both types of individual must be adept at the art of disguise (*dissimulatio*) and simulation (*simulatio*). The 'lover', in such analyses, has become the agent of behaviour, rather than the subject of emotions.[12]

Solodow's emphasis on a potentially serious cultural message in *Ars* anticipated the emphases of two important monographs on the

---

[12] This commonly felt 'essential paradox' is played out in many different ways by different critics, including in this volume. See Rosati on 'Love 1' and 'Love 2'.

poems in the mid-1980s. Labate (1984) argued that the *Ars* rejects earlier elegy's straightforward opposition between Roman civil life and the life of love, and instead sets up love as a serious ethical concern by emphasizing the connections between the relationships of lovers and other Roman social models—in particular, the social bonds between friends, between the *kolax* or flatterer and his patron, and between slave and master. In a central chapter (1984: 121–74), Labate worked through Ovid's adaptation of Cicero's *De Officiis*. Cicero had emphasized the positive personal ethics by which one might earn respect from peers, establish harmonious personal relationships, and, ultimately, contribute to the smooth running of society: importance was placed on mutual gain through reciprocity, personal *decorum*, the arts of persuasion, and the avoidance of excess. Ovid, seeing love as a natural medium for the displaying of 'erotic' social virtues, likewise encourages his students to observe the rules of reciprocity in the giving of gifts, to exercise *decorum* in both their looks and behaviour, and to be attentive to the needs of their beloved and develop the arts of persuasion; acting in this way will win the favour of the beloved and ensure the smooth running of an amorous relationship.

Just one year later, on the other side of the Atlantic, another important, yet quite different, cultural assessment of the poem was advanced by Myerowitz (1985). Whereas Labate had been working within the traditions of Italian and German philology, Myerowitz came to the poem from an American tradition of sociological and cultural approaches to text. Most significantly, she argued that Ovid makes a clear (and potentially serious) distinction in the poem between instinctual love and the culturally determined manner in which this instinctual love is played out: Ovid stresses the way in which *cultus* ('culture', 'refinement') has the power to convert wild and instinctual love (*amor*/*eros*) into an elaborate and dynamic cultural game played by both parties: a 'conventionalised seduction'. The playing of this game is revealed as an art form, and the successful lover is in every sense an artist: both must apply control (*ars*) to a natural energy (be it *eros* and the woman (lover) or *ingenium* (artist)).[13]

[13] Attempts, subsequent to Labate and Myerowitz, to discover a cultural or otherwise 'serious' message behind the poem include Kennedy (1993: 64–82), who re-emphasized the culturally constructed nature of Ovid's love experiences and love

In the present volume, both Katharina Volk and Molly Myerowitz-Levine reassert a (serious) sociological significance to the *Ars*, in that they both ask what Ovid's comments on 'the mating game' have to say about love as a social phenomenon. Volk, concentrating on the rhetoric of the *praeceptor*, argues that lovemaking is presented specifically as a cultural construct, in that the poem's instructions are consciously directed towards a specific audience, namely certain sectors of Roman society, at a (broadly) specific time, namely contemporary Augustan Rome. Myerowitz-Levine, on the other hand, takes her cue from some strands of modern evolutionary science, which argue against a straightforward opposition between Nature and Culture in favour of a system of complex interaction between the two: 'human nature manifests itself on a field of reciprocity between Nature (universal) and Nurture (culturally specific...)' (Ch. 13 below). The process of sexual selection—in other words, 'the mating game', the subject of Ovid's poem—operates at the intersection between nature (physical instinct) and culture (the specific strategies adopted to achieve sexual fulfilment). Myerowitz-Levine argues that, consistent with this philosophy, Ovid shows an awareness of not only the culturally specific aspects of lovemaking, but also those aspects that are universal and paralleled in the natural world. It is suggested, therefore, that the overall tenor of the poem is one closer to the tenets of modern evolutionary science than to cultural specificity. The kind of 'love' taught and reflected in the *Ars Amatoria* has, on this reading, fundamental similarities with the erotic behaviours and feelings of the human animal in any age and place, whereas in Volk's reading it is specific to Ovid's Rome.

Augustan Politics

It is probably fair to say that before the 1970s the potential antagonism between the poem's erotic content and Augustan discourse had been acknowledged but not scrutinized in detail: any politically

---

teaching in *Amores* and *Ars*, and Wildberger (1998), who argued that Ovid teaches a serious lesson in how to enjoy an 'elegiac' love affair without suffering the typical elegiac pitfalls. Broadly speaking, subsequent critics have tended to respond to *either* Labate *or* Myerowitz, but rarely to both. Both, however, appear in the present volume.

controversial aspects to the poem were, on one view, outweighed by the overwhelmingly harmless and 'apolitical' atmosphere of the burlesque.[14]

Holleman (1971) offered a serious and detailed analysis of some of the political implications of *Ars*. In particular, he demonstrated how Ovid champions romantic love by using Augustus' own discourse against him: so, for example, Roman lovemaking is viewed as a consequence of both Augustus' much-vaunted *otium* and the subversive example set years ago by Romulus, a king with close associations with the emperor. In spite of this, the political force of the poem continued to be downplayed in the 1970s.[15] Nevertheless, Holleman's broad approach eventually enjoyed serious, if critical, engagement from Labate (1984: 48–64). Labate argued that, in the *Ars*, there is no clash between the worlds of love and Augustan civil life, but rather the two are harmoniously combined as different sides of the same reality: solemn public joy could now be linked, without irony, to frivolous private joy (as in, for example, the celebration at the *naumachia* at *Ars* 1. 171–6). Clear models for this innovation, Labate (1984: 78–89) suggested, could be found in Hellenistic poetry, where the combination of the mundane (crowds of people, noise) and the public (opulence of public buildings) emphasizes the truly cosmopolitan nature of a city in which all classes of people can prosper. Moreover, the lovers' sharing of space and time with Augustan civil life is 'sanctioned' by the conduct of Romulus against the Sabine women: from that point on, public ceremony and love became intertwined.

The easy combination of unlike attitudes has not suited all readers, however. Myerowitz (1985) argued that Ovid refuses to marry the two Augustan ideals of pride in the present and respect for the past;

---

[14] Wilkinson (1955: 133) speaks of the 'irreverent mind of the poet'; Kenney (1958: 208) labels the poem 'an immoral and subversive work' and suggests that it might foster adultery, but offers no development of these remarks. There is some evidence here, perhaps, of an older critical approach which tended to the opinion that texts could only really have political force if they specifically referred to formal political institutions and their personnel; see Kennedy (1993: 34–9).

[15] Hollis (1973: 86) shies away from the political implications of the poem—'the general atmosphere of the *Ars* was unhelpful to Augustus' policy of moral reform'—emphasizing instead an atmosphere of 'sharpness and detached, ironical humour' (1973: 113). Compare also Barsby (1978: 21), who detects irreverence rather than political force.

moreover, the negative impression stamped on Romulus' orchestration of the first Roman marriages might be read as a criticism of Augustan legislative control over marriage (1985: 57–72). In direct opposition to Labate, Sharrock (1994*b*) put forward a forceful reassertion of the poem's political subversion.[16] In particular, Sharrock (1994*b*: 107–13) stressed the necessarily political nature of Roman didactic poetry after Vergil and the fact that sex was an inextricably political issue in Augustan Rome.[17] She emphasized the Ovidian tactic of using Augustus' maxims against him (1994*b*: 105–6, 108–9) and uncovered a deliberate violation of Augustan legislation in the Mars and Venus episode in *Ars* 2 (1994*b*: 113–22).

If one apparent trend of more recent times has been to revert back almost to the view that the poems are an essentially harmless and witty literary game,[18] this volume rekindles the potential of the *Ars* for political antagonism. Sergio Casali argues that to view Ovid in *Ars* as an intentionally subversive character is an approach fully legitimized by Ovid himself, who tells us in his own (later) works about the anti-Augustan reception of the poem (most notably by Augustus himself): looking for anti-Augustan sentiment in *Ars* is, therefore, a strategy of reading which the poet prescribes for his 'Model Reader'. Focusing on the most overtly 'Augustan' part of the poem—the Parthian expedition of Gaius Caesar (1. 171–228)—Casali invites us to read the event as an episode which exposes tensions in the dynastic family and draws attention to the spectacle and theatricality of the Emperor's Parthian campaign.

Concentrating on *Ars* 3, Roy Gibson assesses the political implications of the *praeceptor*'s advice of moderation in several aspects of women's lives. Instead of observing the traditional stereotypes that linked hairstyle, clothing, and use of cosmetics to either sexual purity or sexual promiscuity, Ovid advocates a principle of individual decorum, whereby each woman must choose the style that best suits her: in short, female appearance is judged to be a matter of

---

[16] See also, along similar lines, Davis (1995). [17] See also Section 4 below.
[18] See Toohey (1996: 162–9); Dalzell (1996: 156) '[The poem's] purpose is not to scandalise, but to tease'; Watson (2002: 143, 149). See also Holzberg (1997: 119–21) (= 2002*c*: 111–13) who argues that the very lack of clarity surrounding the status of the women and messages given militates against the view that the poem is politically subversive.

aesthetics rather than morality. This Ovidian strategy can be felt to clash with Augustus' *Leges Iuliae*, which had reinforced the polar stereotypes for *meretrix* and *matrona* by requiring women to dress according to their sexual status. In rising above these stereotypes, however, Ovid can be seen to criticize the extremities of the Augustan law; on a more general level, this may amount to an implicit criticism of the contradictions of Augustan discourse itself.

The political status of women in the Augustan age is also the focus of Alessandro Barchiesi's paper, which sees both the *Leges Iuliae* and the *Ars Amatoria* as creative attempts to redraw the boundaries for different groups of women. Against a backdrop of widespread anonymity in the *Ars*, Barchiesi focuses on two named individuals—the historical 'first lady' Livia and the mythological Andromache—and demonstrates the ways in which these two women at one time represent polar opposites (the ideal wife and the concubine respectively), and at another appear to occupy a 'middle ground' between the two poles. The instability of female categorization in the *Ars* is, in turn, a (playful) commentary on the negotiation of gender roles in an Augustan age that embraces both the public image of the ideal wife and the ownership and (public) display of erotic, pornographic artwork.

4. GENDER, STATUS, AND THE SPECIALIZED NATURE OF *ARS* 3

For many years, it would seem, little distinction was made between *Ars* 1–2 and *Ars* 3, despite the fact that each was ostensibly addressed to opposing sides in the 'sexual war': or perhaps it would be more accurate to say that *Ars* 3 was largely ignored in general discussions of the poem.[19] In more recent years, however, analyses of the status of the female addressee and the diverse make-up of the internal

---

[19] If it was the case that *Ars* 3 used to be regarded as little more than a literary experiment in reversing tactics from the earlier books, it was a partially misguided view: there are relatively few direct reversals of instruction; see Hollis (1973: 101–4); Downing (1990: 237–8); Miller (1993: 233).

audience of *Ars* 3 have opened up the text to both political and gendered readings.

Myerowitz (1985) offered an important contribution to understanding the difference between the instructions given to men and women in the poem, drawing attention to the way in which Ovid's instructions observe the traditional cultural distinctions between the 'active' male and the 'passive' female. The man's sexual journey is an active exercise that sees him progress (with any luck) from the public forum of the city at the beginning of *Ars* 1 to the private quarters of the girl's bedroom at the end of *Ars* 2;[20] he is taught to rein in his natural instinctual love (*eros*) by converting it into sophisticated seduction (*cultus*); the ship, representative of man's control over nature, becomes a suitable metaphor for his sexual progress. The woman, by contrast, starts and ends *Ars* 3 in her bedroom, and is encouraged to occupy herself in the 'passive' exercise of cultivating her physical appearance and hiding blemishes;[21] her *eros* is destructive and uncontrollable; consequently, the ship metaphor is never used of her role in the games of love. In essence, Myerowitz argued that women were not being instructed in their own right but in order that they might become 'sophisticated accomplices' in the male game of love: they needed to be able to appreciate and comply with the rules of the man's game of seduction.[22] Along similar lines, Downing (1990) read the *praeceptor* in *Ars* 3 as an 'anti-Pygmalion' figure. Whereas Pygmalion famously constructed a statue of the perfect woman, only to desire that it be brought to life, the *praeceptor* works in the opposite direction by starting with the live woman and attempting to turn her into a (passive) living statue by covering her up with all manner of cosmetics and garments, and keeping her movement and speech to a minimum. In short, it was argued that the *praeceptor*, essentially hostile towards the real woman, whom he regards as savage, offensive, and physically flawed, aims to make her more amenable to the male audience by replacing the natural with the

---

[20] For the progression of the instruction in *Ars* 1–2, see esp. Dalzell (1996: 138–9).

[21] Perhaps the only discernible sense of 'progression' for women in *Ars* 3 is the general (but dimly marked) movement from 'elementary' to 'advanced' instruction; see Gibson (2003*a*: 1–7).

[22] Myerowitz (1985: esp. 79–86, 97–101, 123–8, 134–41).

artificial.[23] The issue, although formally it refers to the *praeceptor* not to 'Ovid himself', has close affinities with a perennially intriguing question in Ovidian scholarship: whose side is he on? Such generalizing views on Ovid's treatment of women have been nuanced by other critics who have argued that the *praeceptor* should be viewed as a figure who, whilst serving male interests for the most part, does offer some instruction to women which appears to be principally for their benefit.[24]

Male-oriented instruction in *Ars* 3 implies the presence of a male audience for the book. Miller (1993: 238–41) noted that Ovid often distances himself from his female addressees in *Ars* 3, particularly in self-reflective comments on the progress and appropriateness of the lecture he is delivering; such reflections suggest the existence of a male audience in the background, at least for part of the time. This view received further development by Gibson (2003a: 19–21), who showed that an eavesdropping male audience had long been written into the tradition of erotodidaxis to women.

But ambiguity resides not only in the question of the make-up of the internal audience. The social status of the primary, female addressee is open to question—and this carries political implications in the light of the restrictions placed on the sexual behaviour of certain groups of women under the *lex Iulia de adulteriis coercendis* of *c*.18 BC. What was already a 'golden oldie' in Roman love elegy (the status of the *puella* and the implications of that for the moral and political ambience of the imagined world), becomes even more complex an issue in erotodidaxis, where the reading situation (and hence the implied status of the readers) has gained a new generic foundation. Many have argued against a face-value acceptance of Ovid's frequent disclaimers about married women (as the targets or

---

[23] Downing (1990: 240) 'the calculated, artificial effect must replace the spontaneous, natural given'. The charge of misogyny in *Ars* was prominently levelled at Ovid by Leach (1964). For further differences between the instructions given to male and female, see Sharrock (1994a: 44–6); for further observations on the male orientation behind the advice given to women in *Ars* 3, see Holzberg (1997: 111–15) (= 2002c: 103–7); Wildberger (1998: 343–80).

[24] For such nuanced approaches, see Volk (2002: 165–6); Gibson (2003a: 19–21 *et passim*), who detects 'gender confusion' in the figure of the *praeceptor*, in that he is both male and usurper of the position usually occupied by a woman, the *lena*.

audience of the *Ars*), on the ground that Ovid's advice elsewhere in the poem—as well as the ambiguity of the terms *puella* and *uir*—might well suggest instruction in adultery.[25] This approach was furthered by Gibson (1998) and (2003a: 35–6), who argued that Ovid constructs a hybrid female addressee for *Ars* 3—a mixture of both *matrona* and *meretrix*—which provocatively eschews the categories of women largely accepted by society and enshrined in the Augustan legislation.[26]

5. *REMEDIA AMORIS*: ANTIDOTE OR POISON?

Remedia has not traditionally received as much attention in its own right as *Ars*. For a long time, *Remedia* seems to have been regarded largely as an exercise in reversing the strategies of *Ars*—one experiment too far in the eyes of some.[27] Granted that there are some clear examples of reversals of advice in *Remedia*,[28] it is now widely acknowledged that this strategy constitutes only a small part of a poem that develops in directions quite distinct from *Ars*.

This is most obviously the case in the poem's use of imagery and metaphor. In stark contrast to (male) passions in *Ars*, love in *Remedia* is consistently viewed as a destructive force, comparable to a disease or wound. Fittingly, Ovid assumes the identity of the medical doctor bringing relief to a patient. The doctor-poet makes regular use of medical terminology, and *Remedia* itself is structured along the lines of a medical assessment: the 'doctor' starts by dealing with the disease from incubation period, through to critical period and cure; he then moves to caring for the patient whilst he/she[29] is in convalescence.[30] In treating love in this way, Ovid draws on a variety of different

---

[25] See Miller (1993: 233–6); Sharrock (1994b: 109–13); Davis (1995).
[26] See also Section 3 above.   [27] See esp. Fränkel (1945: 67–72).
[28] See Hollis (1973: 101–4); Henderson (1979: p. xvi).
[29] Though the instruction is purportedly offered to women as well as men (e.g. *Rem.* 51–2), the overriding impression is that the instruction is predominantly aimed (once again) towards men: see Henderson (1979: 42); Davisson (1996: 242); see also (John) Henderson in this volume.
[30] For the medical imagery in general, see esp. Henderson (1979: p. xiii *et passim*); Pinotti (1988: 15–23 *et passim*); Toohey (1996: 171); Watson (2002: 162–3).

traditions: Hellenistic didactic cure-poems, such as Nicander's *Alexipharmaca* (on poisons and antidotes) and *Theriaca* (snakes and remedies for snakebites); Roman love elegy, which constantly speaks of the pain of love; and philosophical contemplation on the ruinous nature of love from Lucretius' fourth book.[31]

In more recent times, scholars have looked for deeper messages from *Remedia*. Detecting a strong metaliterary consciousness running through Ovid's love-elegiac output, Conte (1989) viewed *Remedia* not simply as a rejection of love, but more specifically as a renunciation of elegiac love and, by inference, the composing of love elegy itself. The elegiac form of love, which involves both suffering and an unwillingness/inability to relinquish the pain, is totally dismantled by a text purporting to teach a cure to willing patients.[32] Coming to the poem from a different angle, Davisson (1996) argued that the *exempla* in *Remedia*, both mythological and non-mythological, fail to serve their outward function of acting as character role models for those seeking a path out of love. Instead, the reader is presented with predominantly negative foils (usually female), and many of the positive role models proffered are dubious, in that they suffer beyond love in the established mythical tradition.[33] The (playful) implication for the reader is either that love cannot be easily cured, or that the cure itself may turn out to be fatal: either way, the reader may become reluctant to abandon love after such instruction.

Underlying Davisson's piece is a view of *Remedia* as a didactic poem which, to some extent, deliberately 'backfires', in that it fails to offer convincing instruction on how to fall out of love. It is this general view of the poem which has produced some of the most interesting scholarship of the present decade. Brunelle (2000–1) has argued that *Remedia* cannot escape erotics on any level: it is not just its erotic content—handled either directly or through allusion and innuendo—that is a problem, but also the pleasurable sound and rhythm of the elegiacs themselves, a metre inextricably linked to

---

[31] See Wilkinson (1955: 136); Henderson (1979: pp. xii–xvii).
[32] This view is endorsed by Holzberg (1997: 115–18) (= 2002c: 107–11).
[33] For a reassertion of Ovid's logical use of mythological *exempla* in *Remedia*, however, see Jones (1997: 50–9), who conducts a detailed analysis of Ovid's rhetorical strategy of offering an enjoinder to his readers accompanied by arguments/proofs.

love.[34] All this is at odds with Ovid's purported attempt to rid the reader of thoughts of love. In effect, then, Ovid has created 'a poem whose elegiac form is diametrically opposed to its didactic goal' (2000–1: 129). If we want a way out of love, then, we are ultimately compelled to separate out the inseparable: be a *reader*, enjoy the poetry and be drawn into love, or be a *student*, and avoid such poetry in the first place (but how can we learn this advice without being a reader?). Taking a different approach, Fulkerson (2004) has argued for the inescapable circularity of Ovid's advice in *Remedia*. Ovid's list of apparently unerotic pursuits designed to take the lover's mind off love—forensic work in the law courts, warfare, farming, fishing, hunting, travelling—are, for the reader of Ovid's elegiac poetry, by now so tainted with erotic overtone and potential as to draw him/her back to love, and back again to the *Ars*. What ultimately emerges is the painful truth that any cure is relative: the only escape from a bad love is to replace it with another (one hopes) less painful love.

Recent scholarship stimulates both Philip Hardie and Gianpiero Rosati in their differing readings of *Remedia* in this volume. Both are concerned with Ovidian repetition and intertextuality, and with the apparently contradictory claim in *Remedia* both to cancel and not to cancel the teaching of *Ars*. Rosati, consonant with Brunelle and Fulkerson, detects in the poem's intertextual resonances a reaffirmation of the overriding power of love. Hardie, by contrast, argues for a serious and constructive message in *Remedia*: he suggests that Ovid is attempting to undo the teaching of *Ars* and replace it with the (albeit challenging) anti-erotic art of forgetting.

6. MYTHOLOGICAL 'DIGRESSIONS'

Ars and *Remedia* are peppered with various extended mythological 'digressions'—as they are still popularly (if inaccurately) known—which have long proved favourites with many readers. But their

---

[34] Interestingly, the apparent contradiction between *Remedia*'s alleged purpose and the seductive pleasure of the poetic medium was noted almost two hundred years ago by August Graf von Platen; see Brunelle (2000–1: 123 n. 1).

particular function or functions within the poems—beyond being simply an inherited part of the didactic tradition going back to Hesiod—have been a matter of some debate over the past fifty years. Owing to the length and colourful subject matter of some of these episodes, some scholars have viewed them purely as entertainment, with little or no connection to the contexts in which they were placed.[35] By contrast, the first systematic analysis of fourteen of the mythological digressions, conducted by Weber (1983), argued for the strong logic and integrity of these episodes within Ovid's overall didactic strategy. Few, however, were convinced by the neatness of Weber's theories,[36] and the debate has since developed into analyses of the *complexity* of the relationship between 'digression' and 'main text'.

Myerowitz (1985: 151–74) argued that the mythological digressions involving Daedalus and Icarus and Calypso and Ulysses demonstrate that the controlling force of *ars*—as represented by Daedalus' craftsmanship and Ulysses' eloquence—has limitations, in that it is ultimately fixed by nature's absolutes. As such, these episodes can be seen to deepen the arguments of the main text— which champions the power of *ars* in the sphere of love—by introducing paradoxes and limitations. Myerowitz also identified the metaliterary potential of the Daedalus and Icarus episode by reading Daedalus as the didactic poet himself: both Daedalus and the poet offer creative ways of attempting to control nature by *ars*.

These same two mythological digressions received fuller attention from Sharrock (1994*a*: 78–83, 87–195), who argued for much greater complexity in the didactic function of these episodes. The Calypso and Ulysses episode is ostensibly introduced as an example of how to keep hold of a girl, and yet it is immediately problematized by the fact that Ulysses actually wants to leave. The reader has to work hard for a lesson here: if we are being taught the merits of good speaking,

---

[35] For views along these lines, see esp. Wilkinson (1955: 123–7), who speaks of these digressions as delightful and vivid narratives that help break the monotony of the poem's instructional sections; see also Galinsky (1975: 42). For a more balanced early view of these episodes, see Hollis (1973: 104–10).

[36] See E. J. Kenney's review in *CR* 35 (1985: 389–90). For separate attention to the mythological episodes prior to Weber, note (e.g.) the unpublished Michigan dissertation of J. D. McLaughlin, 'The Relevancy of the Mythological Episodes to Ovid's Ars Amatoria' (1975).

are we meant to follow the example of Ulysses (who entrances his girl with his speaking) or Calypso (who manages to detain her lover by her own rhetorical powers)? The Daedalus and Icarus episode is even more dynamic, in that it teasingly invites the astute reader to pursue a sustained metaliterary reading. Daedalus may be seen as the exiled/exilable poet, Icarus as the daring/doomed poem (*Ars*), the sun as the disapproving Augustus. But the mapping of myth onto reality is by no means exact, and the reader is encouraged to enter into playing with different meanings.

Such appreciation for the dynamic relationship between digression and main text has had a strong influence on scholarly treatment of several other mythical episodes in *Ars* and *Remedia*,[37] and the present volume strives to push such negotiation further. Mario Labate argues that the first digression of the poem involving Romulus and the Sabine women, which draws attention to the absence of *ars* in the process of selecting a mate, acts as an effective anti-exemplum to make more prominent the positive teaching of the *Ars* as a whole. Taking a rather different approach to the issue, Alison Sharrock invites us to rethink the relationship between 'digression' and 'main text' by concentrating on the poem's 'narrative' and, more specifically, on the temptations offered by the text to narrativize. By looking at both the narrative 'digressions' and the 'action' of central characters implicit in the instructional parts of the text, Sharrock argues that both parts can be seen to work together, rather than in opposition, in the creation of an 'implied narrative'. It might even be said, Sharrock contends, that it is the instructional parts that are obstructive, in that they slow down the instructional momentum of the 'digressional' stories.

7. THE ROLE OF THE READER

One of the first to set forth an extended analysis of the role of the (sophisticated) reader in the construction of meaning in Ovid's

---

[37] Digressions in *Ars*: for Mars and Venus, see Sharrock (1994*b*: 113–22); for Cephalus and Procris, see Gibson (2003*a*: 356–60) with his bibliography. Digressions in *Remedia*: for Circe and Ulysses, see Brunelle (2002).

erotodidactic poems was Sharrock (1994*a*). Sharrock identified two types of reader of *Ars*: the (internal) addressee of the text ('Reader') and the (external) addressee ('reader'), loosely defined as an educated Roman man with a mildly subversive air (1994*a*: 5–10). She suggested that, because the *Ars* does not have a named addressee, there is greater potential for slippage between 'Reader' and 'reader'. The text, then, creates both 'naive' and 'sophisticated' readings/readers, and we can enjoy both acting as the naive, first time reader (like the lover) and looking down with superiority on the 'Reader' (1994*a*: 16).

By looking closely at three passages from *Ars* 2, Sharrock argued that it is the 'reader' who brings his own literary knowledge to bear on the poem to produce pleasant 'hidden' meanings. Thus, for example, to the reader well-versed in the traditions of erotodidaxis, and Tibullus Book 1 in particular, Ovid shows, through simile and metaphor, that he is trying to establish a pederastic relationship with his pupil (1994*a*: 27–32). To the same literate reader, Ovid shows himself, in his use of language, to be adopting the role of the love magician (1994*a*: 61–86). It is not so much the (naive) 'Reader' who is being seduced here, but the knowledgeable literate 'reader' who is prey to this 'magical and pederastic seduction' (1994*a*: 86).

Sharrock's critical approach has helped to open up the dynamics and complexities of the text, and its influence is strongly felt in this volume. In a novel piece, Duncan Kennedy focuses on the female reader/Reader of *Ars* 3, and takes up the invitation offered by the *praeceptor* to (re)read the *Heroides* as part of an implicit love-lesson: by 're-enacting' the scenarios in the letters with a certain level of detachment, Ovid suggests that the pupil may be able both to empathize with the heroine's words and to assess their erotodidactic significance. Focusing on two of the letters—those of Ariadne and Phyllis—Kennedy demonstrates how the *Heroides* can be used by the female reader both to reinforce the *praeceptor*'s advice and to offer additional, 'extra-curricular' instruction.

Other contributors to this volume focus more specifically on historical post-Ovidian readers. Markus Janka argues for creative intertextual dialogue between Martial and Ovid's erotodidactic poems, whereby Martial can be seen to test the strengths and weaknesses of Ovid's advice when the latter is applied to the more 'extreme' amatory environment of epigram. Ralph Hexter and Genevieve Liveley analyse the fluctuating ways in which Ovid's erotodidactic corpus has been received in more recent times. Hexter charts the curious history of Ovid's erotodidactic works as school texts over the past thousand years, in which the poems became popular for either their (innocent) Latinity or their raunchy messages. Focusing on a single poem from twentieth-century poet Robert Graves, Liveley explores Graves's close critical engagement with Ovid's *Ars* and *Remedia*—an engagement that, on a more general level, comments on the challenges of reading (and misreading) Ovid's poetry over the past millennium.

Part I

Poetics

2

Love in Parentheses: Digression and Narrative Hierarchy in Ovid's Erotodidactic Poems

Alison Sharrock

Ovid's *Ars Amatoria*: a love story. So what kind of 'story' do we have here? A reader might object that surely the *Ars*, as a fully paid-up didactic poem, does not in any normal sense partake in a narrative genre. As Ovid's last elegiac trial run before he launched into the *Metamorphoses*, the erotodidactic cycle has been admired for its narratives (digressions), but not normally credited with a Narrative.[1] I shall so credit it, and I shall take support for such a critical move from authorities both ancient and modern, both literary scholars and creative practitioners, for in their different ways both classical Graeco-Roman culture and modern Western culture display a strong drive towards finding narrative in all things and valuing narrative above all things.

As is well known, there was in antiquity a high valuation of narrative, with epic representing the top of the generic hierarchy and drama being defined by its manner of specifically narrative presentation (people doing things, Arist. *Poet.* 1448^{b}); modern criticism maintains the hierarchy and is, moreover, additionally affected by contemporary literature, in which the novel is top genre. This

---

[1] Volk (2002) is one of the few scholars to appreciate the dramatic immediacy of the *Ars Amatoria*, a feature which she deems essential to membership in the didactic genre, but she does not move to the next stage of reading a Narrative out of the poem.

need-to-narrativize (and it is no bad thing) encourages not only a complex theory of narratological levels (narrative and story, narrative, story, and plot, etc.) but also the creative construction of narrative out of textual hints.[2] A case in point is the epistolary novel, where the events of the story, which inevitably happen outside the direct time-frame of the epistolary activity, must be construed by the reader out of the hints offered in the letters themselves. Still more driven by the narratological imperative is the practice and criticism of modern avant-garde poetry. Brian McHale (2001) discusses what he calls 'weak narrativity' in poems such as *The Waste Land* by T. S. Eliot, which he takes as emblematic for this form.[3] He describes this kind of poetic construction as having a narrative that underlies the surface of the text rather than one that hits you in the face: 'Narrative, while not utterly banished, shifts to another level, becoming the invisible "master-narrative" that, present nowhere in the text, nevertheless ensures the text's ideological (if not formal) coherence.'[4] It is in part with this reading-in of narrative into 'non-narrative' poetry that I am concerned in this chapter.[5] I am going to be particularly interested in two different (but, I hope, related, and indeed interwoven) manifestations of narrative in the erotodidactic poems: the narrative interludes or mythological excursuses which add so much colour and so much disruption to the didactic text, and the quasi-narrative of the love story which I will argue arises from the implied action of the central characters manifested through the directly instructional parts of the text. These two elements in the poem have traditionally been placed in a slightly odd mix of hierarchies. On one level, narrative (storytelling, exempla, mythological excursuses)

---

[2] I discuss these matters in more detail in my contribution to Sharrock and Morales (2000).

[3] Interestingly for my study of the way in which narrative and non-narrative forms may combine, *The Waste Land* has been turned into a classic narrative comic book, by the device of combining it with a Philip Marlowe detective story. I am grateful to Roy Gibson for this reference.

[4] McHale (2001) quotes Ron Silliman, *What* (1988): 'It is not that there is no narrative here (each sentence is a narrative, each line moves) but that there is no hierarchy of narratives (not even the story of the poem), no sentence to which the others (all the others) defer and are ranked (the map is not built about the city).'

[5] Perhaps I might even call it, in honour of Hardie (2002b), the 'absent presence' of narrative.

is deemed to be best, in an absolute sense. On the other hand, didactic poetry is meant to be about instruction, so passages that say 'do this and do not do that' would on this reckoning be the central point of the *Ars*. So the narratives would be absolutely best, but relatively inferior, since they are in some sense digressions from the main purpose of the poem, while the instructional elements would be absolutely inferior, but relatively best (since they are the main purpose of the poem, but 'not so good'). It is this double-edged hierarchy that I seek to subvert in the present chapter, by reading from the narratives back into the instruction rather than the other way round, and by reading the instruction as narrative. I am not at the moment concerned so much with how the content of the mythological narratives links to and reflects the overall project of the poems, or how the stories are 'relevant because metaphorical', important though these points are. Rather, I am interested in (1) how the explicit narratives might be seen as central to the books they are in, either alone or when taken as a group, and might even be taken as 'main text'; (2) how the poem subliminally offers an implied narrative of a love story; (3) how the excursuses may function to help the story of the affair and the instruction along, in formal or structural ways rather than merely in thematic ways; and (4) how the prevalence of directly narrative material (excursus) might interact with the levels of narrativity in the instructional parts of the text (or, simply, why there are so few narratives in *Ars* 3 and the *Remedia*).

In thinking about the interactions of narrative and non-narrative modes of communication with regard to the erotodidactic poems, it occurred to me to wonder whether this interaction might be at all illuminated by the translation of texts into different media, as in the case of novels into film.[6] If you were to try to represent the material of the poem visually, how would you go about it? At first sight, it

---

[6] Filming the unfilmable piece of literature has a long and distinguished tradition. The 1965 film of *Finnegan's Wake*, directed by Mary Ellen Bute, is also known by the significant alternative title *Passages from James Joyce's Finnegan's Wake*. The use of the term 'passages', rather than 'scenes', is marked. Conversely, screen and TV versions of epistolary novels (such as the 1991 BBC adaptation of Richardson's *Clarissa*) tend to occlude the epistolary mode entirely, and simply translate into the medium of visual narrative. I am very grateful to Roy Gibson for much useful information on these topics.

might sound like a ridiculous idea to make a film of a didactic poem, but actually it raises in a startlingly direct way some of the issues with which I am concerned. How does Ovid write a love story in these poems? What is the relationship between the narratives and the Narrative? One way of making a film would be to intersperse a narrative of the relationship between avuncular Ovid and his eager pupil (and, assuming this was not for consumption by the innocent, you might well put an erotic spin on that) with a narrative of the pupil's progress in his own affair. If this were Hollywood, the film would probably end up with the young couple rejecting Ovid's cynical and devious instruction and going off to live happily ever after. You might even have three separate teaching narratives going on at once: male lover, female lover, rejected lover, who could all be involved in an erotic triangle with each other (and also the teacher). But what would you do about the digressions? An easy approach would be to make the teacher also a storyteller, and cut from the scene of telling into a cinematic presentation of the stories themselves. But maybe that would be rather a boring way to do it, and one that would perpetuate the myth that the so-called digressions are simply adornment. An alternative would be to have the main characters in the mythic sections played by the actors of the erotic sections. Better still, perhaps, would be somehow to set the erotic narrative within one of the mythic narratives. Daedalus could be the *praeceptor*, and his crime against Minos could be explicitly his success in this area (as the Pasiphae digression at *Ars* 1. 289–326 might seem to suggest). Or the whole story could be set within the overall context of the early Sabines, which Mario Labate's paper in this volume shows to be a particularly fertile ground for visual erotodidactic narrative. Alternatively one might link together Ulysses from *Ars* 2 and from the *Remedia*, with Achilles on Scyros in *Ars* 1, and make those the main setting.[7]

---

[7] In fact, there has been at least one film loosely based on the *Ars*: 'Ars amandi' (Francia/Italia 1983) by Walerian Borowczyk, in which a Roman noblewoman attempts to play out the erotic advice of Ovid. I have not seen the film myself, but from the accounts of others I have ascertained that it was no great work of art, and in particular the story was distinctly weak. Perhaps the producer made the mistake of basing his story on *Ars* 3, without setting it in its context both within the didactic cycle and of its mythological excursus. I shall argue that the third book is the least conducive to narrative reading.

To return, then, to my four points. I will address the first very briefly, because its main purpose is to contribute to the later points. I want to suggest looking at the major mythological narratives of the *Ars* not as digressionary but as central. Let me start with Book 1, the main narratives of which are the Sabine Women, Pasiphae, Ariadne, and Achilles on Scyros.[8] I do not suggest that these four tell a story all together in any obvious way, although there clearly are direct links between Pasiphae and Ariadne, and an indirect link between the Sabine Women and Achilles.[9] They do, however, all tell at some level the same 'story', in the sense of 'message', which is the romanticization of force.[10] This, perhaps, is what *Ars* 1 is all about. We could say that, when the chips are down, the rest of the book is just an illustration of this point. The stories are the main text; the instruction is the digression. Stories have been used for teaching purposes since the beginning of recorded history, so it should not surprise us if the stories were to be our central moments, and the directly instructional parts just illustrations of how the great messages of these

[8] A problem inevitably arises here, over what we are going to include in the category of 'major mythological narratives', and why choose 'major' ones anyway. Throughout the erotodidactic poems, but especially *Ars* 1 and 2, Ovid uses a range of different presentational methods for his exempla: some take on a life of their own as huge digressions in which we can easily get lost (such as Daedalus and Icarus), while others are brief hints in less than a couplet. Since my interest is in narrative (more even than it is in content), I tried to make the distinction between the major stories and the hints on the basis of whether we are actually told anything about what happened beyond the, we might say, implied title. Making distinctions like that, and expecting them to hold, is asking for trouble from Ovid, but they will, I think, more or less do as a working method. As regards *Ars* 1, Busiris (647–56) would be the next in line: maybe he also fits into the argument I am suggesting for the major narratives, although there is nothing very romantic about being burned alive in a metal bull!

[9] On which see Labate in this volume, Ch. 10. With regard to links between apparently disparate narrative interludes, Steve Green made the very useful suggestion to me that a possible previous example of ongoing narrative within 'digression' is provided by Apollonius, *Argonautica* 1. The two major digressions in Book 1 are the song of Orpheus (496 ff.) and the depictions on Jason's cloak (730 ff.). Orpheus' song ends with detail about the Cyclopes making a thunderbolt for Zeus, which is precisely the detail that forms the beginning of the next digression on Jason's cloak. In a poem where the apparent Narrative (story of the Golden Fleece) is constantly 'interrupted' by scholarly digression, Apollonius may be encouraging the reader to see the Narrative within the extended ecphrases.

[10] Both Labate and Volk, Chs. 10 and 12 in this volume, take a rather gentler line on the Sabine narrative than I allude to here. Perhaps I might put the stress on 'romanticization' rather than on 'force'.

stories work in practice. We will see how this matter cashes out in more detail below, and more importantly still we will, I hope, see how the narratives also have a central function which does *not* depend directly on their own content.

The function and manner of the excursuses is different in each book of the cycle. I have argued in the past for the central importance of the outrageously disproportionate narrative of Daedalus and Icarus,[11] which we may also see thematically as a continuation of both the Pasiphae story (which is why Daedalus is in trouble in the first place), while the following Ulysses story is quite an obvious double and trumping of the Achilles story from Book 1. Apollo's intervention in the poem makes explicit (partly by contrast!) one of the major messages of all the other narratives of Book 2—the central importance of *ars*. But the point about the stories of Book 2 which surprised me most is the way in which the high density of digressionary material is reflected by a high density also of implied narrative, rather than, as one might expect, the other way round.

By contrast, the only extended narrative in *Ars* 3 is that of Procris and Cephalus (687–746). I would suggest that one of its important underlying messages could act as a key to the reading of the whole book. Women are supposedly being taught how to catch and keep (and exploit) a lover, but it is hard to resist the feeling that what they are actually being taught is how to let their men have it all ways. They should love their men to distraction, but let them get away with playing around and any other bad behaviour. All this about *malae meretrices* and their devious ways is just a distraction—it isn't the point of *Ars* 3 at all. That is the lesson which Procris' story tells us, because she is not only a model for the genuinely loving partner, but she also suffers the consequences (and even accepts those consequences) of trying to impose the constraints on her lover that love imposes on her.[12] The book without a story, by contrast, is *Remedia*

---

[11] Sharrock (1994*a*).
[12] Cf. *Ars* 2. 447–8 *o quater et quotiens numero comprendere non est | felicem, de quo laesa puella dolet!* The male lover is advised only *fac timeat de te* (2. 445), whereas the female lover must *fac timeat speretque simul* (3. 477). On the Cephalus and Procris story, see Gibson (2003*a*: 357–8), who makes a powerful case for reading a central theme of this narrative as being 'control of the self and the emotions', which he rightly sees as crucial to the poem as a whole. Another theme, as he points out, is credulity, which is always at issue in dealing with Ovid.

Amoris. There are thousands of possibilities for narrative development, and hundreds of hints, but only one proper excursus, that of Ulysses and Circe (261–88)—where Circe is very clearly playing the role of Dido. This, it seems to me, is because the story which the *Remedia* refuses to tell is precisely that one. Dido, although she is rarely mentioned, is central to the *Remedia Amoris*. Her near-absence makes a very telling gaping hole.

The second prong of my argument rests on 'implied narrative', a phrase I coin on the basis of the now well-accepted terms 'implied author' and 'implied reader'. Those sections of the poems not structured from narrative digressions are presented to the reader as instructions, descriptions, quasi-philosophical *sententiae* etc., using grammatical forms such as the imperative and future tenses, and giving high priority to the second-person forms of verbs. This is in contrast with conventional narrative, which prefers third-person or first-person verbs and past or historic present tenses. Conventional narrative is dominated by the indicative, implied narrative by the subjunctive. I suggest that we are invited to construct our own narrative (driven by the text) out of the textual hints that Ovid provides at various levels. The first, most obvious level is the narrative of instruction, which we actually see happening before our eyes. More subtle is the erotic narrative that can be teased out of the instructional mode. We are watching teaching and practice developing side by side. If we accept the possibility for a narrative to be written in the second person, and in future tenses or other imperatival expressions of various forms, then we can see narrative developments throughout the books. One of the great riches of such implied narrative is that, because it is currently unfulfilled, it can contain a host of alternatives, dead ends, retreats, and leaps. It is not bound by the normal pedestrian paths of conventional narrative realism and chronology. The value and the trouble with implied narrative, as with any other 'implied' notion, is that it is a dynamic, self-fertile hydra. Narratives not bound to the most simplistic of representational methods can jump up and shoot off all over the place—there's no stopping them.[13] I am sometimes going to use the

---

[13] Once you go down this route, there is always the question of 'how far can/do you go?' I considered making a distinction to answer that question by using the opening couplets of *Ars* 3. We could say that *arma dedi Danais in Amazonas* (3. 1) is a

past tense to describe events that are 'narrated' in present, future, or even imperative or conditional mode in the text, and consequently I am sometimes making factual statements out of things that are only mentioned in the text as potential or even occasionally in the negative.

The story began with a young man setting off on a tour of the erotic hotspots of Rome. There are a few alternative narratives offered, including the possibility of the lover pursuing his Quest all over the world (1. 51–4), but he ends up in the theatre (1. 89). Incidentally, this kind of alternative storytelling reminds me of *Monty Python and the Search for the Holy Grail*, where Arthur and his men arrive outside Camelot, launch into a crazy song in which they act out, in situ, all the delights of being there, until Arthur says 'on second thoughts, let's not go to Camelot; it's a silly place'. Now the theatre, of course, is a great place for acting out alternative narratives, and the lover duly enjoyed a performance of the Rape of the Sabine Women (1. 101–30). For my purposes at the moment it is not so much the content that matters (though it does), as the way in which the mythological interlude actually moves the story forward. Before arriving in the theatre, our young lover was just wandering vaguely, looking at girls in crowds. Immediately after the excursus, he has moved on several notches in his amatory adventure, and is sitting next to a particular girl at the races (1. 139–40). Narrative interlude causes quasi-narrative development. He has, no doubt, followed the action of the Romulean soldiers, who

> respiciunt oculisque notant sibi quisque puellam
> quam uelit   (1. 109–10)

(They look back and mark out with their eyes, each for himself, which girl he wants).

---

piece of narrative, in this case the narrative of instruction which is at some level the primary narrative of the poem. *Ite in bella pares* etc. (3. 3) would then be a rudimentary implied narrative, inviting us to invent the story of the male and female pupils putting their lessons into practice. *Non erat armatis aequum concurrere nudas* (3. 5), for all its sexual suggestiveness, would then be not narrative but comment. Readers will probably have spotted that even the third line contains the potential for implied narrative, because of the hydra-effect. But reading requires the imposition of order onto a text, so I shall try not to be distracted by all the manifold possibilities.

The text does not explicitly say this, but I am granting the poem a slippage in which the Rape is the subject matter of a play which our young lover sees there.[14] He is now at the races with an individual girl—termed *domina* (which could just mean 'lady' but is bound to suggest 'mistress' in the erotic sense)—joining side on side (!—1. 140); he is even touching her (1. 142) and, in a rather puerile piece of playfulness, sneaking a look at her legs (1. 156). So what has happened? When the lover was still uncertain about his choice, still looking out for the—er?—girl of his dreams, he took the opportunity offered, and found *socii sermonis origo* (1. 143) with the old 'speck of dust' trick (1. 149–52). This is quite a development, and it is all thanks to that interlude in the theatre.

Perhaps I may put the argument of the previous paragraph in rather more pedestrian terms. I am suggesting that the sections from *Ars* 1. 41–88, where Ovid tells the pupil to go looking for girls, and makes a series of suggestions about good hunting grounds, can be read at the implied-narrative level as recounting the young man's quest around these very places. The alternative strategy introduced at line 51, of pursuing the search abroad, which is proclaimed unnecessary by the Roman poet, serves as a brief alternative narrative, in the manner of flashback (or flash-forward) techniques of visual narrative media such as film. The final place recommended for hunting is the theatre, at which point Ovid pauses the tour in order to reflect on how the theatre has always been a good environment for catching girls, ever since Romulus engineered the Rape of the Sabine Women there at the beginning of Rome's history: Ovid tells the story at delightful and very visual length. I am suggesting, first, that this narrative is itself a suitable story for performance in the theatre, and so is doubly (meta-)theatrical here; and also that the telling of this story performs a functional role in the development of the young lover's affair, for it is after this section that he has first clearly moved a long way forward in his erotic adventure, from 'just looking' to 'chatting up', which happens in the scene 'At The Races'. This is what I mean by the interaction between 'digression' and 'main text' at a purely structural level.

---

[14] In the second theatre visit, the content of the mime being performed exactly parallels the desired behaviour of the would-be lover.

Now, before we follow the narrative further, here's a little narratological problem. We are used to the idea that the mythological excursus creates a pause in the development of the poem as a whole, and we might even think the poem goes into stasis during passages such as the Rape of the Sabine Women, whereas we would tend to see the scene at the races as fully Main Text, because it contains Advice on What To Do. But there is a sense in which this scene, which is indeed a great narrative of beginnings, might itself constitute a kind of pause in the development of the book as a whole. 'Illustrations' can move the story forward, while 'instruction' may keep it in waiting. The beginnings of gallant behaviour are all very well, but we have to move on.

And move on we do, or don't—with more of the same. The scene at the races constituted a development in itself (after the scene in the theatre/excursus on the Sabines: *post hoc* and, I suggest, *propter hoc*) but did not cause any development *of* itself, since what we get afterwards is a repeat for gladiatorial games (1. 163–70), and repeat again for Augustus' naval extravaganza (1. 171–6) and the ensuing orgy of Eastern conquest and projected triumph (1. 177–228)—an alternative narrative even within the narrator's scheme of things.[15] Incidentally, if we are wondering how Ovid writes a love story in these poems, we might wonder what this (grotesque?) outpouring is all about, and whether *this* is really the one big irrelevance in the poem.[16] But this story too is a romanticization of force, as I characterized all the digressions of Book 1, and it is a story of the conquest of the female (i.e. feminine East), just as is the whole book. The lover watches and plays out the Rape of the Sabine Women in the theatre, and watches and plays out the conquest of the East in the triumph.

Be that as it may, the triumph gave our lover a great opportunity to show off (1. 228 *si poteris, vere, si minus, apta tamen,* 'truthfully, if you can, but if not, at least appropriately'). To return to my story: all

---

[15] I mean: Ovid relates the triumph of Gaius as something potential for the future, rather than as something concrete in the past, thus making a narrative out of what we might loosely call a prophecy. I am suggesting that his treatment of hypothetical narrative here is not many stages removed from my treatment of hypothetical narrative throughout this chapter.

[16] For a powerful reading of the political import of this passage, see Casali, Ch. 11 in the present volume.

these public shows, which in a sense constitute a digression from the business in hand, aid the young lover in his progress through the poem, because he comes out of them much further developed, and afterwards he gets to a party (1. 229). This is looking good. He nearly slipped that night, however. Taking more of the Dutch courage than his master thought advisable when you are still looking, and seduced by the soft lighting and the ambience of the party, he almost got involved with the wrong woman, until his mentor came to his rescue and dragged him off home (1. 245–52). In order to get over this awkward moment, he went off (against the teacher's advice) to sample the delights of Baiae and the almost equally notorious temple of Diana Nemorensis at Aricia (1. 259). And there he fell in love. I am, of course, inventing that last event. It seems to me, however, worth noting that the Virgin Diana's responsibility for many an affair is the last thing mentioned before the heavily signalled move from *legenda* to *capienda* at 1. 263–8.[17] The implication of a major narrative event—falling in love—is hard to resist.

Okay, so far the lover has looked around, sounded out a few possibilities, tested the water, had the odd minor repulse, chosen a girl to work on, and still believes he can win her (1. 269–70). Now begins the narrative of seduction. Readers who know the poem well will be able to construct their own narrative out of the whirlwind of activity going on in this section. Very briefly, it goes something like this. There is a bifurcation of narrative first: down one route, the lover gets involved in an affair with the *puella*'s maid (1. 351), and uses both her compliance and his power of blackmail (cf. Cypassis, *Am.* 2. 7 and 8) as a way of getting close to the mistress; while on the other, he avoids that temptation, and just gets her help anyway.[18] So: once the lover was caught by this woman, and believed her to be catchable too, he sent a letter with a coded declaration of love (1. 437, 455 ff.), deceptively promising things he didn't really intend to deliver (or at least, so he thinks), and using all the resources of a Roman

---

[17] The narrative moment is accompanied by a series of bizarre stories of excessive or perverted love on the part of women, culminating with Pasiphae. It is told as a generic love story, but this story is heavily hedged around by its frame—this is a love which might titillate the lover as a story, but for which he really is not ready yet.

[18] At the same time, there is another extra narrative of the beloved's hurt at the breakdown of a previous relationship (1. 365–74).

rhetorical education, artfully disguised. The letter was sent back, but he persevered (1. 469). The next letter was read, but no reply was made. The next elicited a reply, but only to tell him to cease and desist (1. 483). This is definitely making progress (!). Then he approached her in her litter, still using *ambiguis...notis* (1. 487–90), and 'happened' to bump into her when out walking (1. 491–6).[19] A second theatre visit (1. 497) more explicitly links the content of the play with the situation in hand, as Hollis (1977 ad loc.) has shown. All this seems to be working towards the climax of the story. At this point, however (1. 505), there is a *digression* on the cultivation of the self. Although this passage might seem like Main Text because it contains advice, it really diverts us from the love story which had been doing nicely without instruction on basic personal hygiene. Far less digressive is the love story of Bacchus and Ariadne which follows (1. 525). This story will move the lover's erotic narrative to a new stage, towards the dinner party which will finally get him together with his girl. In its content also the Bacchus and Ariadne story is a nice miniature of the lover's own story, including the bit about approaching a girl when she is upset over a previous failed relationship (cf. 1. 365).

So, when we come out of this excursus, the story has moved on, as it did when we came out of the Sabine excursus. Now the lovers are at a party (1. 569). I paraphrase (creatively): 'As they left the room, in the confusion he managed briefly to brush against her, which sent an electric shock through them both.' And so on. That night, our young man pulled out all the classic elegiac stops, even down to charming the beloved girl's *vir*. After this magical evening, the lover moved closer and closer to his goal. A kiss (at 1. 663) was rejected, but it was an important step.

Not surprisingly, there is an increasing tendency in the final couple of hundred lines of the text to delay the narrative—the oldest trick in

---

[19] These are all typical courtship rituals, as suited to modern teenagers as to Jane Austen's silly girls, but do they suggest particularly outrageous behaviour in Roman terms? See Gibson (2003*a*: 259, 269–70, 288–9). He argues that, in *Ars* 3, Ovid teases his pupils with the prospect of street prostitution, but is careful to chaperone them away from any actual contact in person on the street. 'First contact' comes by the more decorous method of the letter. Likewise, in *Ars* 1, if there is a hint at something indecorous, it is certainly no more than a hint.

the narratological and sexual book. One of those delaying tactics, the excursus on Achilles on Scyros (1. 681–706), nonetheless moved the lover on again, and gave him the confidence to pop the question at 1. 711. This again is an example of how the big narrative movements happen directly after narrative excursuses. Even though the initial reaction was outrage, the lover believed, on Ovid's advice, that it was encouraging (1. 715–22). You might think it would be plain sailing from here on, but in fact instead of driving the narrative directly towards its consummation, Ovid causes a deflection at the last moment—the lover's enthusiasm fired an excessive interest on the part of his best friend, who became a rival (1. 739 ff.). At the moment, Ovid won't tell us how that story ended, and instead goes into a digression about various types of girl, and the approaches appropriate to each—thus generalizing when we thought we were making progress on a particular story. The erotic narrative has to be put on hold for the moment, because this is the cliff-hanger at the end of Episode 1. *Ars Amatoria* 2 will be coming to a cinema near you on 21 June.

Book 2 is if anything even more susceptible to narrative analysis, because it has a fairly straightforward and quite specific love story lurking among the beautiful excursuses and the unnecessary advice. The narrative has now settled down into a love story of two individuals, with only limited recourse to narrative alternatives. For example: the advice on sweet-talking (2. 145 ff.) implies a narrative like this—in the early weeks of their relationship, they were untroubled by serious arguments or by any intrusions of financial and social reality (2. 153–8). Sometimes she was a bit prickly, being that kind of person, but he managed to win her over by his devotion (2. 177–8). For he was completely besotted, and fawned on her like a lapdog (2. 197–202)...skip a bit...but after the honeymoon time, there were occasionally problems. He suffered a cold night outside (2. 237), which he liked to believe was the result of an over-zealous guard. One time, he was so desperate to be with her that he even came in by the roof (2. 245). The story unfolds not only in her house (2. 251), but in his also, where she has become a part, if not an entirely licit one, of his establishment, who even influenced the way he treated his slaves (2. 287–94). The bit of advice, at 2. 295 ff., on how to praise, seems almost like a distraction from this story. After it comes the first real crisis, the girl's illness (2. 315), which heralds the beginning of a series of obstacles which love must (that is, 'had to') overcome. The later period of the relationship was dogged by infidelity: first a minor indiscretion, which she found out about despite his attempts to hide and to deny (2. 410), but he won her round in the usual way (2. 413: there follows a didactic digression at this point on aphrodisiacs), then another fling which he deliberately let her know about, since the original accident had gone so well (2. 427 ff.).

Indeed, I would say that the only element in the story of Book 2 which, paradoxically, does *not* make neat narratological sense is the great climax at the end. From a structural but not strictly narratological point of view, it is natural and appropriate that the climax of the two books should be a celebration of sex. This is the great achievement, after all, the goalpost towards which the whole enterprise has been directed. This is the climax that ought to have been there at the end of Book 1, but was elided and deferred until the great moment at the end of Book 2.[20] To end on a high like this is fine structurally, but it is not particularly well motivated narratologically—there would have been other points in the story better suited to a bedroom scene. But my point here is that this is one of the few episodes in *Ars* 2 which do not fit a clear narrative trajectory. We might say it fits better to narrative than to story, perhaps, or structure than narrative. As is well known, we can see its separation from the rest signalled in the text:

> conscius, ecce, duos accepit lectus amantes:
> ad thalami clausas, Musa, resiste fores   (2. 703–4)

(See, the knowing bed has welcomed the two lovers: Muse, stop outside the closed doors of the bedroom.)

The question must remain, however, as to whether this story has a happy ending. It is certainly given a powerful sense of ending,

---

[20] It is abundantly clear that the affair was consummated long before, since the episode with the 'cure' for anger at sexual indiscretion (more sex) implies a well-established sexual relationship. The exact point at which consummation took place, however, is occluded, as in all the best love stories, or at least *Amores* 1. 5. The climax will be repeated when the story is told from the other point of view in Book 3. Even the *Remedia*, to which it is even less directly appropriate, plays the same game subliminally.

closural force, and so on, through the climactic bedroom scene, but do the lovers live happily ever after? Or is this orgasmic ending just a timeless moment that defers resolution of the never-ending struggles of relationships? Our aim was to make love last a long time, but that is a narrative type which can only find its conclusion in failure, or death, or a cop-out (sailing off into the sunset)...

All this intense narrative action in Book 2 is to be found in the book which also carries the most prominent and digressive mythological excursuses. By contrast, as is generally well known, *Ars* 3 contains far fewer excursuses of the types which add so much colour to Books 1 and 2.[21] I grew up believing that one reason for this was the teacher's need to get through the material of two books in the space of one. In that case, one would expect to find that the implied narrative of Book 3 would be much more intense than that of the earlier books, and that it would not be padded out with mythological narratives because it has got plenty of narrative of its own. But this turns out not to be the case. There is, in fact, very little narrative indeed in the Book, while what is there is particularly well hidden and requires a lot of creative work on the part of the reader to tease it out. Much of the book is, indeed, taken up in Advice, which makes it look like Main Text, but it is advice that is going nowhere, and is a distraction from or an occlusion of a story that hardly manages to happen at all to any degree of specificity. Most of the time there is no true primary character, just a generalized mass of girls of every variety.[22] The addressee remains non-specific, often present in the plural, often split into many different possibilities that are not personal alternatives but individual cages. The reason for this is, perhaps, rather predictable. Very little happens in *Ars* 3, because there is very little for the primary character to do, except to adorn herself and wait.

---

[21] See Gibson (2003*a*: 6–7) on cataloguing and other aspects of density in the text, and the relative paucity of excursuses. Could the catalogues be taking the place of narratives? Gibson points out that the catalogue style has a long tradition in didactic poetry (and *Ars* 3 begins with an allusion to the ps. Hesiodic *Catalogue of Women*), so the presence of cataloguing as such should not surprise us, but it is significant that the full catalogue style is reserved for *Ars* 3 rather than *Ars* 1 and 2, where narrative prevails.

[22] See Gibson (2003*a*: 87, 146, 404).

As a result of this general lack of narrative in the Book, there is surprisingly little temporal development, considering that the material of two packed books is fitted into one. For example, already at 3. 209, the lover is not to see the beloved putting on make-up, but we have had no indication of how he might be in a position to do so anyway, and in fact Ovid explicitly draws attention later to the fact that he has run away with himself. Nothing much happens at all until about halfway through the book, when Ovid suddenly notices that his chronology is all over the place, and is going nowhere. (This is not intended to imply that he has made a mistake, of course, but that he is responding to a problem of his own significatory making.[23]) Suddenly he pulls a brake on the poem (3. 467–8), with a grand couplet making entertaining allusion to (or prophecy of) the opening of the *Metamorphoses*:

> fert animus propius consistere: supprime habenas
>   Musa, nec admissis excutiare rotis

(My spirit prompts me to take up a closer position; check the reins, Muse, and be not hurled headlong with the wheels in full career),

(Gibson's adaptation of H. T. Riley's 1864 translation ad loc., which nicely conveys the mock-elevated tone of the original.)

And then we move on to specific advice about how to receive a lover's address, with some quite clear consequent narrative movement. He has asked; now she can do something. Perhaps we should not be surprised: of course nothing could happen until the man popped the question.

Another, more congenial, effect of the socio-narratological situation in Book 3 is that instead of a continuous narrative, what we get is a whole series of snippets, which offer mini-narratives of their own:

---

[23] See ibid. 3–6. He notes that 'the linear progress of the affair becomes increasingly hard to trace towards the end of the book' (ibid. 5). He also points out that the passage on the party (3. 747–68) seems a bit out of place at this late stage in the book, but suggests that 'no awkwardness is felt' because the long Cephalus and Procris episode immediately before the party 'helps to remove from the mind of readers any strict concern with the stage-by-stage progress of the affair' (ibid. 6). Such comments suggest a nice misfit of *Ars* 3 with the case I made above for the role of excursuses in moving the affair along: in this case, the excursus would have the effect of shooting the affair back almost to the beginning! These observations, then, would support my case for reading *Ars* 3 as narratologically challenged.

the anti-make-up scene (3. 209), a snippet about laughing (3. 287) and lisping (3. 293), a cautionary tale about an attractive con-man who stole his trusting girl-friend's gown (3. 445–50), the scene when the lover was made to hide in the cupboard (3. 608), and so on. These snippets do not have a context, a wider scenario that might encourage us to fit them into a story, but they do tell miniature stories of themselves, and contribute to the wider message of the lack of female control of narrative, which is crucial to the *Ars*. Perhaps I might even characterize Books 1 and 2 as a novel, and Book 3 as a series of short stories.[24] In that sense, it might even be Book 3 that most closely reflects the narrative challenge identified by McHale in lyric narrative. Be that as it may, I find it striking that levels of mythological excursus narrativity should reflect so closely the levels of 'main text' internal narrativity, and that the two together should make it clear that women are not in the business of narrative.

[24] I note again here my observation that perhaps Borowczyk's film made the mistake of basing itself on *Ars* 3, which does not have enough extended narrative for a movie. By contrast, we might compare the short stories inspired by Ovid's *Ars* and *Remedia* in Philip Terry's (2000) collection of modern responses to Ovid.

3

Staging the Reader Response: Ovid and His 'Contemporary Audience' in *Ars* and *Remedia*

Niklas Holzberg

Rounding off Book 2 of his *Ars Amatoria*, Ovid, who at the beginning of Book 1 had undertaken to furnish male readers with a course in erotic education (1. 35–40), announces that he has reached the *finis* of his opus (2. 733). He calls on the *uiri* to pay tribute to him and expresses the wish that all who now manage to 'conquer an Amazon' with the 'weapons' their teacher has provided will etch the words *Naso magister erat* on their booty (2. 733–44). It sounds at this point as though Ovid is 'signing off' with a form of *sphragis*. But the *Naso magister erat* is followed—still in Book 2—by one more distich:

> ecce, rogant tenerae sibi dem praecepta puellae:
> uos eritis chartae proxima cura meae. (2. 745–6)

(Well, look at this! The delicate young ladies are asking me to give them lessons! I shall take care of you in the next book.)

This transition to Book 3, i.e. the promise of more coaching, comes as a complete surprise considering the agenda announced at the start of Book 1 and the 'seal' just affixed to the opus. The intended

---

I would like to thank the three editors of this volume for their constructive comments. I am also much indebted to Gerlinde Bretzigheimer, as it was our lively exchanges during the preparation of her book on the *Amores* that provided me with the initial idea for this chapter.

effect is without question a comic one; the two lines even sound a lot like an ἀπροσδόκητον at the end of an epigram. Given that the *Ars*, like all Ovid's writings, sparkles with wit, a surprise of this kind is not wholly out of place here. Biographical readings take a very different view of the couplet, however, being by their very nature more concerned with the history of the text's composition than with any humour it might contain. These lines are seen to indicate that the *Ars* was originally published as a man's manual in two books, and that there later followed a second edition with additional material. This would mean that, in preparation for his introduction of a third book, Ovid had revised the first and second, tacking the said verses on to the end of what is now for us Book 2.[1]

We can safely dispense with any long and involved refutations of such 'archaeological' analyses and of an approach that has its roots in nineteenth-century scholarship. Modern critical readers—for example, Gerlinde Bretzigheimer, Markus Janka, and Alison Sharrock—have long since applied their genuinely interpretative skills to the *Ars Amatoria*, and they have demonstrated very convincingly that the three books were conceived from the start as one unit, and that, consequently, the transition from the second to the third book in no way 'contradicts' the specifications at the beginning of the first.[2] The 'turn up for the books' effected by the two verses which follow the *sphragis*[3] is not only a comic device, but also one further

---

[1] For a particularly ardent supporter of the 'second edition' theory, see Murgia (1986). For more cautious approaches, see Hollis (1977: p. xiii) and Küppers (1981: 2533–4), who regard 2. 745–6 simply as a later addition to Book 2.

[2] Bretzigheimer (1981: 3 n. 7, 7); Sharrock (1994*a*: 18–20); Janka (1997: 501–2); see also Holzberg (1997: 111–12) = (2002*c*: 103); Bretzigheimer (2001: 167 with n. 8); Volk (2002: 160).

[3] Henderson in this volume demonstrates the unexpectedness of 2. 745–6 with particular effect. Also important here is R. K. Gibson's observation (2003*a*: 87–8) that the book intended for the *puellae* is implicitly likened in 3. 1–2 to the *Iliad*'s 'sequel' *Aethiopis* and is thus presented as an 'epigonal afterthought'. However, neither Henderson's discussion nor Gibson's discovery mean that we must assume Book 3 to be a later addition tacked on to Books 1 and 2. What we have here is simply another humorous and belittling swing at women, one entirely consistent with the opinion articulated repeatedly between the lines of the *Ars* by the comic *persona* of the *praeceptor amoris*: the female sex is just not as equal as the male. (In *Ars* 1. 55 ff., for example, the *puellae* are classified from the start in a *laus urbis* as part of Rome's assets, like the temples, houses, bridges, etc. usually listed in this genre: see Holzberg (2000*b*: 51). A book for the *puellae*, then, seems not to have been part of the original

application of the principle behind Ovid's arrangement of the individual lessons. He does not set forth his course of instruction in any systematic way, but presents it instead as a loosely connected sequence of ideas for possible manoeuvres within the framework of an erotic discourse. If performed strictly according to the *praeceptor amoris*'s book, these manoeuvres will lead directly to the happy union of the male or female pupil with the desired partner, or, in other words, to bed. Like the contents of comedies or of erotic novels, the programme of study, then, is geared in terms of structure to a happy outcome and, correspondingly, the separate lessons resemble not so much chapters in an academic treatise, but scenes in a drama.[4] The *praeceptor* frequently combines the expounding of his erotic theories with enactments of their practical application, in which he shows us his pupils apparently already busy putting their lessons to good use. Thus he surprises his readers on occasion with the type of unforeseen turn otherwise sprung on them principally on the stage or in narrative fiction. An example: the advice given to male pupils in 2. 702—*si modo duraris, praemia digna feres* ('if you just hang on in there, you will get the deserved reward')—is immediately followed by the stage 'direction' *conscius, ecce, duos accepit lectus amantes* ('Look, the bed, their confidant, has taken in the two lovers'). In this quick 'cross-fade' we[5] suddenly 'see' the *iuuenis* currently receiving his 'deserved reward'. Just as unexpectedly, we later 'witness' the request put by the *puellae* to the *praeceptor* as he finishes instructing his male pupils. And since the young women clearly ask him for lessons because they have heard or read his lectures in Books 1 and 2,[6] we may infer that a reader response is being staged at this point.[7]

---

plan: those who 'count less' obviously do not immediately occur to those who 'count more' and so they have to draw attention to themselves—which is precisely what the *puellae* do in 2. 745–6.)

[4] On 'simultaneity', 'spontaneity', and 'staging' in the *Ars*, see now Volk (2002: 173 ff.).

[5] It is hardly possible to say where exactly the author would have 'us' be in all this—merely watching from the auditorium or on stage as 'chorus' in the midst of the goings-on as prompted by the lessons.

[6] We could think of the *puellae* as present from, at the latest, the end of Book 1's lessons onwards, as they are addressed in 1. 617–18: see Bretzigheimer (1981: 4) and (2001: 167).

[7] Steve Green has quite rightly drawn my attention to the fact that this 'reader response' differs from the audience reactions mentioned below in one important

The string of 'chapters' in the didactic *Ars Amatoria* is reminiscent not only of scene sequences in a comedy or episode chains in a novel, but also of the arrangement of poems in a *carminum liber*. There, one poem often alludes to another that has preceded it, and such references can take the form of remarks which reveal that one or more persons involved in the later poem have read the earlier one. This is a device already detectable in the oldest extant book of Latin poems, the poetic book of Catullus. I share the opinion now voiced in the majority of studies on Catullus, that the order of the texts as we know them represents the poet's own configuration of his collection.[8] Working on this premise, we can observe two instances of reader response there: in poems 16 and 93. In poem 16 we learn how two readers—Furius and Aurelius by name—have reacted to poems 5 and 7, the 'kiss' poems. The poet remarks quite generally at the beginning of poem 16 that the two men have declared him lacking in moral propriety on account of his 'camp' *uersiculi*, and he is later more specific about what they have said:

> uos, quod milia multa basiorum
> legistis, male me marem putatis?   (Catullus 16. 12–13)

(Because you have read about the many thousand kisses you think me not a real man?)

His own view of himself is a contrary one, however, and he stresses this in the poem's final line by threatening the two judgemental readers with anal and oral penetration. Catullus's central concern in poem 16 is his response to what Furius and Aurelius have said

---

point: here the readers are in agreement with the poet, there they are critical, even admonishing. And *puellae* who have evidently been 'overlooked' up until now (see n. 3) could be expected to berate the *praeceptor*. But perhaps their implicit enthusiasm for this sexologist's *praecepta* is meant to convey a touch of irony, perhaps they are supposed to illustrate yet again the truth of the ancient gender discourse's time-honoured belief: women take the 'passive' role, as opposed to the men's 'active' part, and always bow to the 'superior' authority. Furthermore, women were, in ancient times, believed to be more lascivious than men and were thought to flaunt this too. This is discussed at some length in the *Ars*: at the beginning of the second course of lessons for men (1. 269 ff.). The *puellae* are, therefore, simply doing what would be expected of them when they clamour for their own special lessons after the *uiri* have had theirs.

[8] See now Holzberg (2000*a*: 37 ff.); Claes (2002).

about his verses: he does not deny that these are *molliculi* because this is, after all, the way he has to write them if he wants to mix *sal* with *lepos* and, at the same time, provide for his readers erotic stimulation. The poem thus offers both a defence of Catullus's poetry and a programmatic declaration for the poetic book. This suggests that the reader response which prompted the poem has been deliberately staged by the poet as an opportunity for him to announce his poetic agenda.[9]

The assumption that Catullus is simply inventing the two men's reaction to the 'kiss' poems is especially plausible for this reason: Furius and Aurelius have implied that he is an obscene poet, but, instead of proving them wrong, Catullus now confirms their allegation by making his language more obscene than ever before. Something quite similar happens in poem 93, at least if we accept—as I choose to—Severin Koster's punctuation:[10]

> 'Nil nimium'. Studeo, Caesar, tibi uelle placere,
>   nec scire utrum sis albus an ater homo.

('Nothing in excess!' I am keen, Caesar, to please you and not to want to know whether you are a white or a black man.)

If Koster is right to take *nil nimium* as words spoken by the *imperator* to the poet—they do represent a rendering of μηδὲν ἄγαν and so it seems reasonable to read them in a double sense as 'quotation'—then no guesses are needed as to what is 'in excess' here: Catullus has already made fun in poems 29 and 57 of Caesar's sexual practices, portraying him there as, amongst other things, *cinaedus* ('faggot'). A biographical approach to the text would conclude here that the historical Caesar had read those poems when they appeared in separate publications prior to their inclusion in a poetic book,[11] but it is more probable that this, like the reaction shown by Furius and Aurelius to the 'kiss' poems, is a staged reader response. Here again we find Catullus answering the insinuated charge that his verses are obscene by piling on more obscenity. Admittedly this is something we can only read between the lines in poem 93, but it is in my view nevertheless quite unmistakable there. Catullus alludes to terms sometimes used in

---

[9] See Holzberg (2000*a*: 41; 2002*a*: 26–7).   [10] See Koster (1981: 133).
[11] A conclusion drawn, for example, by Koster (1981: 133–4).

the Rome of his day to describe the active partner—*ater homo*—and the passive one—*albus homo*—in a male–male relationship,[12] and we could paraphrase his words roughly as follows: 'I seriously do want to please you [*placere* has obvious erotic connotations too] and I don't even need to know whether you are the one who'll do the penetrating or who'll be the *cinaedus*.' Or, more drastically: 'I'm quite happy to turn you on and I don't care who rams whom, you me or I you!' Assuming that my reading of the poem does hit the mark, then the text illustrates very nicely for us an aspect of ancient lyric poetry that presents itself more and more clearly with every new interpretation: the authors speak through the mouth of a fictitious *ego* and allot to the other persons addressed a role that makes of them figures living and moving in a fictional world.

One thing, at any rate, we can be sure of: the comic effect of poem 93 is greater if the reader response 'cited' there is taken to be an imaginary scene invented by the poet—if, in other words, the offence caused by poems 29 and 57 is a reaction merely imputed to Caesar—than if we assume that the poem is Catullus's answer to criticism which (as was apparently already believed by Suetonius, *Iul.* 73) the historical *imperator* had actually voiced. After all, hearing a Caesar comment on obscene poetry with a μηδὲν ἄγαν sounds, in connection with this kind of literature, more like an advertising ploy on the part of the author, one similar to the way in which publishers today like to quote in their blurb the enthusiastic reactions of eminent readers. In poem 93, then, Catullus puts in a plug for his poetic book, and I believe that Ovid does exactly the same for his own work in the poetological excursus we find in his *Remedia Amoris* (361–96). This comes just after Ovid has announced that he is about to give his pupil some practical pointers for acquitting himself/ herself as a lover. The text at this point reads:

> nunc tibi, quae medio Veneris praestemus in usu,
>   eloquar: ex omni est parte fugandus Amor.
> multa quidem ex illis pudor est mihi dicere, sed tu
>   ingenio uerbis concipe plura meis.   (*Rem.* 357–60)

---

[12] See ibid. 133.

(Now I am going to tell you straight from the shoulder what we have to do during the act of love: *Amor* must be routed from every quarter. Many of these things propriety in fact prevents me from uttering, but just use your imagination to understand more than my words can say.)

There then follows the excursus:

> nuper enim nostros quidam carpsere libellos,   361
>   quorum censura Musa proterua mea est.
> dummodo sic placeam, dum toto canter in orbe,
>   qui uolet, impugnent unus et alter opus.
> ingenium magni liuor detractat Homeri;   365
>   quisquis es, ex illo, Zoile, nomen habes.
> et tua sacrilegae laniarunt carmina linguae,
>   pertulit huc uictos quo duce Troia deos.
> summa petit liuor: perflant altissima uenti,
>   summa petunt dextra fulmina missa Iouis.   370
> at tu, quicumque es, quem nostra licentia laedit,
>   si sapis, ad numeros exige quidque suos.
> fortia Maeonio gaudent pede bella referri:
>   deliciis illic quis locus esse potest?
> grande sonant tragici: tragicos decet ira cothurnos;   375
>   usibus e mediis soccus habendus erit.
> liber in aduersos hostes stringatur iambus,
>   seu celer, extremum seu trahat ille pedem.
> blanda pharetratos Elegia cantet Amores
>   et leuis arbitrio ludat amica suo.   380
> Callimachi numeris non est dicendus Achilles,
>   Cydippe non est oris, Homere, tui.
> quis ferat Andromaches peragentem Thaida partes?
>   peccet, in Andromache Thaida quisquis agat.
> Thais in arte mea est: lasciuia libera nostra est;   385
>   nil mihi cum uitta; Thais in arte mea est.
> si mea materiae respondet Musa iocosae,
>   uicimus, et falsi criminis acta rea est.
> γ rumpere, Liuor edax: magnum iam nomen habemus;
>   maius erit, tantum, quo pede coepit, eat.   390
> sed nimium properas: uiuam modo, plura dolebis,
>   et capiunt anni carmina multa mei.
> nam iuuat et studium famae mihi creuit honore;
>   principio cliui noster anhelat equus.
> tantum se nobis elegi debere fatentur,   395
>   quantum Vergilio nobile debet epos.   (*Rem.* 361–96)

(Recently, you see, certain people have been picking holes in my little book; in their critical opinion my poetry is shameless. As long as I can give pleasure in this way, as long as I am sung throughout the world, let the odd one or other attack my work if they will. Envy runs down great Homer's genius; whoever you are, Zoilus, you have your name through him. Even your poems wicked tongues have torn to pieces, you under whose guidance Troy brought her defeated gods over here. Envy aims at the highest targets; the winds bluster around the highest peaks, the thunderbolts dispatched by Jupiter's right hand seek out the highest peaks. But you, whoever you are, whom my uninhibited manner offends, if you have any sense, then measure each (poem) according to its numbers. Spirited battles like to be reported with the Maeonian metre: what place can there be there for erotic delights? The tragedians speak in grand tones: passionate intensity is suited to the tragic buskin; the slipper of comedy should be worn in the spirit of normal everyday life. In the face of enemies outspoken iambics should be drawn, either the fast-running kind or those that limp with their hind foot. Winsome elegy should sing of quiver-bearing Amores and play the flighty lass just as the mood takes it. In the metre of Callimachus Achilles should not be besung; Cydippe is no subject for your mouth, Homer. Who could bear to have Thaïs playing the part of Andromache? Anyone doing a Thaïs in Andromache's role would be making a serious mistake. Thaïs has her place in my art: my skittishness is unrestrained; I have no truck with the (matronly) head-band, Thaïs has her place in my art. If my poetry adapts itself to suit its erotic content, then I have won and it stands accused of the wrong crime. Burst, voracious envy: I already have a great name; it will become greater still if it will only keep on going with the foot on which it started out. But you are much too hasty: if I can just stay alive, you will have more to feel sorry about, and my coming years hold many poems yet. After all, it feels good, and my appetite for fame increases with every tribute; my horse pants eagerly at the beginning of the climb. Elegy acknowledges that it owes as much to me as does noble epic to Virgil.)

After finishing his excursus Ovid explains what measures a man should take when making love to a *puella* from whom he wishes to free himself (397–440).

The common assumption is that this digression is Ovid's answer to concrete criticism brought forward against him in real life.[13] There

---

[13] See e.g. Küppers (1981: 2515–20); Barchiesi (1993: 173) = (2001: 96) ('Ovid was responding to literary-critical charges'; but cf. n. 22 below); Holzberg (1997: 118) = (2002c: 110); Woytek (2000).

has been much speculation as to the identity of the *quidam*, and some scholars even think that the person addressed in verse 371 is Augustus.[14] For my part, however, I am more inclined to believe that the excursus is another staged reader response, designed by Ovid as a marketing strategy. By maintaining that *censura* has frowned upon his permissive verses, he is merely furnishing himself with an excuse to introduce some poetological thoughts on the genre he has chosen, to blow his own trumpet a little,[15] and to hint at his plans for future poetic works.

That Augustus was the addressee of the excursus has seemed quite likely, because in the second book of the *Tristia*—Ovid's long elegy to the emperor—the poet uses very similar arguments to justify his work and defend his *Ars Amatoria* in the process.[16] It was therefore perhaps only natural to conclude that the criticism responded to in the *Remedia* was the critics' reaction to the *Ars Amatoria*, especially since Ovid twice stresses, at 385–6, *Thais in arte mea est*. A parallel in the poet's vocabulary was taken as confirmation of this: in v. 371, Ovid writes *at tu, quicumque es, quem nostra licentia laedit*, and *laedere* is the word he often uses when talking about the umbrage Augustus had taken at the *Ars*.[17] However, in *Tristia* 2. 211 ff. the emperor is explicitly named as 'plaintiff' in Ovid's case, whereas the censure in the *Remedia* excursus has been voiced by a person or persons about whom Ovid is so vague that one almost automatically begins to wonder whether the latter did not simply invent the 'charges' himself for his own purposes. The criticism too remains somewhat nebulous: did it have to do solely with the lack of *pudor*, i.e. was it purely a moral issue? Or had Ovid displayed *licentia* in his handling of the genre, in other words, was his art at fault? Or was it a bit of both? Ovid's account of the matter tells us no more than that

---

[14] See e.g. Geisler (1969: 345–6); Henderson (1979: 88). Most recently Woytek (2000: 200–7) and Casali, Ch. 11 in this volume: cf. the brief outline of my thoughts on Casali's views in n. 21.

[15] Roy Gibson has kindly pointed out to me that, in antiquity, self-defence would have been a legitimate pretext for self-praise, occasioned either by a real or an imaginary attack. Gibson (2003b: 238–41) offers a useful overview of 'self-praise in the ancient world' (with the relevant passages from Cicero, Quintilian, and Plutarch).

[16] For comparison of the *Remedia* excursus with *Tristia* 2 see esp. Barchiesi (1993: 173–5) = (2001: 96–8) and Woytek (2000: 204–5).

[17] Geisler (1969: 345 n. 2); Lazzarini (1986: 149).

his poetry was labelled *Musa proterva* (362) by 'certain' people and that someone took offence at his *licentia* (371). Over and above this, we could take *lascivia* (385) and *materia iocosa* (387) to be 'quotations' from the 'arraignment'. Book 2 of the *Tristia*, by contrast, makes it crystal clear what Augustus's grievances were. Ovid says there in verse 212: *arguor obsceni doctor adulterii* ('I am accused of being a teacher of indecent adultery'), and in 345–6:

> haec tibi me inuisum lasciuia fecit, ob artes,
> quis ratus es uetitos sollicitare toros.

(My friskiness has made me hateful to you, on account of the arts with which you suppose me to have brought turmoil into forbidden marriage beds.)

There can be no doubt here that the *Ars Amatoria* has given rise to the charges, but in the *Remedia* the things Ovid has to say in vv. 385–8 about his elegiacs do not apply to the *Ars* alone, even if v. 386 does allude to v. 1. 31 of that particular work.[18] After all, elegiac *puellae* of the Thais sort also appear in the *Amores*, the *Medicamina Faciei Femineae* and the *Remedia Amoris* and, if we are just considering the phrases *lasciuia libera* and *materia iocosa*, we must include the *Epistulae Heroidum* on the list of suspects because, in *Ars* 3. 339–46, Ovid recommends this work along with the *Amores* and the first two books of the *Ars* as titillating reading.

Ovid's excursus in the *Remedia Amoris* is not, then, meant to be a vindication of his *Ars Amatoria*. It represents instead: (1) some of his thoughts on the definition of elegy as a literary form, as compared to the genres of epic, tragedy, and comedy; (2) Ovid's styling of himself as the elegiac poet par excellence; and (3) the promise of more poems to come in the future. With items 2 and 3, Ovid is creating intertextual dialogue with the proem in Book 3 of Virgil's *Georgics*:[19] this older text stands in the middle of the didactic poem, just as Ovid's excursus forms the centrepiece of the *Remedia*, and not only do both poets discuss poetological matters in these passages, but they also each introduce there the motif 'more to come in the future'. The last couplet of Ovid's excursus, in which the poet presents himself as the elegiac genre's Virgil, finally modulates properly into the *recusatio*

---

[18] Cf. *Rem.* 386 *nil mihi cum uitta* with *Ars* 1. 31 *este procul, uittae tenues...*
[19] Discussed by Woytek (2000: 192–9).

key already audible in the admonishment of his critics: their *liuor* must clearly conjure up the φθόνος motif used by Callimachus in the prologue to his *Aetia* and, after him, time and again by other poets in their *recusationes*.[20] It is only the emphatic 'pledge of allegiance' to elegy as a genre, however, that the excursus in the *Remedia* and a 'proper' Ovidian *recusatio*—like *Amores* 3.1—have in common. In this latter text the poet also introduces a critical reader: Lady Tragedy. She complains that the *poeta* exceeds the bounds of *pudor* in recounting his deeds and calls on him to switch to the genre that she represents; he promises that he will, but wants to devote a little more time to elegy first. In the *Remedia* excursus, by contrast, nothing is said of any calls by the critics for the poet to change genres, neither—correspondingly—does Ovid mention which literary shape the planned poems of the future will take. From first to last verse here he is on parade as an elegist and nothing else, and this probably has a lot to do with a concern that is, as we shall now see, central to his thinking here: a desire to highlight *lasciuia libera* as a characteristic of the genre.

Let us take another look at the verses from the *Remedia* (quoted above) immediately preceding the excursus. One reason why the poet chooses this particular point to interrupt his lessons for a poetological pause could be this: here of all places, in a book of remedies for the 'lovesick' where he is explaining to the reader ways to cure sexual longing for a particular female, Ovid has to talk now about the best procedures during intercourse! An absurd situation really (and, of course, extremely amusing too). Anyone aware of this incongruity will perhaps initially be 'relieved' to find the poet following up the announcement of his next topic with a note that *pudor* prevents him from saying many of the things he should now be saying, and that the reader must therefore use his imagination.[21] After he has opened his

---

[20] Geisler (1969: 353–4, 368–9) lists the most significant ones.

[21] Casali, Ch. 11 in this volume reads these lines not so much as encouragement for the readers to draw on their own imaginations and sexual fantasies when obscenities are merely hinted at (see also n. 22), but rather as a veiled signal that criticism of Augustus forms the undertone here. This seems reasonable if one takes *ingenio uerbis concipe plura meis* to refer primarily to the excursus and not (as I would read it) to the *praecepta* offered in 399 ff. (even if *pudor* in 359 does, I believe, suggest such a reading). Ovid's contemporaries were naturally at liberty to interpret the excursus in a political sense, whether the *quidam* mentioned be identified as Augustus or not.

excursus by reporting that certain critics have accused him of *proteruitas* and *licentia*, one might then expect Ovid to declare: 'And that is why, when giving said lesson, I shall be displaying the restraint that *pudor* dictates.' What follows, however, is a theoretical discussion of elegy, with Ovid essentially at pains to show that *lasciuia libera* and *materia iocosa*—the very things, that is, which *pudor* would normally shun—are in fact an intrinsic component of the genre. Having dubbed himself as a classic exponent of this *pudor*-eschewing form, he then launches into a lengthy stretch of elegiac couplets that could quite easily be classified as the most obscene of Ovid's entire erotic production,[22] not only as regards content, but also in terms of the language used.[23] This naturally brings Catullus to mind, with the two poems in which he responds to criticism of his obscene verse and issues even worse obscenities than those of which he has (allegedly) been accused. This parallel once again makes it appear probable that Ovid too is staging his reader response. Moreover, just as Catullus had done in poem 16, Ovid extends here his 'reaction to criticism' to include programmatic declarations for his use of the genre. And then he even goes one step further than his predecessor, combining his poetological outing with a self-assured ego trip.

The two texts have begun to diverge at this point, and the difference becomes clearer still when we come to the instructions that follow Ovid's excursus. The pupil keen to cure himself of his love for a *puella* is offered one especially effective remedy: he should

---

One word of caution here, however: the *persona* of the *praeceptor amoris* speaks to his audience through a text that belongs to the 'minor' genres which, whatever numerous classicists from the 1960s onwards have thought, were in their day perhaps not automatically looked on as possible vehicles for political statements. Lorenz (2002) has now shown how shaky interpretations are that approach *Kleinpoesie* in search of *Kaiserkritik* (even Martial has been accused of this); see also Holzberg (2002b: 63 ff.)

[22] Similarly Barchiesi (1993: 175) = (2001: 97) '... a passage where the *Remedia* displays the same irreverence as its antecedent, the *Ars*. The poet is relapsing into his old ways. True, he shows some modesty (359: *pudor est mihi dicere*), but the last line before the apology, *ingenio uerbis concipe plura meis* (360), undermines the entire self-defence. The poet wilfully provokes readers' malice, and invites them to imagine more than what is really said. This is to say that Ovid's didactics... is concerned to construct a lascivious reader.' But not only readers are constructed: critics too, who 'have recently been picking holes in the little book'.

[23] Cf. esp. *ineas*, a verb normally reserved in this sense for animals (Lucke (1982: 402) ad loc.).

purposely concentrate during their intimate moments on the little details that can be so offensive to the eye in 'fleshly dealings'. The possible unsightly sights named by Ovid are all *turpia*, otherwise only verbalized in scatological literature and the like: ugly bits on a naked woman's body (417–18), the external female genitals (429–30)—always an eyesore for the delicate ancient male and his aesthetic standards[24]—traces of sperm and vaginal secretion on the bed (431–2), and bowel movements (437–8). True, Ovid is less than explicit here and does leave the full-colour picture to the readers' imagination, as he said that he would. But he provides more than suggestive snapshots to set this imagination in motion, even just by making his well-versed readers associate this section with other texts from iambic poetry, comedy, and the epigram, the authors of which did not let *pudor* stop them from producing graphic descriptions of any αἰσχρά connected with a female body; cf. e.g. Horace's *Epodes* 8 and 12.[25] By actually telling readers to focus on such irritations, Ovid leads them over the edge, as it were, and beyond the confines of elegy. And for those who sense this, something will now click: before launching into the sort of allusive lewdness that is normally only permitted in iambics, in comedy, and in epigrams, Ovid had just declared himself the Virgil of elegy. The irony is obvious: a moment ago the self-professed 'elegist of elegists', now he seems to be wilfully disregarding the laws of his genre.

These last arguments ought to have shown that the parallels I have traced between the staged reader responses in Catullus and in Ovid's erotic-didactic poems are indeed justified. Final confirmation comes in the shape of Martial's *Epigram* 1. 35.[26] This is immediately preceded by a poem in which the last word is the first obscene one of the book: *futuere*. In the first verse of 1. 35 Martial has a reader

---

[24] One of many passages that document such sensitivities is the description of Corinna in Ovid's *Am.* 1. 5, which, like the description of a woman in *Anacreontea* 16, follows the rule of rhetoric and moves down the body, but stops just before it comes to the *pudenda*. The description of a boy in *Anacreontea* 17, by contrast, does not pass over his αἰδώς (36–7).

[25] See esp. Grassmann (1966) and Siems (1974). Siems shows variously that, far from being stimulated by the kind of αἰσχρά hinted at in *Rem.* 419 ff., antiquity's men were 'turned off' by them, especially if simultaneously confronted with the sight of the female *pudenda* (see also n. 24).

[26] See now Holzberg (2002b: 110–11); Lorenz (2002: 24–7).

reacting to this and he then responds himself to this feedback in a way that clearly betrays Catullus's poem 16 and Ovid's *Remedia* excursus as pretexts:[27]

> Uersus scribere me parum seueros
> nec quos praelegat in schola magister,
> Corneli, quereris: sed hi libelli,
> tamquam coniugibus suis mariti,
> non possunt sine mentula placere.
> quid si me iubeas thalassionem
> uerbis dicere non thalassionis?
> quis Floralia uestit et stolatum
> permittit meretricibus pudorem?
> lex haec carminibus data est iocosis,
> ne possint, nisi pruriant, iuuare.
> quare deposita seueritate
> parcas lusibus et iocis rogamus,
> nec castrare uelis meos libellos.
> Gallo turpius est nihil Priapo.

(I write verses that are not sober enough and that no teacher can read out in school, you complain, Cornelius. But these little books, like husbands with wives to delight, cannot satisfy without a dick. What if you were to tell me to sing a nuptial song in words unsuited to nuptials? Who dresses the Floralia (dancing-girls), who allows whores the modesty of a wifely stola? This law has been laid down for humorous poems: that they cannot amuse unless they titillate. I ask therefore that, with your sobriety discarded, you indulge me in my games and jokes and stop wanting to castrate my little books. Nothing is fouler than a eunuch of a Priapus.)

---

[27] Even clearer than this (cf. *pudorem* with *Rem.* 359 *pudor* and esp. 10 *lex haec carminibus data est iocosis* with *Rem.* 387 *si meae materia respondet Musa iocosae*) is Martial's allusion to *Rem.* 356 ff. in the *epistula* at the beginning of Book 1 (which is taken up again in 1. 35): cf. esp. 1 *epist.* 5 *inprobe facit qui in alieno libro ingeniosus est* with *Rem.* 359–60 *sed tu ingenio uerbis concipe plura meis* and 1 *epist.* 5 *lasciuam uerborum ueritatem* with *Rem.* 385 *lasciuia libera nostra est*. On Martial's intertextual dialogue with Ovid, see also Janka, Ch. 14 in this volume.

4

Vixisset Phyllis, si me foret usa magistro
Erotodidaxis and Intertextuality

Duncan F. Kennedy

The defining premise of the *Ars Amatoria* is that (if one does not know already) one must *learn* how to love (1. 1–2). The classic statement of how this is to be achieved is addressed to the male pupil in 1. 611–12:

> est tibi agendus amans imitandaque uulnera uerbis;
> haec tibi quaeratur qualibet arte fides.

'You must *act the part* (*agendus*) of the lover,' we are told, 'and credibility (*fides*) must be sought by whatever skill it takes.' This is a world of *make-believe*, in a very strong sense of that phrase: you are out to make the world believe that you are what you say you are. The would-be lover is thus instructed to become a *simulator*, a role-player—whilst being aware of the danger that, if you submerge yourself too fully in the role you are playing, you may end up making *yourself* believe that you are what you had started out by pretending to be:

> saepe tamen uere coepit simulator amare;
> saepe, quod incipiens finxerat esse, fuit. (1.615–6)

(Often, however, the one who puts on a pretence really begins to love; often he has turned out to be what at the start he had pretended to be.)

Similarly in the *Remedia*, to fall out of love, you must no less be a role-player, a *simulator*: *quod non es, simula positosque imitare furores* ('pretend to be what you are not, and simulate frenzy laid aside', 497). In Ovid's didactic books, didaxis is equated with mimesis in such a way as to offer a subtle and, from a post-structuralist point of view, very plausible inversion of most of the ('Platonic') assumptions about truth, knowledge, reality, and appearance, and the relationship between world and text that are taken for granted in the Western educational tradition.[1] Learning takes place through imitation, in particular the imitation of words. When one 'plays the role of lover', one is to 'imitate the wounds of love *in words*' (*imitandaque uulnera uerbis*, 1. 611): love is viewed as a discursive construct.[2] A corollary of this is that if social and cultural practices—including love—are seen as discursive constructs, then Life itself is an intertextual phenomenon.[3] In Book 3 of the *Ars Amatoria* (329–38), the *praeceptor amoris* offers his female pupil a bibliography of further reading, including Callimachus, Sappho, Gallus, Propertius, Tibullus, Virgil, and last, but by no means least (339–46),[4] Ovid. The primary intertext, the essential reading, is always, of course, going to be the *Ars Amatoria* itself (341–2; cf. 1. 1–2), but there is much more where that came from. 'Choose', he says, 'from the three books of the *Amores* what you may read,' appropriately for a pedagogical exercise, *docili... ore* ('with a practised voice', 343–4); or one of the *Heroides* (*uel tibi composita cantetur epistula uoce*, 345). The would-be lover is instructed to *perform* these epistles (*cantetur*, 'let it be sung'), and so practise the role of the lover lamenting her abandonment. The *Heroides* therefore offer the pupil the opportunity to practise by acting the part, with a ready-made script penned (at least in part) by someone not unconnected with the *praeceptor amoris* himself. But what might our putative female pupil learn from the exercise, and how? At first sight, Ovid's heroines seem at best negative role models,

---

[1] Argued for in detail in Kennedy (2000).
[2] See Volk's essay in this volume, Ch. 12; also Kennedy (1993: 64–82).
[3] For this textualization of life, and its implications in terms of intertextuality, cf. Fowler (2000*a*: 119–120): 'this "opening out" of the relationship between texts has an even broader implication when coupled with Derridan pan-textualism: if nothing is outside text in the sense that we can only speak and think of anything in language, then intertextuality is not simply about the relationship between this or that literary production but a central feature of human life'.
[4] As Roy Gibson points out (2003*a*: 236 on 3. 339 ff.), the Ovidian syllabus is given almost as much space as the rest put together.

not conspicuously successful at the art of catching and keeping their men. After all, 'Phyllis would have stayed alive, if she'd had the benefit of me as her teacher' (*uixisset Phyllis, si me foret usa magistro, Rem.* 55): the *praeceptor* would hardly state as the 'learning outcome' of an exercise of reading the second of the *Heroides* that his pupil should promptly hang herself as Phyllis did.[5] So, surely total identification is not what is called for—indeed, it would be positively dangerous.

There are lessons here, the *praeceptor amoris* assures us, for would-be lovers, but there are lessons as well for lovers of Ovid's writings. Many of the distinctive intertextual effects we experience in the *Heroides* can be usefully analysed by heuristically seeing the authorial voice as a complex one, an amalgam of the heroine writing and of Ovid writing.[6] Perhaps we can learn more by carrying out a similar heuristic exercise at the level of the reader, and I shall return to consider the theoretical implications of this move at the end of this essay.

Our female pupil is asked to perform the epistle *composita ... uoce.* What might this phrase mean? The *Oxford Latin Dictionary* cites it in the guise of an adjective (s.v. *compositus* 4b) and offers the relatively neutral definition '(of expression) practised, studied',[7] but there could be more than this going on in a text in which simulation and the blurring of distinctions between 'appearance' and 'reality' can be foregrounded as pervasive themes. The verb *componere* is found in

---

[5] That this is the 'outcome' of *Heroides* 2 is foreshadowed in Phyllis' reference to her belt (*zona*, 116; cf *Rem.* 602 and see Barchiesi (1992) ad loc.), in her fantasy that Demophoon should look upon the result of her suicide (133–6; cf. *Rem.* 602, *uiderit*), and in her contemplation of possible modes of making away with herself, culminating in hanging (139–42). It is also implied by what Ovid says about Sabinus' 'replies' to the *Heroides* in *Am.* 2. 18. 32 (*quodque legat Phyllis, si modo uiuit, adest,* 'and there's one for Phyllis to read, *if she's still alive*'). Versions of the Phyllis story also contain her metamorphosis into an almond tree. See the scholiast to Pers. 1. 34: [*sc.* Phyllis] *laqueo uitam finiuit et conuersa est in arborem amygdalum* ('she ended her life with a noose and was turned into an almond-tree'); and Servius on Virgil *Ecl.* 5. 10 recounts that, when she was turned into a leafless almond tree, *postea reuersus Demophoon, cognita re, eius amplexus est truncum, qui, uelut sponsi sentiret aduentum, folia emisit* ('afterwards, when Demophoon returned and recognized what had happened, he embraced its trunk which, as if it sensed the approach of its betrothed, put out leaves'). This detail provides an aetiology for leaves from Phyllis's name. Ovid, as we shall see, was familiar with this detail (*Ars* 3. 38).

[6] See Kennedy (2002*b*).   [7] See also Gibson (2003*a*: 238–9).

the sense, to use the words of the *Oxford Latin Dictionary* once more (s.v. 11a), 'to modify one's appearance (so as to give a particular impression)', and, with the object *uultum* ('face'), 'to modify one's expression (so as to mask one's true feelings)';[8] as a perfect passive participle (*compositus*) it takes on the sense 'having put on a studied or masked expression'. The writings of Tacitus are, not unexpectedly, a good place to look for such usages. Thus when Nero dresses up to roam the streets at night, he does so *ueste seruili in dissimulationem sui compositus* ('disguised in slaves' clothes so as to conceal his true identity', *Ann.* 13. 25). On the death of Augustus and the accession of Tiberius, consuls, senators, equestrians rapidly degenerated into abject slavery:

quanto quis inlustrior, tanto magis falsi ac festinantes, uultuque composito ne laeti excessu principis neu tristiores primordio, lacrimas gaudium, questus adulationem miscebant   (*Ann.* 1.7)

(The more pre-eminent each was, so much the more false and forward, and with their expressions fashioned so as not to appear overjoyed at the departure of the old regime, nor too sorrowful at the inauguration of the new one, they intermingled tears with gladness and laments with adulation)[9]

So, we may perhaps take it that the pupil's voice is to observe that distinction between inner thoughts and outward expression, and is thus to be, if the play is allowed, a 'composite' one, partly empathizing with the past heroine's words, but simultaneously distancing herself so as to scrutinize those very same words for their present erotodidactic significance.

A really assiduous pupil of the *Ars Amatoria* might work through all the *Heroides* systematically, but for present purposes I will confine

---

[8] See also the *Thesaurus Linguae Latinae*, which adduces the examples that follow, and many others, under the rubric *cogitatione fingere, mentiri, simulare* (iii. 2128. 15 ff.).

[9] In an erotic context, we might adduce [Tib.] 3. 6. 33–6 (*ei mihi, difficile est imitari gaudia falsa,* | *difficile est tristi fingere mente iocum,* | *nec bene mendaci risus componitur ore,* | *nec bene sollicitis ebria uerba sonant,* 'alas, it is difficult to imitate joys you do not feel; it is difficult to make up jokes with a sad mind; a smile is not well put on by a lying mouth; not well do drunken words sound to the worried') or 3. 13. 9–10 (*sed peccasse iuuat, uultus componere famae* | *taedet,* 'but it is pleasing to have sinned, and it is boring to compose one's features for reputation'), though in this latter case, Sulpicia's sentiments about the distinction between appearance and reality have a rather un-Ovidian ring to them.

myself to a couple of heroines who are favourite exempla in Ovid's erotodidactic works, Ariadne and in particular Phyllis—a useful pairing, since, as Ovid suggests (*Ars* 3. 459–60), they were similarly abandoned by, respectively, Theseus and his son Demophoon:

> et tibi, Demophoon, Thesei criminis heres,
> Phyllide decepta nulla relicta fides.

(You too, Demophoon, heir to the crime of Theseus, lost all trust with the deception of Phyllis).

Let's start with Ariadne, so frequently treated that the author of the *Aetna* was moved to remark (21–2):

> quis non periurae doluit mendacia puppis
> desertam uacuo Minoida litore questus?

(Who has not grieved over the lies of the treacherous ship, lamenting the abandonment of the daughter of Minos on the empty shore?).

We might remark in passing that the poet's words could be applied to her appearances in scholarly studies of intertextuality and Latin poetry as well: she has become the intertextual heroine par excellence, but plenty remains to be said of her. Indeed, the very triteness of the theme can be turned to pedagogical ends, as we shall see. As our pupil reads *Heroides* 10, she will find herself impersonating Ariadne as she describes herself running to and fro along the shore (19–20). Ariadne herself then tells how she did what she was to become most famous for doing, shouting out the name of Theseus over the sea as, she informs us, the hollow rocks send back his name to her:

> interea toto clamanti litore 'Theseu'!
>   reddebant nomen concaua saxa tuum,
> et quotiens ego te, totiens locus ipse uocabat:
>   ipse locus miserae ferre uolebat opem.   (21–4)

(And all the while as I shouted out 'Theseus' along the whole shore, the hollow rocks sent back your name, and as often as I called out for you, so often did the place itself. The place itself wanted to bring help to me in my wretchedness.)

Now, if our pupil has read John Hollander's *The Figure of Echo: A Mode of Allusion in Milton and After* (1981), she will know that the motif of the echo has been identified as one of the most hallowed tropes of allusive self-annotation. She might thereby catch the familiar tones of the epistle's Ovidian author as well, and recognize that her teacher has marked the text for her benefit. If she has further read the works of Gian Biagio Conte,[10] or, for that matter, Alessandro Barchiesi[11] or Stephen Hinds,[12] she will be aware that this allusive self-annotation can set off a chain reaction which reverberates through, amongst other texts, Ovid's own *Fasti*, where Ariadne laments her desertion for a second time, this time by Bacchus:

> en iterum, fluctus, similes audite querellas.
>   en iterum lacrimas accipe, harena, meas.
> dicebam, <u>memini</u>, '<u>periure</u> <u>et</u> <u>perfide</u> <u>Theseu</u>!'
>   ille abiit, eadem crimina Bacchus habet.
> nunc quoque '<u>nulla</u> <u>uiro</u>' clamabo '<u>femina</u> <u>credat</u>';
>   nomine mutato causa relata mea est.   (*Fasti* 3. 471–6)

(For the second time, you waves, listen to like complaints. For the second time, you sand, receive my tears. I used to say, I remember, 'treacherous and deceitful Theseus'. He went away, and now Bacchus is facing the same charge. Now again I shall cry out 'let no woman trust a man'; my case has been reopened, with the name of the defendant changed.)

As Conte has argued, *memini* ('I remember') tropes Ariadne's textual reminiscence of her 'earlier' exclamation in Catullus 64. 132–3, and her statement in 143–4 that no woman should thereafter trust a man who swears to her:

> atque haec extremis maestam dixisse querellis,
> frigidulos udo singultus ore cientem:
> 'sicine me patriis auectam, <u>perfide</u>, ab aris,
> <u>perfide</u>, deserto liquisti in litore, <u>Theseu</u>?
> sicine discedens neglecto numine diuum
> immemor a! deuota domum periuria portas? ...
> nunc iam <u>nulla</u> <u>uiro</u> iuranti <u>femina</u> <u>credat</u>,
> nulla uiri speret sermones esse fideles'   (Catullus 64. 130–5; 143–4)

(And this she sadly uttered in final complaint, summoning up chill sobs, face wet with tears: 'Is this how you have left me on a deserted shore, faithless, faithless Theseus, having carried me away from my ancestral altars? Is this

---

[10] Conte (1986: 57–69).   [11] Barchiesi (1986: 93–102).
[12] Hinds (1998: 3–5).

how, departing contemptuous of the gods' wills, ah heedless! you carry home the curse of perjury?... From now on let no woman trust a man's oath, nor let her expect that his words will be trustworthy')

Were she to follow this chain, our pupil might learn a lot of useful lessons—not to trust a man, as Ariadne advised, not to repeat your mistakes, as Ariadne did—but I am more immediately concerned about how her reading of *Heroides* 10. 19–24 specifically can help her to distil a practical lesson from this plethora of material. If she failed to pick up the trope of echo in line 22, her enunciation of line 23, *et <u>quotiens</u> ego te, <u>totiens</u> locus ipse uocabat*, should provide an immediate reminder of it. For Ariadne as author of this epistle, the echo is interpreted as pathetic fallacy in line 24: *ipse locus miserae ferre uolebat opem*, 'the very place felt the will to bring aid to me in my wretchedness.' There is a further echoic emphasis on *locus ipse* (23) in *ipse locus* (24) which might encourage our pupil to hear something else here especially relevant to her, attuned as she will be from the *Ars Amatoria* to the slippage between erotics and rhetoric.[13] Ariadne's exclamations have become a commonplace now, a *locus*, indeed, but a *locus* capable of bringing aid to the unhappy. How? When Ariadne shouts out, a key word is almost immediately repeated. Listen again to Catullus 64. 132–3:

> sicine me patriis auectam, <u>perfide</u>, ab aris,
> <u>perfide</u>, deserto liquisti in litore, Theseu.

A gorgeous epanalepsis, to be sure, but perhaps a bit more than that. This may be a sin of omission on my part, but I have never seen it remarked, by Catullus' commentators or elsewhere, that this kind of epanalepsis between the fifth foot of one hexameter and the first foot of the next occurs no less than three times in the curse-poem, the *Dirae*, and thus can be seen to take on the attributes of a formal curse:

> diuisas iterum sedes et <u>rura</u> canamus,
> <u>rura</u> quibus diras indiximus, impia uota. (2–3)

(Once again let us sing of our divided homes and lands, lands on which we have pronounced our curses, unholy prayers.)

The epanalepsis functions here as a performative utterance, and is effectively glossed by the phrase that follows, *quibus diras indiximus*. Twice more in the poem we find the same pattern:

[13] See Kennedy (2000: 170).

Erotodidaxis and Intertextuality 61

> Sic precor, et nostris superent haec carmina uotis:
> 'undae, quae uestris pulsatis <u>litora</u> lymphis,
> <u>litora</u>, quae dulcis auras diffunditis agris,
> accipite has uoces: migret Neptunus in arua
> fluctibus et spissa campos perfundat harena'   (47–51)

(Thus I pray, and in my prayers let these spells prevail: 'Waves, that with your waters beat the shores, you shores that spread sweet breezes over the fields, listen to my words: let Neptune with his waves move on to the fields, and cover the plains with thick sand')

> piscetur nostris in finibus <u>aduena</u> arator,
> <u>aduena</u>, ciuili qui semper crimine creuit.   (80–1)

(Let the foreigner ploughman fish on my lands, the foreigner, who has always grown wealthy from civil strife.)

By attending to the echo—in all its ramifications—our pupil can learn how to curse. Ariadne's 'invention' of the technique is somewhat fortuitous—the accident of being in a responsive landscape—and its consequences will not be immediately evident to her (curses need time to take effect, and may only be recognized as such in the light of their consequences); but our pupil can observe Ariadne's use of language, note those consequences, and so extrapolate a technique that can be applied systematically in the future.[14]

We might see this as a good example of student-centred learning: give the pupil a bibliography of further reading and let her follow it up. With *Heroides* 10. 19–24, we see an example of what she might be able to do with a bit of initiative. One aspect of teaching is the contingency of its outcomes, a theme that I have argued elsewhere is taken up in the programmatic Chiron/Achilles *exemplum* with which Book 1 of the *Ars* opens: the behaviour of Achilles with Priam could not be foreseen at the moment of Chiron's teaching, and yet in hindsight could be credited to it.[15] Set a pupil to read one

---

[14] The *praeceptor amoris* commends knowledge of Greek as well as Latin (*Ars* 2. 121–2, *nec leuis...| cura sit... linguas edidicisse duas*, 'nor should it be a concern you hold light to learn the two languages'; cf. Sharrock (1994*a*: 49–50)), and our pupil may detect in Ariadne's phrase *patriis... ab aris* a Catullan bilingual pun (duly 'annotated' by *patriis*) on *ara* (Latin: altar/Greek: curse) which, as in *Dirae* 3, effectively glosses for our benefit (if not for Ariadne's) her performative utterance.

[15] See Kennedy (2000: 160–2).

of the *Heroides*, and she may come up with things her *praeceptor* may never have dreamed of. We are frequently reminded in the *Ars Amatoria* that *ars* is an ever-emerging phenomenon; crude techniques are rendered more sophisticated in the course of time to counter the enemy's advances in the 'arms race' constituted by the battle of the sexes (cf. *Ars* 3. 1–2). For example in 1. 101 ff., the behaviour of the Romans of Romulus' time is characterized by primitive manifestations of *ars* in a number of areas, not simply the erotic, which have their obvious counterparts in the more sophisticated practices of Ovid's day; the theatre, the stage, the seating, the music, the applause.[16] Ovid may congratulate himself that he was born when he was (*Ars* 3. 121–8), but we should not therefore assume that his poem is the last word on what it has to say, or that his pupils are not going to take his ideas on to the next stage.

Having probed in some detail what our pupil might do with a short passage, let's look in as much detail as space permits at what she might do with one of the *Heroides* overall. The names of Theseus and Demophoon are often linked in the literary tradition, on the basis of 'like father, like son', for example in Propertius 2. 24. 43–4 (*paruo dilexit spatio Minoida Theseus, | Phyllida Demophoon, hospes uterque malus*, 'Theseus loved the daughter of Minos for a short time, and Demophoon likewise Phyllis, each of them a bad guest'), but more significantly for our purposes in *Ars* 3. 35–8, so the epistle of Phyllis, *Heroides* 2, might be a good exercise to set our pupil. Particularly as it occurs earlier in Book 3, that reference in the *Ars* and its context should be especially familiar to her, so let's remind ourselves of it, and of the lessons the *praeceptor amoris* might expect her to take away from it:

> saepe uiri fallunt, tenerae non saepe puellae,
>   paucaque, si quaeras, crimina fraudis habent:
> Phasida, iam matrem, fallax dimisit Iaso;
>   uenit in Aesonios altera nupta sinus.
> quantum in te, Theseu, uolucres Ariadna marinas
>   pauit in ignoto sola relicta loco.
> quaere, Nouem cur una Viae dicatur, et audi
>   depositis siluas Phyllida flesse comis.
> et famam pietatis habet, tamen hospes et ensem

---

[16] See Labate, Ch. 10 in this volume.

praebuit et causam mortis, Elissa, tuae.
quid uos perdiderit, dicam: nescistis amare;
defuit ars uobis: arte perennat amor.
nunc quoque nescirent! (3. 31–43)

(Men often deceive, not so gentle girls; if you look into it, they incur few charges of treachery. Deceitful Jason dumped Medea, when he'd already made her a mother, and a second wife filled the gap in the son of Aeson's embraces. And, for all you cared, Theseus, Ariadne was food for the seabirds, left all alone in a place she didn't know. Just ask why the Nine Ways are so called, and hear how the woods wept for Phyllis by dropping their leaves. He has a reputation for upright behaviour, but your guest, Dido, provided you with both the sword and the motive for your suicide. I'll tell you what did for you all: you don't know how to love; you don't have the technique, and it's technique that makes love last. Would that they still did not know!)

Men frequently deceive (31), not so often tender girls; seldom do they stand accused of deceit. Recall the injunction to the male in Book 1 (611 ff.) to play the role of the lover, and to achieve trust (*fides*) by whatever means it takes. The female is thus all the more in need of systematic study of this particular topic so as to counter male strategy. Four examples of male deception follow, Jason, Theseus, Demophoon and Aeneas,[17] all of whom could be lumped together as ungrateful guests. That point is not made wholly explicit (though cf. *hospes* in 39), but in all forms of didaxis, not to speak of erotodidaxis (and intertextuality!), we are encouraged to see similarities and extrapolate from them. Phyllis is evoked in 37–8 aetiologically through the name of the route of her nine visits to the shore to watch for Demophoon, and through an allusion to her metamorphosis into an almond tree after her suicide by hanging, wept over by her fellow trees as they drop their leaves.[18] What destroyed these women,

---

[17] Lines 39–40 contain a clear echo of the concluding couplet of *Heroides* 7, a further reminder of the relevance of this collection to the *Ars*; cf. Gibson (2003*a*: 98–9) on 3. 29–42. All the figures named here are implicated in that collection.

[18] It is widely, and certainly correctly, assumed that *Heroides* 2 is based on Callimachus' treatment of the story of Phyllis and Demophoon in his *Aetia*, which is lost to us except for one line (fr. 556 Pf. νυμφίε Δημοφόων, ἄδικε ξένε ('Bridegroom Demophoon, treacherous guest'); cf. Jacobson (1974: 58–9). Barchiesi (1992) has painstakingly tracked a number of passages in *Heroides* 2 that reflect Callimachean language or themes. He remarks (1992: 109) of the phrase *quaere... et audi* in *Ars* 3. 37 that it reflects the structure of aetiological question and answer, and so may function as a

we are told, is that they didn't know how to love; they lacked *ars*—or maybe even the *Ars*. Recall how in *Remedia* 55, we were told how Phyllis would have lived had she had the benefit of the *magister*'s teaching. So, girls are less likely to deceive—or were so in the days of Phyllis—though things have since changed (to the discomfiture of the *praeceptor amoris*: *nunc quoque nescirent!*, 43) and are likely to change even more, we may surmise, if the *Ars* is to have its desired effect. Thus primed to see Phyllis as a victim of *fraus* and not privy to the amatory techniques that will be developed in the future, our pupil can embark on playing her role ready to empathize with—but also practise the convincing display of—the emotions of being deceived, whilst simultaneously alert to the lessons she might draw. Some of these lessons she may very well have learnt from the *Ars Amatoria*, and so the exercise functions as a form of revision and reinforcement. Others, however, she might well develop herself...

As we saw, the male lover was instructed to play the part of the lover, and to seek *fides* ('trust') by whatsoever means (1. 611–12). Our female pupil will find the Phyllis of *Heroides* 2 peculiarly defenceless in the face of male deception: Demophoon was, it appears, very successful in instilling *fides*—at least until now. Her attention cannot fail to be drawn by the remarkable concentration of *fides* and related terms of belief and deception in the epistle. Lines 25–6 of her epistle encapsulate this tone:

> Demophoon, uentis et uerba et uela dedisti;
> uela queror reditu, uerba carere fide.

(Demophoon, to the winds you gave at once your words and your sails; my complaint is that your sails are without return and your words without faith.[19])

---

marker of authorial indebtedness to Callimachus. In his note to *Her.* 2. 22, where Phyllis remarks *ad causas ingeniosa fui* ('I have been ingenious in finding causes' [for Demophoon's absence]), he draws attention to a similar sentiment in Acontius' letter (*Her.* 20. 23 ff.) and its extant point of reference in Callimachus *Aetia* fr. 67. 1–3 Pf., commenting 'il tema potrebbe avere in qualche modo precedenti callimachei' (1992: 131). Just so; but, given the clever ways in which he exploits his major source texts in the other *Heroides*, if we hearken to the Ovidian author's voice here rather than Phyllis', we may perhaps detect a similar claim in respect of his appropriation of Callimachus' prototype: 'I have been ingenious in respect of the *Aetia* (*causas*)'. If so, it is very frustrating not to know exactly how.

[19] *Verba dare* is a favourite Ovidian phrase for 'to fool'. For Phyllis' other references to *fides* cf. 31, 102.

The aim of the male lover in Book 1 is *capere*, to ensnare, and Phyllis has walked straight into the trap (she uses this verb of herself in 54 and 74). Our pupil might note that, in *Ars* 1. 613, it needs no great effort to win a woman's confidence since *sibi quaeque uidetur amanda* ('each woman seems loveable in her own eyes'), and might see in Phyllis' words in 65 (*sum decepta tuis et amans et femina uerbis*, 'as both a lover and a woman, I have been taken in by your words') evidence for this statement. 'Tell me', she complains, 'what have I done wrong, except that I have loved not wisely' (*dic mihi, quid feci, nisi non sapienter amaui*, 27): loving *wisely* (*sapienter amare*) is precisely what Ovidian erotodidaxis is all about.[20] One who has been *capta* and *decepta* is sorely in need of *praecepta*. Our pupil might be particularly struck by lines 49–52, with their threefold repetition of *credidimus*.[21] 'I had faith in your soft words, and you had a supply of them,' she begins, 'I had faith in your lineage and their names':

> credidimus blandis, quorum tibi copia, uerbis;
>   credidimus generi nominibusque tuis;
> credidimus lacrimis—an et hae simulare docentur?
>   Hae quoque habent artes, quaque iubentur, eunt?

But as our pupil mimes Phyllis' indignant questions in 51–2 ('I had faith in your tears—or is it the case that these too are taught [*docentur*] to feign [*simulare*]? Do these too have their techniques [*artes*] and flow where bidden?'), she cannot help but notice the didactic register of the language. What for the ingénue Phyllis are incredulous questions, our more knowing pupil will be prompted to note as standard items of erotodidactic wisdom from that very section of the *Ars* in which the male lover is instructed how to be a *simulator*:

> et lacrimae prosunt; lacrimis adamanta mouebis:
>   fac madidas uideat, si potes, illa genas.
> si lacrimae, neque ueniunt in tempore semper,
>   deficient, uncta lumina tange manu.   (1. 659–62)

---

[20] Cf. *Ars* 2. 511–12, *quisquis sapienter amabit, | uincet et e nostra, quod petet, arte feret* ('whoever loves wisely will prevail and will get what he seeks from my expertise/*Ars*').
[21] The verb appears also in 9, 10, 53, and 63.

(Tears too are useful; you'll move adamant with tears: make sure, if you can, that she sees your cheeks wet. If your tears won't flow, and they don't always come on cue when you want them, touch your eyes with a greasy hand.)

A particularly assiduous pupil, who had been reading her *Amores* as she has been told, *docili . . . ore*, would already be familiar also with the advice of Dipsas in 1. 8. 83–4 (*quin etiam* discant *oculi lacrimare coacti,* | *et faciant udas illa uel illa genas*, 'furthermore, let your eyes learn to shed tears when you demand it of them, and let "this rival" or "that" make your cheeks wet') and familiar also with McKeown's note ad loc.,[22] which catalogues feigned tears as one of the great conventions of the lover's discourse—modern no less than ancient, as she will recall from her reading of the prologue of *The Taming of the Shrew* (124–8): 'And if the boy have not a woman's gift | To rain a shower of commanded tears, | An onion will do well for such a shift, | Which in a napkin being close conveyed | Shall in despite enforce a watery eye.' Once the distance to recognize something as a convention has been achieved, it can be transferred to fresh situations as knowledge.[23] And, as *The Taming of the Shrew* suggests, this is a skill that over time has become associated more with women than men, a situation the *praeceptor* perhaps anticipated in *Ars* 3. 291–2:

> quo non ars penetrat? discunt lacrimare decenter
> quoque uolunt plorant tempore quoque modo

(Where does technique not find its way? They [i.e. females] learn to shed tears becomingly, and they cry at the moment, and in the manner, they want).

Our pupil may conclude that Phyllis, like the Romans of Romulus' time, is at a fairly rudimentary stage of erotodidactic awareness, though experience, a powerful motivating force in this area (cf. *Ars* 1. 29), is beginning to lead her painfully in that direction. The capacity for identification is a vital element of erotodidaxis, both identification *of* (recall how we were invited to see Jason, Theseus, Demophoon, Aeneas as all *alike* in some respects) and identification *with*. Phyllis knows about Theseus' desertion of Ariadne, and our pupil may reflect that

---

[22] McKeown (1989: 244).
[23] *Mutatis mutandis* think of the epanalepsis which we have, only just now, recognized as a curse.

Phyllis is far enough advanced to see Demophoon's behaviour in terms of role-playing (cf. particularly *Her.* 2. 78): 'you act (*agis*) the heir of your father's treachery, perfidious one (*perfide*)'. She has detected that Demophoon is acting out the role of Theseus, but how aware is she, as she utters the imprecation *perfide*, that she is acting out the role of Ariadne, let alone drawing all the lessons she might from the experience of Ariadne? Phyllis has got as far as apostrophizing Demophoon with the adjective Ariadne applied to Theseus, *perfide*, but here, as our pupil will have noticed also from *Rem.* 597 ('*perfide Demophoon' surdas clamabat ad undas*), she hasn't quite mastered the technique of cursing him (the waves are not listening)—a point our pupil will have observed did not escape the poet of the *Culex*, who curses Demophoon on Phyllis' behalf[24] with the now obligatory epanalepsis:

posterius cui Demophoon aeterna reliquit
perfidiam lamentandi[25] mala—perfide multis,
perfide Demophoon et nunc deflende[26] puellis.   (*Culex* 131–3)

---

[24] The context of this difficult passage is the poet's catalogue of the trees in the grove in which a shepherd will be stung by the gnat of the poem's title. Most of the trees are associated with stories of metamorphosis as, allusively, the almond tree is here: neither the almond nor Phyllis are named, and the only oblique reference to the metamorphosis, which confers a kind of immortality, comes in the adjective *aeterna* (cf. *Met.* 10. 164, where Orpheus says to the transformed Hyacinthus *aeternus... es*). Hence the poet must enunciate her ongoing curse for the transformed Phyllis.

[25] All the manuscripts and Clausen in the Oxford Classical Text (1966) read *lamentandi*, but the genitive dependent on *mala* offers an idiomatically unusual sense. *mala* is the term regularly applied to the grief and distress of lovers, and is usually not further defined (as e.g. in Virg. *Ecl.* 10. 61, *Aen.* 4. 549, Tib. 1. 2. 87, 1. 8. 64, 2. 6. 19, Prop. 1. 5. 28, 1. 7. 14, 1. 9. 18, Ov. *Her.* 11. 33, 21. 53, *Rem.* 138, 526, 768). I have a preference here for Weber's *lamentanti* (1832, ad loc.), i.e. 'to whom, lamenting his treachery, Demophoon left eternal misery'. Erotic *mala* were normally ended by death (cf. Tib. 2. 6. 19, *iam mala finissem leto*, 'I would by now have put an end to my woes by death'), but although Phyllis killed herself by hanging, her metamorphosis into the almond tree ensured that her grief was everlasting.

[26] The manuscripts all read *defende*, which is meaningless here. The only plausible conjecture is Scaliger's *deflende* (1573), though one normally bewails the injured party or the injury itself, rather than the injurer. Who are the 'many girls'? In the context of the grove description, we might take it to connote other trees (cf. Ov. *Rem.* 606, *non flesset positis Phyllida silua comis*, 'the wood would not have wept for Phyllis by shedding its foliage'); for *puella* in such a context as the equivalent of *amygdalum*, cf. Cat. 64. 290–1, where the poplar is referred to as *lentaque sorore | flammati Phaethontis*, 'the swaying sister of burnt Phaethon'), but as well as admiring this choice example of Alexandrian allusivity, our female pupil might see in *et nunc*

(Next along was the one to whom Demophoon left the everlasting woe of lamenting his perfidy—treacherous Demophoon treacherous, even now bewailed by many girls.)

For one prepared (if we follow Palmer's interpretation of *Her.* 2. 13) 'to consign Theseus to perdition by magical arts' (*Thesea deuoui, quia te dimittere nollet*)—a practice, by the way, the *praeceptor* would most certainly frown upon (*Ars* 2. 99 ff., *Rem.* 249 ff.)[27]—Phyllis' failure to curse *Demophoon* is remarkable, and has been duly remarked upon by many commentators on this poem, who point to the centrality of Phyllis' curse in the version of the myth transmitted by Apollodorus. Phyllis' epistle arises out of her recognition, and complaint, that Demophoon's words lack faith (*queror... uerba carere fide*, 26); in lines 31–2, Phyllis asks where now is that faith he pledged (*pacta fides ubi nunc*), the right hands joined, and the talk of god ever on his lying lips (*quique erat in falso plurimus ore deus*). Phyllis assumes that the many gods by whom Demophoon has falsely sworn will see to his punishment (43–4): 'Should each and every one of the many gods you have wronged take vengeance, your one life will not be sufficient to pay the penalty.' It may be that Phyllis is naive enough to believe that her own curse is not required: our pupil might recall how in the *Ars*, the male lover was advised boldly to make promises, and to back them up with an oath by the gods, who were indulgent to such behaviour (1. 630–6). Although the school of hard knocks is giving her inklings of an emergent *ars amandi* which in its developed form will long after her be codified by the *praeceptor amoris* for the benefit, and elaboration, of future generations, she doesn't know what to do with that incipient knowledge.

Could that rudimentary awareness even be leading her to disaster? Is a little learning a dangerous thing? She sees Demophoon as acting out the role of heir to his father Theseus' treachery (*heredem patriae, perfide, fraudis agis*, 78). Why? Because he has not returned to her at the time he said he would (*te... | ultra promissum tempus abesse queror*, 'I complain that you are away beyond the time you promised to come back', 1–2; *at tu lentus abes*, 'but you are taking your time

---

deflende puellis an invitation to herself to maintain the tradition of memorializing the abandoned heroine's *aeterna... mala*, not least by perpetuating the curse.

[27] And see also Barchiesi (1992: 128) ad loc.

away', 23). The time at which she writes her letter is thus vital: how long is Demophoon now overdue? At this point our pupil will need to play the role of textual critic. The crucial passage is close to the start of the letter:

> cornua cum lunae pleno *semel* orbe coissent,
>   litoribus nostris ancora pacta tua est—
> luna quater latuit, toto quater orbe recreuit;
>   nec uehi Actaeas Sithonis unda rates.
> tempora si numeres—bene quae numeramus amantes—
>   non uenit ante suam nostra querela diem. (3–8)

(When *once* the horns of the moon should have come together in a full orb, your anchor was due for our shores: the moon has waned four times, four times it has waxed with its orb complete, but the Sithonian wave does not bring the ships of Attica. If you were to count the days—which we count well who love—my complaint does not come before its time.)

Commenting on *semel* (3), Palmer in his commentary remarks 'If the better MSS. permitted, I would gladly read *quater* with Burmann', who felt that one month was not long enough for Demophoon to go to Athens, get his affairs in order there, and be able to get back to Thrace, and that anyhow it was more appropriate to an impatient lover that she demand the fulfilment of the promise when it was due, not that she should wait for three months before writing.[28] Some versions of the story, which may of course be dependent on Ovid's, stress Phyllis' impatience. So Hyginus, who states that 'when [Demophoon] did not arrive on the day that had been agreed, [Phyllis] on that very day is said to have run to the shore nine times, which from her is called "the Nine Ways" in Greek. Phyllis moreover from longing for Demophoon breathed her last' (*Fab.* 59).[29] The scholiast to Persius 1. 34 (see n. 5 above), who mentions that she hanged herself, says she did so through impatience brought about by love

---

[28] Burmann (1727) ad loc.: *Non uidetur tempus mihi satis longum, ut Athenas ire, ibique res suas componere, & rursus in Thraciam redire potuerit... Conuenit etiam melius puellae impatientius amanti, ut ad ipsum tempus pactum promissa exigeret, non ut tres menses ultra constitutum cessaret, antequam scriberet.*

[29] *Qui die constituta cum non uenisset, illa eo die dicitur nouies ad litus cucurrisse, quod ex ea Enneados Graece appellatur. Phyllis autem ob desiderium Demophoontis spiritum emisit.*

(*amoris impatientia*). Those who favour *semel* draw attention to Phyllis' own protestations of patience,[30] or see the delay of three months as showing Phyllis to be over-credulous.[31] Had Callimachus' version survived, it might have been possible, as our pupil will have noted from her reading of Penelope's letter which immediately precedes this in Ovid's collection (*Her.* 1), to catch from its intertextual resonances with its 'source' text the exact moment at which Phyllis is envisaged as writing; certainly the importance of this issue in reading any of the collection will have been impressed upon her by its importance in the first.[32] She also cannot have failed to have taken into account Laurel Fulkerson's shrewd observation:

> It is significant that no extant version of this story (besides *Heroides* 2, according to most scholars) features a Demophoon who unambiguously abandons Phyllis; he generally wants to return but is prevented by circumstances. His deliberate abandonment has been taken as an Ovidian innovation; perhaps it is rather an innovation of Phyllis.[33]

Phyllis' description of her actions, climbing the cliffs and scouring the horizon for sails (*Her.* 2. 121–2), and running into the breakers

---

[30] Cf. Barchiesi (1992) ad loc. Laurel Fulkerson (2002: 150 n.16) counters this by arguing: 'yet much of the irony of *Heroides* 2 derives from the fact that, to Phyllis, waiting this long to write [i.e. the *four* months agreed] *does* show restraint'.

[31] Jacobson (1974: 71).

[32] See Kennedy (1984). As Steven Green has pointed out to me, there are many ways in which the first two *Heroides* constitute effective contrasting exempla for the female pupil. Penelope provides a fitting contrast to Phyllis' deficient *ars*. They are both faced with men who, they complain, are 'slow to return' (Ulysses is *lento* in *Her.* 1. 1; Phyllis complains of Demophoon *at tu lentus abes* in *Her.* 2. 23). Our pupil might read the discrepancies in detail between Homer's *Odyssey* and *Heroides* 1 as a consistent tactic on Penelope's part to deceive Odysseus in an attempt to get him to return home (e.g. she shows her concern by suggesting that she initiated the search for her husband, and makes conscious errors (e.g. line 15) to convince him that she has little real knowledge of events far away); see Green (2004). 'Might, therefore,' he continues, 'the female student see Penelope as an ideal role-model? (i) she mixes hope of her fidelity with fear of the future (*Ars* 3. 477, *fac timeat speretque simul* ['make him apprehensive and hopeful at the same time']) and feigns rivals (*Ars* 3. 677); (ii) the final word of the epistle, *anus*, may explain a lot: Penelope has resorted to the tactics suitable to her, i.e. trickery, rather than the beauty tips which Ovid reserves for younger women (*Ars* 3. 59 ff.); (iii) as she is eventually successful in getting her man back, she is someone to whom Ovid's students can aspire. In the process, Penelope's situation "corrects" *Ars* 3. 69–70, which suggests that old women are destined to lie alone.'

[33] Fulkerson (2002: 148).

on the shore (*Her.* 2. 127–8), recalls those of Ariadne (Cat. 64. 126–9; *Her.* 10. 25–8).[34] She accuses Demophoon of playing the role of his father (*Her.* 2. 78), not least from her perspective in the latter's abandonment of Ariadne:

> de tanta rerum turba factisque parentis
> sedit in ingenio Cressa relicta tuo.   (*Her.* 2. 75–6)

(From the host of events and deeds associated with your father, it is the abandoned Cretan that has impressed itself on *your* mind.)

But does she see Demophoon as a second Theseus only because she herself has completely internalized the role of Ariadne? We only have Phyllis' word for it that Demophoon is 'his father's son'. Perhaps from the host of deeds associated with the father, it is the 'abandoned Cretan' that has impressed itself on *her* mind, to the extent of taking over her very identity and determining her actions, with catastrophic results.[35] In some ways, as our pupil has detected, Phyllis makes a disastrous Ariadne, learning little from the latter's experiences.[36] But in the make-believe world of role-playing, she has, albeit perhaps inadvertently, made the world, or at least the literary tradition, believe her. In that sense, Demophoon remains truly accursed, however faulty Phyllis' technique is in this regard. Nonetheless, total identification at best leads nowhere (and can be disastrous); no two sets of circumstances are precisely the same. By contrast, our pupil, miming Phyllis, though with sufficient distance to reflect upon what she says, might conclude that, while Phyllis has made the step of recognizing Ariadne's situation as a (possible) parallel to her own, she is simply *replicating* her behaviour—to the extent of also damning

---

[34] When Ariadne depicts herself as running to and fro along the shore with the deep sand slowing down her girlish feet (*nunc huc, nunc illuc, et utroque sine ordine, curro;* | *alta puellares tardat harena pedes, Her.* 10. 19–20), we also have the prototype for the behaviour that will give the 'Nine Ways' their name.

[35] As noted above, versions of the story have Demophoon return distraught to find Phyllis dead. *Heroides* 11, in Gareth D. Williams's reading (1992), suggests that Ovid was not averse in the *Heroides* to cliffhanger plots infused with the irony of over-hasty action, and it is possible that the interaction of Ovid's version with Callimachus' may have afforded readers fortunate enough to have had access to the latter the opportunity of seeing something similar going on with *Heroides* 2.

[36] To be fair, Ariadne also makes a very bad Ariadne, as Ov. *Fast.* 3, discussed above, makes clear.

Theseus—rather than observing it, theorizing it, and learning from it—the 'transferable skills' that are the essence of a progressive *ars*, and the object of the very exercise our pupil has been engaged in, miming her heroine *composita...voce*.

There may be lessons here for us as well from the figure I have somewhat cavalierly been calling 'our' female pupil.[37] How we envisage this reader will reflect the theoretical agenda served by an appeal to the notion of intertextuality. At first sight, as her existence is prompted to us by the *praeceptor amoris* himself, she might seem ideally suited to 'playing the role' of Conte's 'reader-addressee':

> The model of the reader in my studies is quite simple, and it is only the current situation of literary criticism which obliges me to comment on it. I could define my operative notion as the idea not of a *reader-interpreter* (which seems to have become prevalent in contemporary hermeneutics), but of a *reader-addressee*. The reader-addressee is a form of the text; is the figure of the recipient as anticipated by the text. To this prefiguration of the reader, all future, virtual readers must adapt themselves.[38]

As Lowell Edmunds remarks, this figure is one that the poet 'had in mind' or 'intended', and so 'stands in for the intention of the poet that Conte elsewhere repudiates'.[39] It makes of you or me—the 'reader-interpreter' of 'contemporary hermeneutics' viewed with such suspicion by Conte—a 'virtual' reader. Conte's 'reader-addressee' represents a strong recuperation of traditional philological practice, and of the configuration of historicism championed by it, what Conte elsewhere terms the rediscovery of 'the text's true historical intentionality'.[40] For 'contemporary hermeneutics', however, meaning is a readerly construction, and is only fully realized at the point of reception, by you or me, here and now.[41] From this perspective, it is Conte's reader-addressee that is the 'virtual reader', who finds his or her realization only in some actual historically situated reader, ultimately the present interpreter. This metaphysical scrap over

---

[37] For a wise analysis of the scholarly use of the first person plural and the way in which it is deployed to blur the distinction between past and present see Edmunds (2001: 40).

[38] Conte (1994: p. xx).   [39] Edmunds (2001: 41).

[40] Conte (1994: p. xix).

[41] For a clear statement of this position in relation to intertextuality see Fowler (2000a).

'appearance' and 'reality' will sound oddly familiar to anyone who has persevered with this essay thus far. These two extremes offer different configurations and evaluations of the relationship of 'past' and 'present'. If, with Conte, the goal of interpretation is to 'discover' the literary work's original intentionality (without which, as he remarks with some justification, if somewhat hyperbolically, 'our very relation with these works loses its genuine interest'[42]), the historicizing assumptions at work focus attention upon the 'past'. Interpretations (including Conte's own) 'discover' things 'there in the text' that, regardless of the historical moment of their revelation, are assumed to have been ontologically there all along if deemed, according to whatever prevailing criteria, 'true'. Consider in this light the suggestion made above about Ariadne's 'invention' of the curse. This may never have existed for Ovid, but in a world of make-believe in which we have convinced ourselves, it has now (*quod incipiens finxerat esse, fuit*).[43] If with Fowler, meaning is 'constructed' at the point of reception (i.e. 'now', whenever that is), the—no less, but differently—historicizing assumptions at work privilege the 'present' moment in the ever-emerging meaning of the text, which floats free of the intentions of its author and of its subsequent interpreters.[44] Consider—in this light—the suggestion made above about Ariadne's 'invention' of the curse. The discussion of *Heroides* 2 presented here can help to crystallize the issues. The process of *learning* requires the drawing of a distinction between 'past' and 'present', so as to set up a dialectical interplay of epistemological lack and plenitude. Perhaps we can learn a lesson from our female

---

[42] Conte (1994: p. xix). Note again the rhetoric of 'reality' in the terms 'very' and 'genuine' deployed in favour of his preferred interpretative model.

[43] Contrariwise, what existed then (Callimachus' *Aetia*) as part of the text's 'true historical intentionality' is for us the stuff of fantasy.

[44] Moreover, 'past' and 'present' are not dates in history so much as temporal markers of epistemological change. If I may be allowed an Ovidian gesture, let me commend my own discussion of these issues. See Kennedy (2002a, Essay 1 *passim*, esp. 33): 'The present is... not a date in history (though it can be assigned a date "in" history). Rather, the cohesive ordering of those entities (physical, sociological, philosophical, and the rest) deemed transcendent, an ordering that places figures far removed in date shoulder to shoulder (Lucretius and Perrin; or Protagoras and Michael Dummett, as it may be), constitutes *a* present; and it is the replacement of those entities by others rendered no less coherent in the subsequent period that works to create a sense of time that passes.'

pupil, who, in playing the role the *praeceptor amoris* has set for her, seeks, in the spirit of Conte, to enter into an empathetic identification with the past heroine's words as they were written, but simultaneously distances herself, in the spirit of Fowler, so as to think about those same words in terms of their present erotodidactic significance. We too for our part, so as to negotiate the relationship between the 'past' of Ovid's texts and the 'present' of our interpretative assumptions, might seek to play our role as readers likewise, *composita... uoce.*

Part II

Erotics

5

In Ovid With Bed (*Ars* 2 and 3)

John Henderson

1. METHOD

ulteriora pudet docuisse

(To take my teaching any further means blushes.)

(3. 769)

This chapter focuses on the join between the two main units of the poem, the two book panel addressed to males, and the third book 'for women'. The diptych culminates in a page of sex in bed, as the youth finds that women in their prime (over 35, he specifies) make better sexual partners, whether in terms of erotic technique and experience, or in terms of physical maturation. The manual presses upon readers the goal of simultaneous, mutual, reciprocal orgasmic intercourse. This involves full recognition of the necessity, for the realization of Ovid's training programme, that his male graduands should incorporate parity between self and female other. The point is put in terms of the metaphor of 'winning', as if in battle, of 'victory' (*uinco, uictoria*). Male partners must be 'defeated' by their females if they are themselves to 'overcome'. The logic that 'Women must overcome, too' is, to all appearances, a surprise twist, as the conclusion to two books of all-out predation, assault, seduction, and sexploitation.[1] It

---

This is down to Roy Gibson and Alison Sharrock. Fancy luring me on all these years. The conference paper was called 'OVID CYBORGS, INC.' until I realized it would give the Amatorians a bad name; in the event, the working title was 'fucking.Rome.com', and began: '*quis cetera nescit?* It had to come.'

[1] James (2003: esp. 207) politely nails the poser dead: 'The desire to give a woman pleasure, however, is rather undercut by the pleasure the *praeceptor* himself takes

also serves as a step towards the even huger surprise of the third book 'for women', which was not anticipated in the programme at the start of Book 1, or anywhere else along the way before the bolt from the blue explodes in the final couplet of Book 2.

The essay rereads through Books 1 > 2 to search for disguised, de-emphasized, troped, incidental items in the pedagogy that would serve as preparation/grounding for the revelation of the need for the 'special relationship' of the sexual politics of that 'parity in ~~victory~~'. A backgrounded but interwoven narrative of amatory temporality is traced from the very first lesson's listing of the omni-availability in Rome of females for boys to bed in a catalogue arranged so as to lead up to the older woman as its final entry, right through to the last lesson before our now-indoctrinated lovers get between the sheets for perfect sex, which admonishes males to be careful not to bruise feelings by making tactless personal remarks, the last instance of which is mentioning age to the ageing.

If this is a winning analysis, and I think it is (rather than me fucking over the reader), then it follows that Book 3 will *not* seem anywhere near so much of a bolt-on extra, a supererogatory appendix, or second thought, or later botch-up (the writer fucking up himself). It may even be billed for us as an attempt to achieve the vital parity in winning which has just emerged as the pinnacle of erotic nirvana. But, in that case, Book 3 is one book light, outnumbered 2 to 1. How dumb is that?

The chapter looks back, once again, for a third way, and fixes on the schedule of works as programmed and implemented in Books 1 > 2. This review at once confronts the foregrounded oddity that Book 1 sets out three aims for the male tripos, and marks the achievement of each objective as faithfully as you could wish, at the rate of 2 out of 3 in Book 1, and the remaining 1 out of 3 monopolizing Book 2. A tripartite course in a bipartite manual which debouches into a supplementary third volume makes for a suggestive

from seeing her conquered by sensation. [317 n. 149: This undercutting is reinforced by the final instruction of *Ars* 3, to the women: to fake their climax convincingly, if they don't actually experience it (797–804). Thus the *praeceptor*'s preference for simultaneous climax (*pariter uicti*, 728) may be more ideal or theoretical than practical or even necessary....] Female sexual pleasure, in other words, is a sign of male sexual prowess, as will be made clear again in *Ars* 3.'

textual fusion of premature rush to readerly satisfaction with progressively maturing slowing to readerly collusion with the poem, as experience transforms *it* from sex-object to equal partner in the quest for jouissance. The fit of sex to text is tight but well-lubricated, as the erotic curriculum dashes from its all-out thrash of a start taking on all-comers, through the premature ejaculation of Book 1, and into Book 2's undivided story of continuing persistence, endurance, and eventual pacing to match the partner in perfection.

So three peaks scaled in two books overachieves, leaving a third book free for the work of supple-mentation that is only announced when its necessity has been realized. The third book presents its own set of tropes and logics for its relationship to its preceding predecessors, including the precedent of the poetic 'palinode', which promises to reverse and re-verse earlier work. This ineluctably extends our field to embrace the whole range of Ovid's erotic pedagogy, since the *Remedia Amoris* must suggest itself as 'palinode' for the *Ars*. Inspection of the relationship turns up many continuities, both stated and enacted, between *Ars* and *Remedia*. In a sense, *Remedia* supplements *Ars* 3, thus evening up erotic parity with *Ars* 1–2;[2] and thus achieving a four-book package in all. So the essay is put to bed with notes in a brief 'appendix' on Ovid's play with numbers, of books, aims and objectives, around the topic of *amor* and the *Ars*; and bounces this play off both his own and other classical poets' practice and play with quadripartite publication. A good time is had by all.

2. INTRODUCTION

sed repetamus opus: mihi nudis rebus eundum est

(Hold on. Let's make it over: I'll have to get to it in stark reality.)

(3.747)

Ovid's men and women come together when *Ars* 3 joins *Ars* 2:

...2. 744 > the bridge couplet, 745–6 > 3. 1,...

[2] See esp. R. K. Gibson (2003*a*: 39 n. 106); he adds, *per litteras*, that *Ars* 3 × 812 verses and *Rem.* × 814 contrast with *Ars* 1 × 772 and *Ars* 2 × 746.

The couple—he and she—bed down at 2.703: *duos accepit lectus amantes* ('One bed, two lovers').[3] The twosome first touch her up digitally, slow and easy, through 720. Lingering Latin gets busy. Eyes tremble and flash, moans, mutters, groans, fun words, to 724. It turns out this has turned into two-way genital sex between the 'fingering' of 707 and the 'touching' of 720 or so. The crunch is coming. At 2. 725–8 we are told both parties should stay in time, not leave each other behind or go on ahead. Togetherness is full pleasure, parity between female and male:

> sed neque tu dominam uelis maioribus usus
>   desere, *nec* cursus *anteat* illa tuos;
> ad metam properate *simul*: tum plena uoluptas,
>   cum *pariter uicti femina uirque* iacent
>
> (Don't you run up bigger sail, don't leave the madame
>   in your wake; nor should she pip you in your race.
> Quicken pace together, past the post: brimming joy's
>   when woman and man lie done in par defeat.)

This jouissance is the opus and the end of the opus is the 'victory' that overcomes *both male and female*: *u i c t i* ('beaten', 728; 730, 733).[4] So far, however, Ovid has to all appearances taught males to 'overcome'; he has not come out and taught them that they must learn to be 'overcome'.

So the finalized project is incomplete. The female must (have) 'overcome', too, for 'parity' to be achieved, everyone a winner (3. 3):

> ite in bella pares; uincant.

(Into battle you go, on a par. Let 'em win.)

Now (how?) to pitch female nudity against male rocketry—fairly (3. 5):[5]

---

[3] See the excellent notes in Janka (1997: 486–501), '703–32. Vergnügen beider Partner als Ziel und Inhalt des Liebesspiels'.

[4] The Zweiwortverbindung *femina uirque* = Ovid territory, pair-shaped, cf. *Am.* 1. 10. 36, *Ars* 2. 478, 682, 728, 3. 800, *Rem.* 814, *Tr.* 2. 6 (Janka (1997: 355–6)). Feel the savagery of Murgatroyd's selection when *Ars* 2 is cut between 595–6, ... *nec uos | excipite arcana uerba notata manu*, and 733, *finis adest operi*; but cf. Murgatroyd (1982: 1), quoting Patrick Wilkinson, ' "the prurient will read on with increasing disappointment, and may never reach their first meagre reward at the end of Book II" (there is also a rather naughty bit at the end of Book III)'.

[5] Myerowitz (1985: 122), 'The sly sexual innuendo undercuts all pretense at equality.' For *uinco*—and *faueo* (4)—as *sermo amatorius*, cf. Henderson (2002: 55–8).

> non erat armatis *aequum* concurrere nudas.

(It wasn't even stevens—loaded guys and disarmed gals.)

Either Ovid has ruined his syllabus in the run-in, or else we must go back over the coursework, and learn how come this feat of simultaneous defeat by both parties is the due climax of the sex manual's strategy. If Ovid hasn't fouled up, a sustained and persistent subliminal induction must lurk embedded between the covers, the debouchment of which issued in re-conceiving the telos—just as the text was making it. According to our best intuitions, Ovid's 'cyborgasm' is out to mate *ars amatoria* with *amor artis*, packaging 'Erotic Technique' within 'Affect Analysis'.[6] If the overt line of instruction did not lay out the 'victory for parity' for all to read, was it building to a surreptitious climax of narration? Underneath, the *form* of the poem undergirds its lesson for loins, the mannered *impetus* of epic didactic melding into the phoney *ratio* of elegiac mindfuck?[7]

The alternative would be paradise lost once glimpsed from the gate. Have three objectives in two books (outlined in the proem, 1.35–40) proved to be too few? Did The End come all too soon? If the Last Waltz is to fit the bill, *Ars* 3 will, it seems, have to do double duty: since it starts outnumbered 2 : 1, it must carry twice the punch. Otherwise, this inexact science will need further, still-to-come, supplementation to even up the odds—unless, conceivably, we can find brute quantities qualitatively redressed closer toward parity by undercutting the male-led programme of *Ars* 1–2.

---

uinco: Ars Armata 1. 168, 190, 192, 201 *bis*, 205, 211 *bis*, 248, 278, *femina uicta*, 302, 394, 462, *puella uicta*, 477, 666, 684, 699–700 *bis*, 2. 181, 197, 205, 406, 512, 539–40, 716, 728, 742 *bis*, 3. 3, 6, 366, 648; *Rem.* 668, 678, 712 (cf. John Henderson (1991: 46), on *Am.* 2. 7. 1). For tumbling dice on the way to [so to] bed, Ovid did sneak in counsel of 'Harmonie durch *Assentatio* und G e w i n n e n l a s s e n beim Spiel' (197–8, with Janka (1997: 176–8)).

[6] Cf. Hinds (1998: 131–5), on 'the sexually frank end-zones of the *Ars Amatoria*' (2. 703–10, 3. 769–78), at 134, 'Ovid's behind-the-door Muse embodies a principle of narrative coyness which is programmatic for the *Ars*' whole approach to sex.'

[7] From wild hunt of the beast to cultured choreography: Green (1996), cf. Watson (1984) on 2. 467–92. Heady sex is in the head: e.g. *Ars* 1. 357–8, *mens bis*, 2. 112, *ingenium*, 119, *animus*, 145, 501, *sapienter*, 3. 25, *hae mentes* (~~heroines~~), 57, (poet's) *ingenium*...; cf. Wildberger (1998). But we should [not] blank out the thriller kill of the game, the hate knotted in Ovid's games of love:... love Ovid, hate love, love poetry, hate [wo]men, love reading, hate being read, love learning, hate to be taught, love hating [wo]men, hate knowing it, love an alibi, hate demotion to voyeur, love sophistication, hate to be told how, love desire, hate stereotyping... love-hate R. D. Laing/Ovid.

- Amatorious Articulation: Ovid's games with numbers are summarized in the *Appendix* below.

3. ESSAY: BED-WRITTEN OVID

'praecipue nostrum est, quod pudet', inquit, 'opus'

('That's my speciality', said She, '—make it, and blush'.)

(3. 770)

We need both approaches: parting of the legs *and* parting of the ways at/between 2. 744 >< 3. 1. And this because of the premature completion of a triple objective, as a pair of books is spent. 'Parity' *could* suggest a second pair ahead—and in *Remedia* Ovid *does* insist on declaring, at the outset, that he is still the lover he was in *Ars*.[8] Ovid yesterday, Ovid today, Ovid forever (71–2):[9]

Naso legendus erat tum cum didicistis amare,
    idem nunc uobis Naso legendus erit.

(Ovid was required reading when you learned to be lovers.
    More Ovid will be your required reading. Encore.)

The model of Stesichorean palinode invoked to gloss the complementary role of *Ars* 3, as supplement to *Ars* 1 + 2 (3. 49–50),[10] serves as *internal* precedent for an external supplementarity and complementarity of *Remedia*, as the remainder of the dose from Ovid's pharmacy.[11] If *Ars* 3 + *Remedia* combine to complete the course,

---

[8] Cf. Green (1996: 232).

[9] Ouroborous Ovid is *still* chasing his tail when *Remedia* has the gall to refer back to *Ars* for help in bailing out of one beauty by capturing new booty (487): *quaeris ubi inuenias? Artes tu perlege nostras.* When you begin the beguine again, Michael Finnegan. Cf. Henderson (1979: 27) for triangulation between the preliminaries of *Remedia, Amores*, and *Ars*. Repetition < > differentiation = artistic *amor*. Sharrock (1994*a*).

[10] Helen and Stesichorus' palinode: Woodbury (1967); Gibson (2003*a*: 106–7).

[11] See Rosati, Ch. 8 in this volume. In the *Regius*, the heading actually reads: *Remediorum Liber Primus*. And at 397, the *Puteanus* even marks a book division. Cf. Henderson (1979: p. xix).

however, they do so by *un*doing the foundation module of *Ars* 1 + 2. (Stesichorus himself wrote not one palinode but *two*: the concept is intrinsically recursive—palindromous, *en abyme*...)

There is every incentive to try this one on: the final score of the male project is undone by its own unforeseen incompleteness. It was *not* the only show in town it supposed itself, after all. This is a self-inflicted puncture that is not to be repeated when *Remedia* arrives to supplement the triptych *Ars* 1–3: for *Remedia* proclaims itself readable for girls *through* its address to men, *mutatis mutandis* (49–50):

> sed quaecumque uiris, *uobis quoque dicta, puellae,*
>   *credite*: diuersis partibus arma damus.
>
> (Come, the instructions for men were also for you, babes,
>   Trust me, appointed arms dealer to both sides.)

Thus undoing, and indeed scotching, with one devastating swipe of 'What's sauce for the gander is sauce for the goose', the [superficial] switch of address to women pupils between *Ars* 2 and 3.[12] Lo! Women only get the 'left-overs' that hadn't been needed to overcome the Amazons (*supersunt*, 3. 1).[13]

Now *Achilles* has been, and remains, a chief type for the male trainee from the start (*Ars* 1. 11).[14] He is joined by his partner *Penthesilea* across the divide between *Ars* 2 and 3 (3. 2; cf. only *Rem.* 676). In myth, Achilles + Penthesilea signifies sex-n-death, when she is overcome by the ultimate orgasm [death], and he is overcome by [love for] the woman he has overcome, as he overcomes her.[15] And in *those* terms, as I have hinted, the male project of *Ars* has

---

[12] *Remedia* addresses women, in tandem with men, at 607–8 (the moral for the story of Phyllis), 813–14 (The End). Even up front, *Ars* 3 is very often insecure in directing its address to women: from *ite*, 3 onwards (cf. *parcite*, 9, and its gender destabilization by 10); and from 5–6 onwards, instructs men: *uiri*... (in 7–8, *aliquis* is already a male interlocutor figure: see Gibson (2003a: 21, 35–6), 'The *puellae* and the male audience of *Ars* 3'). *Amores* 2. 1 already modelled the layering of reading constituencies which ensures that there is *only* 'over-reading', reading the readings of other readers—the only game in love town.

[13] On Ovid's positioning of *Ars* 3 vis-à-vis 1–2: Gibson (2003a: 85–7).

[14] *Ars* 1. 441, (682), 689, 701, 743; 2. 711, 741; cf. *Rem.* 381, 473, 477, 777.

[15] For this myth, with or without necrophilia: Frazer's note on Apollodorus, *Epitome* 5. 1. For the (Homeric) supplementarity of an Amazonenbuch, hosting a regiment of female losers, cf. Gibson (2003a: 86, 87).

already culminated in its own sexological flunking: *pariter uicti*. Not so fast. If our teacher must spurt for the finishing line rather than run that occupational risk of the lecture that runs out of time before reaching its conclusion, his *point* is that the pair of lovers in bed should *not* rush the rush of it. Gently does it, this copulation in couplets, hexameter to pentameter, the near parity of 6 : 5. Yet, lo! *Ars* 1 + 2 came too far too soon: to hit all three targets in what will stand as two of three books is in fact to overshoot the mark, by a third.

The time has come to look back over the series of lessons that have come to a head with this self-deflating revelation. To take a shot at seeing how the defeat of male predominance in sex, despite superior capability, was written into its exegesis all along. Long before any surprise post-war bombshell announced the necessity for 'parity through *female* defeat' for the whole project to count as fulfilled. Mission, not just emission, achieved. Long before we could possibly have seen it coming.

The poem's simplest model for an 'equalizing' of the amatory male through giving him his head is the Hesiodic-Stesichorean-ubiquitous mythic paradigm of Helen of Mycenae: the boy who begins as *Paris* is a *Menelaus* in the making (e.g. 2. 358–72). In time, he will be conditioned to take the rough with the smooth in a world of mass-produced Parises, and of ageing Parises like him. There is, however, one consolatory teaching folded into the finale of the training schedule for boys. It turns on the dynamics of keeping an 'extra', follow-up, manual under wraps until its necessity has been revealed. The 'parallel' lines of the [Gibsonian] story of [Sharrockian] womanufacture: *Ars* 3.

First, however, we need to recap the erotonarratology of *Ars* 1 + 2. Narrative 'drive', teleology, *impetus* will come first; pleasure will have to slow and defer before it can 'reasonably' become *ratio*. *Ars* 1 prodded the freshman into a world that was his oyster. Countless women, all ages available, every one of them is on, they're all mad for it on the bangbus, female lust wins hands down. Just collect your yesses; the odd no is no problem because lads always hanker after the next thrill, the grass is always green(er). Method-act the lover, and soon you'll be doing it for real. For, yes, the gent must 'go first, break the ice, get it on, start up' (*coepisse priorem*..., *alio*... *incipiente*,...

principium..., 1. 705–12).[16] And that is what is happening in the structure of the poem, as it wades through the laddishness of the go-getting first strike to second base. Whether this is seen as nature at work, or culture's construction of nature, the male is taking the lead; his claim to monopolize narrative focalization is founded on the unchallenged postulate of his anteriority in 'courtship'. Gently does it: notice, nonetheless, the muffled *sous-entendu* in Ovid's rhyming phraseology (1. 707–10):

> a nimia est iuueni propriae fiducia formae,
>   exspectat siquis dum *prior illa* roget!
> [*uir prior* accedat, vir verba precantia dicat:
>   excipiet blandas comites illa preces.]
>
> (Too, too much faith has the lad in his personal profile,
>   [if he hangs fire till *she* pops the question!]
> *He's* to come on first, and pop it – his to begin the begging:
>   beg hot, she'll play ball and cop the suggestion.)

It takes two, baby, whereas one is one and all alone.

Yes, we could sense that it takes at least twice as long to hold on to love and make it last.[17] The whole of Book 2 'endures, sticks it out, persists': e.g. *duret*, 119, *permanet*, 120, *mansuri*, 242... The *Ars* is a *perpetuum carmen* ('unified composition')—a 'drawn-out, stitched together, aggrandized, running version of *Amores*' (*longus*... *amor*, 1. 49), and *Ars* 2 is, quintessentially, ἓν ἄει σμα διηνεκὲς ('one unified composition'). First off, Ovid doubles back to the theory test of 'gaining access [to women]'. This time, though, the yes or no hustle of the Plenty More Fish in the Sea mentality, 'all gagging for a male, any male (though maybe, this time, all but you)', is displaced by

---

[16] *Ars* 1. 277–80 should have left us in no doubt that this is a cultural contract that overlies the natural call of the female animal on heat: *conueniat maribus, nequam nos ante rogemus, | femina iam partes uicta rogantis agat. | mollibus in pratis ammugit femina tauro: | femina cornipedi semper adhinnit equo.* If Call of the Wild noises can serve *homo sapiens* as their How about It, the question arises—*do they*? See Myerowitz Levine Ch. 13 in this volume. But *Ars* 2. 481–8 equivocates some more on this: way back when, *femina uirque* did without a tutor; but any salivating documentary on the Birds and the Beests will show how The Female 'gets/finds', 'chases', and 'is held by' their Male, ... [so as] to 'get mounted, enjoy, bear up, get sent delirious': *ales habet quod amet; cum quo sua gaudia iungat, | inuenit in media femina piscis aqua; | cerua parem sequitur; serpens serpente tenetur; | haeret adulterio cum cane nexa canis; | laeta salitur ouis; tauro quoque laeta iuuenca est: | sustinet immundum sima capella marem; | in furias agitantur equae... sequuntur equos.*

[17] 'How long does a relationship have to be to rate as "long"?' (Sharrock 1994a: 49). Habituation, *longue durée* in love, is dismantled at *Rem.* 503.

persistence from the boy, who must try every trick in the book on one elusive, resisting, target. He should let what he does appear as if it is by request from her. The complaisance does work still—as well as flattering everything else about her, he should verbalize his carnal pleasure, the joy of sex avowed, out l o u d (2. 307–8).[18] But this is now an *effort*. Getting her *used* to him takes time, getting used to not rushing into the china shop can't be rushed, and takes Ovid time to articulate in ever more tortuous narration, and he must put up with the tedium (from 339 ff.).[19] Yes, he can have lots of women on the go at any one time, separately (from 387 ff.); and some women *need* a rival (435 ff.). But there is 'pain in love', (the pain *of* love): *in amore dolores* (from 519 ff.). Endure, don't be a bore—the cause, now, of tedium (530). *difficilis labor* is part of Ovid's new deal—be patient, now, with a rival (537–8):

> difficilis nostra poscitur Arte labor.

(Hard labour. Such heavy demands on my pArt.)

The drift wends onwards, to pull up short at 647:[20]

> quod male fers, assuesce, feres bene.

(Hard to take? Get broken in, you'll take it good.)

So even for the experienced doctoral graduate of Romeo University, each she steadily commandeers the time of his life. *Amor* turns out to bring its pay-off 'if the male can only last it out' (702): *si modo duraris*. By this stage, the he has been programmed for sharing that double bed (703 ff.). He has been imprinted with the superiority of conjoined 'parity' of pleasure between man and woman (682):

> quod iuuat, *ex aequo femina uirque* ferant.

(The joy's for woman and man to take on a par.)

What released this denouement was, first, the turn of the tide when Ovid exercised his right to double back on his tracks, pointing out

---

[18] Cf. Janka (1997: 246), 'Begeisterung und Komplimente im Bett (anlässlich der *munera Veneris*, die er freilich erst gegen Ende des Buches eingehender behandelt, vgl. u. V. 703–32).'

[19] See ibid. 269, cf. 271–2. Ovid's *ars moratoria*: Heyworth (1992). *Remedia* will recommend non-stop monopolizing of the girl you want, to bring on boredom soonest (539): *taedia quaere mali: faciunt et taedia finem*.

[20] 'Die "Wunderwirkung" der *assuetudo*' (Janka (1997: 450–1)).

that the customized advice he gives may call for retuning or reversal when circumstances change (427–8):

> qui modo celabas monitu tua crimina nostro,
>   flecte iter et monitu detege furta meo.
>
> (You were just using my manual to hide your crimes?
>   Now change tack, use my manual to bust your scams.)

For this Ovidian double-cross will call the poor amoralist back to suspicious rereading and re-versing the pages of his manual. And second, the slide from 'long-term habituation' in *amor* (*uetustas*, 647)—which can talk its way out of trouble by euphemism—to specially underscored emphasis on never reminding her of her *age*... which then triggers special recommendation of the mature woman:[21] she is worth the investment, the 'effort' ploughed into her, the 'endurance' (669): *tolerate labores*. For *both of them*, see, are not getting any younger, by the page. But wearing yourself out pays dividends because (besides contortionist acrobatics any way you want it, 679–80), mutuality in sex depends (hey presto!) on equal response in sex (682–3):

> odi concubitus, qui non utrumque resoluunt.

(I can't stand sex that doesn't cut both partners loose.)

For wominids (listen to the man) mature like wine (695–6).[22] The sexually non-responsive woman who lets him, but thinks of her knitting or does her duty, is no good. Not compared with women who verbalize the joy of sex, and request slow and easy, who do the Mad Eyes Overcome thing, and the Flopped Out Tantalizing bit (685–92). The weird wired-in magic (you *must* know) of the over-35-year-old watershed crossed by the majority of the female of the species (693–4):[23]

> ... bona ...
>   quae cito post septem lustra uenire solent.

---

[21] 'Gelenkfunktion', see ibid. 462, on 663–702.
[22] Cf. Labate (1984: 98–101). For the complementary 'Benefits of a Mature [male] Lover': Gibson (2003*a*: 317–18) on 3. 555–76.
[23] The pose of 'collective' address to women as well as men in *Remedia* wears thinnest at moments such as 399, *ubi concubitus et opus iuuenale petetur*.

(...the candy...
  that generally comes soon upon turning thirty-five.)

Worth the wait; worth the effort; the persistence; the endurance; therefore worth nothing even conceivable by the graduand of *Ars* 1, nothing realizable by his grooming for boys playing the field: Hollists can know and teach nothing of this.

Of course, you're thinking, the instructor's guidance of the male towards women of a certain age only *happens to be* through the discipline of long-term dedication and perseverance. So a loophole may yawn. Maybe it's just possible to skip straight to pretty well any woman in her prime—here's one we prepared earlier. But it may not be possible to stop boyish hustle *except* by letting it rush ahead, and then coaxing it into biding its time until steady enough to listen to reasons for working towards a different sexual orientation. Even though it *was* actually on offer from the start (1. 65–6):

> ...seu te forte iuuat sera et sapientior aetas,
>   hoc quoque, crede mihi, plenius agmen erit.

(...or maybe you go for the late, more clued-up, crop?
  This formation, trust me, spills over as well.)

The full-grown woman of the world was already specially recommended here, but darkly, without amplification or comment, as the clincher to a muffled programme of narrative in prospect, set out in terms of stages in her ageing process. Only a second-time reader could second-guess this. And, when I read it, the *Ars* is playing at playing another game, too—the conceit that the disciple *lives* the plot, so reading ahead for a sneak preview is, imaginarily, verboten. Of course, we student readers *of the reader student* can't be held to *that* contract with the Reader in Latin Libido; but the pleasurable game of pretend seduction into living by the book [of Ovid] depends on the illusion that we have indeed been hunted down, netted, and bagged for keeps, for real.

Now to cross the great divide between *Ars* 2 and *Ars* 3. Validation of the claims of woman to sexual 'parity' through the taming of raw testosterone, the fight back, may be the point of departure for *Ars* 3, but it proves to be very much the point *from* which it departs. The book satirically feasts on the imperfections that saturate the female sexual subject/object.[24] Here, her ageing is not the promise of twin peaks of sharing sex, but blemish, regret, disgust (esp. 3. 59–82).[25] Her translation into Ovid's cyborg creation,[26] the Living Doll/Private Dancer/Supermodel Mannequin designed to service him and simultaneously the Poet's Masterpiece and Icon for the Poem,[27] *already* poisons—inoculates—the predatory male against her reality: eat your heart out, pseudo-philosophizing, mock-renunciatory, *Remedia* (remedying *what*? What will be left of amorous affect?).[28]

What *Ars* 3 does to our 'romanticized' scene of a properly together healthy fuck as the climax of *Ars* 2 is of course to double-take it, going over the same ground to make a difference (a cancellation...). In the reprise, 'with the gloves and every other stitch off' (*nudis rebus*, 3. 747: cf. 747, above, *sed repetamus o p u s*), we get to sexual acts via the crashed-out drunk who deserves all she gets, down on the floor and out to the world (765–6):

> turpe iacens mulier multo madefacta Lyaeo:
> digna est concubitus quoslibet illa pati.

(Disgusting! A horizontal She, awash, molto vino.
Deserving the sex inflicted, at your pleasure.)

Next to her, stuffed, her sister is lost in a dream, but was it a dream? Ugh, whichever (767–8):

> nec somnis positâ tutum succumbere mensâ:
> per somnos fieri multa pudenda solent.

(No, it's unsafe to surrender to post-prandial naps:
In naps plenty can happen to cause blushes.)

---

[24] So, succinctly, Leach (1964: 147–8).

[25] Sharrock (1994a: 44).

[26] For Woman as 'cyborg' cultural monstrification, see esp. Haraway (1997); cf. Latour (2002); Graham (2002: esp. 200–20), 'Cyborg writing'; Gray (1995). Erosion-erasure of distinctions between human and artificial intelligence is invading-pervading minds and bodies, erotics and fiction: Lodge (2001).

[27] See the fine detailed reading by Downing (1990) picking out the 'anti-Pygmalion' degradation processing of woman in *Ars* 3 from its weave into the book's hard sell of man-serving robotics/self-serving poetics. Myerowitz (1985: 97) shows how this make-over of woman-as-masquerade starts and finishes inside her bedroom; where we snoop, and males can but intrude: cf. Gibson (2003a: index s.v. boudoir).

[28] For *Ars*' 'anti-Lucretian didactics', see Shulman (1981: esp. 250–3).

Ugly abjection. Suffering sex, sex to *suffer*. Then, the way to realize Ovid's touchstone of '*equal* pleasure for a hetero-couple'—*ex aequo res iuuet illa duos* (794)—is, face it, for her to pick the position that flatters her best. Yes, again, the cue calls, verbalizing the joy of sex is good (795–6). But some in the freshwomen class will be faking every whimper and yell of ecstasy. Sex ought to be enjoyed 'equally' by hers and hims (800):

> quo *pariter* debent *femina uirque* frui

(that woman and man should enjoy on a par)

—but such is life. Those Mad Eyes can be faked; +/− optional Panting; if the body can't lie, nevertheless its secrets may be hers, not yours... (804). *Post coitum omne animal triste est*, someone said. She may already be planning to claim her rake-off, *instanter*. Keeping the curtains drawn because she's a sight and a fright (805–8). Even so, Ovid may declare, 'the story has managed an Ending'—[some more] sex has been *had* (809): *lusus habet finem* (cf. *finis adest operi*, 2. 733). Finally, ultimately, *Ars* 3 attains underlined, slide-rule, 'parity' with *Ars* 1 + 2 as we hit the closural couplet that writes *finis* as triumph (3. 811–12 ∼ 2. 743–4).[29]

> ut quondam iuuenes, ite nunc, mea turba, puellae
>   inscribant spoliis NASO MAGISTER ERAT.
> sed quicumque meo superarit Amazona ferro,
>   inscribat spoliis NASO MAGISTER ERAT.
>
> (As one time the lads, so now come all ye lasses, my group
>   -ies must write on the winnings: OVID WUZ COACH.
> ∼
> Come on, anyone overcome their Amazon with my blade?
>   He must write on the winnings: OVID WUZ COACH.)

Only for the double agent's double-dealing *Remedia* thereafter to amplify and exacerbate these ugly 'thought bubbles' already supplied for Amatorians in Bed by the Professor of Sexology. Copulation degrades some more. (Don't) Think about it. Not only is he cheating

---

[29] See esp. Gibson (2000). It appears that these winsome women's winnings, after successfully faking orgasm, must celebrate their—agreement not to press for payback afterwards! (Gibson (2003a: 404))

on her all over town, every minute that he is not devoting to this particular long-term nest-egg dividend, but he has only just got through screwing someone else, anybody else, so as to make sure the sex doesn't go too well and risk letting *her* catch *him* (*Rem.* 399– 404).[30] The amateur gymnastics will be *least* flattering to her physique if he has anything to do with it. Virtually a non-contact sport. He'll be after opening those curtains she is keeping shut, to catch her in the least attractive light (411–12). Post-coital blues are livid: the instant that ecstasy is done and dusted, he'll be bored—and regretting ever having touched a woman and vowing he'll never touch one again, and focusing on anything he can find wrong with her body, to store up against the threat of any repetition in the future. Once bitten. Thinks...: 'Some men are freaked out by seeing a woman during sex, and some by damp patches, or [   ], fouling the sheets' (429–32).[31] Maybe 'erotic parity' only amounts, in the end, to him having the proverbial 2-on-1 sex romps (441):

> hortor ut pariter binas habeatis amicas

(I strongly recommend: a brace of playmates on a par.)

(cf. *bipertito*... *utroque*, 'halved... both', 443). Conceivably, there just is no 1-on-1 sex for him. And all too probably, that is 'the final', last gasp, 'conclusion' about 'Ovid's' Rome 'a-Fucking' (811): *hoc opus exegi.*

A full programme of aversion therapy, for *femina uirque*, 'woman-an'-man' (814).

Here is the war-zone between body politics and the body politic. By the time Grand Master NASO is finished with *amor*, there is no primal authenticity left to the sexual scene of the Augustan world.[32] Intersecting, overlaid, multiple narratives, self-serving and otherwary, recount and re-count blurred tales of distrust and demonization. Undecidably strung between fallen bodily truths of nature and the cyborg programming of imperialized society. If *Ars* 1 + 2 finally *demanded Ars* 3 for its completion, then 3 already makes a start on

---

[30] This 'responds' to 2. 413–14, where the boy is urged to fuck hard, because *concubitu prior est infitianda Venus.*

[31] Scat put into scat by Holzberg, Ch. 3 in this volume.

[32] Love or theft? No honour among she's: the Swedish au pair, of course, and the French maid... but also your best friend who gave you the use of a bed has had the run, the best, of your man in it (3. 663–6).

the project which *Remedia* is charged to carry off.[33] As a four-book package, the ensemble inserts its conditioning between the minds and bodies of its trainees, substituting complex sexual-textual tales for drive, instinct, need, act. At the very least, rape becomes 'rape', physical carnality perverts into readerly body-snatching. Our pleasure in the poetry seals terms for the registration of an extremely circumscribed, highly conformist, mapping of sexual relations, in line with both official *mores* and their Augustan (re)codification. By the same token, the very textualization of these sexual subjectivities ratifies the dependence of sexual norms on their own constitutive 'perversion'—or rather, in the name of modernity, on the recognition of their own complicit post-naivety.

If everyone in Rome now slept with Augustus in the bed beside them, now there was Ovid, too, training his people to practise their inculcated mutual infidelities, in the self-consciously cosmopolitan name of Fucking Rome.[34]

> You know everything is said in the bed, everything,
> And it shouldn't change just cos you win.
> That's right.
> I know it is.
>
> (Williams, 'Beyond Games' (1969))

APPENDIX: OVID IN-BRED

1. Doh-Re-Mi-*Doh*, 1–2–3–?

In Cambridge, Part I + Part II Make Up a Tripos
(Faculty of Classics Handbook)

- Ovid will pin the number three to the *Ars Amatoria* triad: *Tr.* 1. 1. 109–18: 'the rest, vs. the 3 . . . none of the 3 . . . , vs. the 5 × 3 books' of *Metamorphoses*; cf. *Tr.* 2. 246, '1 of the 3 books'.[35]

[33] See Rosati, Ch. 8 in this volume.

[34] On the theory that no one could ever legislate for what was *really* going on in any given *concubitus*, maybe Robert Graves was right to propose that I, Augustus never got it on with I, Livia, and maybe our Amatorians and Exilics are all currently all wrong to suppose that *Il Principe* was *really* the worst ever reader of *Il Poeta*'s bible of Erotic Technique. Alternatively/As well, Augustus taught Ovid all he knew...

[35] See Sharrock (1994*a*: 18–20), 'How many books make 3?'.

Readers can hardly fail to begin *Ars* 1 without knowing full well that there will be [at least] one more book: *Liber Primus*... But (how m)any more than that?

- The internal division for *Ars* 1–2 is prominently displayed at 1. 35–8:

> principio, quod amare uelis, reperire labora,
>   qui noua nunc primum miles in arma uenis;
> proximus huic labor est placitam exorare puellam;
>   tertius, ut longo tempore duret amor.

i.e. '[1] = search; [2] = win; [3] = last' (*ut longo tempore duret amor*) This breakdown is declared complete and conclusive (1.39–40):[36]

> hic modus, haec nostro signabitur area curru,
>   haec erit admissa meta terenda rota.

- We move from first to second base at 1. 263–6:

> hactenus, unde legas quod ames
> [...]
> nunc tibi quae placuit, quas sit capienda per artes
> [...]

i.e. 'so far, picking [1]; now, catching [2]'.

- Book 1 closes tidily with 771–2:

> pars superat coepti, pars est exhausta, laboris;
>   hic teneat nostras ancora iacta rates.

i.e. 'part remains [2], part done [1]; stick'. (Do overtones of 'half' and 'half'—as at Verg. *Georg*. 3.286 *hoc satis armentis; superat pars altera curae*—unbalance *pars... pars*? Note *teneat*, suggesting [3]?)[37]

- *Ars* 2. 1 begins by singing a refrain of 'twiceness', '× 2' (1):

> dicite io Paean et io bis dicite Paean.

- At 2. 11–12, we move on from: 'caught' [2], to 'holding' [3]:

> non satis est uenisse tibi me uate puellam;

---

[36] But *meta* = turning-post/finishing-line (End/climax in sex) (ibid. 20).
[37] Cf. 2.98, *detinuisse*, ibid. 23–4.

> arte mea capta est, arte tenenda mea est.

This is written up as 'the big one, the start of art, lasting, the limit' (2. 13–20):

> nec minor est uirtus, quam quaerere, parta tueri
> ...hoc erit artis opus,
> [...]
> ...remanere...,
> [...]
> ...imposuisse modum.

- The surprise intrusion of the bridge to *Ars* 3, after the closural formula of dedication at 744, is (copula) 2. 745–6:

> ecce, rogant tenerae sibi dem praecepta puellae:
> uos eritis chartae proxima cura meae.

i.e. female applicants: next [4]. Out of the blue.

- Into the blue, *Ars* 3. 1:

> arma dedi...arma supersunt.

i.e. Greeks (men) done, Amazons (women) extra ([4]).

- So, too, at 3. 47–8:

> illos artifices gemini fecere libelli;
> haec quoque pars monitis erudienda tuis.

i.e., quoth Venus, 'twin books done for men, women need tutorial'. Followed by incitement to 'do a Stesichorus' (49–50), and write a Palinode or two.[38]

2. Quadratipoetic Books: Fourplay

One-Two-Free-Four

(R. Waters: Pink Floyd (1972), 'Free Four')

---

[38] *Ars* 3 pulls in the spread of Ovid's texts on/of *amor*: 205–8, cf. *Medic.* 1–**100**, with *faciem commendet cura...forma...cultus...cultus...culta*, 1–7 ~ *Ars* 3. **101**–5, *cultu; cultis, culto, forma, cura dabit faciem*. At 3. 341–5, Ovid recommends his poems for both sides (*carmina quis partes instruit ille duas*: halves, armies/tutorial groups) = *Amores* 1–3..., *Heroides*,...?; not *Ars* 1 + 2.

But Ovid's œuvre plugs him into an ongoing game of numbers that crosses to Roman poetry with Hellenistic editions and new works. Did *four books* make the best number of units for the perfect verse classic? Did *coming close, but aiming off* this magic total, distribution, articulation, patterning, make for writerly sport?

- Thus the prelusory *Epigramma* to the *Amores* claims that the author has cut down '5 books > 3' (before 1. 1. 1–2 chime in with the conceit that Cupid has cut down 'every 12th foot > 11', to convert epic > elegy).
- *Amores* opens with a second book's *hoc quoque... hoc quoque...*, and opens its readership out to include a mix of 'maid and boy + one of the lads' + 'for girls' (2. 1. 1–10, 37–8).
- The last book is in a rush, to clinch and climax the *Amores* climax, for Tragedy is already on its way, big, sexy, and *a tergo* (*a tergo grandius urget opus*, 3. 1. 69–70). The End is loudly signalled (*ultima meta*, 3. 15. 1–2).
- For a quasi-norm of '4 books', consider the Aristophanic edition of Pindar's 'Victory Odes' (× 4); Callimachus, *Aitia* (= 2 + 2 ?); Apollonius, *Argonautica* (2 + 2 =? Or 2 + 1 + 1 ?); Gallus (× 4: = ?); Virgil, *Georgics* (= 2 + 2; if ~~gardening~~ would count: 4 < 5); Horace, *Odes* 3; + 1 (? + *Carm.Saec.*); Propertius (1 + 1 + 1; + 1), etc.[39]

---

[39] For these quadratic equivocations: Barchiesi (2001: 161), Henderson (2002: 61–4), etc. For the '4-book package' of Callimachean elegy: Gibson (2000).

6

Women on Top: Livia and Andromache

Alessandro Barchiesi

PART ONE: THE NAME OF LIVIA

Neither marginal nor central to Roman society,[1] Roman women are a notoriously difficult topic for historians. They are also a contested category in the interpretation of Ovid's *Ars Amatoria*: it has proved difficult to find agreement on how far the representation of women in the poem is based on realism. Some of the best recent studies agree, although with significantly different emphases, that what is peculiar to the *Ars* is a program of moderation and mediation between extreme stereotypes, and an ideology of modernization.[2] Yet the ideal woman who would fit the ideology of the work is someone who fits neither of the stereotypes promoted in Roman society by the Augustan family laws, the *leges Iuliae*. If the typical woman of the poem is a *matrona*, the poem is about adultery; if she is a courtesan, the poem is a witty cover-up for a financial transaction.[3]

Many thanks to Roy Gibson, Alain Gowing, and Ann Kuttner for their suggestions, and to the participants to discussions in Manchester, Rome II, and Rethymno. Latin translations are taken or adapted from the relevant volume of the Loeb Classical Library: Ovid (G. P. Goold); Lucretius (M. F. Smith); Vergil (H. R. Fairclough).

[1] Mc Ginn (1998) accepts prostitutes and other low-born women, but not women as a whole, as a marginal group.

[2] Labate (1984); Gibson (2003*a*).

[3] Mentions of *munera* and gift-giving are one of the crucial, ambiguous issues: when women are being advised not to ask for presents after intercourse, this can be argued to be a crude behaviour worthy of a prostitute (Gibson (2003*a*: 402), on 3. 805–6). Yet, on the one hand a streetwalker would probably stipulate *before* sex, and on the other the link between adultery and gift-giving is surprisingly regular in

If we view the text from this angle, all the talk about moderation, mediation, and modernization is still important, but we begin to feel that what the poem does is not a reflection of a realistic image of Roman society, but an intervention in a contested area.[4] This is in fact a step forward, because if we look again at the *leges Iuliae* and their impact on Roman society, it should become clear that they are not a realistic image of contemporary society either:[5] just like Ovid's work, the laws are an ambitious and bold experiment in redrawing boundaries and fashioning ideal women. This is not to say that social change did not exist: I will try to be more precise about Ovid's project by focusing on two emerging tropes in the representation of women in society, which are both about visibility and exemplarity: the empowered woman, and the woman of pleasure.

I am painfully aware that it would be possible to drive a triumphal quadriga between the arguments of this paper: it is unlikely that I will demonstrate any sensible link between my two women, Livia and Andromache, and the general outlook will be far from coherent. Yet, with some luck, I will be able to get away with the idea that the gap in the argument, the mutual irrelevance of Livia and Andromache, is precisely the focus of my research.

My initial approach derives from a brilliant paper by O'Gorman (1997), in which *Love and The Family* emerge as a crucial polarity for the understanding of Ovidian poetry. This polarity opens the way to a question about the role of the Family in this poem about Love.

Roman mentality (see McGinn (1998: 182–6)). Once again—and 3. 805–6 is emphatically placed at the closure of the work—we are somewhere in a grey area between the prostitute and the untouchable woman (for the approach in general, see Sharrock (1994*b*)).

[4] This is true even if we decide to argue that the Woman of the *Ars* responds to stereotypes that are in fact much more traditional than Ovid's insistence on 'modern' and 'urban' values would admit. In fact it would be worth trying out, if only by experiment, an interpretative model in which Ovid's 'traditional' sexual politics conflicts with the 'modern' agenda of the Augustan cultural change and *mutatio morum*—probably less inadequate than the widespread view that Ovid the innovator confronts Augustus the traditionalist.

[5] On legal discourse not being evidence for social evolution, but more like evidence for attempts to influence social evolution, see McGinn (1998).

A couple of preliminary points are already evident in the initial couplet of Book 1:

> siquis in hoc artem populo non nouit amandi,
>   hoc legat et lecto carmine doctus amet.   (*Ars* 1. 1–2)

(If anyone among this people knows not the art of loving, let him read my poem, and having read be skilled in love.)

The *Ars* begins as the most demotic text in the history of Augustan poetry. The sequence *ars-carmen-doctus* in a preamble would normaly suggest Callimachean and Catullan elitism, and a polarization vs. *populus* or *uulgus*, but this is flatly contradicted by the prosaic incipit *siquis in hoc populo*. Horace, still the most authoritative of recent poetic voices in the years immediately prior to the publication of the *Ars*, would never use *populus* in such a user-friendly way, yet it is true that references to the *populus* are more frequent in his own *Ars*, the *Ars Poetica*, than in the rest of his work, and they are linked to the stage, in particular the comic stage.[6]

This immediately raises the question of affinities between the Ovidian poem and comic spectacle, but there is also a question to be asked about something that is absent in the *Ars*. This absence is an absence of naming, an absence of individuals and names. It almost looks as if the initial mention of *siquis in hoc populo* has managed to oust from the poem references to individuals.

First of all, talking about absences, the *Ars* is unique, I think, in ancient didactic poetry for the combined absence of a dedicatee and of a named addressee. No Perses, no Memmius; and no Octavian, no Maecenas. This is already enough to make the *Ars* a very anonymous poem. But more is to come: the *Ars* is full of action and characters, but none is named and recognizable, with one important exception to be mentioned again later.

The structure of the poem is coherent with the proemial mention of the *populus*: it stresses open access, interchange, and availability as crucial issues. Books 1–2 and then 3 move from public places to bedrooms and closets and even to loos—and public as we shall see will become pubic. But in the meantime something gets lost, and this is individual identification. The *Ars* is exceptional among all genres

---

[6] Cf. Hor. *Ars* 81, 153, 185, 206, 321.

of ancient poetry for the absence of identification and personal names, for its degree of de-individualization.[7] The two main generic sources of the work, elegy (with epigram) and comedy (with mime), are not identical in their politics of naming, but both are different from the *Ars*, and different again is another kindred genre, satire. Didactic offers of course yet another different template, where it can be argued anonymity is more regular. Yet even so, the constant focus on individuals living in an urban society would seem to require some amount of identification, and the absence of a named addressee is not easy to reconcile with didactic traditions.

The complete absence of personal names,[8] combined with the absence of a dedication and of an identifiable didactic addressee, has the result of empowering two important sets of references: references to the *domus Augusta*, and to mythological characters. We will return to mythological characters later: but for now, what the two categories have in common is that they provide some amount of identification in a poem which is otherwise more anonymous than a chatroom. The only other individual who receives full identification is of course the author himself, *Naso* (2. 744 and 3. 812).[9]

We can approach the problem of identity and individuality in the *Ars* from the related point of view of family. The *Ars* is not only unique in its absence of personal identities: it is also unique in offering a treatment of eroticism which has been completely stripped of family implications. The plot of the poem manages to do without references to husbands and wives, brothers and sisters, fathers and mothers, daughters and sons, procreation and kin—all the specific embedding of human lives in Roman society. This is remarkable in a world where the paradigm of metropolitan individualism of $9\frac{1}{2}$ *Weeks* and of *Sex and the City* has yet to be invented. It must have been hard for Ovid to conceive a panoramic text about love in Rome without reference to family ties—exactly the stuff that made it possible and

---

[7] I am not of course arguing against the fact that the poem is a very 'localized' one: on the Roman features of the *Ars* see e.g. Volk, Ch. 12 in this volume.

[8] On the importance of the rhetoric of naming in Ovid see (e.g.) the brilliant studies by Oliensis (1997) and Hardie (2002*b*: 239–57).

[9] On the naming of Gaius and Lucius Caesar, see Casali, Ch. 11 in this volume.

effective to transplant to Rome the scripts of New Comedy.[10] In fact the position of the narrator in the *Ars* is closer to authorial positions in comedy than to the traditional ego-voice of elegy, and the exclusion of family contexts sounds even more anti-realistic than it does in subjective Roman elegy. (The link with comedy touches on one of the main concerns of contemporary discussions of the *Ars*: the question of the social status of the *Ars* woman. Comedy, New Comedy, was too restricting for Ovid; it was precisely the genre that polices the boundaries of legal distinctions between family women, concerned with reproduction of the citizen body, and hetairae or slaves. Mime, with its favourite theme of adultery, was too loose. Elegy was suitably vague, but also too subjective to fit the new project. The result is that the instability of social status for the poem's women[11] is matched, at the formal level, by eclectic invocations of different genres.)

The elision of the Roman family is of course a programmatic choice when Ovid decides at *Ars* 2. 473–80 to write a follow-up to the Lucretian account of the history of sexuality (Lucr. 5. 962–5, 1011–23). The main difference, in short, is that in Ovid sex leads to civilization, while for Lucretius sex leads to *family* and *family* leads to civilization. The effect of the imitation is to highlight the suppressed mediating term, *family*, and its suppression: note for example how the two poets, brought to interface by a clear Ovidian allusion, appear to say respectively that humans stopped wandering around in order to have sex, and more exactly a very spontaneous kind of sex (*Ars* 2. 477–80 *blanda truces animos fertur mollisse uoluptas:* | <u>con-stiterant</u> <u>uno</u> <u>femina</u> <u>uirque</u> <u>loco</u>; | *quid facerent, ipsi nullo didicere magistro:* | *arte Venus nulla dulce peregit opus*, 'beguiling pleasure is said to have softened those fierce spirits: a man and a woman had tarried together in the same spot; what they were to do, they learnt themselves with none to teach them: artlessly did Venus accomplish the sweet act'), and that humans stopped wandering around when they started a nuclear family (Lucr. 5. 1011–14 *inde casas*

---

[10] Family relationships are also typical of the 'quick and dirty' plots of mime, where relational designations seem to be preferred to naming, cf. Petron. 80. 9 *grex agit in scaena mimum: pater ille uocatur* | *filius hic*..., with the analysis of a new Greek text by Elliott (2003: 60).

[11] As argued by Gibson (2003*a*), building on the work of McGinn (1998); see also Gibson, Ch. 7 in this volume.

postquam ac pellis ignemque pararunt | *et <u>mulier</u> <u>coniuncta</u> <u>uiro</u> con-cessit <u>in</u> <u>unum</u>* | ... | *cognita sunt, prolemque ex se uidere creatam,* | *tum genus humanum primum mollescere coepit,* 'next, when they had got themselves huts and skins and fires, and woman joined with man moved into one [...] became known, and they saw offspring born of them, then first the human race began to grow soft').

It may be argued that the effect of this strategy is to keep the family out of sight in a work that is not respectable enough—but I am more interested in the fact that Augustan power is represented in this poem, precisely, within or as a family structure. The *domus Augusta*, precisely, not Augustus, is what emerges from the *Ars* as the new form of power in this poem of love not family. Consider the two passages from Books 1 and 2 where the cruising lover intersects with the monuments of contemporary Rome:

> tu modo Pompeia lentus spatiare sub umbra,
>   cum sol Herculei terga leonis adit:
> aut ubi muneribus *nati* sua munera *mater*
>   addidit, externo marmore diues opus.
> nec tibi uitetur quae, priscis sparsa tabellis,
>   porticus auctoris *Liuia* nomen habet:
> quaque parare necem miseris *patruelibus* ausae
>   Belides et stricto stat ferus ense *pater.*   (*Ars* 1. 67–74)

(Only walk leisurely beneath the Pompeian shade, when the sun draws nigh to Hercules' shaggy lion, or where the mother has added her own gifts to her son's, a work rich with marble coating. Nor should you avoid the Livian colonnade which, scattered with ancient paintings keeps its founder's name, or where the daughters of Belus dare to plot death for their wretched cousins, and their fierce father stands with drawn sword.)

> quaeque *soror coniunxque* ducis monimenta pararunt,
>   naualique *gener* cinctus honore caput;   (*Ars* 3. 391–2)

(And the monuments which the sister and wife of our Leader have erected, and his son-in-law whose head is wreathed in naval glory.)

These twin passages feature a number of family terms that are otherwise utterly unfamiliar to the reader of this poem: the only occurrence of *mater* outside mythological reference, the only occurrence of *patruelis*, the only occurrence of *gener*, the only occurrence of *soror* outside mythological reference, and the only occurrence of *coniunx* ouside myth or comparison. We might say that in this poem family exists only in the official representation of the *domus Augusta*. And family is even mapped onto the urban territory of Rome: now all those levels of family affinity are represented in the cityscape of Rome as it is offered to the wandering lovers of the poem.

Those monuments are not just identified by individual figures of the *domus Augusta*; they are identified by relatives who enter the text in their relational denominations; *the monuments have a family relationship*.[12]

It is time to mention that the *Ars* is one of the first Roman texts where the idea of a *domus Augusta* becomes truly important. The construction of this idea must have been slow and laborious, and shaped by improvisations and corrections—although, in hindsight, two factors emerge, and both are related to flukes of biology and anomalies of family situation. First, the fact that Augustus and Livia had a married life of unexpected length, and Augustus a very unusual lifespan. The fluke is thus summarized by Scheidel (1999: 279–80):

When the future Augustus married Livia in 38 BC he was twenty-five and his bride twenty years of age. Of every sixty couples of twenty-five year old men and twenty year old women joined in matrimony at that time, only one could still have been together fifty years later. By AD 13, Augustus and Livia had become that one couple. When Augustus died the following year, five out of six inhabitants of the empire were unable to remember a time when he had not been their sole ruler. It is hard to overestimate the extent to which the successful launch of the Principate, depending as it did on Augustus' ability to outlive both his rivals and their memory, was facilitated by a statistical fluke. It took four centuries for another emperor, Theodosius II, to rule that long, and if we consider Octavian as co-regent from 43 BC onward, his luck was without parallel in Roman history.

To complete the picture of the emerging *domus*, the above needs to be combined with a second factor: the absence of male progeny, and

---

[12] In previous Roman culture, some kind of family network among monuments existed, but was limited to all-male genealogical associations—victories of relatives and descendants would reverberate glory on, or invoke comparison with, other relatives and ancestors, and temples *ex manubiis*, inscriptions and honorific statues could enter a dialogue, combining memory and topography: but who had ever heard of a sister, a wife, a mother being compared and linked to their male kin via public monuments?

Augustus' habit of outliving his successors while having no biological sons. The specific nature of the *domus Augusta* can be understood only if we take into account both factors: it depends on the need for succession created during a long life without an obvious, direct male heir.

Now we can see one reason why the cluster of family names is so important. There is a paradox here. *The family is what unites Augustan power to Roman society and also what makes Augustan power extraneous and 'unheimlich' for Roman society.* Family is a very Roman institution, but by 'coming out' in public it becomes a shock to the Republican system; besides, it is not the predictable structure of your grandad's family anymore. Note for example that the first monument (1. 69) is linked with a mother and a son, but the mother is actually the sister of the emperor, and the son his deceased nephew and failed successor, while Livia, who has some claim to be the *mater familias*, is only represented as Livia (we will come back to this exceptional case of naming later), while *her* son (and co-author of that monument), Tiberius, is of course not represented on the map, being a glaring absence in contemporary Rome; in the meantime Augustus, the only real *pater*, is actually substituted by *pater Danaus*, the threatening father Danaus who organized a very peculiar family (here again I am indebted to O'Gorman's (1997) ideas).[13] That was one special family in which (from what we can speculate about Aeschylus' Danaid tragedies, texts to which the Romans had full access) a father uses violence to stifle a rising family of fifty daughters (not a single son) and sons-in-law, and death is substituted for marriage in order to preserve the life of the father, who was fated to die if his daughters had had intercourse, and thus presumably a dangerous progeny, with their husbands. As a result of this clash between fatherhood and reproduction, sex and family, Danaos becomes the sole ruler of Argos.

In short, Ovid represents *the public appearance, the façade of power* in contemporary Rome through family links, but they are not so traditional and exemplary as one would expect. About the second passage, 3. 391–2, Michael Haslam (*apud* Gibson (2003*a* ad loc.))

---

[13] On fatherhood and Augustus note Fowler (2000*a*: 218–34), drawing on the research by Stevenson (1992) on evergetism and paternalism.

has wittily observed that after the reference to the victory over Alexandria (*Paraetonium*) it takes a moment for the reader to decide that *soror coniunxque ducis* are not one and the same person, a Ptolemaic brother–sister marriage—in fact, one of the few schemes of succession not actually experimented with by the enterprising emperor. (And indeed I could show on another occasion that *all* the references to urban monuments in the poem are insinuating a comparison between Rome and Alexandria.)

But let me focus on Livia. From my whole mountain of discussion emerges one little mouse, one that deserves attention. Through her appearance at *Ars* 1. 72 Livia becomes the only living woman, the only historical Roman woman—and one of the very few Roman individuals—to be named in this very anonymous poem. Small wonder that her name *Livia* is accompanied by the self-reflexive comment about *nomen*. As we saw, she does not even need the relational term, she is not styled a wife or mother. She is Livia. She has her name, and she has her monument. (It would be important to ask whether there is something to be renegotiated about the very category 'woman' when dealing with Livia, but that is too difficult for me. One thing is for sure: in Rome, Man is both a category and a sum of individuals, while the idea of individual women is just beginning to appear when Livia enters the public arena: woman is less individual than man (at least in traditional ideology).) If we look at other Augustan poets, we see that Ovid is exceptional in his propensity for naming the wife of Caesar: 'The frequent obtrusion of Livia cannot have been to the liking of the princeps (or of her son). Horace, the personal friend of the ruler, had shown the proper tact and reserve. He nowhere names Livia' (Syme (1978: 44)).

Now of course studies of visual representations and image management have not been slow in pointing out the exceptionality of Livia as a subject and object of representation: 'Livia Drusilla was the first woman in the history of the West to be depicted systematically in portraits' (Bartman (1999): p. xxi: perhaps we should add 'in public locations'); cf. Flory (1993: 287) 'the grant of 35 BC marks a striking innovation in Rome... [296] [it] is not part of any Roman tradition... [306] the issue for Augustus was clearly how to represent women in his family in public without violating his scruples or societal conservatism'; and Purcell (1986: 89) 'Livia's actions are unprecedented. The *monumenta* of an increasingly monumental Rome had been the political display pieces of the great *men* of the state, and Livia as builder was adding her contribution to that process.'

In the *Tristia*, Ovid offers a very precise poetic equivalent of this cultural shock: as she enters the delicate system of elegiac catalogues and paradigms, she is the one who (as Hinds (1999) has explained) wrecks the entire system of exemplarity and comparisons because she embodies a paradox never seen before, the existence of a *femina princeps*. The power of *princeps* as a designation politicizes the womanhood of Livia to an extent never imagined before in Roman society, and crushes attempts at primacy expressed by *prior* or *prima*: she is the first woman of Rome not only in terms of excellence, but also of logical sequence, because the category 'woman' has been reinvented and 're-started' to fit her model. At *Tr.* 1. 6. 21–3, Ovid's wife is 'first among women' because, we finally discover, she has been shaped by the example set by the Principal Woman, Livia, who is above the usual parameters of hyperbole: a great woman may be an example for others, but Livia is the example-*maker*, the matrix. This is in fact why, the author of the *Consolatio* for Livia argues, this woman has been set on a pedestal: she must be visible, displayed, and talked about, all of which is of course a paradox in the context of the Roman tradition of the restrained and self-effacing *matrona*:

> imposuit te alto Fortuna locumque tueri
> iussit honoratum: Liuia, perfer onus.
> ad te oculos auresque trahis, tua facta notamus...
>
> (*Cons. Liuiae* 349–51)

(Fortune placed you high and bade you guard an honoured station; bear your burden, Livia. You draw to yourself eyes and ears, we mark your doings...)

This is not 'just' panegyric, it is about acknowledging the new status of a woman who is visible in person and in statuary replicas: not by chance the emergence of Livia is accompanied by a change in the typology of public representations of *matronae*[14] and backed up by the sharp *visual* distinctions between woman and 'woman of pleasure' enforced by the Julian laws.

[14] Trimble (2000).

What is more—and here I am surprised by the silence of commentators, and by the time it took me to understand that there is something unfamiliar about the 'name of a woman' in a public Roman setting—the implication in the *Ars* passage (1. 72) is not only that the portico bears the name of Livia as her author (significant per se, with the intentional paradox of attaching the Augustan word *auctor* to a female).[15] We are also being told that the name was officially inscribed on the monument.[16] From what we know about Roman public architecture, the *porticus Liuia* must have been one of the first (conceivably, the second, if we start from the appearance of Octavia) public places in Rome to be inscribed and dedicated in the name of a female citizen. Not a small step. Livia is really, as Stephen Hinds (1999: 140–1) would say, one of a kind, one who outgrows the traditional expressions and formulas of power. Especially in a society where women do not even have a true name, an individual name, and the formulaic expectation raised by a name such as *porticus Liuia* would have been 'a portico dedicated by/honoring some male individual among the Livii'.

The innovation is so striking that we tend to minimize it half-consciously. Moderns are so attuned to monarchy that not everybody readily acknowledges what Fergus Millar (2000: 33) says so clearly about the impact of Livia: she is not the beginning of a gradual progression towards a public role of a Roman empress, but the very

---

[15] There is a note of political innuendo if we accept the idea that the word *auctor* would have started a process of allusion to the male individual who should have been held responsible for the monument alongside Livia, that is the absent Tiberius, now at the nadir of his fortunes; cf. the problems raised by Ov. *Fast.* 6. 637–8 *te quoque magnifica, Concordia, dedicat aede | Liuia, quam caro praestitit ipsa uiro*.

[16] Again we can compare the mention of the *aedes Concordiae Augustae* in the *Fasti* (see previous note). I would imagine that *Fast.* 6. 637–44 reflects at least some of the language of the dedicatory inscription (and there surely was one, cf. e.g. *CIL* 6. 36908, the dedicatory inscription for the *porticus Gai et Luci*): that is, such an inscription would have probably featured *Concordia, dedicat Livia*, maybe *aedes*, and perhaps even 'Augustus', extrapolating from the Ovidian *quam caro praestitit ipsa viro*. Dio (54. 23. 6, cf. 55. 8) seems to suggest that the *porticus Livia* was built by Augustus (on the site of Vedius Pollio's house), but he too puts Livia's name on it: 'Augustus razed Pollio's house to the ground, on the pretext of preparing for the erection of the other structure, but really with the purpose that Pollio should have no monument in the city; and he built a colonnade, inscribing on it the name, not of Pollio, but of Livia.' If true, this might be paralleled in the *basilica Aemilia*, which he is said (again by Dio) to have rebuilt but in the name of an 'Aemilius'.

climax of this process: 'Livia occupied a more prominent public role than any subsequent member of any Imperial family.'

I conclude that this poem about the availability of women has been written in a time of complex change for the public image of Roman women—a time in which increasing demand for accountable separation between wives and courtesans[17] is accompanied by a seemingly unrelated, but shocking change in the public status of one woman: Livia Augusta enters the public space in which she will be the object of uninhibited public gaze.[18] But what about another more traditional typology of women that had always been subjected to public inspection and visual availability? They are Greek, and have little to fear from public scrutiny. Romans had always felt free to stare at them. They are not, however, the courtesans: they are the women of Greek myth and mythological art.

The fortunes of Livia in the poem make a telling contrast with the fate of one of them, Andromache. Like Baudelaire, although for different reasons, the author of the *Ars* might have said about his poetic inspiration *Andromaque, je pense à vous*.

PART TWO: THE BODY OF ANDROMACHE

I choose Andromache as an example of what can happen to a lady, a Greek lady, in the mythological, the non-Roman hemisphere of the poem. Here names are legion, identification is constant, and some of the details are utterly degrading. Commentators are duly puzzled by some of the sexual material in the mythological *exempla*, and I choose Andromache for two reasons. First, she occupies a structural position of some kind: she is the final mythological vignette in book 3. 777–8, and has a parallel position (but this is not the most innocent word in context) at the end of Book 2, together with the equally programmatic Briseis (2. 709–16). Secondly, and more importantly, she is singled out in the *Remedia Amoris* as the woman

---

[17] See McGinn (1998).
[18] But against a clear-cut opposition of private and public in Roman society, note the power of Purcell's comments on Livia's own voice (Purcell (1986)).

who is extraneous to the lascivious world of Ovidian elegy: Thais belongs to the *Ars*, Andromache does not (*Rem.* 381–6). Elegy is for Thais, and she is like comedy, while epic and tragedy are for Andromache. Courtesan vs lady means genre vs genre.

The entire passage about genre and various sexual topics in the *Remedia* (361–88) should raise suspicions. Hinds has already pointed out that the rule 'Achilles is not good for elegiacs' is a strange one if uttered by the author of *Heroides* 3.[19] One might add, if this is not too literal-minded, that Achilles, together with Andromache, is the most frequently mentioned character in the mythological world of the *Ars*—while Thais the comic courtesan is mentioned only once in the whole *Ars*.[20]

There are not less than five passages about Andromache in the *Ars* (2. 645–6, 707–11; 3. 107–10, 517–23, 777–8) and perhaps their distribution is significant. In Books 1–2, for men, she starts as the reactionary woman who cannot make love, and ends up as a scandalous symbol of foreplay. In Book 3, for women, she appears first (again) as a non-erotic woman, but ends up as the final erotic mythologeme of the poem, right in the middle of the only downright pornographic section of the *Ars*, the sequence of 8 or 9 *figurae Veneris*. It almost looks as if she serves as a model for the reader and pupil of the *Ars*: she begins as a resisting reader and ends up as a transformed pupil.[21]

By entering the world of the *Ars*, Andromache loses something of her traditional rigidity, associated with epic. But by naming her *longissima... Thebais* in the final bedroom cameo in *Ars* 3, Ovid wittily insinuates that this large,[22] old-fashioned woman has problems in entering the world of his elegy: *longissima Thebais* is indeed a threatening definition for a post-Callimachean and anti-Antimachean

---

[19] Hinds (2000: 224–5).
[20] On the significance of Thais in Roman elegy see the thorough analysis by Traill (2001).
[21] On the importance of taking paedagogy and its dynamics seriously in the *Ars* see the fundamental paper by Kennedy (2000). On the methodology for reading 'plots' into didactic texts, see Fowler (2000*b*).
[22] This detail could be based on a specific tradition about Andromache, but also on the conventional impact of tragic heroines on stage: they must have been rather towering 'women', played by male actors, and equipped with high-soled buskins.

poet.²³ It is not by chance that Martial (11. 104) has chosen this passage for his programmatic attempt to turn his own wife into a foxy lady, as Hinds has demonstrated.²⁴ (Cf. esp. *Ars* 3. 777–8 *quod erat longissima, numquam | Thebais Hectoreo nupta resedit equo*, and Mart. 11. 104. 14 *Hectoreo quotiens sederat uxor equo*.) The fact is that the Ovidian passage, before the staining and debasing appropriation in Martial, is itself already deliberately scandalous. The sexual position that Andromache considers but rejects for reasons of physical fitness (and of masculine vested interest, one suspects) is constantly associated with degradation and the sex trade in all other sources.²⁵ There are of course multiple reasons for this: the woman on top position inverts the symbolism of domination, allows and encourages initiative from the woman, favours 'egalitarian' eye-contact during sex, can be imagined as an anti-pregnancy strategy: more importantly for the context of *Ars* Book 3, this position services the male partner with sexual pleasure *plus visual* pleasure. (In the world of the *Ars*, women are unusually close to being admitted to sexual pleasure, therefore it is fitting that a new separation should begin to appear— now that genital pleasure can be shared, the male prerogative shifts to the visual.)

Andromache shouldn't even know about such things. Perhaps the truth is that *Thebais* is only a couple of letters away from the unruly *Thais*. (In a famous story narrated both in the *Ars* and the *Metamorphoses*, Ovid makes capital out of the two letters separating different kinds of women: Aura/Aurora.²⁶) The topos of the *mulier equitans* immediately invokes the traditions of comedy and epigram, where the names of the characters often trigger multiple jokes. *Hectoreo* presupposes a horse 'consisting of Hector' not the expected 'belonging to Hector' (see Gibson (2003*a*: 393)) and the reference is to the famous epithet *hippodamoio* which concludes the *Iliad*.²⁷

---

²³ For references to the *Thebaid* as a very long poem, cf. e.g. Cic. *Brut.* 191, *magnum illud quod nouistis uolumen suum*: on the derogatory nuance and the link with Catullus 95. 10 *tumido... Antimacho*, see Matthews (1996: 66, 72).

²⁴ Hinds (1998: 130–5).

²⁵ Major discussions include e.g. Jeffrey Henderson (1991: 164–5); Heath (1986: 33–5); Davidson (1997: 196–7); Pretagostini (1997); and Kurke (2002–3: 38).

²⁶ See Gibson (2003*a*: 358).

²⁷ Unless this conclusion is supplanted by the variant 'the Amazon (!) arrived', and the Amazonomachy as a coda to the *Iliad* has been already evoked by the end of book 2 (see Janka (1997: on *Ars* 2. 741–4); Gibson (2000)).

The subtle joke challenges the tradition of whore episodes in comedy, such as the reference to 'the *tyrannis* of Hippias' in Aristophanes' *Wasps* (500–2). The tamer of horses needs a rider.

So the final mention of Andromache compromises her into a position which mixes epic parody, sexual misconduct, and pornography. Indeed, the entire sequence of *figurae Veneris* has a programmatic ring and should be considered with attention by scholars pondering the sociology of the *Ars* woman. Readers focusing on this problem, discussions of which are among the best recent scholarship on the *Ars*, will find something of interest in the sequence of positions:

> ... non omnes una figura decet.
> quae facie praesignis erit, resupina iaceto:
>   spectentur tergo, quis sua terga placent.
> Milanion umeris Atalantes crura ferebat:
>   si bona sunt, hoc sunt accipienda modo.
> parua uehatur equo: quod erat longissima, numquam
>   Thebais Hectoreo nupta resedit equo.
> strata premat genibus, paulum ceruice reflexa,
>   femina per longum conspicienda latus.   (*Ars* 3. 772–80)

(... one position does not suit all alike. Let she who is fair of face recline upon her back; let those whose backs please them be seen from behind. Milanion bore Atalanta's legs upon his shoulders; if they are good, they should be taken thus. A small woman should ride on horse: because she was tall, his Theban bride never sat on Hector's horse. A woman whose long flanks deserve to be seen should press the coverlets with her knees, her neck bent back a little.)

The mention of Andromache implies the curious idea of a position that could be designated in the negative—the 'not-Andromache' position as it were, although Martial will ride roughshod over the distinction. The following position has no name attached, yet via a scandalous allusion (3. 779 *ceruice reflexa*) to Virgil it could be named 'the she-wolf':

> fecerat et uiridi fetam Mauortis in antro
> procubuisse *lupam*, geminos huic ubera circum
> ludere pendentis pueros et lambere matrem
> impauidos, illam *tereti ceruice reflexa*
> mulcere alternos et corpora fingere lingua.   (Verg. *Aen.* 8. 630–4)

(He had fashioned, too, the mother she-wolf outstretched in the green cave of Mars; around her teats the twin boys hung playing and mouthed their mother without fear; she, with shapely neck bent back, fondled them by turns and moulded their bodies with her tongue.)

ceruice reflexa is reminiscent of the position analysed in Greek art by Stewart (1996: 147–8) (a fitting commentary on what, with Gibson ad loc., we may call the 'ecphrastic quality' of this text, with the Virgilian intertext from the shield of Aeneas and the model of Lucr. 1. 35 *ceruice reposta*). This position may have been known as *more ferarum*, since it is styled 'the lioness' in some Greek sources. Gibson (2003*a*: *ad* 8 and 419) has already commented on a somewhat disingenuous use of *lupa* in the poem:

> 1. 118 ut fugit inuisos agna nouella lupos

(As the little lamb flees from the hated wolves)

> 2.148 ... et pauidum solitos in pecus ire lupos

(... and the wolves that make a practice of rushing upon the startled flock)

> 2. 364 plenum montano credis ouile lupo?

(Do you trust a full sheepfold to a mountain wolf?)

> 3. 8 ... et rabidae tradis ouile lupae?

(... and betray the sheepfold to the mad she-wolf?)

> 3.419 ad multas lupa tendit oues, praedetur ut unam

(The she-wolf draws nigh to many sheep, to prey on one)

There is nothing striking in the symmetry between wolves and she-wolves in the animal similes, if one looks at the structure of the poem: but the problem is, of course, that *lupa*, unlike *lupus*, also suggests a particular type of woman, a whore.

Before Andromache, who is the last mythological *exemplum* in the poem, we find what we are entitled to call Atalanta's position. This is stimulating because, while Andromache has a career in epic and tragedy, Atalanta has a claim to be the most elegiac of *puellae*. In fact, her sexual position has closural force in the poem because she is the mythical exemplum of 'playing hard to get' in traditional Roman elegy. Her cameo appearance in Book 2 of the *Ars* (2. 185–94 *quid fuit asperius Nonacrina Atalanta?* etc.) was in turn based on a foundational text of Roman elegy, Prop. 1. 1. 9–17 *Milanion nullos fugiendo, Tulle, labores*, etc. (Hence, of course, the reflexive force of the Ovidian *flesse...Milaniona ferunt* at 2. 188.) The allusion to the Propertian passage turns Propertius (via 1. 1. 17 *in me tardus Amor non ullas cogitat artes*) into not only a failed precursor of the *Ars Amatoria*,[28] but more specifically a clueless loser who should be contrasted with the victorious lover of the *Ars*. The pliant symplegma of *Ars* 3. 775 *crura ferebat* (legs on the shoulders, instead of the nets burdening the neck of the pretender at *Ars* 2. 189 and 194) is clearly a form of revenge over the Propertian image of Atalante as a *uelocem... puellam* (Prop. 1. 1. 15), as well as a closural allusion to the previous imitation of *Am*. 3. 2. 27–9 *(bona crura...*/*talia Milanion Atalantes crura fugacis* | *optauit manibus sustinuisse suis)*, the *Ars* passage being a realization of those erotic phantasies.

So we have Ovid's revenge over elegiac asceticism through the position of Atalante, and then Andromache, a wife who inspects then rejects for practical reasons the sexual fitness of a *meretrix*, and finally an allusion via Virgil to a *lupa*—the bluntest Latin expression for a sex-worker. The sequence well expresses the instability of categories in the poem: the ideal *puella* of elegy and Greek myth in the process of becoming a sexual icon; the ideal wife trying out a pornographic scenario; and the *meretrix* enjoying her liberated role in the most shameless of ways.

There is no doubt that the sequence is as pure a form of pornography as we can find in antiquity, if we consider three aspects that are normally acknowledged as important in modern definitions of

---

[28] On the intertextual trope by which a predecessor becomes someone who 'invokes' the new text as a necessary realization of a wish or resolution of a problem, see Hinds (1998: 119) 'against all the odds, one of the most famous speeches in Virgil's *Aeneid* has become, for just a moment, *pre-Ovidian*' (his italics). Propertius is a particularly good candidate for this Ovidian strategy because of his poetics of excess and contradiction (see Gibson (forthcoming); on Ovid constructing Propertius as 'already passé', see Barchiesi (1991: 2–3)). In the context of Ovid's elegiac career the composition of Book 3 may well have had some kind of closural significance: therefore the success of Milanion's chase has a programmatic effect, after the *seruitium amoris* of Prop. 1. 1 and the lust of *Am*. 3. 2.

pornography: (1) autonomization of body parts, (2) insistence on visuality, blurring the distinction between viewer and male sex-partner, (3) the use and abuse of analogies with the visual arts. As a crowning touch, the last *figura Veneris* is the (un)conquered Parthian archer, the ultimate icon of modern Imperial art in Augustan Rome.[29]

If we go back to Andromache, we can easily see why she is the most popular example of a woman in the poem. Already in the homonymous Euripidean tragedy Andromache's *persona* is an interesting combination of concubine/slave and wife. In the prologue she juxtaposes her present status as a 'slave' (12) to her former social position, while Hermione also underscores Andromache's status within Neoptolemus' house: 'a slave and a spear-won woman' (155). While explaining her relationship to her 'master' (25) Andromache repeats the word 'given' (15) she used earlier to refer to her betrothal to Hector (4), imparting thus 'an air of legitimacy to her relationship with Neoptolemus'.[30] Meanwhile the fact that she has fulfilled the conjugal duty by supplying Neoptolemus with an heir (24) 'places her in the position of legitimate wife'.[31] Her position as such is confirmed when she is later addressed as a 'mistress' (56–9), while the process of her identification with the legitimate wife is enhanced by her loyalty to Neoptolemus' *oikos* in contrast to Hermione's desertion/betrayal of it. In her next appearance in literature, which is also the next step in her biography (Verg. *Aen.* 3. 321–9), Andromache resurfaces both as a widow of Hector and as a special and inferior kind of wife, the widow given to a *levir*, the slave married to a slave through enfranchisement, then raised again to some level of dignity through the donation of a 'mini-Troy'.[32] This character well represents and anticipates the feature of the *Ars* to which we now turn: the urge to resist a polarization between the ideal wife and the concubine. In the catastrophic and unruly world of Greek literature, Andromache had been everything: princess and war slave, concubine and *matrona*.

---

[29] See Casali, Ch. 11 in this volume on Parthians in the *Ars*.
[30] McClure (1999: 169).   [31] Ibid.
[32] See Bettini (1997); Hexter (1999: 77, 316–17).

PART THREE: LIVIA MEETS ANDROMACHE

Safely removed from the downward spiral of Andromache (a princess who became a slave and a concubine, and finally a character in lascivious *tabellae*), Livia has a unique status in the poem and even offers a counterexample. Many scholars have already suggested that the sequence of *figurae Veneris*, and indeed the whole strategy of projecting mythological characters into sexual scenarios, has something to do with the tradition of porn-mythological *tabellae* and frescoes in Roman private rooms. We know a little about that tradition of art objects,[33] and we know the names of some possessors.

This casts an interesting light on one detail of Ovid's presentation of the porticus Livia (*Ars* 1. 71; cf. Part One above). It is sometimes inferred that the paintings there had something to do with early Rome, or that they were by old masters. But the *tabellae* are not just old or precious, they are *priscae*, a word normally (and certainly in the works of this poet) associated not only with antiquity but with traditional authority,[34] anti-modernism,[35] and repression of vice: note the slightly twisted expressions *nec tibi uitetur* and *Liuia porticus*

---

[33] In general, see Clarke (1998: esp. 91–118). The specific problem I am addressing in Ovid is not the idea that erotic art was per se scandalous; it is the absence of a socially sanctioned discourse where one could freely mix references to official monuments and the *domus Augusta* with suggestive recreations of aphrodisiac art.

[34] Pianezzola (1991: pp. xxi–xxii) nicely quotes Horace, *Carm. Saec.* 57–60 *iam Fides et Pax et Honos Pudorque/ priscus et neglecta redire Virtus | audet adparetque beata pleno | Copia cornu*, noting the substitution of *rusticus* for *priscus* at *Ars* 2. 607–8 *fuge, rustice, longe | hinc, Pudor...* and the capping and sapping of *redire audet* through *fuge... longe hinc*; note also how Ovid reacts to the dramatic enjambement *Pudorque | priscus* with the emphatic word distribution *rustice... | ...Pudor*. In the *Fasti*, *Pudor* sits next to *Metus* in the Olympic court, supporting the imposing *Maiestas*, daughter of *Honor* and *Reverentia* (5. 23–30): see the illuminating reading of Nicola Mackie (1992).

[35] The adjective marks two important programmatic passages: *Ars* 3.121 *prisca iuuent alios*, and 3. 128, announcing the demise of *rusticitas priscis illa superstes auis* (see Gibson (2003a: ad loc.) and (forthcoming) for the important revision here of Horatian models). Note also that Ovid expels *rusticitas* from present-day Rome precisely when inventing it, that is when innovating at the lexical level, and making sure that the Latin language finally has a match for the sophisticated Greek concept of *agroikia*: the innovation thus generated complements and improves on famous discussions of 'old-fashioned' rustic culture by the likes of Catullus, Cicero, Horace. Compare the passage on *rustica munera* at *Ars* 2. 263–8, where the echoes of bucolic

auctoris nomen habet, the first expressing a potential reluctance, the second perhaps implying the suppression of the name of the male *auctor* of the monument, Tiberius:[36]

> *nec tibi uitetur* quae, **priscis** sparsa tabellis,
> porticus auctoris Liuia nomen habet   (*Ars* 1. 71–2)

(Nor should you avoid the Livian colonnade which, scattered with ancient paintings, keeps its founder's name.)

In the submissive world of the *Ex Ponto*, Ovid's wife will have to realize (3. 1. 113) that Livia is the only Roman woman who still manages to keep the standards of *prisca uetustas*; the poet advises his wife to wait for the appropriate moment to talk to her, which is a topos in letters about recommendations, but he also inverts the usual emphasis on choosing the appropriate moment of relaxed *otium*. There will be none: Livia is remarkably indifferent, Ovid tactlessly observes, to *corporis cultus* (3. 1. 141–2).[37]

---

passages in Virgil, Tibullus, and Propertius (see Labate (1984: 221–2)) are ironically undermined by the suggestion that it is a good idea to *pretend* that the simple gifts come from a *suburbanum rus*, while in fact the lover has just bought them in the *Sacra Via* in downtown Rome. The simplicity of rustic economy is doubly vulnerable, since on the one side it can be easily simulated with a little cash in a metropolitan setting, on the other hand it ultimately denotes wealth and property, not *autarkeia* and austerity. The word *priscus* is absent from the *Amores*; in the *Metamorphoses* it appears in a context suggestive for the *Ars* and the *leges Iuliae*. Atalanta and Hippomenes have sex in a sanctuary of Ceres: the violation happens in the stern presence of old-fashioned *lignea simulacra* (an exceptional type of art in this art-obsessed poem, see Barchiesi (2005 p. clv n. 2) *religione sacer prisca, quo multa sacerdos | lignea contulerat ueterum simulacra deorum; | hunc init et uetito temerat sacraria probro* (10. 693–5)). Hippomenes is an extremist reader of the *Ars*, who goes beyond the advice to pick up girls in temples and public monuments: his decision to have intercourse in the Ceres precinct will attract divine punishment and turn him and his partner into a lion and a lioness.

[36] On the *aedes Concordiae Augustae*, and on *Concordia* in the *Fasti* and the *Ars*, see the impressive paper by Kellum (1990).

[37] The poem is a masterpiece of poetic *lasciuia*. Livia, Ovid explains to his wife, is *not* Procne, Medea, a Danaid, Clytemnestra, Scylla, Circe, Medusa (3. 1. 113–16: readers are implicitly invited to consult the *Metamorphoses* about most of those violent women): she has the beauty of Venus and the *mores* of Iuno (117) yet for some reason (and with good official backup, cf. *ILS* 120) it is Iuno whom Ovid's wife will have to confront and adore (145 *uultum Iunonis*), and that sounds like a tall order for readers of the *Aeneid* and *Metamorphoses*. In fact, Ovid's wife will have to perform a unique ritual of self-abasement, one that, we are told, Livia's *maiestas* will enjoy: tears, trembling voice, broken words, arms stretched to her sacred feet. On Livia and exile see especially Johnson (1997).

As we know from Dio (54. 23. 6) and from Ovid's own *Fasti* (6. 639–48), the new *porticus* could be read as a programmatic monument, a deconstruction of the Palace of Vice by Vedius Pollio. By a nice coincidence one of the few details we know about Vedius is that he embarrassed some aristocratic wives by being found travelling around with certain images of them (*imagunculae matronarum*). In one of the most enjoyable pieces of gossip in the history of dandyism, Cicero digresses on him at *Att.* 6. 1. 25. The epiphany of Vedius was an omen of imperial decadence, and Cicero instantly finds the appropriate, Petronian style: the baboon in his wagon and the wild donkeys set the stage for the discovery of Vedius' travel-kit: compromising portable images, a baggage of adultery (*C. Vennonius... in Vedianas res incidit. in his inuentae sunt quinque imagunculae matronarum*). Perhaps Vedius was also famous as a possessor of *figurae Veneris* of the kind we later find in classy Imperial brothels. We can ponder the implications of Livia's *priscae tabellae* and of their obverse, the pornographic images of Atalante and Andromache, the pleasure-dome of Vedius, and we will find that the *Ars* is only marginally about pornography yet implicitly refers to the repression of pornography. More crucially, the *Ars* is a poem whose social background combines an increased public visibility of respectable women and a growing market for private consumption of women's sexualized images. Livia and Andromache are the poster-women for those two tendencies.[38]

Yet there is another story to be told. Livia should be allowed to speak for herself, because she was not a passive player in an all-male field of competing icons.[39] A Roman elite woman must have had some interest in a text such as Euripides' *Andromache*, a crucial example of how literature can experiment with ambiguities and role-playing that even elite women cannot afford in real life.[40] In a

---

[38] Gibson, Ch. 7 in this volume, explains very well how the discovery of a middle ground in the arena of womanhood can be expressed by Ovid in terms of moderation and mediation, yet also be incompatible with Augustan sexual politics.

[39] Purcell (1986) is a fundamental discussion of the problem of dealing with Livia in a post-feminist world, and subsequent invocations of Jackie Kennedy in the literature about Livia are rather stale when compared to his deconstruction of the traditional alternative models, the cynical scheming woman in a men's world, and the female empowerment icon.

[40] Even Plautus had not been very daring in this area: his choice and transformation of New Comedy plots (a genre profoundly indebted to Euripides' *Andromache*) show a preference for plots about courtesans over plots involving traffic in free-born women and modifications of their status.

shocking passage, Andromache tests the limits of the categories 'legitimate wife' and 'concubine'. As a concubine, she stands her ground against the aggressive would-be queen Hermione, and explains to her that it is never about sex only, it is about how much you are willing to endure for a 'marriage'. As a famous epic wife, now she remembers, this is exactly what she has had to suffer and dissimulate with Hector; she reads back comedy into the plot of the *Iliad*, as she teaches Hermione how to keep her own man, who is also by chance Andromache's man, Pyrrhus:

> This is what you call my love magic: it is not beauty, woman, it is virtue that gives pleasure to bedmates... A woman, even if she has not a very good husband, must love him, and avoid being competitive with him. If you had as a husband a tyrant of snowy Thrace, where a man shares his bed with many women in turn, would you kill your rivals? That would mean demonstrating that women are sexually insatiable. This is shameful. We do suffer more than men in this respect, but we are able to disguise the suffering well. Dearest Hector, in order to please you, I accepted to share you with other women, when Aphrodite attacked you, and I often offered my breast to your bastards, only to spare you conflicts—that was my way of keeping my husband close to me. (Eur. *Andr.* 207–8; 213–27).

It is a relief to discover that there is a good chance that Livia had meditated on the importance of a middle ground between the wife and the concubine. There are two striking quotations from her anecdotal life in Cassius Dio's *Histories* (58. 2. 4). In the first instance she argues that innocence is in the eye of the beholder: 'There are many good apophthegms of Livia, in particular when she spared the life of some men who had had the misfortune of running into her when they were naked—she said that to a wise woman naked people are no different from statues.' This is the very argument that Ovid echoes and also deconstructs, with the help of examples from the visual arts, in *Tristia* 2. There are images of vice as well as lofty tragedies in the house of the aristocracy (*domibus uestris*, v. l. *nostris*), yet Augustus has done nothing to enforce *prisca uirorum corpora* over *concubitus uarios* as a subject for private art:[41]

---

[41] Note the splendid lasciviousness of *Venus uda* and the irony of contrasting two respectable examples based on tragic characters, Ajax and Medea, who are the heroes of, respectively, the only (aborted) tragedy by Augustus, and the only (hugely successful) tragedy by Ovid. On the use of *priscus* in such a context, see the beginning of Part Three of this paper.

> scilicet in domibus uestris ut *prisca* uirorum
>   artificis fulgent corpora picta manu,
> sic quae *concubitus uarios Venerisque figuras*
>   exprimat, est aliquo parua tabella loco.
> utque sedet uultu fassus Telamonius iram,
>   inque oculis facinus barbara mater habet,
> sic madidos siccat digitis Venus uda capillos,
>   et modo maternis tecta uidetur aquis.   (*Tr.* 2. 521–8)

(Surely in your houses, even as figures of old shine, painted by an artist's hand, so in some place a small tablet depicts the varying unions and figures of love: there sits not only the Telamonian with features confessing wrath and the barbarian mother with crime in her eyes, but wet Venus as well, wringing her damp hair with her hands and seeming barely covered by her maternal waves.)

To a respectable woman, suggestive images and texts are not dangerous, but find her a malicious one and everything will appear in a different light:

> 'at matrona potest alienis artibus uti,
>   quoque trahat, quamuis non doceatur, habet.'
> nil igitur matrona legat, quia carmine ab omni
>   ad delinquendum doctior esse potest.   (*Tr.* 2. 253–6)

('But a matron can use arts intended for others and has something to tempt her, though she be not herself the pupil.' Let the matron read nothing then, for from every poem she can gain wisdom for sin.)

> quis locus est templis augustior? haec quoque uitet
>   in culpam si qua est ingeniosa suam
> (...) omnia peruersas possunt corrumpere mentes;
>   stant tamen illa suis omnia tuta locis   (2. 287–8; 301–2)

(What place more august than temples? But these too should be avoided by any woman whose nature inclines to fault... All things can corrupt perverted minds. All things stand harmless in their own proper places.)

> nec tamen est facinus uersus euoluere mollis;
>   multa licet castae non facienda legant.
> saepe supercilii nudas matrona seueri
>   et Veneris stantis ad genus omne uidet.
> corpora Vestales oculi meretricia cernunt,
>   nec domino poenae res ea causa fuit.   (2. 307–12)

Women on Top 119

(Nevertheless it is no crime to read tender verse: the chaste may read much that they should not do. Often matrons of serious brow behold women nude, ready for every kind of Love. The eyes of Vestals behold the bodies of courtesans nor has that been the cause of punishment to their owner.)

In *Tristia* 2, all the occurrences of the legally sanctioned word *matrona* (a word never used in the *Amores*) are in a context of malicious viewing and reading.

In the second instance, Livia seems to echo the weary wisdom of Andromache the concubine-cum-princess (in her ambiguous address to Hermione, the princess already bound for a glamorous Helen-style adultery):[42] 'When someone asked how she had managed to keep Augustus under control, she answered—by being always in control of her reactions, by pleasing him in all circumstances, and by leaving him in control of his own private life, especially by pretending not to hear or perceive his sexual entertainments.'

To come back to Ovid. One of the best results of recent scholarship on the *Ars* has been the emphasis on mediation, flexibility, and a new rhetoric of civilized moderation. I think the importance of this work is even better appreciated if we remember that the poem is confronting two implicit, but important extremes, which are both about the issue of representing women, and their representability in a time of social and cultural change: the rise of the public image of the *femina princeps*, and the impact of the lascivious *tabellae*. The poetics of the *Ars* has something to do with the space that separates and connects Livia and Andromache. This is precisely the territory in which the realistic poetics of the poem—with its typical exploitative and manipulative strategies regarding women's behaviour and images—was bound to have an impact, with disastrous effects, on the manneristic poetics of the *leges Iuliae*. In the artificial world of the *leges*, a dramatic, hysterical polarization was being constructed: the *materfamilias* received an 'elevated sexual and social status' (McGinn (1998: 168)). On that imposing pedestal, she was now going to be scrutinized all the time, and for her there was going to

---

[42] On the subtle exploration of marriage in that tragedy see McClure (1999) and Foley (2001: 97–102).

be no middle ground or grey area.[43] The alternative to the panoptic visibility of the respectable *mater* was, quite simply, the visible degradation of becoming—in terms of social status and public image—a prostitute, that is, of adopting the *toga* and being forbidden from the *stola*. The dress code was now divided sharply between honour and shame. To this visual alternative, which was about visibility and availability, the *Ars* responds by creating an opportunistic, but ultimately impossible, mediation, and by using anonymity and evanescence as the defining feature of its Woman.

[43] I do not deny the importance of the vested interest of elite Roman males, who find in the fuzzy social image of the 'potentially available woman' of the *Ars* their ideal target, and are disturbed by the effects of the polarization between adultery and sex trade which is bandied about in the Julian laws: this is convincingly argued by Gibson (2003*a*: 29).

Two important works that appeared too late for my paper are K. Milnor, *Gender, Domesticity and the Age of Augustus: Inventing Private Life* (Oxford 2005), and A. Keith, 'Women's Networks in Vergil's *Aeneid*', *Dictynna* 3 (2006), 211–33.

7

Ovid, Augustus, and the Politics of Moderation in *Ars Amatoria* 3

Roy K. Gibson

In this chapter, I bring together some arguments on moderation and excess sketched out in my commentary on *Ars* 3.[1] This will allow me to achieve something to which the commentary format is not generally sympathetic: focus and expansion on a single theme or set of interrelated themes.[2] I conclude the chapter with a new reading of the significance of Ovid's emphasis on moderation in the light of contemporary and later perceptions of the character of the *princeps*.

POET OF EXCESS

Within a generation of his own death, Ovid had begun to be characterized as a poet who knew nothing of restraint—a writer of

Versions of the paper that became this chapter were given in Glasgow, Manchester, and at the *Ars Amatoria* bimillennial conference. My thanks to the audiences on all those occasions for suggestions, and particularly to Alison Sharrock for invaluable help with revision.

[1] Gibson (2003*a*). Some of the material in this chapter also appears in somewhat different or substantially expanded form in Gibson (forthcoming), where greater emphasis is placed on poetological aspects, on the theme of *decorum*, and on the importance of Horace. Translations in the chapter are taken or adapted from: K. Galinsky (Julian), G. P. Goold (Propertius), P. Nixon (Plautus), S. B. Pomeroy (Xenophon), J. P. Postgate (Tibullus), J. H. Mozley (Ovid, *Ars*), J. C. Rolfe (Gellius), A. L. Wheeler (Ovid, *Tristia*), M. Winterbottom (Seneca).

[2] I also recognize that, outside the guild of commentators, few read commentaries from cover to cover; cf. Kraus (2002: 11, 18) on the range of ways in which commentaries are used.

excessive ingenuity who lacked self-discipline, who could not leave well alone, who was much too fond of his own cleverness (Sen. *Contr.* 2. 2. 12, 9. 5. 17; cf. Quint. 10. 1. 88 <u>nimium</u> *amator ingenii sui*). Hand in hand with this reputation for stylistic excess went a reputation for moral licence, above all in the *Ars Amatoria*. In *Tristia* 2, Ovid cites the main charge against this poem as being one of teaching adultery (*Tr.* 2. 212), although he goes on to insist that the attribution of such viciousness to his poem stems from a kind of critical excess in the reader (*Tr.* 2. 278 *et* <u>nimium</u> *scriptis arrogat ille meis*). Recent critics have been inclined to make Ovid's stylistic excess the object of critical recuperation: Sharrock (1994*a*: 295), for example, talks of the 'functionality' of Ovidian excess in the Daedalus and Icarus episode of *Ars* 2. But the reputation of the *Ars* for other kinds of excess has lingered. In 1962 J. P. V. D. Balsdon (1962: 257) remarked of the *Ars* that in it 'Ovid glorified and sought the refinement of every pleasure which the flesh affords'. Balsdon meant this as a sly criticism, of course, but rephrased in more friendly terms (e.g. 'cheerfully sensualist'), this remark might fairly reflect perceptions of the character of the *Ars Amatoria* even at its bimillennium. But I want to point to the existence of another Ovid—Ovid the poet of 'moderation' (unexpected and ultimately subversive moderation, but moderation all the same). I do so in the context of a contemporary academic culture which endorses the postmodern, ultimately romantic, celebration of the sublimity of excess. In the library of my own university, Georges Bataille's *Visions of Excess* (1985) is virtually unobtainable during term time, while other, more moderately titled works lie gathering institutional dust. However, I can offer the reader hope of finding an Ovid who plays the role of moderate to excess.

Even allowing for the shrink-wrapped reputation of the *Ars Amatoria* for immorality, it is not hard to see how some knowledge of the contents of *Ars* 3—the book on which I concentrate here— might encourage a belief in the excesses of its text.[3] Ovid's 'persuasion to love' at *Ars* 3. 88–98—a discourse common to lovers and the *praeceptor amoris*—includes the injunction: 'refuse not your joys to eager lovers. Even should they deceive you, what do you lose? All

---

[3] For excess and moderation in the first two books of the *Ars* and in the *Remedia*, see chs. 1, 3, and 4 of Gibson (forthcoming).

remains the same. Were a *thousand* lovers to partake, nothing is wasted therefrom [i.e. your vagina].' In the first block of instruction proper, Ovid deals with the controversial subject of *cultus* and its various constituent aspects: hairstyles, clothing, and, most scandalously of all, cosmetics (129–234). Later, he passes on to personal 'accomplishments' associated with the unproductive *otium* of the lover (music, poetry, dancing, board games: 311–80), before manoeuvring his pupils out of the home into the public spaces of Rome, where the model of the prostitute-streetwalker in search of (multiple) customers lurks threateningly (381–432). Finally, after much manipulation and mutual infidelity between the sexes, Ovid ends the book with instruction on the pleasures of the table and of the bedroom (747–808). The overwhelming impression of licence and excess gleaned from this bare summary of subject matter appears to chime with the Ovid we think we know. With this sort of material at his disposal, surely Ovid, the notoriously playful poet of the *Amores*, will not pass up the opportunity to resist or overturn Augustan and Roman discourses on the restraint, personal simplicity, and decorum proper to women?[4] But a closer look at the text reveals something more complex.

POET OF MODERATION

The significance of Ovid's opening passage of instruction on hairstyles, clothes, and cosmetics (129–234) can be understood only when read against the 'anti-cosmetic' tradition. This venerable tradition, which begins in earnest in classical Greece and survives in rude health well into the Middle Ages and beyond, condemns women's cosmetics, dress, and hairstyles with enthusiasm and consistency.[5] The *locus classicus* occurs in Xenophon's *Oeconomicus*, where a certain Ischomachus reports a conversation with his own wife, in which he

---

[4] For these discourses, see (e.g.) the introduction of Nisbet and Rudd (2004: 98–100) to Hor. *Odes*. 3. 6.

[5] On the development of the tradition in classical times, see esp. Knecht (1972: 39–55); on the anti-cosmetic strain in elegy, see Heldmann (1981*b*: 153–9), also Wyke (1994).

asks her whether she would prefer him to have a genuinely healthy complexion or one that cosmetics make appear so (10. 7–8):

Wife, you must understand that I too do not prefer the colour of white powder and rouge to your own, but just as the gods have made horses most attractive to horses, cattle to cattle, and sheep to sheep, so human beings consider the human body most attractive when it is unadorned. These tricks might perhaps succeed in deceiving strangers without being detected, but those who spend their lives together are found out when they get out of bed before they have got dressed, or they are detected by a drop of sweat, or convicted when they cry, or are revealed as they truly are when they take a bath.

Many of the features of this passage play significant and often enlarged roles in later attacks on cosmetics and beauty aids, including the emphasis on deceit, concealment, and detection, and even such details as the damage wrought by tears or sweat. Entirely typical of the anti-cosmetic tradition is Ischomachus' stark binary opposition between cosmetics and unadorned nature. But it is not only powder and rouge that attract the condemnation of traditional morals: fine clothing, elaborate hairstyles, and jewellery are likewise criticized as symptoms of moral decadence, of luxury, or self-indulgence and vanity. However, Ovid's rejection of this tradition in *Ars* 3 does not adopt the mode of going to the opposite extreme from 'unadorned nature'. In fact, his carefully nuanced handling of his subject matter carries an implicit refusal to accept the binary oppositions characteristic of anti-cosmetic discourse.

Advice on Ovid's very first subject takes the form, as often in didactic poetry, of a catalogue.[6] A representative sample of eight hairstyles is set out (135–48). The 'anti-cosmetic' tradition regularly targets over-elaboration or excessive attention to the hair;[7] set over

---

[6] Like a lover praising his beloved, or a doctor writing on the treatment of the body, the *praeceptor amoris* starts with the head, before moving down the body. For Ovid's ordering of his description of Corinna's beauty according to the rhetorical rules for 'from head to foot', see McKeown (1989: 116–17) on *Am.* 1. 5. 19–22. For the similar ordering principle in medical works of treating subjects *a capite ad calcem*, cf. Celsus 4. 2–32, 6. 1–19, Galen 12. 379 K., ps. Galen 14. 390 K. (I owe these references to David Langslow.)

[7] Cf. e.g. Plaut. *Most.* 248–55, Manil. 5. 140 ff., [Lucian] *Am.* 40, Galen 12. 434–5, 445 K. (and in elegy, cf. Tib. 1. 8. 15–16, Prop. 1. 2. 1, 1. 15. 5–6, 2. 18b. 27–8, Ov. *Am.* 1. 14).

against this is an understood preference for simplicity. Ovid, however, recommends neither simplicity nor highly elaborate hairstyles to his pupils *en masse*. Instead he offers a range of styles—from which a *puella* must choose according to personal suitability—starting with the plain central parting and patriotic '*nodus*' (frontal knot) styles (137–40), and ending with a more elaborate (but not over-elaborate) *coiffure* displaying waves in the hair (148).[8] The emphasis on individual decorum is crucial. The vain Aphrodite of Callimachus 'frequently twice re-arranged the same lock of hair' (*On the Bath of Pallas* 22), and writers in the anti-cosmetic tradition routinely criticize women's habit of changing hairstyle.[9] By contrast Ovid, despite ending his treatment with the observation that the number of available styles exceeds the multitude of bees on Mount Hybla (149–52), is not in fact inviting his female readers to try out a new hairstyle every day; cf. 135–40:

> nec genus ornatus unum est: quod quamque decebit,
>   eligat et speculum consulat ante suum.
> longa probat facies capitis discrimina puri:
>   sic erat ornatis Laodamia comis.
> exiguum summa nodum sibi fronte relinqui,
>   ut pateant aures, ora rotunda uolunt.

(Nor is there but one form of adornment: let each choose what becomes her, and take counsel before her own mirror. An oval face prefers a parting upon the head left unadorned: the tresses of Laodamia were so arranged. Round faces would fain have a small knot left on top of the head, so that the ears show.)

Far from constantly changing style, the *puellae* are invited to choose the one that best becomes their features. And whether that style be less or more elaborate is reduced to a matter of indifference. Rather than reversing the terms of the anti-cosmetic tradition, Ovid is denying its relevance.

A warning that Ovid intends to target the polarities of the anti-cosmetic tradition appears immediately prior to the 'hairstyles'

---

[8] For these styles, see Gibson (2003*a*: 151–2, 154–5) on *Ars* loc. cit.
[9] Cf. e.g. Tib. 1. 8. 9–10, Clem. Alex. *Paed.* 3. 11. 2, Tertull. *Cult. Fem.* 2. 7; also Ov. *Met.* 2. 412, *Fast.* 4. 309–10.

passage. The *puellae* are instructed to avoid the usual trappings of feminine *luxuria*, such as expensive earrings and gold-embroidered clothing:

> uos quoque nec caris aures onerate lapillis,
>   quos legit in uiridi decolor Indus aqua,
> nec prodite graues insuto uestibus auro:
>   per quas nos petitis, saepe fugatis, opes.
> munditiis capimur: non sint sine lege capilli.   (129–34)

(You too burden not your ears with precious stones, which the discoloured Indian gathers from green water, and come not forth weighed down with the gold sewn upon your garments; the wealth wherewith you seek us oft-times repels. It is with elegance we are caught: let not your locks be lawless.)

The wearing of costly jewellery and expensive clothing is regularly placed by moralists in opposition to personal simplicity.[10] Ovid's female pupils are likewise warned to eschew *luxuria*. But it is clear from Ovid's earlier and provocative 'hymn' to *cultus* (101–34),[11] and from instruction which follows in *Ars* 3 on hairstyles, clothing, and cosmetics, that Ovid does not accept that his pupils must therefore travel to the opposite 'extreme' of simplicity. In any case, the ground of Ovid's opposition to jewellery and clothing differs from that of the moralists. The latter saw in these items evidence of corrupting *luxuria*, while for Ovid they lack the qualities of taste and elegance (*munditiae*).[12] That is to say, what for others is a matter of ethics, for Ovid is aesthetics: such displays of wealth repel lovers (132).

---

[10] Compare (e.g.) the condemnation of *luxuria* in *matronae* at Sen. *Contr.* 2. 5. 7 *gemmas et ex alieno litore petitos lapillos et aurum vestemque nihil in matrona tecturam* ('pearls and precious stones sought on foreign beaches, gold, and clothes that will hide nothing of a married woman's body'), with the recommendation of how a *matrona* ought to dress in public, at *Contr.* 2. 7. 3 *prodeat in tantum ornata quantum ne immunda sit* ('let her go out dressed up only so far as to avoid unkemptness').

[11] On this important passage, see Watson (1982), Mader (1988), Gibson (2003a: 128–9).

[12] For the malleability of the concept of *munditia* and its association with 'moderate' attitudes to self-adornment, and for Ovid's significant engagement here with the Pyrrha of Horace's *Odes* (1. 5. 5 *simplex munditiis*), whereby Ovid embraces *munditia* while rejecting Horatian *simplicitas*, see ch. 3 of Gibson (forthcoming).

Ovid skilfully manoeuvres himself out of the moral polarities of argument associated with strictures on *luxuria* and women's hairstyles. The use of the principle of 'individual decorum' in the latter case has one further significant implication. Despite his earlier injunction that women take many lovers (87–98), it is not to every *puella* that Ovid recommends erotically charged hairstyles, such as those linked with 'bacchants' (145); but only to women whose features they become. Ovid is driving a wedge into the traditional association between artful attention to the hair and sexual availability or prostitution. If Ovid's female readers may freely choose—again on the basis of aesthetic principles—between 'respectable' styles (such as the '*nodus*' of 139–40) and more 'erotic' styles, then how will the good citizen know how to distinguish the moral from the immoral? Any (apparently) respectably dressed and tressed *puella* may be playing Ovid's games of love.[13]

A response to anti-cosmetic arguments spiked by Ovid with similar subversive intent informs the advice on clothing. The earlier elegists have much to say on women's dress, most of it predictably negative. Typically they pour scorn on beautiful (i.e. expensive) clothing, on the ground that such garments are a manifestation of female greed or desire to attract (other) lovers. The elegists are inheritors of traditional (male) morality, which likewise denounced diaphanous fabrics, or the wearing of gold and expensive purple.[14] Given the near-hysteria which the subject of clothing provokes in the austere moralist or jealous elegist, the mere fact that Ovid includes it in his programme for *Ars 3*—a book dedicated to seducing lovers— must appear to be a bid for controversy. This expectation appears confirmed, when the poet provides a list of eleven or more dyes for the *puellae* to use (and these are said to be a mere sample at 185–7).

---

[13] For this conventional association of elaborate hairstyles with sexual availability and prostitution, cf. e.g. Plaut. *Truc.* 287–8, Herter (1960: 92 nn. 424–8). For the association of the *nodus* and plain central-parting styles (*Ars* 3. 137–40) with Livia and other respectable women, see Bartman (1999: 36–9, 114–16).

[14] For the negative attitudes of the elegists towards such clothing, cf. e.g. Prop. 1. 2. 1–2, 2. 16. 55–6, 3. 13. 6 ff., 3. 14. 27, 4. 5. 57–8, Tib. 1. 9. 69–70, 2. 3. 57 ff., 2. 4. 27 ff., Ov. *Am.* 1. 10. 61. Cf. on diaphanous fabrics, Sen. *Contr.* 2. 5. 7, Petron. 55. 6, [Lucian] *Am.* 41, Philostr. *Epist.* 22; and, on gold and purple, above all the provisions of the *lex Oppia* as quoted at Livy 34. 1. 3.

But in fact Ovid is refusing to accept the traditional binary opposition of luxury versus simplicity of dress:

> quid de ueste loquar? nec uos, segmenta, requiro
>   nec quae de Tyrio murice, lana, rubes.
> cum tot prodierint pretio leuiore colores,
>   quis furor est census corpore ferre suos?
> aeris, ecce, color, tum cum sine nubibus aer
>   nec tepidus pluuias concitat Auster aquas;
> ecce tibi similis, quae quondam Phrixon et Hellen
>   diceris Inois eripuisse dolis... (169–76)

(What shall I say of clothes? Flounces, I need you not, nor you, o wool that blush with Tyrian dye. When so many cheaper colours walk abroad, what madness to carry whole incomes on one's body? Look, here is the colour of the sky, when the sky is cloudless and warm Auster brings no rainy showers; look, here is one like you who are once said to have rescued Phrixus and Helle from Ino's wiles...)

Ovid explicitly rules out the use of gold[15] and Tyrian purple and other costly dyes among his pupils (169–72), and deals only with wool—to the exclusion of diaphanous and other expensive fabrics (170; cf. 187). Perhaps this is not so different from the attitude of miserly love-elegists, who notoriously do not wish to buy expensive clothing for their beloveds. What is arresting, however, is that the usual (preferred or understood) alternative of simple dress is nowhere to be found in Ovid's text. The *praeceptor amoris* delights in the extraordinary variety of dyes available to his *puellae*, ranging from muted greys (175–6) to sexier sea-greens and yellows as worn by sea nymphs and the ill-famed goddess of the dawn (177–80). As in the previous passage on hairstyles, emphasis is laid on 'individual decorum':

> lana tot aut plures sucos bibit: elige certos,
>   nam non conueniens omnibus omnis erit.
> pulla decent niueas...
>
> alba decent fuscas... (187–9, 91)

---

[15] For costly *segmenta* (169), pieces of fabric embroidered with gold or silver and sewn onto garments, see Gibson (2003a: 164 ad loc.).

(So many dyes and more does the wool drink up; choose individual dyes, for not every one suits every woman. Dark colours suit snow-white skins... whites suit dusky skins...)

Moralistic attacks on women's alleged fondness for constant change—in the colour, style, or fabric of their clothing—provide the context for comprehending the force and direction of Ovid's verses here.[16] Where others denounce variety or change as part of a moralistic argument for simplicity and restraint, Ovid drives a (deeply ironic) aesthetic middle path between these two opposed categories. Unlimited choice and variety for the sake of change receive no support as principles from the *praeceptor*; but neither are his addressees expected to embrace simplicity—or restraint per se—in their choice of colour. A select number of shades from Ovid's long and varied catalogue will be suitable for each *puella*: the darker shades will be appropriate for some complexions, and the lighter shades for others. But it is not only the straitjacket of binary opposition that is being refused here. Ovid succeeds in uncoupling the brighter colours from their conventionally lurid associations. Traditional values linked such colours with *meretrices* and lax morals,[17] and it might have been anticipated that these clothes would be recommended by Ovid to his pupils. But instead he insists that colours should be chosen only for their personal suitability. However sexually liberated his pupils intend to be or erotically alluring they want to appear to potential lovers, they must choose between the muted colours associated with respectable women (e.g. 175–6) and the brighter hues associated with prostitutes (e.g. 179–80) only on the basis of the colour of their complexion. Once more, a 'moral' issue has been converted into a question of aesthetics. Ovid also begins to rise above the traditional polar stereotypes of *meretrix* and *matrona*—a point I shall develop at the end of the chapter.

---

[16] Cf. e.g. Plaut. *Epid.* 229 ff. *quid istae, quae uesti quotannis nomina inueniunt noua?* | *tunicam rallam, tunicam spissam, linteolum caesicum,* | *indusiatam, patagiatam, caltulam aut crocotulum* etc. ('what are they at, sir, those women that invent new names for garments every year? The loose-knit tunic, the close-knit tunic, the linen-blue, the interior, the gold-edge, the marigold or crocus tunic...').

[17] For the regular association between prostitutes and bright colours; cf. e.g. Plaut. *Epid.* 213–34, Sen. *Nat.* 7. 31. 2, Herter (1960: 93 n. 436).

A pattern has begun to emerge. Ovid deals with subjects that attract outspoken criticism from both more traditional moralists and Roman love elegists. But, rather than up-ending their arguments and encouraging his pupils to change hairstyle and dress frequently or to wear expensive and diaphanous clothing, Ovid emphasizes the importance of restricting oneself to a limited range of personally becoming styles and bans the use of expensive fabrics and other luxury items. The acute intelligence behind this 'moderate' approach to *cultus* can be glimpsed in the reflection from a story told about the republican orator Hortensius. Attacked for his *munditia*, the excessively fussy attention to his dress, plus the effeminacy of his theatrical delivery, Hortensius responded defiantly:

> sed cum L. Torquatus, subagresti homo ingenio et infestiuo...non iam histrionem eum esse diceret, sed gesticulariam Dionysiamque eum notissimae saltatriculae nomine appellaret, tum uoce molli atque demissa Hortensius 'Dionysia,' inquit 'Dionysia malo equidem esse quam quod tu, Torquate, ἄμουσος, ἀναφρόδιτος, ἀπροσδιόνυσος. (Gell. 1. 5. 3)
>
> (But when L. Torquatus, a man of somewhat boorish and uncouth nature ...did not stop with calling Hortensius an actor, but said that he was a posturer and a Dionysia—which was the name of a notorious dancing girl—then Hortensius replied in a soft and gentle tone: 'I would rather be a Dionysia, Torquatus yes, a Dionysia, than like you, a stranger to the Muses, to Venus, and to Dionysus.')

Like Ovid, Hortensius supplies an aesthetic response to moralistic criticisms. Such a shifting of ground is a common manoeuvre, as a dictum of Oscar Wilde—'There is no such thing as a moral or an immoral book. Books are well written, or badly written. That is all'— perhaps may serve to testify.[18] However, Ovid and Hortensius differ in one crucial respect. The polarity set up in Gellius between the (masculine) unrefinement of Torquatus, and the effeminacy of Hortensius, is one that the orator's proto-Wildean response, delivered in an appropriately '*mollis*' tone, ultimately leaves intact. If the choice is between being graceless and uncultured like Torquatus, or remaining as his refined (and effeminate) self, then Hortensius will choose the

---

[18] This dictum is quoted by Markus Janka (1997) as the epigraph to his commentary on *Ars* 2.

latter.[19] The orator accepts the polarity offered, albeit evaluating its extremes differently; but Ovid, for his part, refuses to recognize the polarity altogether. Instead he drives a middle path where none is envisaged, much less offered. Why Ovid's response is a more powerful one—despite the accompanying hints of moderation—I will come to later.

Ovid has sustained a paradoxical rhetoric of moderation in his *praecepta* on clothes and hairstyles, but it must seem difficult or impossible for a similar rhetoric to be maintained in the treatment of the most controversial of all subjects included in *Ars* 3. Cosmetics, more than any other subject involving women's personal adornment, provoke outrage, and from one end of antiquity to the other. They are decisively condemned already in Xenophon's *Oeconomicus* (quoted earlier), but his sentiments find echoes in a very wide range of authors stretching from Aristophanes to Alciphron and beyond.[20] Writers typically condemn make-up on the ground that it reveals a desire to attract men sexually (hence a frequent association between prostitution and cosmetics), or it offers a beauty that is unnatural, or it is an invitation to *luxuria* and *mollitia*. Contrast Ovid's advice to his pupils at *Ars* 3. 199–204:

> scitis et inducta candorem quaerere creta:
>   sanguine quae uero non rubet, arte rubet.
> arte supercilii confinia nuda repletis
>   paruaque sinceras uelat aluta genas.
> nec pudor est oculos tenui signare fauilla
>   uel prope te nato, lucide Cydne, croco.

(You know, too, how to gain a bright hue by applying powder: art gives complexion if real blood gives it not. By art you fill up the bare common borders of the eyebrow, and a little leather patch covers the cheeks so they appear unblemished. Nor is there shame in marking eyes with powdery ash, or with saffron born near you, O shining Cydnus.)

These lines offer the only recommendation to be found in pagan and Christian antiquity of cosmetics such as rouge, powder, and

---

[19] Broad (and illuminating) context for Hortensius' 'effeminate' choice is provided by Corbeill (2004: 120–1, 133–7).
[20] See the passages cited by Gibson (2003a: 174) on *Ars* 3.199 ff., and see further esp. Grillet (1975: 97–114), Rosati (1985: 9–20).

eye-liner.[21] Shockingly, Ovid fails to condemn his pupils' efforts to cover their blemishes, to acquire 'unnatural' beauty, or to add embellishment to their looks. He both gives prominence to the role of *ars* (and hence the *Ars*) in his pupils' transformation of themselves, and underlines the fact that the deficiencies of nature find reparation in artifice. Of course writers in the anti-cosmetic tradition—deploying the traditional polarity of 'art' versus 'nature'—are provoked to anger by ideas of falsity and artificiality.[22] Has Ovid abandoned his previous practice of refusing binary polarities, and simply moved from one extreme of the anti-cosmetic discourse (nature) to the other (art)? What kind of 'middle way' is it to reply to attacks on cosmetics by, remarkably, actually advocating them? Ovid, however, is not recommending the deliberate cultivation of artificiality, but rather the convincing imitation of nature. Care is taken to underline this point at *Ars* 3. 210 *ars faciem dissimulata iuuat* ('your looks are aided by dissembled art'). The role of Ovidian *ars/Ars* is not to usurp nature (much less to foster the creation of deliberately 'unnatural' looks), but rather to bring nature to perfection (cf. 3. 200). Artifice is made to serve the interests of, ultimately to blend with, its binary opposite of nature. The poet takes a subject stigmatized as an extreme by the anti-cosmetic tradition and handles it in a notably restrained manner. Elsewhere Ovid takes a middle path between conventional binary polarities; here he applies moderation to a subject where, by traditional thinking, it cannot belong.

PROPERTIUS AND OVID: FROM INCONSISTENCY TO MODERATION

For all the illumination provided by reading *Ars* 3 against the general background of the 'anti-cosmetic' tradition, the richest context for viewing Ovid's commitment to moderation is to be found, of course,

---

[21] The surviving portions of the *Medicamina* do not recommend make-up, but rather describe face-packs to improve the complexion or remove blemishes; see further R. K. Gibson (2003a: 174–5 and 180) on *Ars* 3.199 ff. and 207 respectively.

[22] Cf. e.g. Plaut. *Most.* 258 ff., *Truc.* 289 ff., Mart. 9. 37, [Lucian] *Am.* 41, Philostr. *Epist.* 22.

in Propertius. A common reason for rejecting cosmetics and fine clothes is that such things destroy natural beauty—an argument that Propertius reproduces in a disquisition to Cynthia on the subject of self-adornment in his first book:

> quid iuuat ornato procedere, uita, capillo
>   et tenuis Coa ueste mouere sinus,
> aut quid Orontea crines perfundere murra,
>   teque peregrinis uendere muneribus,
> naturaeque decus mercato perdere cultu,
>   nec sinere in propriis membra nitere bonis?
> crede mihi, non ulla tuae est medicina figurae:
>   nudus Amor formae non amat artificem.   (Prop. 1. 2. 1–12)

(What avails it, my love, to step out with the latest hairstyle and to swing a sheer skirt of Coan silk? What avails it to drench your locks with Syrian perfume and to vaunt yourself in foreign finery, to destroy your natural charm with purchased ornament, preventing your figure from displaying its own true merits? Believe me, there is no improving your appearance: Love is naked, and loves not beauty gained by artifice.)

This poem was obviously in Ovid's mind in the first half of the book, since he refers to it directly on a number of occasions, and its order of treatment informs some of the structure of *Ars* 3.[23] But, so far as the female addressees of *Ars* 3 are concerned, the argument found in Propertius 1. 2, happily, is useless to the point of meaninglessness. To learn why is to discover differences between earlier Roman love elegy and the *Ars Amatoria*. It makes sense to assume some basic continuities between 'subjective' love elegy and the *Ars*. After all, they share the same metaphors for love, the classic triangle of lover, beloved, and rival, plus stock characters (doorkeeper, chaperon, go-between—although, of course, no *lena*), and stock situations (accusations of infidelity, the locked door), etc. But—something rarely emphasized—the *puellae* of the *Ars* cannot be identified very closely with Cynthia, Delia, and Corinna.[24] The latter are figured in earlier elegy as creatures of legendary beauty, all but superior to goddesses (Prop. 2. 2. 13–14) or worthy of comparison to the semi-legendary Semiramis (Ov. *Am.* 1. 5. 11).

---

[23] See Gibson (2003a: 24, and notes on *Ars* 3. 101 ff., 107 ff., 205). On Ovid and Propertius more generally in this context, see above all La Penna (1979).

[24] The point was made two decades ago by Labate (1984: 181 ff.).

Ars 3, by contrast, following a didactic tradition of address to a wide audience (such as the *agricolae* of *Georg.* 1. 101, or the *si quis in hoc...populo* of *Ars* 1. 1), takes as its addressees 'girls whom shame and the laws and your own rights allow' (57–8), later characterized as a *turba* (255, 811). The description of Ovid's pupils as an undifferentiated 'mass' (i.e. all the same) is obviously somewhat at odds with his insistence on individual decorum (i.e. all are different, requiring individually appropriate hairstyles and clothing). Nevertheless, rather than leaving readers to work out for themselves the probable differences between the semi-divine Cynthia and the common herd, Ovid highlights it for us—and not just once:

> forma dei munus; forma quota quaeque superbit?
>   pars uestrum tali munere magna caret.
> cura dabit faciem...   (103–5)

(Beauty is a divine gift; how many a one prides herself on her beauty? A great part of you is wanting in such endowments. Care will give good looks...)

> non mihi uenistis, Semele Ledeue docendae,
>   perque fretum falso, Sidoni, uecta boue
> aut Helene...
> turba docenda uenit pulchrae turpesque puellae,
>   pluraque sunt semper deteriora bonis.
> formosae non artis opem praeceptaque quaerunt;
>   est illis sua dos, forma sine arte potens.   (251–8)

(You have not come to learn from me, Semele and Leda, or you Sidonian, borne on a false bull over the sea; or Helen... It is the crowd that come to be taught, women both fair and ugly; and always is the worse more numerous than the good. The beautiful do not seek for the help of art and precepts; their dowry they have, beauty that without art is powerful.)

Such 'insensitivity', amusing as it is to the (male?) reader, also has a pedagogic role to play: straightforward talking, in the style of Hesiod or Lucretius, arrests the attention of the addressee. But, since in both contexts Ovid is about to justify the embellishment of beauty or concealment of defects, these lines also conspire to reduce the arguments of Propertius 1. 2 to redundancy. If the naturally beautiful Cynthia can do without artifice, as Propertius alleges, then Ovid's pupils—naturally 'ugly' (255 *turpes*) as most of them are implied to be—surely require it. The quasi-ethical Propertius is easily outmanoeuvred by the (pragmatically) aesthetic Ovid.

To focus more closely on what Propertius 1. 2 can tell us about Ovid's rhetoric of moderation, one must ask an obvious—if rarely posed—question: what is this poem doing in Propertius' first book at all? The elegies of that book are, to a large extent, about marking the poet's difference from conventional values. Propertius is a man who prefers to be *mollis* rather than *durus*; who would rather stay in Rome with the faithless Cynthia (like a loyal wife!) than cross the seas with Tullus on public service; and who cries aloud his preferences for self-indulgent love elegy over military epic. His commitment in 1. 2 to an old-fashioned standard of personal adornment for women looks odd. Readers could have expected a more defiant—and certainly more coherent—'Hortensian' attitude to *cultus*. Of course Propertius is neurotically anxious lest Cynthia's expensive dress and elaborate hairstyle be evidence of her desire to be unfaithful to him. But his espousal—in a programmatically significant position—of sentiments that sit comfortably with the conservatism of Xenophon's Ischomachus, is in counterpoint to much of the *monobiblos*, which proclaims its author's alienation from mainstream society. As Mario Labate emphasizes, the rhetoric of Propertian elegy is thoroughly 'contradictory'.[25]

I argue that these contradictions and conflicts in Propertius provide a background against which Ovid's development of a carefully nuanced response to the anti-cosmetic tradition makes particular sense. Propertius has a pronounced tendency to take up positions that are at a polar extreme from those of his opponents. In a sense he is like Hortensius, preferring to be *mollis* (or a Dionysia) rather than its opposite. On the other hand, the elegist is capable of flitting to the opposite extreme and adopting Ischomachean rather than Hortensian attitudes to dress. To this double and self-contradictory 'extremism' Ovid offers a deliberate contrast, characterized by both (unexpected) moderation and consistency. The *praeceptor* is eager to advise women on subjects associated with *mollitia* and *luxuria*, but does so in a paradoxically restrained manner. The *puellae* of *Ars* 3 are effectively asked to take up a position intermediate between the simplicity

---

[25] See Labate, Ch. 10 below.

apparently desired by Propertius and the luxury displayed by Cynthia. Encouraged to apply *ars* to their hair, clothes, and faces, they are nowhere invited to try on Cynthia's Coan garments or Syrian perfume.

Where Propertius' behaviour is 'extreme', Ovid displays a respect for the 'mean'. Indeed, in a significant passage on a recommended style of walking 'intermediate' between the rustic's lolloping waddle and the excessive *mollitia* of the artful walker, Ovid announces that this mean is to be of general and consistent application: 305 *sed sit, ut in multis, modus hic quoque* ('but, *as in many things,* let there be moderation here too').[26] Ovid delivers on this promise that 'moderation' is a principle of general application, deploying it in both 'normal' and highly 'abnormal' contexts (where conventional thinking assumed a basic lack of restraint). In *Ars* 3 he goes on to insist, for example, that his pupils smile in restrained fashion (283 *sint modici rictus*), adopt a 'middle' writing style (479–80 *munda sed e medio consuetaque uerba, puellae, | scribite*), display moderation in handling the emotions of lovers (i.e. the *puellae* must be neither too indulgent nor excessively obdurate towards men: 471–8, 511, 577–610), control their own anger (237–42, 369–80, 501–8, 683), and eat and drink neither too much nor too little (757–64).

MODERATION, AUGUSTUS, AND THE *LEX IULIA DE ADULTERIIS*

What are the source and significance of all this emphasis on moderation? I have already pointed to one kind of answer—that part of Ovid's agenda is to poke fun at the characteristic 'extremism' of earlier love elegy, particularly Propertius (the more systematized extremism of the *Amores* notwithstanding). The *persona* of the *praeceptor* is not irrelevant. The 'teacher of love'—from Theognis to the Philetas of *Daphnis and Chloe* and beyond—is usually an older and more experienced person. This is a persona that Ovid sustains in the

---

[26] For this passage as programmatic for the *Ars*, and for the extensive engagement in the immediate context with *Am.* 3. 1, Cic. *Off.* 1. 128–31, and Prop. 2. 4. 5–6, see ch. 3 of Gibson (forthcoming).

Ars, and it is part of this persona that the older, more experienced lover should offer advice from his longer, and presumably more balanced, perspective. Immoderation is left to the passionate young 'boys' of earlier love elegy (including again Ovid's own *Amores*).[27] Viewed from a slightly different angle, the commitment to moderation characteristic of *Ars* 3 must also be a statement of poetics. The earlier elegists, fond of identifying the *corpus* of their poetry with the body of their mistress, use hair, clothes, and (the presence or absence of) cosmetics—the core subjects of *Ars* 3—as bearers of poetological meaning.[28] The emphasis placed in *Ars* 3 on the avoidance of extremes in personal *cultus* must then reflect the generic identity of the *Ars*, as an erotic-didactic work halfway between the poetological 'simplicity' of elegy (as reflected in the Propertian ideal of a Cynthia who avoids over-ornamentation), and the altogether grander pretensions of epic poetry.[29]

But the full significance of Ovid's development in *Ars* 3 of the idea of the 'middle way' is hardly exhausted by poetics. Overshadowing the latter stand politics and the law. I mean the relationship between the *Ars* and the *lex Iulia de adulteriis coercendis* of 18 BC, which made adultery and some other sexual acts a criminal offence.[30] This relationship I have already dealt with in the introduction to my *Ars* 3 commentary, so here I emphasize only the points most salient to the argument of this chapter, and refer the reader to the earlier discussion for the broad view of the *lex Iulia* and the *Ars*.[31] However, I also

---

[27] For Ovid's characterization in the *Ars* of the violent behaviour of the elegiac lover as immature, including his own behaviour in the *Amores*, see Gibson (2003a: 317–18 (on *Ars* 3. 555–76), 320–1 (on 3. 565 ff.), 321–2 (on 3. 565–71)). For the additional generic pressure to adopt a balanced or moderate perspective exerted by didactic poetry, see ch. 3 of Gibson (forthcoming).

[28] See especially Zetzel (1996) on Prop. 1. 2, and Wyke (1989) = (2002: 115–54) on Ov. *Am.* 3. 1.

[29] This point is made *in nuce* in Gibson (2003a: 34) and developed at greater length in ch. 3 of *idem* (forthcoming). A rather similar conclusion is reached by Sharrock (1994a: 133–46) on the poetological dimensions of the Daedalus and Icarus tale in *Ars* 2, where the teacher-father offers his pupil-son stylistically significant advice: *inter utrumque uola* (2. 63). Such overtones are more emphatically present in *Ars* 3 than earlier in the poem, as the female body is rather more amenable to poetological freighting than the male body of *Ars* 1 and 2.

[30] On the law, see (e.g.) Treggiari (1991: 277–98), Edwards (1993: 37–42), Galinsky (1996: 128–40), McGinn (1998).

[31] See Gibson (2003a: 25–37).

put together a new argument which suggests a link between the characteristic 'moderation' of *Ars* 3 and the 'extreme' personality of Augustus.

The *cultus* recommended to the women of *Ars* 3 corresponds to no known literary stereotype for women. On the one hand, a range of luxury items is omitted or placed under ban; on the other, Ovid does recommend that sustained attention be given to all aspects of *cultus*. As a result, women who follow Ovid's advice will resemble neither the traditional matron nor the stereotypical whore. The binary polarity between these two types of woman is firmly fixed in ancient thought, as may be seen most readily in the portraits of Tragedy and Elegy in *Amores* 3. 1, where each is assimilated to her status counterpart of *matrona* and *meretrix* respectively.[32] Here the contrasts (*Am.* 3. 1. 7–14) between their modest versus revealing dress (12 *palla* vs. 9 *uestis tenuissima*), and simple versus perfumed and elaborate hairstyles (12 *fronte comae torua* vs. 7 *odoratos... nexa capillos*) reflect the traditional opposition of austere or simple matron to gaudy whore. Yet in *Ars* 3 Ovid drives an aesthetic middle path between this ethical binary polarity and its associated hairstyles and clothing, and goes on to create a paradoxical 'intermediate' between matron and whore.[33]

Such aesthetic 'moderation' gains a strong political edge if a recent reconstruction of the *lex Iulia de adulteriis coercendis* is accepted. Tom McGinn has argued that the *lex Iulia*—as part of its attempt to define who was subject to prosecution (for various sexual offences)—divided citizen women, in a highly symbolic manner, into two categories: (1) prostitutes and *lenae*; and (2) the rest.[34] The latter group was to be made up of *matres familias* and those who ought to aspire to be of this quasi-moral status.[35] This is a context of potentially great importance for understanding the significance of Ovid's failure to pander to conventional stereotypes of *meretrix* and *matrona* in *Ars* 3.

[32] See Wyke (1989: 125–6) = (2002: 132–3).

[33] There is a partial correspondence here with portrait types of Livia, who is similarly depicted without expensive clothes or excessive jewellery; see Bartman (1999: 44–6). Unlike the *puellae* of *Ars* 3, however, Livia is depicted with other unconventional but prestigious attributes which emphasize her status, such as veil, floral wreath, beaded fillet, and crown. (For caution, however, about whether iconographical subtleties were widely recognized by ancient viewers, see Bartman (1999: 22).)

[34] See McGinn (1998: 194–203).   [35] See ibid. 147–56.

In the Julian law's provisions for this division of society into prostitute and *materfamilias*, each group was awarded its own type of distinguishing dress. The latter group of respectable women were to put on the matron's distinctive markers of *stola* and *palla*, while prostitutes were to assume the *toga*. The presumable purpose of this rather heavy-handed provision was to separate the two groups in an unmistakable and visible manner: no longer could they blend together seamlessly in public.[36] Here the author of the law may have seen himself as 'responding to the chaos of the late Republic, when the dividing line between respectable and non-respectable had become blurred. The polarity of *meretrix* and *matrona* sought to restore a sense of order and clarity to women's status' (McGinn (1998: 209)). But it is precisely this polarity—this clarity—which is rejected in Ars 3.

The orator Hortensius, introduced earlier, accepted the polarity offered him by his opponent Torquatus. Accused of effeminacy, Hortensius did not refuse the binary opposition of masculine versus feminine appearance; rather, he effectively reinforced it by announcing that he preferred to remain effeminate. Ovid, by contrast, refuses to accept such a polarity. He rises above the opposition of dowdy matron and lurid whore found in ancient moralistic thought and reflected in the Julian law, and creates a world characterized by a deliberately restrained *cultus*. Important here also are Ovid's attempts, identified earlier, to break down the traditional association between particular hairstyles (or shade of clothing) and sexual availability by asking that a style or shade ('respectable' or not) be chosen on the basis of personal 'decorum'—not as part of a conventional code for signalling sexual availability. Like Hortensius, Ovid shifts ground from ethics to aesthetics; but quite unlike the former, the elegist refuses to fight on the 'either/or' terms offered by his opponent, and creates instead a third way. Here 'moderation' is deployed as a wholly unexpected weapon in a refusal of the polarities of the *princeps*.

---

[36] See ibid. 154–5, 156–71, 209–11. For anxiety in the jurists about the difficulties of telling apart respectable women and prostitutes by their dress in the street, cf. *Dig.* 47. 10. 15. 15 (with ibid. 331–5, also Gibson (2003a: 269–70)).

Such moderation packs a strong punch—and for two reasons. First, there is the fondness of two poets closely associated with Augustus for versions of the same theme, namely Horace's emphasis on the ethical, rather than aesthetic, middle way in his *Satires, Odes,* and *Epistles*,[37] and Vergil's portrait of an Aeneas who struggles to impose restraint on himself in the *Aeneid*. To these more orthodox treatments of temperance and the middle way Ovid adds his own rather different version, one that is now at odds with Augustus' vision of the good society. Secondly, there is the perceived personality of Augustus himself. As Karl Galinsky has recently emphasized, in both private and public life Augustus appeared to contemporaries and to later generations as a man of strong contradictions;[38] or, to rephrase it in terms more sympathetic to my argument, a figure of unreconciled polarities and extremes of behaviour. Here was a man who proposed draconian laws governing sexual behaviour, yet whose own adulteries were not denied even by his friends (Suet. *Aug.* 69); a man whose literary tastes were severe (*Aug.* 89. 2), but who was also genuinely devoted to popular entertainment (*Aug.* 43–5); and the saviour of the republic who was Rome's monarch in all but name. The greatest distance traversed, however, between extremes of behaviour was to be found in the miles between the bloodthirsty excesses of the young Octavian (*Aug.* 13–15, 27. 3–4) and the clemency of the mature Augustus (*Aug.* 51; cf. 21. 2–3, Galinsky (1996: 84–5)). Writers of the post-Augustan era ring various changes on this theme of the contradictions and extremes of the *princeps*. Seneca disapprovingly notes that Augustus became *moderatus et clemens* only after he had achieved power through bloody civil war and proscription (*Clem.* 1. 11. 1–2); the emperor Julian, in his satirical *Caesares*, introduces an Augustus who, among other evidence of inconstancy, is 'changing colours continually, like a chameleon, turning now pale, now red' (309b–c); and ps. Aurelius Victor describes a *princeps* who, a slave to *luxuria* himself, nevertheless exiles Ovid on the very same charge (*Epit. Caes.* 1. 24).

In *Ars* 3 does Ovid likewise comment (indirectly) on the polarities and contradictions of Augustus the man? The mature *princeps* worked hard to foster an image of moderation and temperance. In

---

[37] See Gibson (forthcoming). [38] See Galinsky (1996: 370–5).

addition to his vaunted political *clementia*, Augustus, so Suetonius' *Life* informs us, practised moderation and restraint in style of house (72. 1 *aedibus modicis*), country estates (72. 3 *sua... modica*), furniture (73 *suppellectilis parsimonia*), and bed (73 *toro... modice instructo*); wore a toga and stripe that struck a middle path between too full and too narrow (73); and served modest meals, ate plain food, and drank sparingly (74, 76. 1, 77). Yet the same man could sponsor a law that operated with the crudest of binary polarities, dividing women into two opposed 'extremes' quite at odds with the graduated spectrum of social and legal status that elite opinion normally liked to find in society.[39] Here was a potential contradiction ready for exploitation—at least by a poet such as Ovid. In his poetic 'immaturity',[40] Ovid countenanced in *Am.* 3. 1 the division of the world into the simple polarities of matron and whore, Elegy and Tragedy (the genre onto which he was to move next according to *Am.* 3. 15). In the greater poetic 'maturity' of the *Ars*, Ovid refuses to repeat this scenario, but rather blends aesthetic aspects of matron and whore into one in a way that is consistent with his larger emphasis on the middle way. Augustus, by contrast, though claiming to practise personal and political moderation in his own maturity, nevertheless commits in the *lex Iulia* an 'extreme' act that reinforces the ethical categories of matron and whore rejected in *Ars* 3. It is precisely this fissure in Augustus' behaviour and ideology which *Ars* 3 is designed to work open: the great moderate's adultery law is portrayed as a work of extremity and polarization, while Ovid appears as the consistent proponent of the middle way.[41]

Such—perhaps—is one significance of the insistence on moderation in *Ars Amatoria 3*. Even without the Julian law, Ovid's new and subversive 'middle way' would possess both meaning and weight, so enshrined is the polarity of matron and whore in ancient thought. But the context provided by that law gives *Ars* 3 special resonance. As a 'message' Ovid's emphasis on moderation is powerful, albeit expressed with great subtlety. It appears deeply unfortunate for Latin

---

[39] For development of this point, see Gibson (2003*a*: 30–2).
[40] For the typical characterization in the *Ars* of the *Amores* as 'immature', see above n. 27.
[41] For other fissures in Augustan 'ideology' explored in *Ars* 3, see Gibson (2003*a*: 134–44) on *Ars* 3. 113–28.

literature that such a message had little or no time to emerge before the poet's exile to Romania—and the consequent burying of the poem for almost 2,000 years under a landslide reputation of the rather more straightforward moral noxiousness of teaching adultery. Or is the poem's blurring of the boundaries between *meretrix* and *matrona* entirely without influence or afterlife? The answer to this question—if it be thought worth answering—I leave to others.

8

The Art of *Remedia Amoris*: Unlearning to Love?

Gianpiero Rosati

> *dediscit animus sero quod didicit diu*
> 'the mind takes a long time to unlearn
> what it learned a long time ago'
> Sen. *Tro.* 633

1. A TEACHER UNDER GUARD

The opening lines of the *Remedia Amoris* present a confrontation between the text's aspiring author and the god Love, who reacts angrily to the very title of the book:

> legerat huius Amor titulum nomenque libelli:
>   'bella mihi, uideo, bella parantur' ait.   (*Rem.* 1–2)

(Love had read just the name and title of this little book: 'Wars, I see, wars are being prepared against me', he said.)

The poet immediately beseeches the god to be merciful towards his *uates* (3), recalling his service under Love's command (*tradita qui toties te duce signa tuli*, 'I who so often have borne arms entrusted under your leadership', 4) and his lifestyle, both past and present, devoted to love (*ego semper amaui,* | *et... nunc quoque... amo*, 'I have always been in love, and... now also... I am in love', 7–8).

Indeed, he boasts to the god of his skill in teaching the art of 'obtaining a lover' and of having made rational what was once a primitive and instinctive practice (*quin etiam docui, qua possis arte parari, | et, quod nunc ratio est, impetus ante fuit,* 'moreover, I have taught the arts by which you can be acquired, and made into an act of reason what was previously a matter of impulse', 9–10). The poet reassures Love of his intentions, and that he is not a traitor (11) but merely a devoted subject who is advocating that Love exercise a 'softer power' in order to avoid the path of blood and violence.

This scene of confrontation between the poet's burgeoning intentions and the god's intervention (aimed at sabotaging those designs) vividly recalls an analogous moment at the outset of Ovid's poetic career.[1] *Amores* 1 begins with the intervention of Love who removes one foot from each second hexameter and forces the powerless poet into the genre of elegy, without explanation (or even the justification of self-defence, as in the *Remedia*), but rather mocking the artistic ambitions of the apprentice poet:

> arma graui numero uiolentaque bella parabam
>   edere, materia conueniente modis.
> par erat inferior uersus; risisse Cupido
>   dicitur atque unum surripuisse pedem.
> 'quis tibi, saeue puer, dedit hoc in carmina iuris?
>   Pieridum uates, non tua, turba sumus'   (*Am.* 1. 1. 1–6)

(I was preparing to speak of arms and violent wars in heavy measure, with metre to match the matter. The second verse was equal; but Cupid is said to have laughed and to have snatched away one foot. 'Who gave you, savage boy, this power over song? We bards are the crowd of the Muses, not yours.')

This famous scene of literary initiation is repeatedly brought to the attention of Ovid's readers whenever the poet wishes to underline a turning-point or the beginning of a new phase in his poetic career, like a yardstick against which the struggle between the poet and the divinity who inspires him is measured time after time. The scene also directs the genre of the poet's new work—it operates to position the

---

[1] For analysis of the comparison between these two passages see Henderson (1979: 27–8). Hardie, Ch. 9 in this volume, is also concerned with the relationship between the *Remedia* and previous Ovidian (and other poetry), and although the emphases of the two chapters are different they may be read as complementary.

poet with respect to his previous work and with respect to literary tradition. Such positioning happened also in the *Ars Amatoria*, where the poet 'rejects' the inspiration of Apollo and the Muses (1. 25 ff.) and describes the hard struggle fought with Love (1. 9–10, 21–4) for control,[2] and it will happen again in the *Metamorphoses* (1. 2), where the poet finally realizes the epic project which he had been forced to abandon in the *Amores*.

An interaction with the *Amores* takes place in the *Remedia* opening also, and comparison between the initial scenes of the two poems highlights the different powers of negotiation with which the poet now credits himself. In the first passage, Love first thwarts an epic (*arma... uiolentaque bella parabam dicere*, 'I was preparing to speak of arms... and violent wars', *Am.* 1. 1. 1–2); in the second, a poetic war against himself (*bella mihi... bella parantur*, 'wars... wars are being prepared against me', *Rem.* 2).[3] At the moment of his first entry into the literary world Ovid claimed a theoretical freedom of artistic choice—without success. But in the proem of the *Remedia* he demonstrates straight away the skills he has obtained either from practical experience or, more likely, from his poetic career. He no longer pretends to be the *Pieridum uates* but instead he calls himself the *uates* of Cupid (*tuum uatem*, 3), whose lifestyle, like a good elegiac poet, is consistent with his literary leanings: he has 'always been a lover' (7)[4] and has written love poetry, even taught it (*docui*, 9). Posing now as a 'political adviser' to Love himself (whom he 'teaches' like a pupil, putting to proof, as it were, his skills of persuasion), he demonstrates that it is much better for this god to exercise his power mildly (*mollia regna*, 24), to be peaceful (*inuidiam caedis pacis amator habes*, 'a lover of peace, you are accused of slaughter', 20), and leave his warrior-like stepfather, Mars, to take pleasure in bloodshed (28). Love should content himself with the tears of disappointed lovers (37) and stay away from the hateful sphere of death.

The reader of the *Remedia* quickly realizes that the initial dialogue with Love is a false proem, employed by the poet to calm the wrath of the god rather than to obtain that inspiration or help which the

---

[2] Cf. also n. 35.
[3] Wills (1996: 64) sees a tone of 'martial alert' in the words of Cupid.
[4] On this common elegiac marker, cf. Pinotti (1988: ad loc.).

didactic poet usually invokes in such circumstances. A little further on, in a 'second proem', the poet will invoke another god, Apollo, as tutelary deity of both poetry and medicine:

> te precor incipiens; adsit tua laurea nobis,
>   carminis et medicae Phoebe repertor opis;
> tu pariter uati, pariter succurre medenti:
>   utraque tutelae subdita cura tuae est.   (*Rem.* 75–8)

(To you I pray as I begin: may your laurel be present to me, Phoebus, founder of song and healing arts. Aid the bard and the healer equally: each care is subject to your protection.)

The *dux operis* and *doctor* which will be recalled a number of times throughout the poem (704; 767 and especially 489–90 *siquid Apollo* | *utile mortales perdocet ore meo*, 'if Apollo teaches anything useful to mortals through my mouth').[5] The first proem, including the dialogue of the poet with Love, does indeed serve to define the relationship of the author with his previous erotic poetry, with the *Ars* in particular, but also with the work that he is now beginning. Above all, however, it operates to frame an important theme in Ovidian poetics: the struggle for power between the poet and Love. This *ius*, which was contested by the young poet in the proem of the *Amores* (1. 1. 5), is now in a sense recognized by the older and more skilful poet as Love's right—although he does make a timid request for autonomy on the grounds of being a faithful subject (that is, a lover). However, admitting that he is in love is equivalent to saying that he is under the control of Love. Even if the poet starts to write his new work when the god has flown away (39), an act which, as we shall see, signifies an alleviation of Love's control, in fact the poet-lover, who 'always loves', can do nothing but write more elegiac poetry: in other words, he remains under the power of Love.

In any case, it is clear that the poet comes out of each skirmish with Love significantly worse off, as in the *Amores*, notwithstanding the superior powers of negotiation he now attributes to himself. From the initial threats of the god (2), the poet immediately asks for indulgence and he seeks to assure Love that he does not intend to challenge

---

[5] Even if perhaps the real protective deity of the poem is another one, *Amor Lethaeus*, as Hardie argues in Ch. 9 of this volume.

him or betray him, but rather he renews his declaration of total devotion. If every didactic relationship is based on a balance of power between the teacher and the disciple, here another relationship intervenes in which the divinity exercises power over the teacher keeping him under control. The author of the *Remedia* therefore writes 'under guard': his conduct as *magister* is strictly limited by the 'qualified freedom' that Love, as a sceptical tyrant, concedes to him. Such subordinate and submissive behaviour certainly does not create the best introduction for a 'sick' reader who is relying on the *remedia* to free him from the slavery of Love. To the intended audience of his new work, the *iuuenes* deceived by love and therefore potentially at risk of dying, the poet promises salvation as compensation for the 'injury' which he himself has caused them (in the *Ars*):

> ad mea, decepti iuuenes, praecepta uenite,
>   quos suus ex omni parte fefellit amor.
> discite sanari per quem didicistis amare;
>   una manus uobis uulnus opemque feret.   (*Rem.* 41–4)

(Come to my teaching, deceived youths, whose love has cheated you on every side. Learn healing from him through whom you learned to love; let the same hand bring you the wound and the cure.)

The poet who has himself been the instrument of divine deception (*decepti, fefellit*) now presents himself as saviour: the wordplay *decepti-praecepta* interweaves the past blame and the present promise of cure[6] (but at the same time plants not unreasonable doubts in his readers' minds). He will teach the cure (*discite sanari*) in the same way as he taught love-sickness (*didicistis amare*). His teaching now is contrary to that which he gave in the *Ars* (contradicting therefore, in part, the promise made to Love). The poet-*magister* stresses the destructive power of his work and the actions of *dediscere* to the intended reader of the *Remedia*. Instead of learning new *praecepta*, the recipient must above all 'unlearn' that which he learnt in the previous poem, according to the principle that learning what is right consists of unlearning what is wrong,[7] and freeing oneself from a

---

[6] Cf. Henderson (1979: ad loc.); cf. also Kennedy (2000: 174).
[7] Sen. *Epist.* 50. 8 *uirtutes discere uitia dediscere est*, 'learning virtue is unlearning vice'.

negative knowledge. 'Unlearning', *dediscere*, is the action that characterizes the reader of the *Remedia*,[8] who must free himself from and empty himself of love (752). Instead of being a learner, the reader of the *Remedia* is an 'un-learner', because the poem presumes the reader has already read the *Ars* and learnt its teaching.[9]

The fact that the work presupposes a recipient who has already been instructed is a paradox that makes the *Remedia* unique within the didactic tradition, in which it is normally expected that the reader is ignorant and in need of the knowledge that the poet-*magister* undertakes to disseminate.[10] Ovid's decision to produce a work of *remedia*, of antidotes to the 'poisons' that his erotic poems (in particular, the *Ars*) have previously spread, is usually explained as following the precedent of Nicander (second century BC), a Greek author of two didactic poems, the *Theriaka* (*Remedies for Venomous Animals*) and the *Alexipharmaka* (*Antidotes*), in which he 'illustrates first the poisoning caused by animal bites, plants and minerals, and then their respective antidotes'.[11] There is a significant difference, however, between the 'curative poems' of Nicander and Ovid's poem; in the case of Ovid, the author himself is responsible for the poisons. Through his teaching he provoked the very illness of his readers whom he now addresses as therapist and saviour.

Rather than Nicander, a genre to which Ovid might have had recourse as a model is that of magical texts, where there is a similar strategy of intervention *à rebours*, in other words, of undoing what one has built.[12] Within the world of magic one can reverse the effects of a spell and return things to their original state. An example that comes to mind is the metamorphosis of Ulysses' companions brought about by Circe (in Ov. *Met.* 14. 277 ff., based on the

[8] *Rem.* 211 *donec dediscis amare*; 297 *tu mihi, qui, quod amas, aegre dediscis amare*; 503 *intrat amor mentes usu, dediscitur usu.*

[9] Hardie, Ch. 9 in this volume, makes a similar point.

[10] On the 'teacher–student constellation' as a typical requirement of the didactic genre cf. Volk (2002: 37–9).

[11] So, Pinotti (1988: 15); but cf. also Hollis (1973: 110); Henderson (1979: p. xiv).

[12] Especially if the conjecture of Sharrock (1994a: 65) on the existence of magic didactic poems is right.

Homeric model of *Od.* 10. 234 ff.) which is followed by their restoration to their original form by means of a formula reversing that which caused their transformation:[13]

> spargimur ignotae sucis melioribus herbae
> percutimurque caput conuersae uerbere uirgae,
> uerbaque dicuntur dictis contraria uerbis.   (*Met.* 14. 299–301)

(We are sprinkled with the better juices of an unknown herb, and we are struck on the head by a blow from a rod reversed, and words are spoken in opposition to the words spoken previously.)

Another example is the metamorphosis of Apuleius' Lucius into an ass, the involuntary result of a magical mistake reversed by a rectifying intervention (the famous bush of roses) which returns the ass to his human form. Photis, the maid who introduces Lucius to the mysteries of magic, reassures him that the process of turning people into animals, which the witch Pamphile taught her, allows the subject to be returned to the human form:

> nam mihi domina singula monstrauit, quae possunt rursus in facies
> hominum tales figuras reformare. Nec istud factum putes ulla
> beniuolentia, sed ut ei redeunti medela salubri possem subsistere.
>
>   (Apul. *Met.* 3. 23. 6–7)

(For my mistress has shown me in detail how such shapes can return to human form. You should not think that she did so out of kindness, but so that I could aid her with the healthful cure when she returned.)

Medela, a synonym of *remedium*,[14] is a medical term, which defines the corrective intervention that cures the anomaly caused by magic. This is the same term that Photis will use, after the mistake, in order to convince Lucius that *reformatio*, the return to human form, is easy

---

[13] But the principle of 'reversal', echoed in the form of the lines (which opposes *dicuntur* with *dictis* and places *uerba* and *uerbis* at opposite ends of the line), is already implied in *melioribus* (which recalls the nefarious *suci* of 275) and is symbolically applied to *uirga* (cf. *conuersae* with respect to 278 *tetigit... uirga*). In Homer (*Od.* 19. 392) the re-metamorphosis is possible thanks to an ointment with 'another medicine', an antidote which nullifies the effects of the 'deadly medicine' (236) which caused the metamorphosis. For other examples of the process of 'anti-magic' or the 'magic of remedy' (*soluere*) cf. e.g. Horace, *Epod.* 7. 17; 5. 71; *Odes* 1. 27. 21 ff.

[14] Cf. *TLL* 8. 517. 61, 518. 19, 45, etc.

(*facilior reformationis huius medela suppeditat*, 3. 25. 3).[15] The correction is exactly that practice described as *recantare*, a rare verb which recurs with this meaning only in Horace's 'palinode' in *Odes* 1. 16 (*dum mihi | fias recantatis amica | opprobriis*, 'until you become friendly to me through insults recanted', 26–8, where the rejection of the past attacks in iambics is given in the phrase *mitibus mutare... tristia*, 'to swap sad things for mild', 25–6), and in the passage of the *Remedia* which recalls the Horatian phrase. The inefficacy of magic is compared with the more concrete utility of the *magister*'s precepts, for he affirms that *nulla recantatas deponent pectora curas* ('no hearts will put aside their cares through recantation', 259): the pain of love, once exorcized, will leave the soul of the patient free, not thanks to magic but rather through the teaching of the poet-*doctor*.[16] *Recantare* is a calque of the Greek παλινῳδεῖν, a typical magical term,[17] in the sense of 'eliminate with a spell, exorcize'. It has as 'its point of departure [...] *cantare* (= 'cast a spell, bewitch'[...]), with a prefix which functions in a similar way to that in the word *retexo* (cf. ad 12: 'to undo the web')' (Pinotti (1988: ad loc.)). The two actions, practical magic and its reversal, have a close relationship, however, just as Ovid links together the two phases of his teaching and his two works, the *Ars* and the *Remedia*, while nonetheless insisting on their opposing purposes. After having reassured Love, in the proem, of his desire not to disown the *Ars*, in discussion with his readers Ovid actually endorses the idea of undoing the work that provoked their suffering. The fact that numerous precepts in this manual of cures form an exact reversal of the precepts set out in the *Ars*[18] once seemed to lend weight to the idea that the *Remedia* was a true palinode of the

---

[15] It is noteworthy that in one of the two other occurrences of this term in the novel (9. 18. 2), the meaning is that of *remedium amoris*. It is used of an antidote for the passion of Philesitherus for the *matrona* with whom he is in love, to the extent of threatening suicide. He seeks to satisfy this passion through the help of her slave (*ei amorem suum aperit et supplex eum medelam cruciatui deprecatur*).

[16] The rejection of magic is also an important theme in the *Ars*, and one of the reasons for this is the fact that the real magic, which really does work, is the poetry itself: cf. Sharrock (1994a: 63–4).

[17] Cf. Geisler (1969: ad loc.).

[18] For an accurate description of this comparison, see ibid. 83 ff.; cf. also Henderson (1979: p. xvi).

previous work;[19] but this conclusion is now rightly rejected by scholars.[20]

2. AN ADDRESSEE WHO IS *DOCTUS* ALREADY

The ambiguity of the nature of the *Remedia* (to be understood as a 'reversal' or conversely as a 'sequel and development' of the *Ars*) is encouraged by Ovid himself. It is an ambiguity resulting from that which is inherent in the Ovidian concept of love (and which the *Remedia* will explain):[21] the ambiguity between love seen as the technique of courting, in other words, as a particular form of social behaviour (the rationality and efficacy of which the poet-*doctor* demonstrates and praises)[22] and love as an emotionally destructive experience (the *miser amor*, 21), whose irrational and asocial characteristics are condemned (*Rem.* 17–22, 37–8).[23] It is against this second type of love (which cannot be taught) that the poet wages his battle, but by playing on the ambivalence of the terms he in fact insists on the 'recovery' that the poem will procure with respect to the illness caused by the *Ars* (*Rem.* 43–4), with the effect of closely linking the two poems, rendering them interdependent.

Even a superficial analysis of the poem shows continuity with the *Ars* rather than a simple reversal, a continuity that is not camouflaged and is, at times, boldly exhibited.[24] Far from apologizing for the damage caused, the *magister* of the *Remedia* seems to expect credit from his pupils for the harmful but efficient teaching which he imparted to them previously. The 'bad teacher' does not

---

[19] On this interpretation, see the bibliography in Geisler (1969: 39 n. 1).
[20] Cf. certain considerations in Lucke (1982: 36 n. 10).
[21] On this point, see the observations of Volk (2002: 168–71).
[22] On the particularly Roman nature of this cultural practice, see Volk, Ch. 12 in this volume.
[23] The fact that sociability and appropriateness, in the sense of *decorum*, are criteria which form the basis of the *Remedia* also (demonstrating again a strong affinity and continuity with the *Ars*) is shown above all in vv. 655–6 (*Sed modo dilectam scelus est odisse puellam:* | *exitus ingeniis convenit iste feris*), 669–70, 439–40, where it is stressed that the 'cure' should not be at the expense of proper behaviour.
[24] On points of continuity between the two works cf. e.g Küppers (1981: 2530 ff.); Wildberger (1998: 344–7).

seek to justify the harm done (*herbas... nocentes*, 45; *urtica*, 46), but rather presents it as the best guarantee of his didactic skills. The poet-*doctor* presents himself, as author, as his own antidote: he had to be read then and must be read now:

> Naso legendus erat tum cum didicistis amare;
> idem nunc uobis Naso legendus erit.   (*Rem*. 71–2)

(Naso was to be read when you were learning how to love; and the same Naso is to be read in the present situation.)

Ovid puts himself in the centre of a universe of readers (the repetition *legendus erat... legendus erit* marks the continuity between past and future),[25] among whom there is also Love (*legerat*, the first word of the poem). An author who has an answer for everyone, for the various requirements of his public: for those who want *parare amorem* (9) as well as those who want to free themselves from love (*o qui sollicitos modo das, modo demis amores*, 'o you [sc. Ovid] who both give and take away troublesome love', 557), just as he had an answer for women longing for a course of poetry readings (*Ars* 3. 329 ff.) or for advice on their make-up (*Ars* 3. 205–8).[26]

In crediting himself as teacher of *remedia*, the author finds a way of promoting himself again as the poet of the *Ars*: he is not only a bad teacher, but also an unrepentant recidivist. First, he has no scruples in exhibiting here and there the libertine spirit of the *Ars* (as, for example, when he observes that he would not have acted any differently from Agamemnon in his treatment of Briseis: 779–81).[27] He even teaches that the method of freeing oneself from one love is to find another (462): in other words, he detains the patient within precisely the space that the patient seeking a cure for love should avoid. When he comes to suggesting the way to find a woman in order to put this precept into practice, he does not waste a moment in advising his reader to consult the *Ars*:

---

[25] On this 'serpentine' distich cf. also Hardie, Ch. 9 in this volume.

[26] On the relationship between Ovid and his readers see Citroni (1995: 431–74) who speaks of the presence of a 'lettore affezionato'.

[27] The impertinence of the expression (*fecit Atrides, | quod si non faceret, turpiter esset iners. | certe ego fecissem*, 779–81) recalls that of Paris who made malicious insinuations about the behaviour of Theseus when he abducted Helen, and comments on what he would have done in the hero's place (*Her*. 16. 160 *nec Venus ex toto nostra fuisset iners*).

> quaeris ubi inuenias? Artes tu perlege nostras:
> plena puellarum iam tibi nauis erit. (*Rem.* 487–8)

(You ask where to find one? Read my *Ars Amatoria*: your ship will be full of girls.)

When illustrating the precept that pupils should show themselves indifferent to rejection, the teacher explains that when faced with such behaviour women will lose their arrogance and become compliant (511), advice that is evidently adapted not to those who wish to free themselves from passion but to those who want to yield to it. The following verse—*hoc etiam nostra munus ab arte feres* ('this gift also you will take from my art')—seems almost to suggest that the author is returning to the logic of the *Ars*.[28] This is confirmed by the successive lines, which stress the 'conquest' and the advantages of a *remedium* which in case of necessity can offer—'as a *bonus*' (Henderson 1979: ad loc.)—a comfortable way out from a painful cure, transforming itself into its opposite, in other words into a gratifying erotic methodology:

> nec sibi tam placeat nec te contemnere possit;
>   sume animos, animis cedat ut illa tuis.
> ianua forte patet: quamuis reuocabere, transi;
>   est data nox: dubita nocte uenire data.
> posse pati facile est, ubi, si patientia desit,
>   protinus ex facili gaudia ferre licet.
> et quisquam praecepta potest mea dura uocare?
>   en, etiam partes conciliantis ago. (*Rem.* 517–24)

(She won't be so pleased with herself nor will she be able to scorn you. Get your spirit up, to make her yield to your spirit. The door happens to be open: pass by, although you are invited in; a night is given: hesitate to come on the appointed night. It's easy to put up with suffering when, if your patience fails, straight away you can get easy pleasure. Can anyone call my precepts hard? Look, I'm even playing the role of peacemaker for you.)

---

[28] Even if it is excessive to see, as Henderson (1979: ad loc.) does, an explicit reference to the *Ars* ('this is a profitable lesson you will learn from my *Ars Amatoria* too').

A real 'peacemaking'[29] and permissive doctor, so indulgent towards his patients that he becomes an accomplice to the very illness from which he should free them. The reader of the *Remedia* is asked therefore to continue to practise the very 'poisons' to which the text should form the antidote.[30] An attitude lacking in 'coherence' and similar to that exhibited in the poetry of exile, which, as Alessandro Barchiesi points out, '[is]a strange sort of elegiac palinode: the reader always has to hesitate between effacing and re-evoking the elegy of the past'.[31] The author's apparently sound propositions are thus completely denied in practice. There is much more truth in the initial reassurance to Love than one imagines in the clearly purposive and self-justifying intention of the poet:

> nec te, blande puer, nec nostras prodimus artes,
>   nec noua praeteritum Musa retexit opus   (*Rem.* 11–12)

(I am not betraying you, alluring boy, nor my arts, nor does my new Muse untie the previous work.)

The new work is not in any way a denial of the *Ars* (and of the *artes* that it teaches): the image of unweaving a work, the previous 'text', bears a clear reference to the actions of Penelope[32] and might suggest a deception (Ov. *Am.* 3. 9. 30 *tardaque nocturno tela retexta dolo,* 'late weaving undone by a nightly trick'), a suspicion the poet clearly wishes to dispel in front of Love: he (his *noua Musa*) will not cause damage to his god, unlike Penelope with her suitors.

The *Remedia* is not therefore a deconstruction of the *Ars*: and moreover, whilst the text stresses repeatedly the idea of unlearning (*dediscere*) on the part of the reader, it does not imply a parallel

---

[29] The meaning of the verb in the sense, familiar to comedy, of 'matchmaking' (cf. Pinotti 1988: ad loc.) suggests the return of the author to the old role of *magister amoris* (cf. *Ars* 2. 554 and Janka (1997: ad loc.)).

[30] Lucke (1982: ad loc.) observes that the advice of the author 'steht...im Widerspruch zu der Passage 757 ff., wo er vor der Lektüre der *teneri poetae* (757), zu denen er sich auch selbst zählt (758. 766), warnt'.

[31] Barchiesi (2001: 179 n. 18 = 1993: 163 n. 18); but cf. also (2001: 102 = 1993: 181) 'When we recall that *Tristia* 2 is, officially, a palinode of erotic elegy, Ovid's persistence is impressive.... The intertextuality connecting *Tristia* 2 to erotic poets like Catullus, the bucolic Virgil, and Tibullus maps out a genealogy of poets who have eluded political powers and the control of imperial police.'

[32] Cf. Geisler (1969: ad loc.). The significance of 'untying' is discussed also by Hardie in this volume.

action of unteaching (*dedocere*) on the part of the *magister*. It is only the reader-pupil therefore who undergoes a negative process (and is *de-discens*), whilst the poet continues to be a *doctor*, even if of a different knowledge: he teaches a different *ars* (16, 233), bestowing *praecepta* (41) that do not involve unlearning those in his previous work but add to or even presuppose them. The poet-*doctor* of the *Remedia* assumes that his readers have already read the *Ars*: he never alludes to the possibility that readers of the new text may not have read the old one.[33] His therapy is corrective, is a 'rehabilitative therapy', addressed to patients who need to free themselves from the unwanted effects of the doctrine of the *magister amoris*;[34] but, at the same time, it is a supplementary therapy which assumes the integration of the previous teaching.

The *Remedia* shows, and also vindicates, a close continuity with the very work it should seemingly be remedying (as well as with all Ovid's previous erotic poetry).[35] This is also confirmed by the author's emphatic defence of himself, in the middle of the poem (361 ff.), with respect to the criticisms made by the 'censors' of his previous elegiac works (above all, presumably the *Ars*). This defence would seem superfluous if the *Remedia* really were a true retraction of the *Ars*, an open disowning of the incriminating work. (Furthermore, in the defence of himself in *Tristia* 2, Ovid is careful not to recall the *Remedia* as proof of his 'repentance': he remains *obsceni doctor adulterii*, 'teacher of obscene love', 2. 212.) The poet rightly therefore reassures Love that his new work does not betray the god; but not to betray Love means he will continue to 'betray' Augustus: a line such as *uiuam modo, plura dolebis* ('if I live, you'll suffer further', 391) sounds like a bold challenge to the *Livor* that personifies the literary defamers of the poet as well as the 'political' censors mentioned above (361 ff.).[36]

---

[33] This is clearly also part of a self-promoting strategy, in that the 'successful' author claims the majority of the *iuuenes* and *puellae* of Rome as faithful readers of his erotic poetry.

[34] Cf. Davisson (1996: 259).

[35] The *Ars* itself constitutes in turn a sort of 'vendetta' of the elegiac lover-poet against the Cupid of the *Amores*: cf. 1. 23–4 and Bretzigheimer (1981: 18–19).

[36] On these important lines, and on their political implications, after Barchiesi (2001: 96–8 = 1993: 173–5) also see, in Chs. 11 and 3 of this volume, Casali and Holzberg; cf. also Woytek (2000).

Scholars maintain that these lines are the response of the poet to the attacks of critics and defamers who accuse him of writing immoral poetry (*Musa proterua*, 362),[37] but it is reasonable to suspect that his protest against censure may be a pretence, or at least that Ovid has emphasized the hostile reaction to his erotic *libelli*, creating, in the same way as Callimachus, the figure of *Livor*, a malevolent and tenacious opponent against whom he is able legitimately to defend himself and claim his own success as the 'Virgil of elegy' (393–6). This self-defence itself seems to have been used, in the literary tradition,[38] as a topical pretext (sometimes totally invented and without real foundation) in order to introduce a self-eulogy which, if introduced without the necessary justification, would have risked being irritating and damaging to the author.[39] As Quintilian teaches (addressing primarily orators but in fact enunciating a universal truth), self-eulogy is not only a violation of the principle of *decorum* but also detrimental to the speaker, because it causes anxiety in the listener making them feel inferior to the speaker (Quint. 11. 1. 15–16). Just as Demosthenes, in the speech *On the Crown*, only speaks of himself because he is forced to do so in 'legitimate self-defence', thereby directing the hostility towards his adversary (Quint. 11. 1. 22) in accordance with a rhetorical strategy well-known to Cicero (*Dom.* 92–3, 96), likewise Ovid might have fruitfully used this rhetorical device.

This expedient seems to work well with another astute form of self-promotion, that of selecting your readers and excluding the more respectable layers of society. The disclaimers that exclude reputable women (the *uittae* of *Ars* 1. 31 and *Rem.* 386)[40] from the group of readers of erotic elegy are, on the one hand, an appropriate, if not a necessary, form of protection against the accusation of

---

[37] Cf. e.g. Geisler (1969: 343 n. 1).

[38] Cf. Most (1989: 124–5).

[39] On this theme, and in general on rhetorical strategy of 'speaking well of oneself' in ancient culture, see R. K. Gibson (2003*b*: esp. 238–41).

[40] According to Woytek (2000: 185 and n. 20), the restrictions concern the female audience since they have 'active roles' in the text and are not excluded from his *audience*, but he does not seem to take into account *Ars* 3. 57–8 *petite hinc praecepta, puellae,* | *quas pudor et leges et sua iura sinunt*, clearly aimed at the male audience: cf. Gibson (2003*a*: ad loc.).

producing 'degenerate art'[41] and also the best editorial *manchette* of 'publicity through your enemy' (that is, the censors) directed at those sectors of society that were supposed to be excluded. Ovid was well aware that prohibition sharpens desire (*quod licet, ingratum est; quod non licet, acrius urit*, 'what is allowed is unwelcome; what is forbidden burns more fiercely', *Am.* 2. 19. 3);[42] and he also knew that proclaiming oneself a victim of censorship is the most effective tool of self-promotion that an artist can possess (anticipating the advertising techniques of modern mass media). By defending his *Musa proterua* from censorship (it is not by chance that these lines are included within a section of the *Remedia* that in terms of audacious content challenges the *Ars* itself—for example, how one can feel contempt for a woman during sexual intercourse),[43] Ovid achieves the promotion of all of his elegiac works, from the *Amores* to the *Remedia* itself, thereby ensuring that even the *Remedia* is included within the genre of erotic elegy.

The *Remedia*, therefore, is anything but a palinode of the *Ars*. Furthermore, in accordance with popular wisdom as recalled by a character of Plautus, to unlearn something does not mean one erases what has been previously learnt, acquiring a clean slate (*Amph.* 687–8 *haud aequom facit | qui quod didicit id dediscit*, 'he does wrong to unlearn what he has learned'): it is impossible completely to cancel what one has learnt. Even according to pedagogues, the act of *dedocere* is difficult once the wrong learning and ensuing *uitia* have become embedded. Quintilian stresses (2. 3. 2) the importance of good teaching from the very beginning and the difficulty of 'cleansing' the shortcomings learnt from bad teaching. Furthermore, the *Remedia* itself is the most persuasive proof of how difficult it is to forget what one has learnt, to free oneself from one's past and from one's memories.[44]

---

[41] For a more thorough analysis of these disclaimers see Sharrock (1994*b*: 110 ff.).
[42] On this theme see McKeown (1998: ad loc. and 406–7).
[43] On the 'construct[ion of] a lascivious *reader*' in these lines cf. Barchiesi (2001: 97–8 = 1993: 174–5).
[44] The function of memory, erotic and poetic, in the *Remedia* is expertly treated by Hardie, Ch. 9 in this volume.

3. THE SPACE OF LOVE

As stated above, the erotic teaching of Ovid is built on the ambiguity of the idea of *amor*: it sways between an 'active' meaning of love in the sense of the art of courting and seducing (the prevalent meaning within the *Ars*), and a 'passive' meaning (more familiar to us) referring to the passion and emotion experienced by the persons involved (and from which the *Remedia* teaches one how to escape). In other words, the *Ars* teaches one how to 'seduce', to conquer a lover, and to manipulate the emotions of the victim (who must fall in love) rather than those of the protagonist (the pupil of the poet-*magister*). However, this does not preclude the seducer from losing control of this operation and becoming the victim of his own game, by ending up in love himself (a risk the teacher points out to his pupils: 1. 615–16); and therefore needing the help of the *Remedia*.[45] So, even in the *Ars*, the author makes space for the importance of self-control and control of one's emotions (the myth of Procris is a model example[46]) and in this sense the *Ars* becomes contiguous with the *Remedia*.

In general, one might say that the above-mentioned difference in the concept of *amor* marks out a distance between the two works, and that 'Love 1' serves to activate and control 'Love 2'. As Wilfried Stroh rightly points out,[47] if the *Ars* teaches the reader not to fall in love, but to inflame love in a partner of the opposite sex, to be a true reversal the *Remedia* would have to teach its readers how not to incite love in another person (or, once love has been provoked, how to dispel it);[48] whereas both texts teach the lover how to free himself from love and from the passion that possesses him. Whilst the *Ars* elaborates the technique of manipulating someone else's emotions,

---

[45] The allusion to the *Ars* in *Rem.* 501–2 is telling: *deceptum risi, qui se simulabat amare,* | *in laqueos auceps decideratque suos.*

[46] Cf. Gibson (2003*a*: 360–1).

[47] See Stroh (1979*a*: 126).

[48] One could imagine what the *Remedia* would be like if it had to 'undo' the *Ars* from vv. 679–82: the renunciation of *placere* suggests the renunciation by men of the will to manipulate the feelings of women, who must not be his only target but rather *e multis una*.

the *Remedia* teaches its readers how to manipulate and control one's own emotions, in other words, both works are focused on teaching a discipline of the self.[49]

While in the *Amores*, in accordance with the motto of the Virgilian Gallus (*Ecl.* 10. 69 *et nos cedamus Amori*, 'let us also yield to Love'),[50] the elegiac poet-lover expresses his resigned subjection to passion (*Am.* 1. 2. 9–10, *cedimus, an subitum luctando accendimus ignem?* | *cedamus*, 'do I yield, or do I fan the sudden fire by struggling against it?—Let's yield'), at the beginning of the *Ars* the poet-*magister* challenges[51] Love with this very phrase (1. 21 *et mihi cedet Amor*, 'and Love will yield to me'),[52] determined to subjugate Love to his pedagogical authority,[53] and thereby himself takes control of the emotions that the god incites. As a metonymy, Love becomes therefore the symbol of all desires, the libidinal potential triggered by passion. In the *Remedia*, that key-phrase is used again:

> ... qui finem quaeris amoris,
>   (cedit Amor rebus) res age, tutus eris   (*Rem.* 143–4)

(... you who seek an end to love (Love yields to business)—do business and you will be safe.)

The different form of the phrase marks out the new and final phase of Ovid's erotic teaching, giving to *res*, the external world, control of the lover's emotions and the curbing of desire. This is almost a declaration of powerlessness from the didactic poet who, instead of giving his own answers (in fact, the first-person form is absent), has to find answers outside himself.

In order to describe the techniques of curbing desire Ovid employs a semiotic of space: the relationship with passion (with *Amor*) is

---

[49] On this point an affinity with philosophical texts on the therapy of the soul has often been suggested: cf. Geisler (1969: 77 ff.); Stroh (1979*a*: 126 n. 47).
[50] According to Volk (2002: 168) 'something like the "motto" of love elegy'.
[51] Cf. ibid. 167–8, and, Ch. 9 in this volume, Hardie.
[52] It is purely by convention (which takes account of our concept of personification of an abstract entity into a mythological figure) that I print this term with the capital letter instead of the lower case letter (cf. on this issue Heldmann 1981*a*); it goes without saying that the distinction, in print and conceptually, is irrelevant to Ovid and his ancient readers.
[53] On the authoritative character of this pedagogical practice, cf. Kennedy (2000); on the vendetta against the *puer* Love of the former lover *praeceptor*, ibid. 173 n. 26.

represented through the degree of proximity between the god and the patient-lover, in terms of contact, of closeness and remoteness, of small and large physical distance. The image of 'movement' in the development of the poem—conveyed through a metaphor of a journey by ship, or by cart, which forms the structure of the poem (vv. 70, 397–8, 577–8, 811–12)[54]—is interwoven with the various movements of Love,[55] which visualize the 'state' of passion, like a diagram of an illness (its 'course' indicates therefore the critical state of the passion: *dum furor in cursu est, currenti cede furori*, 'while the passion is in full flow, yield to the flowing passion', 119). The presence or absence of the god signifies enslavement to passion and inner freedom respectively, such that his entrance and exit (to be precise, his *cedere*, 'yielding') dramatizes the development or decline of the illness.

Leisure, time left empty by *res*, is the most dangerous condition for the arrival and embedding of this god, who conquers and occupies unguarded territory,[56] and on this land a battle develops, the outcome of which is portrayed through the corresponding images of entering and departing. The occupation of space is equated with control and with the exercise of power (*sic uenit ille puer, sic puer ille manet*, 'thus that boy comes, thus that boy stays', 168), whilst the god's departure connotes his concession of freedom (as in the proem when, after the poet's reassuring speech about his intentions, the god *mouit... alas* (39), he goes away and allows the poet to carry out his poetic project).

The renowned mobility of this god, elusive and swift just like desire (*Ars* 2. 19–20), suits the visualization of love as a moving energy, a flux of desire that seizes psychic space (*intrat amor mentes usu*, 'love enters minds through use', 503) and which the teacher-doctor teaches one to ward off and channel into other purposes.[57] Amongst the most effective remedies for avoiding

---

[54] On this see Küppers (1981: 2531 ff.). For the image of the arrival at the 'harbour of salvation' (812) cf. already 610.

[55] On the origins of this image cf. Lucke (1982: 320).

[56] *affluit incautis insidiosus*, 148. On the military character of the language cf. Pinotti (1988: ad loc.).

[57] By contrast, the purpose of the *Ars* was to 'keep hold of' Love: cf. Janka (1997) on 2. 17–18 and 98.

passion and the space in which Love (a notoriously urban god) exercises his influence, are a country life and agriculture:

> cum semel haec animum coepit mulcere uoluptas,
>   debilibus pinnis irritus exit Amor   (*Rem.* 197–8).

(When once this pleasure has begun to soothe your mind, Love, nullified, withdraws on weakened wings.)

The defeat of Love is portrayed in his exit from the stage, in the image which visually symbolizes the efficacy of the *remedium* just illustrated (that followed by the parallel image of Venus who 'withdraws' in front of Diana, in other words in front of hunting, 199–200). Even the section in which another common *remedium*, magic (which the teacher claims to be outdated and ineffectual, 251), is discussed contains two corresponding images which represent the uselessness of this technique. First a general rule is set out, that magic cannot 'repel' Love (*nulla recantatas deponent pectora curas, | nec fugiet uiuo sulphure uictus Amor*, 'no hearts will put aside cares through recantations, nor will Love flee, conquered by living sulphur', 259–60) and then the story of Circe, who is unable to prevent the departure of Ulysses, is used as an example confirming the inability of the witch to protect herself from erotic pain (*omnia fecisti, ne te ferus ureret ignis: | longus et inuito pectore sedit Amor*, 'you tried everything to stop the wild fire burning you: yet Love sits long in your unwilling heart', 267–8). The tenacity of Love, his obstinate 'dwelling' in the heart of his victim is the hurdle against which the doctor must fight, especially while aiming at expelling Love.[58]

In order to remove Love from his mind (752), the patient must avoid physical proximity with the woman who caused his suffering, fleeing from her and the town (213–24, 237–48, 291–2, 529–32). A series of images of contagion at 613–22 show the dangers of proximity, which should be replaced by the exercise of abstinence: keeping the loved person away from the physical and mental space of the patient-lover will cause her to 'float away from your desire' (646). A similar image concludes the recommendation of a gradual

---

[58] Cf. also *Rem.* 108. On the metaphor and its tradition in elegiac poetry cf. Geisler (1969: ad loc.). The objective of causing Love to flee can be obtained through bold strategies, such as focusing on the unpleasant aspects of sex (357–8).

separation as an effective method of getting rid of Love (*in tenues euanidus exeat auras | perque gradus molles emoriatur Amor*, 'let Love slip away into thin air, and die by soft stages', 653–4). A calm parting of the ways is better than a tempestuous split, which can often disguise a risk of the illness 'returning' (661–2).

The achievement of distance, then, is the guidance offered by the *Remedia*;[59] but to achieve this effect, that is, the distancing of Love, one can use the opposite tactic, that of reducing the distance between the lover and his object of desire, forcing the lover to saturation (so that *copia tollat amorem*, 'abundance takes love away', 541).[60] This is achieved particularly by direct contact with the reality of her more crude and unpleasant physical aspects (e.g. 431–2).

On the other hand, physical distance and loneliness do not necessarily cause indifference, which is why the *magister* disapproves of the erroneous belief that it is enough to 'flee' to *loca sola*:

> quisquis amas, loca sola nocent: loca sola caveto;
> quo *fugis*? in populo tutior esse potes.
> non tibi secretis (augent secreta furores)
> est opus; auxilio turba futura tibi est.
> tristis eris, si solus eris, dominaeque relictae
> ante oculos facies *stabit*, ut ipsa, tuos.   (579–84)

(Lover, whoever you are, lonely places are harmful: avoid lonely places. Where are you fleeing to? You can be safer among the people. You don't need privacy (private places increase desire); the crowd will be a help to you. You will be sad, if you are alone, and the face of your abandoned mistress will stand before your eyes as if it were herself.)

In *tristis eris, si solus eris*, the repetition of the verb suggests the idea of insistence and of obsessive repetition, of a closed circle in which the lover is imprisoned and at the centre of which the ghost of the loved one continues to dominate unchallenged.

Memory (*admonitus*, 662),[61] in other words contact with a written word, a place, or a trace of the lover's presence, inflames desire (729),

---

[59] Such distance is seen also as the final goal of the now-healed patient, as is confirmed by the image of the flight 'at full gallop' that heralds the end of the poem: *nunc fortiter ire, | nunc opus est celeri subdere calcar equo*, 787–8.
[60] A condition that recalls the paradox of Narcissus (*Met.* 3. 466 *inopem me copia fecit*).
[61] On this meaning cf. Lucke (1982: 232–3).

just as near-extinct embers when touched with sulphur (731) are revived into a blazing flame. It is necessary to escape one's memories and build 'another world', an alternative space away from the memory of the past:

> quid iuvat admonitu tepidam recalescere mentem?
> alter, si possis, orbis habendus erit.   (629–30)[62]

(What's the point in reheating a tepid mind by recollection? If you are able, you must inhabit another world.)

This includes literary memories, the great texts of love poetry, which like so many recurring echoes, symbolically fill these *loca sola*, in other words the psychological loneliness of the lover unable to distance himself from his past (and from its literature).[63]

4. THE *REMEDIA* AS *RENUNTIATIO AMORIS*

As we have already seen, the emphasis on *dediscere* as a key feature of this text makes this an unusual didactic poem, which, rather than presenting its own message, teaches the reader to undo what its author has already taught, that is, the message of a previous text which is, therefore, a prerequisite and a point of reference for the later text. The act of *dediscere* assumes a 'base-text': if intertextuality is a necessary part of every text, this is even more so in the case of the *Remedia*, which implies and practises a type of specific 'didactic intertextuality', a consequence of the complex nature of 'second degree' teaching (the *Remedia* is a *de-didactic* text).

The *Remedia* is not an autonomous text: it cannot work without the *Ars*, of which it is a natural and necessary supplement, a journey that concludes at the end of the poem (811–12) closing the cycle begun by the *Ars* (1. 3–4, 8). Far from denying the *Ars*, the *Remedia* recalls that text, and at the same time praises and consolidates

---

[62] On the interpretation of *alter orbis* cf. Lucke (1982: ad loc.) and Lazzarini (1986: ad loc.).

[63] This 'flight of literary echoes' is considered by Hardie, Ch. 9 in this volume.

its reputation.[64] The *Remedia* is an integral part of Ovid's erotic teaching: a further step in the understanding of self-control, exploring the consequences of and suggesting opportune corrections to, the methodology illustrated by the *Ars*, but the first and most obvious consequence is that in its turn it expresses and conveys erotic potential as intrinsic and inescapable. The *Remedia* obeys in exemplary fashion the principle of repetition:[65] it is 'the fourth book of the *Ars*'[66] and continues the 'seduction' of the reader.

In the final part of the poem, the poet-doctor warns his convalescent pupil against dwelling in the polluted arena of erotic poetry (*teneros ne tange poetas*, 'don't touch the tender poets', 757). Ovid well knows that 'amorous speech' (especially if made up of 'fragments' from the great erotic poets) is a symptom of latent illness and is itself a source of contagion: to continue to speak of love—even if only to repeat that it is over and that one is no longer in love—means continuing to dwell in the world of desire.[67] Systematically repeating the *Ars* (even while pretending to deny it) indicates that the reader has kept within the space of that poem, which spreads its dangerous contagion and nullifies the act of freedom which the poet claims to promote. The *renuntiatio amoris* is the key feature of erotic poetry which best defines the nature of the *Remedia*: a poem which speaks of love whilst pretending to reject it:

> qui nimium multis 'non amo' dicit, amat   (648)

(Whoever keeps telling everyone 'I'm not in love'—is.)

And so a line such as *et mea nescio quid carmina tale sonant* ('and my poetry has something of the same nature', 766) completing a list of erotic texts to be avoided[68] sounds to the reader of the *Remedia* like a confession (with an ironic wink) of the true nature not only of the previous Ovidian elegy, but also of the *Remedia* itself.

---

[64] See in this regard also Fulkerson (2004: 211), according to whom 'the two texts work in tandem'.

[65] On this feature of the *Ars* see Sharrock (1994a); and more generally on the theme of repetition and desire in Ovidian poetry see Hardie (2002b: esp. 65–70).

[66] Cf. Holzberg (1981: 195–6); cf. also Gibson (2003: 39 n. 106) (with bibliography) about the hypothesis of the concept of *Ars* 3 and *Remedia* as a pair of texts.

[67] Cf. Fulkerson (2004: esp. 221–3).

[68] cf. 757–8 *eloquar invitus* [...] *summoueo dotes impius ipse meas.*

As a true, elegiac *renuntiatio amoris*, the *Remedia* ends by reaffirming the implacable power of Love: with the excuse of unlearning love, what the *magister* ends up teaching his pupils is what every elegiac lover in fact already knows, that *amor non est medicabilis* ('love is not treatable', *Her.* 5. 150). Therein lies the failure of the *Remedia*—and its triumph.

9

Lethaeus Amor: The Art of Forgetting

Philip Hardie

In the prologue of the *Remedia Amoris* Ovid protests to Cupid that he is not making war on Amor (1–4), that he is not a traitor to love (11), and that he is not cancelling or unweaving (12 *retexit*) his earlier work. After a protracted distinction between the acceptable woes of the typical elegiac lover (who is to be encouraged in the arts of love) and the suicidal sorrows of the truly hopeless lover (who is to be cured of his disease), Amor gives his blessing to the new project; cf. *Rem.* 40 *et mihi 'propositum perfice' dixit 'opus'* (' "finish the planned job" he said to me'). Yet in the opening address to the didactic audience of (41) *decepti iuuenes* ('deceived youths') Ovid sets out as his aim the complete reversal (albeit for an audience explicitly limited to those unhappy in love) of the programme of the *Ars Amatoria*; cf. *Rem.* 43 *discite sanari per quem didicistis amare* ('learn from me to be healed, through whom you learned to love'). Modern critics tend to emphasize the continuity rather than discontinuity between *Remedia* and *Ars*, and attribute a (typically Ovidian) duplicity to a work which perpetuates the empire of love in the very act of claiming to undermine it. So for example Alison Sharrock, 'The rejection of love is part of the discourse of love—it *is* love', citing *Rem.* 648 *qui nimium multis 'non amo' dicit, amat* ('anyone who keeps on telling people "I am not in love", is in love').[1] Gianpiero Rosati likewise (Ch. 8 in this volume)

---

[1] Sharrock (1994a: 62–3); see also Sharrock (2002: 160–1). Brunelle (2000–1) argues that the form (elegiac, with inescapable erotic connotations) of the *Remedia* pulls against its avowed didactic function.

stresses the contagious effects of the *Remedia*'s intertextual repetitions of the *Ars*, and concludes, 'as a true, elegiac *renuntiatio amoris*, the *Remedia* ends by reaffirming the implacable power of Love'.

retexit (12) looks at things from the writer's point of view. We might want to say that, so far from 'unweaving' the text of the *Ars*, Ovid 'retraces' (*OLD* s.v. *retexo* 3) the paths of the *Ars*, or even that he 'weaves again' the *Ars*. In this chapter I want to look at things from the reader's point of view. This poem opens with an act of reading: *legerat huius Amor titulum nomenque libelli* ('Love had read the title and name of this little book'). The subject of 'had read' is a reader both unusually well versed in the matter of *amor*, Amor himself, but also a perhaps less than ideally expert reader. His reader-response is based on only the two words of the title of the poem. Amor seems quite unselfconscious of the fact that his first words in line 2 echo the first line of his eponymous *Amores*; he shows no sign of being an assiduous reader of his own poet Ovid. At the end of his dialogue with the author Amor 'moves his wings' (39), a sign of assent like Jupiter's nod,[2] but also a sign that the god is ready to fly away, leaving the field to those other, more expert, readers with whom the *Ars Amatoria* began at 1. 1–2: *si quis in hoc artem populo non nouit amandi, | hoc legat et lecto carmine doctus amet* ('If anyone of the people of Rome does not know the art of loving, let him read this poem and by reading let him be taught to love'). Amor's reading is over before the poem has properly begun (the pluperfect *legerat*).

By the time those other readers come to the *Remedia* they are thoroughly familiarized with the *ars/Ars amandi*. They are learned lovers, but they are also learned readers. Even were it possible for the *doctus amator* to 'unlearn' (*dediscere*) love, it is the characteristic of the *doctus lector* that s/he does not, cannot, forget what has been read before. To the extent that the *Remedia* does mount a sustained campaign against love, it does so through an intertextuality that depends for its effects on the memory of its learned readers. The impossibility of forgetting is highlighted in the paradoxical divinity at the centre of the poem, Lethaeus Amor (*Rem.* 549–78), a virtual

---

[2] So Lazzarini (1986: ad loc.). If Amor flies away, it is to leave clear the way for Apollo (invoked at the end of the 'second proem', *Rem.* 75–8), the god over whom he had triumphed in the reworking in *Met.* 1 of his triumph over the poet in *Am.* 1. 1. 1–2.

personification of the place held by memory and forgetting in the poem as a whole, and an embodiment also of the close connection between textual and non-textual kinds of memory. Lethaeus Amor is an oxymoron, since love is by definition all-absorbing of attention. As a poetic fiction the presiding god of forgetfulness manifests himself in a tissue of intertextual memories.

The *Remedia* is a paradoxical didactic in that it aims not to construct and inculcate a body of knowledge, but rather to deconstruct and evacuate; cf. *Rem.* 752 *dum bene de uacuo pectore cedat amor* ('until love has left you completely fancy free').[3] The didactic poet advises (*moneo*), offering a body of *monita*,[4] but in the area of admonition and teaching Amor may be a rival to the didactic poet. Thus in Bion fr. 10, Eros is brought by Aphrodite to the poet to be taught bucolic poetry, but ends up himself teaching the poet about love: 12–13 'and I forgot everything that I was teaching Love, but I had been taught everything about love that Love had to teach me'. In *Georgics* 3 love presents a serious threat to the poet and his pupil, not just because of the irrational violence it inflicts on the ordered farm, but because love too is a teacher. The defeated bull goes away to give himself a course of military training, spurred on by his sexual desire, before returning to confront his rival; cf. Verg. *G.* 3. 232–4 *temptat sese atque irasci in cornua discit... et sparsa ad pugnam proludit harena* ('he tests himself and learns to toss his horns in anger... and scatters the sand in training for battle').[5] Love's absorbing claim on his victims' mental attention induces forgetfulness of all else, both in the animal world—cf. Verg. *G.* 3. 245 *catulorum oblita leaena* ('the lioness forgetful of her cubs')—and in the poet, oblivious to the passage of time; cf. Verg. *G.* 3. 285 *singula dum capti circumuectamur amore* ('while I explore each detail, the prisoner of love'). The challenge for the poet of the *Remedia* is not so much to convey his

---

[3] Evacuation may create a dangerous void: vacuums ask to be filled, as Ovid knows: *Rem.* 150 *da uacuae menti, quo teneatur, opus*; 166 *uacuum litibus Argos erat* (a vacuum filled for Aegisthus by adulterous love). Cf. *Am.* 1. 1. 26 *in uacuo pectore regnat Amor* (if this means that Love took vacant possession as a squatter).

[4] For *moneo* and *monita* of Ovid's didactic role, cf. *Rem.* 124, 128, 135, 296, 439, 804; see Gibson (2003a) on *Ars* 3. 353–4, '*monere* and *admonere* are not employed by Lucretius or Virgil of their own instruction, but the usage is popular with Ovid.'

[5] See Hardie (2004a: 98–9).

own body of doctrine, as to make the pupil deaf to the admonitions of love, memories that threaten to undo all the teacher's hard work when the pupil is almost safe in port (609 ff.); cf. *Rem.* 629 <u>quid iuuat admonitu</u> *tepidam recalescere mentem?* ('what use is it if your cooling spirit is reheated by a reminder?'); 661–2 *ubi nulla simultas | incidit,* <u>admonitu</u> *liber aberrat Amor* ('when no dispute arises between [the couple], Love saunters off free of any reminder'); 729 <u>admonitu</u> *refricatur amor* ('love is rubbed sore again by a reminder'). At the beginning of the *Ars Amatoria* Ovid had pointedly reversed a long tradition of Ἔρως διδάσκαλος, 'Love the Teacher', by setting himself up as the teacher of the boy-god.[6] If this teacher–pupil relationship has been placed under severe strain by the end of the *Remedia*, one important reason is that to forget the admonitions of love would also be to learn to forget how to be a memorious intertextual reader.

THE SAME AND NOT THE SAME?

Ovid addresses his own faithful readers at 71–2:

> Naso legendus erat tum cum didicistis amare;
> idem nunc uobis Naso legendus erit.

(Ovid you had to read when you learned to love; the same Ovid you will have to read now.)

The typically Ovidian repetitions draw attention to the problem of whether the poem we are now reading stands in a relation of continuity or discontinuity to the *Ars Amatoria*. The idiomatic use of *idem* to refer to a person previously named (*OLD* s.v. 3) receives additional emphasis through the near identity of the first three and last three words of the 'serpentine couplet'. The *Remedia* will be business as usual, this is the same old Ovid. But Ovidian repetition, as also Ovid's use of words such as *idem*, can be tricky.[7] The 'same god', we read at *Metamorphoses* 12. 614 had both given Achilles the

---

[6] See Stroh (1979*a*: 131–2 with n. 60).
[7] Hardie (2002*b*: 8–9). *idem* can also be used to mark an inconsistency between two actions of the same person (*OLD* s.v. 10).

arms which confirmed his military potency, and reduced him to nothing: *armarat deus idem, idemque cremabat* ('the same god had armed him, the same god cremated him'). But the anthropomorphic god of fire, Vulcan, and the flames of the funeral pyre ('Vulcan' by metonymy) are not exactly the 'same'.[8] Yet, from another point of view, that one and the same god, even in the same shape, should both empower and annihilate need occasion no surprise: it is part of the power of a divinity to create opposed effects within his or her sphere of activity. In a line to be discussed more fully below the poet is addressed in language of a kind typically used of a god; cf. *Rem.* 557 '*o qui sollicitos modo das, modo demis, amores*' ('you who now give, and now take away, the troubles of love'). This is a reversibility of function formulated in the prologue through allusion to the powers of the spear of the godlike Achilles; cf. *Rem.* 47–8 *uulnus in Herculeo quae quondam fecerat hoste, | uulneris auxilium Pelias hasta tulit* ('the spear of Achilles that had once wounded his enemy, the son of Hercules, also brought the cure for the wound').

The power of a god both to give and to take away will suggest to Ovid's faithful readers one way in which a poem that set out in earnest to teach how to fall out of love might claim to remain under the patronage of Love. In Book 1 of the *Metamorphoses* we read that Cupid has two arrows 'of different workings: one chases off, the other produces love' (*Met.* 1. 469 *diuersorum operum: fugat hoc, facit illud amorem*). Those are the expressed aims of those two different works, *diuersa opera*, the *Ars* and the *Remedia*. Another divinity may hide behind *Naso legendus erat... Naso legendus erit*. In his discussion of Ovidian 'serpentine couplets', Jeff Wills notes a formal parallel to this couplet ('repeated hemiepes with tense-shift') in the last line of Propertius 1. 12 (20): *Cynthia prima fuit, Cynthia finis erit* ('Cynthia was the first, Cynthia will be the end'). She is the divinity who is the alpha and omega of Propertius' existence.[9] Ovid too is a beginning

---

[8] In amatory contexts arming and burning can function either as figures for the same or for opposites: warfare is an alternative to love (e.g. *Rem.* 153–66), but also a metaphor for love (e.g. arming for love at *Ars* 3. 1–2, echoed at *Rem.* 50); fire is the commonest of erotic images, but also a way of destroying love (Prop. 1. 1. 27; *Rem.* 719–22).

[9] See Wills (1996: 432 n. 81). For the topos of 'beginning and ceasing' in addresses to gods see Hunter (2003) on Theoc. *Id.* 17. 1.

and an end: the initiator into the art of love in the *Ars*, and the provider of a *finis amoris* in the *Remedia* (143 *qui finem quaeris amoris*). The previous line in the Propertian poem points by contrast what is on offer in the *Remedia*; cf. Prop. 1. 12. 19 *mi neque amare aliam, neque ab hac desistere fas est* ('but for me it is neither possible to love another, nor to break off with her').[10] This Propertian intertext points to repetition with a difference: the *Remedia will* attempt to liberate its readers from the Propertian erotic *seruitium* (Prop. 1. 12. 18), but at the same time memory of the uncompromising finality of the Propertian couplet may undermine our confidence in Ovid's ability to make good his promise.

The reader-lover's impossible task of remembering and forgetting at the same time is conducted through intertextuality both with Ovid's own works and with the works of other poets, the subjects respectively of my next two sections. Memories of other works by Ovid in the first proem (1–40) tend to reinforce the poet's rhetorical protests to Amor that the *Remedia* does *not* move in an area radically opposed to the earlier amatory works. But, in what follows, the reader's memories of works by other poets work against the poet's programme of *renuntiatio amoris* and his advocacy of a strategy of forgetting as a cure for love. The history of the *renuntiatio amoris* is a path strewn with good intentions. Oblivion is not easily achieved, since the lover is surrounded by sticky traces of his former passion, not least intertextual traces.[11]

REMEDIA 1–40: OVIDIAN READERS HUMAN AND DIVINE

The prologue to the *Remedia* reveals traces or foreshadowings of other Ovidian amatory prologues or proemial reaffirmations of amatory intent.[12] The interview between poet and Cupid forms a

---

[10] For advice on 'loving another', see *Rem.* 441–88.
[11] The emphasis on the difficulty, and perhaps impossibility, of ridding oneself of love is approached from a different angle by Davisson (1996).
[12] On the parallels between *Rem.* 1–40, *Am.* 1. 1, and *Fasti* 4. 1–8, see Korzeniewski (1964: 184–93).

pair with that in *Amores* 1. 1, in both cases hinging on an opposition of *arma/bella* and *amor*.[13] cf. *Rem.* 2 '*bella mihi, uideo, bella parantur*' *ait* (' "war, I see, war is being prepared against me", he said'); *Am.* 1. 1. 1 *arma graui numero uiolentaque bella parabam* ('I was preparing arms and violent war in a weighty metre'). In the *Remedia* Ovid claims that the preparations for war exist only as a misunderstanding on the part of Cupid—but how real, we might ask, were the preparations for warlike poetry in *Amores* 1. 1? In the *Remedia* the boy Cupid (*puer: Rem.* 23; *Am.* 1. 1. 5, 13, 25) accepts the poet's demarcation of his proper sphere of activity (power over the happy lover, but not over the suicidal lover), as he did not in *Amores* 1. 1 (the empire of love, but not the heights of poetry)—and as he did not in the related confrontation between Apollo and the *puer* (*Met.* 1. 456) Cupid in *Met.* 1.[14]

Amor's closing endorsement of the *propositum opus* (*Rem.* 140) is duplicated in the injunction to the poet at *Fasti* 4. 16—'*coeptum perfice*' *dixit* '*opus*' (' "finish the job you have started", she said')—by a Venus who is surprised to find Ovid still busy with what he claims has never in fact ceased to be his *propositum opus* (*Fasti* 4. 8). On the basis of previous statements of poetic intent by Ovid and also, presumably, of a reading of the first three books of the *Fasti*, Venus has come to the conclusion that Ovid has abandoned her service: 'did I ever abandon your standards?', the poet counters (*Fasti* 4. 7 *numquid tua signa reliqui?*). In the *Remedia* Cupid, on the basis of a reading of the two words of the title, 'Remedia Amoris', is led to an interpretation of the poem as a rebellion against his service: 'I who under your leadership have so often carried the standards entrusted to me', protests the poet (*Rem.* 4 *tradita qui toties te duce signa tuli*). Cupid is persuaded otherwise by the poet, just as Venus in *Fasti* 4 does not dissent from Ovid's account of his unceasing service to her.

saucius an sanus numquid tua signa reliqui? (*Fasti* 4. 7 'wounded or whole, have I ever abandoned your standards?'). In the healing manual of the *Remedia* Ovid, it seems, is still as much the poet of love as he was in the series of amatory works inaugurated with the

---

[13] See Rosati, Ch. 8 in this volume.
[14] For further detailed parallels between the *Am.* 1. 1 and *Rem.* 1–40, see Henderson (1979: 27–8).

wound inflicted by Cupid's bow in *Amores* 1. 1. But are Venus and Cupid taken in by Ovid's weasel words? How expert are they as readers of Ovid? In *Fasti* 4 how aware is Venus that she is to some extent being recast as the Venus of the proem to Lucretius' *De Rerum Natura*, rather than as the patron of love elegy, a division that reflects the difficult duality of Venus in Lucretius' poem (both constructive principle of *natura*, and destructive psychological force)? In the *Remedia* how far is Cupid seduced by Ovid's court-room rhetoric,[15] led on by what Ovid does grant (29–38) to an acquiescence in a radically destructive campaign against love?[16] Cupid appears blind to the division within his own self on which Ovid's argument depends: *amor* as a technique of practical courtship, versus *amor* as an overpowering and destructive emotion.[17] In agreeing to give up his claim to the latter, Cupid might be thought to cede the greater part of his power. As I have suggested, he also seems unaware of the intertextuality of his own words at *Rem.* 2 with the first line of the *Amores*, and unaware of the universal empire of love to which he had laid claim in *Amores* 1. 1 and 1. 2.

Venus and Cupid offer possible models only for Ovid's readers' own response. Ovid's persuasion of Cupid not to oppose his project in the *Remedia* might be read as the first success in his campaign against the god, but a success that depends on the poet's good fortune in finding Cupid to be a less than *doctus lector*.

RENUNTIATIO AMORIS

Katharina Volk has observed that the *Remedia* 'does not operate according to the principle of mimetic simultaneity', whereby the order of the precepts in a didactic poem tracks the development in 'real time' of the learning experience of the addressee,[18] although

---

[15] On which see ibid. 28; Korzeniewski (1964: 186–7).
[16] On the similar tactic in the prologue to *Ars* 3 of a rhetorical diversion of potential opposition to the poet's project, see Gibson (2003*a*) on *Ars* 3. 7–28; for another way in which *Ars* 3 and *Rem.* present themselves as a pair, see ibid. 24.
[17] On the double meaning of *amor* in the *Ars* and *Remedia*, see Volk (2002: 168–71) and Rosati, Ch. 8 in this volume.
[18] See Volk (2002: 184–5).

(as she notes) the major divisions of the poem correspond to the different temporal stages in the 'disease' at which different patients may be offered help: (1) before the disease has taken a firm hold (79–106); (2) once it has become established (107–608); (3) following a relapse (609–794).[19] But more broadly it is possible to read in the *Remedia* the 'plot' of a *renuntiatio amoris*, from a starting-point of erotic enslavement to the conclusion of a farewell to love. Ovid alludes to a number of escapes, or attempted escapes, from painful love in first-person love poetry. But the learned reader's awareness of the difficulty of escape in at least some of these cases throws doubt on the likely efficacy of the Ovidian precepts.

Most prominent, and least problematic, are allusions to the Propertian experience. Henderson suggests that 'The outline of the programme for the *Remedia* seems to have been suggested to Ovid by Prop. 1. 1'[20]: the request for a cure for painful love, the contrast with those who can continue with a happy love. By the epilogue to the *Remedia* we have reached the same point as Propertius in the *renuntiatio amoris* of the penultimate poem of Book 3:

> Hoc opus exegi: fessae date serta carinae;
>   contigimus portus, quo mihi cursus erat.
> postmodo reddetis sacro pia uota poetae,
>   carmine sanati femina uirque meo.   (*Rem.* 811–14)

(Now I have finished this work: hang garlands on the exhausted ship; I have reached the harbour for which I was making. Later you will make pious thank-offerings to the sacred poet, men and women healed by my poem.)

> ecce coronatae portum tetigere carinae,
>   traiectae Syrtes, ancora iacta mihist.
> nunc demum uasto fessi resipiscimus aestu,
>   uulneraque ad sanum nunc coiere mea.
> Mens Bona, si qua dea's, tua me in sacraria dono.
>   exciderunt surdo tot mea uota Ioui.   (Prop. 3. 24. 15–20)

(See, my garlanded ships have reached harbour, the Syrtes are behind me, and I have cast anchor. Now at last, exhausted, I recover from the sea's vast surge, now my wounds have healed over. Goddess of Sound Mind, if you are

---

[19] On narrative and plot in the books of the *Ars Amatoria*, see Sharrock, Ch. 2 in this volume.

[20] See Henderson (1979: p. xv).

a goddess, I dedicate myself to your shrine. So many of my prayers to Jupiter have fallen on deaf ears.)

Here is a definitive closure to the first three books of Propertius; yet there will be a relapse of a kind at the beginning of the fourth book.

Less reassuring are the allusions to Catullan attempts to escape from a painful love. Injunctions to be firm at *Rem.* 218 and 642 (*perfer*),[21] and 245 (*quod nisi firmata properaris mente reuerti*, 'if you hasten to return with mind not yet steadfast'), remind the reader of Catullus' attempt to put the past behind him. Poem 8, lines 11–12 read: *sed obstinata mente perfer, obdura. | uale, puella. iam Catullus obdurat* ('but with resolute mind be firm, harden yourself. Farewell, my girl. Catullus has now hardened to you'). But the following memories of the *puella*'s beauty and kisses suggest that Catullus is far from hardened in his resolution. At *Rem.* 649–50 Ovid advises a gradual cessation of the affair, *sed meliore fide paulatim extinguitur ignis | quam subito: lente desine, tutus eris* ('but it is more reliable if a fire is extinguished slowly rather than suddenly: give her up slowly, and you will be safe'). This seems all too easy a solution to the Catullan predicament of poem 76. 11–16:

> quin tu animo offirmas atque istinc teque reducis
> et dis inuitis desinis esse miser?
> difficile est longum subito deponere amorem,
> difficile est, uerum hoc qua lubet efficias:
> una salus haec est, hoc est tibi peruincendum,
> hoc facias, siue id non pote siue pote.

(Why don't you stiffen your resolve and draw back, and stop being unhappy in the face of heaven? It is difficult suddenly to get rid of a long love, it is difficult, but this you must do somehow or other. This is your only salvation, this you must strive for, this is what you must do, whether you can or not.)

Four couplets later allusion to Catullus 76 is combined with allusion to Catullus 85 *odi et amo*, the most famous expression of Catullan impotence: *Rem.* 657–8 *non curare sat est: odio qui finit amorem, | aut amat aut aegre desinit esse miser* ('not to care is all it takes: he who ends love in hatred, either loves or with difficulty stops being unhappy'). If only not to care *were* enough.[22]

---

[21] Followed by allusion to Cat. 55. 18–20.
[22] For a sustained Ovidian engagement with Cat. 85, see *Am.* 3. 11b.

At the end of the tenth *Eclogue* the Virgilian Gallus (very possibly in allusion to the words of Gallus' own poetry) acknowledges the omnipotence of Love; cf. Verg. *Ecl.* 10. 69 '*omnia uincit Amor: et nos cedamus Amori*' ('Love conquers all: let me too surrender to Love'). At the beginning of the *Ars* Ovid had thrown out a bold challenge, 1. 21–2 *et mihi cedet Amor, quamuis mea uulneret arcu | pectora, iactatas excutiatque faces* ('Love will surrender to me too, however much he wounds my breast with his bow and shakes and brandishes his torches').[23] In the *Ars* the power struggle between Ovid and Amor is a kind of civil war for control of the empire of love. In the *Remedia* it is a struggle between love and not-love. Ovid appears confident in his ability to make love yield at 143–4, *Venus otia amat: qui finem quaeris amoris, | (cedit amor rebus) res age, tutus eris* ('Venus loves idleness: if you want an end to love, be busy (love surrenders to busyness), and you will be safe'); and again almost at the end, 751–2 *at tanti tibi sit non indulgere theatris, | dum bene de uacuo pectore cedat amor* ('but it is important that you not indulge in the theatre, until love properly leaves you fancy-free'). In *Eclogue* 10 Virgil sings of (6) *sollicitos Galli... amores* 'Gallus' troubled loves'; at *Rem.* 557 Lethaeus Amor acknowledges the power of Ovid both to grant and to remove *sollicitos... amores*, and in the passage that follows there is repeated allusion to *Eclogue* 10.[24] Allusions to the last poem of a book reinforce, in formal terms, the closural quality of the echoes of *Eclogue* 10 in the *Remedia* as an end to love. But Gallus' admission of the impossibility of a *medicina furoris* (*Ecl.* 10. 60) qualifies the reader's faith in Ovid's own credentials in this area.

FORGETTING LOVE

The examples of earlier love poets tend to undermine the *Remedia*'s 'plot' of escape from love. The chances of flight for an epic hero may

---

[23] On *et nos cedamus Amori* as 'something like the "motto" of love elegy', see Volk (2002: 167–8); for other programmatic allusions to the Virgilian words see Gibson (2003a) on *Ars* 3. 673–4; Rosati, Ch. 8 in this volume.

[24] See Pinotti (1988) on 549–608, 557–8, 579–80, 597–8. Other allusions to *Ecl.* 10: *Rem.* 15–16 *at si quis male fert indignae regna puellae, | ne pereat, nostrae sentiat artis opem*: *Ecl.* 10. 10 *indigno cum Gallus amore peribat*; *Rem.* 37 *his lacrimis contentus eris sine crimine mortis*: *Ecl.* 10. 29 *nec lacrimis crudelis Amor* [*saturatur*].

be better. One straightforward *exemplum* of escape from erotic entanglement is Ulysses, who was able to leave Circe, just like that, despite her magic and her rhetoric (*Rem.* 263–88). At *Remedia* 70 a specifically epic model is written in to the more general image of the ship of poetry, through reference to the 'companions' of a 'leader': *rectaque cum sociis me duce nauis eat* ('let the ship with my companions sail on a straight course under my leadership'). Not so reassuring to us as readers if the leader is Odysseus, who managed to lose all his companions, but encouraging if we are in the same boat as Aeneas.[25] We will note that Ovid does indeed rewrite Circe in the *Remedia*[26] (as also the love-stricken Calypso at *Ars* 2. 125–42) through the prism of their Virgilian avatar, Dido. Circe's first words are (273–4) '*non ego, quod primo, memini, sperare solebam,* | *iam precor, ut coniunx tu meus esse uelis*' ('I no longer pray for what, I remember, I used to hope for at first, that you should wish to be my husband'). What she remembers, however, are not the dashed hopes of the Homeric Circe, whose mind did not run on marriage, but of Dido, at *Aeneid* 4. 431 (*non iam coniugium antiquum, quod prodidit, oro,* 'I no longer beg for the one-time marriage that he has betrayed') and at *Heroides* 7. 167 (*si pudet uxoris, non nupta, sed hospita dicar,* 'If you are ashamed to have me as your wife, then call me not bride, but host'); the rest of Circe's speech continues to rework the words of Virgilian and Ovidian Didos.[27]

Virgilian *fuga*[28] is a better model than Homeric *nostos* for the Ovidian patient, who must put his past behind him and forget previous attachments. Aeneas must avoid the temptation of a *reciduua Pergama* (*A.* 4. 344, 7. 322, 10. 58: for Virgil, if Troy is to be reborn, it must be in a different form), as the danger of relapse (*Rem.* 611 *reccidit*) is acute for Ovid's readers. Aeneas must also put Dido out of his mind, but she will continue to cast a long shadow both over Aeneas' later history and over the history of Rome; cf. Verg. *A.* 4. 386 *omnibus umbra locis adero* ('I shall be present everywhere as

---

[25] On another example of poet and readers travelling in the same boat (*Ars* 1. 772), see Volk (2002: 180).
[26] On Circe in the *Remedia*, see Brunelle (2002).
[27] See Prinz (1917: 261–2).
[28] Cf. 224 *sed fuge: tutus adhuc Parthus ab hoste fuga est.* Aeneas is repeatedly told to 'flee'; cf. Verg. *A.* 2. 289, 2. 619, 3. 44, 4. 565.

a shadow').²⁹ Memory and forgetfulness, concerns of the epic tradition *qua* tradition from its inception, are in the *Aeneid* charged with new thematic significance, of psychological, historical, and ideological kinds. The *Remedia* has its own erotic agenda when it comes to memory and forgetting, but this intersects in important ways with the Virgilian agenda, nowhere more so than in the epiphany of Lethaeus Amor, the presiding god of the poem.

LETHAEUS AMOR (REM. 549–78)

At the beginning of the *Remedia* Ovid invokes Apollo, suitable for present purposes as god of both poetry and healing (75–8), and Apollo appears in answer to a second invocation towards the end of the poem (704–6).³⁰ But the true presiding spirit of the work is *Lethaeus Amor* who appears in a vision to deliver to the poet, at length and with obtrusive mundanity, a series of specific additional precepts rather than general instruction or inspiration. It may seem paradoxical for a god of love to advise on the elimination of love— and 555 *dubito uerusne Cupido* ('I am in doubt whether it was truly Cupid') momentarily raises a doubt about the authenticity of *this* manifestation of Amor, before line 556 makes clear that the doubt is really as to whether it was a true epiphany or just a dream³¹—but, as discussed above, a god has the power both to give and destroy within his sphere of operation (as, for example, Apollo is the god both of healing and of plague). This is also the power of the poet Ovid, who claims both to inflict and heal the wound of love (43–4). The opening words of Lethaeus Amor reverse the roles, addressing Ovid as if *he* were the divinity; cf. *Rem.* 557 *o qui sollicitos modo das, modo demis*

---

²⁹ Sharrock, Ch. 2 in this volume, notes that 'Dido, although she is rarely mentioned, is central to the *Remedia Amoris*. Her near-absence makes a very telling gaping hole' (above, p. 29). It might be better to describe her as a looming intertextual absent presence.

³⁰ On Ovid's systematic slighting of Apollo as god of poetry, see Armstrong (2004).

³¹ This perhaps echoes the expression of doubt at Prop. 3. 24. 19: *Mens Bona, si qua dea es* (for the relevance of Mens Bona see below).

Lethaeus Amor: *The Art of Forgetting* 179

amores ('you who now give, and now take away, the troubles of love').[32]

The apparition inverts the epiphany of Apollo at *Ars* 2. 493–510 as the god of self-knowledge, advertised in the Delphic precept, itself known throughout the world in fame (*Ars* 2. 499–500).[33] There Apollo advises the lover to remember his own good points in order to attract the girl; cf. *Ars* 2. 501–2 *qui sibi notus erit, solus sapienter amabit | atque opus ad uires exiget omne suas* ('only the man who knows himself will love wisely, and carry the job through in keeping with his own strengths'). Here Lethaeus Amor instructs in the art of forgetting the beloved, although a kind of self-knowledge is used in order to obliterate the awareness of desire; cf. *Rem.* 559 *ad mala quisque animum referat sua* ('everyone should remind himself of his own troubles'). It may seem odd that a poet should be inspired by a god of forgetfulness rather than by a god of knowledge such as Apollo, or by the Muses, daughters of Memory, but Ovid has not in fact forgotten the Hesiodic-Callimachean tradition of the appearance of the Muses to the poet. The power of reminders of one's non-erotic anxieties to induce forgetfulness of the cares of love[34] can be compared with the ability of Hesiod's Μουσάων θεράπων to induce forgetfulness of troubling thoughts and cares through singing of men of old and of the gods (*Theog.* 98–103). The connection between

---

[32] So Pinotti (1988: ad loc.) noting *o qui* introducing the powers of a god, and *modo... modo...* referring to the power of a god both to give and take away. One god whose place Ovid usurps is Bacchus, invoked in a Propertian hymn as a liberating doctor of love, Prop. 3. 17. 3–6 *tu potes insanae Veneris compescere fastus, | curarumque tuo fit medicina mero. | per te iunguntur, per te soluuntur amantes: | tu uitium ex animo dilue, Bacche, meo*. In the oddly anti-climactic final section of the *Remedia* on the role of Bacchus and wine, 803–10, there is, in pointed contrast to the Propertian poem, no hymnic praise of Liberator Bacchus, of a kind that might form a ring with the legal imagery of freedom at 73–4; instead wine is briefly dismissed in a discussion of dietary regime, the power of a divinity to create and destroy reduced to physiology and physical analogy, 807–8 *nutritur uento, uento restinguitur ignis; | lenis alit flammas, grandior aura necat*. No competition for Ovid. More widely, and in contrast with the didactic freedom missions of the *De rerum natura* and Horace *Epistles* 1, the *Remedia* underplays the theme of liberation.

[33] See Prinz (1917: 94–6).

[34] *Rem.* 557 *sollicitos... amores*, as well as the cuing allusion to *Eclogue* 10 (see above), suggests that love is a *cura*, to be crowded out by more material *curae*: cf. 170 *quaelibet huic curae* [agriculture] *cedere cura potest*, but there with *distinctio* of meanings of *cura*: see Pinotti (1988: ad loc.).

the memory embodied in the Muses and forgetfulness of woes is emphasized through the verbal jingle at *Theog.* 53–5: τὰς ἐν Πιερίῃ Κρονίδῃ τέκε πατρὶ μιγεῖσα | Μνημοσύνη, γουνοῖσιν Ἐλευθῆρος μεδέουσα, | λησμοσύνην τε κακῶν ἄμπαυμά τε μερμηράων ('Memory, ruler of the heights of Eleutherae, bore them in Pieria after lying with father Zeus, to bring forgetfulness of troubles and release from cares').

The god of forgetfulness appears in a passage dense with literary, and other, memories and associations (although the god himself, so far as we can tell, appears to be an Ovidian invention). Lethaeus Amor's neighbour Venus Erycina puts the reader in mind of a god of Mind. There were in Rome two temples of Venus Erycina.[35] That by the Porta Collina was dedicated by L. Porcius Licinius in 181 BC. The earlier was dedicated on the Capitol in 215 BC by Q. Fabius Maximus, at the same time as an adjacent[36] temple to Mens.[37] Although the inscriptional evidence for dedications to Mens *Bona* begins in the imperial period,[38] this goddess Mens is presumably the Mens Bona to whom Propertius dedicates himself at 3. 24. 19 in thanksgiving for his safe delivery from enslavement to Cynthia. The Propertian Mens Bona is led, hands bound, in the triumph of Cupid that marks the beginning of Ovid's erotic captivity at *Amores* 1. 2. 31. Now in the *Remedia* Love 'who brings oblivion' returns the lover to his 'Right Mind', in the sense that Lethaeus Amor brings the mind back to the mundane concerns that love makes you forget.[39]

The power of love to distract from the usual business of life is a cliché. Tiberius Donatus comments on Dido's neglect of her city-building at *Aeneid* 4. 86–9: *nam cum in amore multa sint uitia, tum magis quod obliuionem negotiorum omnium parit et nimiam in agendis necessariis neglegentiam* ('chief among the many evils of love is that it brings forgetfulness of all one's business and an excessive negligence of life's necessities'). Earlier in the story of Dido a mindful Love induces in an unknowing Dido a forgetfulness of a former

---

[35] See Henderson (1979) on 549–50; Bömer (1958) on *Fasti* 4. 873; on Venus Erycina see Schilling (1954: 233–6).
[36] See Livy 33. 31. 9 *canali uno discretae*.
[37] See *Fasti* 6. 241–6 with Bömer (1958: ad loc.).
[38] See Latte (1960: 239–40).
[39] See Hardie (1986: 271 with n. 103).

attachment that is at the same time a reanimation of a state of mind that has faded, *Aen.* 1. 717–22:

> haec oculis, haec pectore toto
> haeret et interdum gremio fouet inscius Dido
> insidat quantus miserae deus. at memor ille
> matris Acidaliae⁴⁰ paulatim abolere Sychaeum
> incipit et uiuo temptat praeuertere amore
> iam pridem resides animos desuetaque corda.

(She hangs on him with her eyes and all her heart. Sometimes Dido fondles him on her lap, unhappily oblivious to the power of the god sinking into her. But mindful of his mother Venus he sets about gradually wiping out the memory of Sychaeus, and sets a living love to head off her now long idle spirit, her heart disused to passion.)

Dido herself later comments on the reawakening of memories of desire—cf. Verg. *A.* 4. 23 *agnosco ueteris uestigia flammae* ('I recognize the traces of an ancient flame')—words that, for us, locate themselves in a long chain of intertextual memories stretching backwards and forwards in time.

Lethaeus Amor remembers other Virgilian roles. His first words to the poet—557 '*o qui sollicitos modo das, modo demis amores*'—echo the power of Mercury's rod at Verg. *A.* 4. 244 [*hac*] *dat somnos adimitque* ('with this he gives and takes away sleep').⁴¹ Mercury comes down to rebuke Aeneas for an erotic amnesia and to recall him to his proper concerns; cf. Verg. *A.* 4. 267 '*heu, regni rerumque oblite tuarum*' ('what, have you forgotten your kingdom and your duty!'). Like Mercury, Lethaeus Amor vanishes suddenly in midspeech: with *Rem.* 575–6 *plura loquebatur: placidum puerilis imago | destituit somnum, si modo somnus erat* ('he was about to say more: the boy's image vanished from my calm sleep, if sleep it was'), cf. Verg. *A.* 4. 276–8 *tali Cyllenius ore locutus | mortalis uisus medio sermone*

---

⁴⁰ O'Hara (1990) suggests that the learned reader will see reference to Venus Erycina in the recherché epithet Acidalius (etymologized from ἀκίς 'dart, sting'), with allusion to Cat. 64. 72 *spinosas Erycina serens in pectore curas*.

⁴¹ Pinotti (1988: ad loc.) also cites Hor. *Sat.* 2. 3. 288 *Iuppiter, ingentis qui das adimisque dolores*. Lucke (1982) cites Verg. *A.* 4. 487–8 *haec se carminibus promittit soluere mentes/ quas uelit, ast aliis duras immittere curas*; Ov. *Am.* 2. 9. 50 *gaudia ambigua dasque negasque fide* (a poem that alludes substantially to Prop. 2. 12, very much in Ovid's mind in the Lethaeus Amor episode as well: see below).

reliquit | et procul in tenuem ex oculis euanuit auram ('with these words Mercury vanished from my mortal vision in mid-sentence, and disappeared from my sight into thin air').

Virgil's Mercury appears to Aeneas twice, once in waking reality and once in his sleep. Lethaeus Amor appears once to Ovid, but the poet is in two minds as to whether it is a waking or dreaming vision; cf. *Rem.* 555–6 *is mihi sic dixit (dubito, uerusne Cupido, | an somnus fuerit: sed puto, somnus erat)* ('Thus he spoke to me (I don't know if it was truly Cupid or a dream; but I think it was a dream)'). Some take *somnus* to mean 'dream', but in all other passages adduced for this sense 'sleep' is also a possible, and in most cases an unforced, translation.[42] At the end of the vision in 576 (*destituit somnum, si modo somnus erat*), *somnus* most naturally means 'sleep'. *Lethaeus* most commonly qualifies sleep, or sleep- or oblivion-inducing substances, as at Verg. *G.* 1. 78 *Lethaeo perfusa papauera somno* ('poppies drenched in the sleep of Lethe'), possibly modelled on Callimachus *Hymn to Delos* 233–4 (Iris by the throne of Hera) 'she never forgets her station, not even when sleep plants her Lethaean wing on her'.

The further doubt arises for the reader as to whether the referents of *uerus Cupido* and *somnus* in 555–6 are the same or different. If the latter, we will translate 'Was it the real Cupid, or was it sleep [in which I saw something unreal]?'[43] But we could also translate 'Was what I saw Cupid or Sleep?' This might seem a nonsensical (if grammatically possible) translation, were it not for the fact that a doubt of this kind as to the identity of the vision may be read as an intertextual clue when taken together with the poet's reaction to the disappearance of Lethaeus Amor at 577–8. There, adverting to the seafaring image that runs through the *Remedia* as well as the *Ars*,[44] Ovid gives the particular example of Aeneas' loss of his helmsman

---

[42] So at Enn. *Ann.* 35 Sk. *exterrita somno* ('ablative of separation', Skutsch); Verg. *A.* 8. 42 *ne uana putes haec fingere somnum*; Lygdamus 4. 11–12 *et tamen, utcumque est, siue illi uera moneri, | mendaci somno credere siue solent*; *Met.* 7. 646; *Fasti* 3. 28. However at *Her.* 13. 105 *aucupor in lecto mendaces caelibe somnos*, 'dreams' is the most natural sense.

[43] Cf. Verg. *A.* 3. 173–4 *nec sopor illud erat, sed coram agnoscere uultus | uelatasque comas praesentiaque ora uidebar*; Ov. *Pont.* 3. 3. 2–3 *dum tibi quae uidi refero, seu corporis umbra | seu ueri species seu fuit ille sopor* (a vision of Amor related to that of Lethaeus Amor in the *Rem.*: see Kenney (1965: 46–7)).

[44] See Lucke (1982) on *Rem.* 811–14; Gibson (2003a) on *Ars* 3. 99–100.

Palinurus at the end of *Aeneid* 5.[45] Henderson suggests (on 577–8) that 'it is possible that Virgil's description of Somnus masquerading as Phorbas [in the Palinurus episode] ... gave Ovid the whole idea of the Amor-*somnus* ambiguity'. Virgil's Somnus shakes over Palinurus a 'branch dripping with Lethaean dew' (Verg. A. 5. 854 *ramum Lethaeo rore madentem*). Sleep, the Homeric brother of Death, brings death to Palinurus; Ovid's Lethaeus Amor brings the 'death' of love, hinted at in his extinguished torches at 552. The water that he uses to douse them may be drawn from the infernal river, where 'by the waves of river Lethe they drink the waters that bring freedom from care and ages of oblivion' (Verg. A. 6. 714–15 *Lethaei ad fluminis undam | securos latices et longa obliuia potant*). Ovid's uncertainty as to the identity of the vision dramatizes the intertextual conflation of two individuals (Cupid and Somnus), with the further twist that Ovid alludes to a Virgilian character who himself embodies delusion, appearing to Palinurus in the disguise of Phorbas (Verg. A. 5. 842). The Virgilian Somnus is an obsessive role-player, for he offers to take Palinurus' place as well; cf. Verg. A. 5. 846 *ipse ego paulisper pro te tua munera obibo* ('I myself will carry out your duties in your place for a little while'). Lethaeus Amor's first words already hint at something similar, addressing Ovid 'con uno stile quasi innodico, che disorienta il lettore, presentandogli uno scambio di ruoli fra il dio e il poeta'.[46]

In terms of the Virgilian plot, Lethaeus Amor's impersonation of the manner of Mercury's visitations to Aeneas at Carthage is in line with a story of successful escape. But what does the disappearance of Lethaeus Amor-as-Palinurus mean for the onward 'journey from Carthage'? Does this disrupt the Odyssean-Aenean plan of flight? First, so far from being a failure of divine guidance, the sudden disappearance of Amor is a *leçon par exemple* to the poet, mimicking the experience of forgetfulness: he just drops out of mind. Secondly, Ovid is disingenuous in claiming the need for the god, when he

---

[45] Cf. *Tr.* 5. 6. 7–8 (to an unreliable friend) *fluctibus in mediis nauem, Palinure, relinquis? | ne fuge, neue tua sit minor arte fides.* Love as a steersman: *Her.* 15. 215–16; Meleager, *AP* 12. 157. There is also an element of ring composition, for Ovid had opened the *Ars* (1. 5–8) with an image of himself as Tiphys, an Argonautic 'helmsman' of the ship of erotodidaxis. On Palinurus as Virgil's rewriting of Apollonius of Rhodes' Tiphys, see Nelis (2001: 221–3).

[46] See Pinotti (1988) on 557–8.

himself has been credited by the god with the power to remove love (557), and when the identities of poet and Lethaeus Amor are, as a result, hard to distinguish. Thirdly, the language of 575–6 (*plura loquebatur; placidum puerilis imago | destituit somnum*) recalls an earlier epic exemplum at 285–6 (*illa loquebatur, nauem soluebat Vlixes; | inrita cum uelis uerba tulere Noti*, 'as she was speaking, Ulysses set sail; the winds carried off her futile words together with his sails'). Here is a hero who can all too easily put Circe out of his mind and just slip away, confident of his onward course. Ovid may think that he can no longer find his way, bereft of his helmsman, as adrift as Palinurus himself in the dark of the storm in *Aeneid* 3, in a line 'remembered' at *Rem.* 577–8 *media nauem Palinurus in unda | deserit* ('Palinurus abandons ship in mid-sea'); cf. Verg. *A.* 3. 202 *nec meminisse*[47] *uiae media Palinurus in unda* ('Palinurus [said he did not] remember the way in mid-sea'). But in fact this kind of forgetfulness keeps Ovid well on track.

Propertian memories reinforce a sense that the poet is not in danger of losing his way. At the very moment that he complains at 578—*ignotas cogor inire uias* ('I am forced to enter on unknown paths')[48]—Ovid remembers the poem that provides a blueprint for the *Remedia* as a whole, Propertius 1. 1. 17–18: *in me tardus Amor non ullas cogitat artes, | nec meminit notas, ut prius, ire uias* ('in my case sluggish Love devises no ruses, and does not remember to travel on known paths, as before').[49] The Propertian couplet itself probably uses the language of memory self-reflexively to define the poet's position with regard to his elegiac predecessor, Gallus. Ovid experiences a moment of existential panic as he finds (or thinks he finds) himself on, for him, truly untrodden paths, detached from Amor and amatory themes (an end to the excogitation of further erotic *Artes*?); but, if we take seriously Ovid's several protestations that he has never left the service of Cupid, for this poet escape from love *must* be on an untrodden path.

---

[47] 'a rather unexpected word', remarks Williams ad loc.
[48] Henderson (1979) suggests the influence of Verg. *A.* 5. 871 *in ignota... harena* (Aeneas' epitaph on Palinurus). Cf. also Verg. *A.* 8. 112–13 '*iuuenes, quae causa subegit | ignotas temptare uias?*'
[49] *cogor*, a Propertian favourite (Tränkle 1960: 27–8), is perhaps another allusive signal.

Another Propertian intertext also seems to gainsay the poet's fear of failure and misdirection. Ovid is abandoned by the *puerilis imago* (575) of Lethaeus Amor. This is what Propertius wishes *would* happen in the poem (2. 12) that allegorizes the painted attributes of the boy Amor. Here, despite the poet's plea to the god to aim his arrows elsewhere, 'his darts stay in me, his boyish image stays in me too: but he has surely lost his wings, since, alas, nowhere does he fly away from my breast' (Prop. 2. 12. 13–15 *in me tela manent, manet et puerilis imago; | sed certe pennas perdidit ille suas; | euolat heu nostro quoniam de pectore nusquam*).[50] If the goal of the *Remedia* is indeed to undo the work of the *Ars*, then, although the poet pretends not to realize it, the disappearance of the *puerilis imago* reverses the goal of *Ars* 2. 17–20 (also alluding to Prop. 2. 12):

> magna paro, quas possit Amor remanere per artes,
>   dicere, tam uasto peruagus orbe puer.
> et leuis est et habet, quibus auolet, alas;
>   difficile est illis inposuisse modum.

(My great project is to sing of the arts which can make Love stay, the boy who wanders through such a wide world. He is fickle, and has wings on which to fly away: it is difficult to restrain them.)

A little later the disappearance of love is reprised in naturalistic terms. Best to allow love simply to fade away, by avoiding the triggers to memory, the associations that provoke a relapse of the almost cured subject (609 ff.). Stop talking about her, 'so that she slips out of your desires' (*Ars* 2. 646 *ut desideriis effluat illa tuis*).[51] Love's final trick will be to disappear before you notice it, just as Lethaeus Amor slipped away from the poet's consciousness; cf. *Ars* 2. 653–4 *fallat et in tenues euanidus exeat auras*[52] *| perque gradus molles emoriatur*

---

[50] The contrast with what precedes introduced by 13 *in me* is parallel to that at Prop. 1. 1. 17, *in me tardus Amor*, opening a couplet alluded to at *Rem.* 578. Prop. 2. 12 is an important model for Ovid's staging of his attempt to renounce love, followed by his renewed commitment to love, at the centre of *Amores* 2, in poems 9a and 9b (see McKeown 1998: 170; Hardie (2004*b*: 158–9). In terms of the *Remedia*, *Am.* 2. 9b represents a 'relapse': with 34 *notaque purpureus tela resumit Amor* cf. *Rem.* 612 *et, quae condiderat, tela resumpsit Amor.*

[51] For *effluo* used of memory, cf. e.g. Cic. *Fam.* 7. 14. 1 *ut istuc ueniam antequam plane ex animo tuo effluo.*

[52] Cf. Verg. *A.* 4. 278 (Mercury: see above) *et procul in tenuem ex oculis euanuit auram.*

amor ('let love trick you by vanishing away into thin air, and let him die by soft degrees').[53] The association of Amor and Mors has a long history in love elegy; here at the end love itself dies, thanks to the deathlike oblivion offered by Lethaeus Amor.

Yet, as Alison Sharrock points out to me, can one talk of the death of love without being reminded of love (orgasm) *as* death? There are other words in this couplet that continue to remind us of the erotic, of love's trickiness (*fallat*) and *mollitia* (*molles*). And a slow approach to a final dissolution is a climactic part of Ovid's erotodidaxis, 'believe me, the pleasure of Venus should not be hurried, but drawn out slowly with lingering delay' (*Ars* 2. 717–18 *crede mihi, non est Veneris properanda uoluptas | sed sensim tarda prolicienda mora*).

The casual way in which Lethaeus Amor both enters the text at 549 ff. and slips away at 575–6, mimetic of the supposed ease of the forgetting cure, is, however, belied by the associations of thought that bond the passage to what precedes and to what follows. In the couplet that immediately precedes the description of the temple of Venus Erycina, the precept that anxiety about the beloved increases desire is illustrated with the case of a mother of two sons whose love is greater for the son on campaign for whose safety she fears (547–8). This anticipates the advice of Lethaeus Amor to crowd out the cares of love with other more pressing cares, including 571: *filius hunc miles... angat* ('let this man worry about his son the soldier'). At the end of the episode the poet's anxiety about *ignotae uiae* leads by a natural association into the warnings about the dangers of *loca sola*. The transition is doubly determined: if the disappearance of Lethaeus Amor at 575 reminds us of Ulysses' desertion of Circe at 285 (see above), then we are prepared by intratextual association for the further stories of heroines abandoned in *loca sola* that are to follow.

LOCA SOLA AND LITERARY LOCI

Loca sola are dangerous for the convalescent lover, for in the absence of a distracting crowd images of the beloved present themselves

---

[53] Undoing the trick of love that caused all the trouble in the first place, *Rem.* 41–2 *ad mea, decepti iuuenes, praecepta uenite, | quos suus ex omni parte fefellit amor.*

irresistibly, cf. *Rem.* 584 *ante oculos facies stabit, ut ipsa, tuos* ('her face will appear before your eyes, as if she were there herself'). Literary 'topics of solitude' are also dangerous, for they conjure up for the experienced reader scenes of erotic despair.[54] By this stage in the history of Roman and Ovidian Callimacheanism untrodden paths have become very well worn indeed, and *loca sola* are filled with literary reminiscences. To Lucke's suggestion that *ignotas uias* flags original arguments in what follows, Pinotti responds, apparently without irony,

tuttavia, proprio la sezione successiva, che illustra i pericoli dei *loca sola*, si pone ostentatamente sulla scia di alcuni famosi precedenti, in particolare dell'egloga 10 di Virgilio, e trova la sua ragione d'essere appunto nel rapporto intertestuale con i modelli; perciò sarà più prudente non sopravvalutare tali dichiarazioni, e non estenderne troppo la portata.

We the readers cannot go into those lonely places without being haunted by a crowd of abandoned heroines and star-crossed lovers. This final section of the first main movement of the *Remedia*, which almost brings us safe into port before the relapse at 609 ff., culminates in an extended retelling of one of the foundational stories of the abandoned heroine, Phyllis and Demophoon (591–608), who also headed up the opening catalogue of mythological disasters that could have been prevented by Ovid's healing art (55–6). To judge from the fragmentary evidence, Callimachus' handling of the Phyllis and Demophoon story, possibly in the *Aitia*, was much read and imitated.

Phyllis blazes a trail for all the later feet (metrical?: cf. 600 *pedes*) that wander on lonely ways. Before she hanged herself, she herself had already travelled nine times on her 'narrow path, dark with its long shadow' (599 *limes... tenuis, longa subnubilus umbra*)—casting its long shadow over the later tradition.[55] Her *nouum iter* ('new

---

[54] The plural of the literary and rhetorical *locus* is almost always in *-i*: *OLD* s.v. 23, 24; but cf. *TLL* vii. 1576. 20 ff. for instances of *loc-a* of memory-places in Quintilian. On the tradition of erotic *loca sola*, and in particular on the allusions to *Ecl.* 10, see Pinotti (1988) on 579–80, 583–4, 605–6.

[55] On Ovid's stripping away of the narrative detail from his Phyllis in *Her.* 2 to create a schematic, archetypal, image of the Callimachean and neoteric abandoned heroine, see Barchiesi (1992: 107–11). Phyllis' ejaculation at *Rem.* 597 *perfide Demophoon* is an echo of Call. fr. 556 Pf. and a pre-echo of the complaints of Catullus' Ariadne, Dido's Aeneas, and assorted heroines, particularly Ovidian (see Lucke (1982) on 597). νυμφίε and ξένε are contrasted by Dido at Verg. *A.* 4. 323–4 '*cui me moribundam deseris hospes* | *(hoc solum nomen quoniam de coniuge restat?)*', rephrased at *Her.* 7. 167 *si pudet uxoris, non nupta, sed hospita dicar.* On further episodes in the allusive history of *perfidus* see Wills (1996: 26–30); see also della Corte (1973).

path') is a path on which she travels *nouies* ('nine times', *Rem.* 56); by this time the *nona uia* ('ninth journey', 601) is certainly a *nota uia* ('well-known journey', unlike 578 *ignotas... uias*).

The dangers of memory (*admonitus*) as a counter-agent to the admonitions of the didactic poet are rehearsed most intensively at *Remedia* 715–30:[56]

> exiguum est, quod deinde canam; sed profuit illud 715
>   exiguum multis, in quibus ipse fui.
> scripta caue relegas blandae seruata puellae:
>   constantes animos scripta relecta mouent.
> omnia pone feros (pones inuitus) in ignes,
>   et dic 'ardoris sit rogus iste mei.' 720
> Thestias absentem succendit stipite natum:
>   tu timide flammae perfida uerba dabis?
> si potes, et ceras remoue: quid imagine muta
>   carperis? hoc periit Laodamia modo.
> et loca saepe nocent; fugito loca conscia uestri 725
>   concubitus; causas illa doloris habent.
> 'hic fuit, hic cubuit; thalamo dormiuimus illo:
>   hic mihi lasciua gaudia nocte dedit.'
> admonitu refricatur amor, uulnusque nouatum
>   scinditur: infirmis culpa pusilla nocet 730

(What I have to sing next is a small thing, but this small thing has helped many, including myself. Avoid keeping and rereading your charming girl's letters; rereading letters undermines resolution. Put them all into the fierce flames (you will do it reluctantly) and say 'Let my passion blaze on this pyre.' Althaea burned her absent son with the log; do you shrink from putting the faithless words on the fire? If you can bring yourself, remove her portraits. Why let a mute image prey on you? That was how Laodamia perished. Places, too, are often harmful; avoid the places that remember where you slept together, for they cause grief. 'This is where she was, this is where she lay; this is where I enjoyed her in nights of love.' Remembering rubs love sore again, and opens up the wound afresh; when you're weak even a little slip causes injury. Just as if you were to touch sulphur to embers almost dead, they will come alive and the smallest fire will turn into a bonfire, so, unless you shun things that renew love, the flame which a moment ago was dead will blaze up again.)

---

[56] This is discussed as a catalogue of absent presences in Hardie (2002*b*: 13–15).

Erotic memories are bound up with textual and artistic memory and memorialization, in the first instance texts written by the girl herself. Ovid's own texts are also implicated, both a literal story of erotic infatuation, Laodamia, and a story, Althaea and Meleager, which relates to the erotic through association (maternal/erotic love; metaphorical uses of 'fire'). From texts to wax images (*cerae*), to places, but *loca* that function like textual 'places' of memory. Places and writing-surfaces of wax and paper are compared in the account of the art of memory in the *Rhetorica ad Herennium* 3. 17. 30: *loci cerae aut cartae simillimi sunt, imagines litteris* ('the memory places are very like wax or paper, the images are like letters').

The repeated deictics *hic... hic... illo... hic* themselves point to a textual tradition of using physical places to trigger memories. The *locus classicus* for Ovidian instances of these repeated deictics is Aeneas' account of the Trojans sightseeing in apparently *loca sola* at Verg. *A*. 2. 27–9 *iuuat ire et Dorica castra | desertosque uidere locos litusque relictum: | hic Dolopum manus, hic saeuus tendebat Achilles; | classibus hic locus, hic acie certare solebant* ('they delight in going and looking at the Greek camp, the deserted places and the abandoned shore; here the Dolopes pitched their tents, and here cruel Achilles; this was the place for their fleet, and here they used to fight in battle'): the Trojans' happy memories of their recent grief, filtered through the narrator Aeneas' painful memory of joy turned to grief. Ovidian examples of this pattern are all occasions for erotic yearning and erotic fantasy: old soldiers' recollections renewing Penelope's longing for her absent husband at *Her*. 1. 33–6; Calypso's love-struck request for repeated retellings of the Trojan War at *Ars* 2. 133–8; the younger Tarquin's infatuation with Lucretia at *Fasti* 2. 771–4; Alcyone's memories of the last time she saw her husband, on the beach as he set sail, at *Met*. 11. 712–13.[57]

CODA: MEMORY AND THE RETURN OF LOVE

In *Ex Ponto* 1. 3 Ovid speaks from his own experience as a pupil, not a teacher, of the incurability of a love that cannot forget, in the face of

---

[57] On these passages see Barchiesi (2002*b*: 197–9); Hardie (2002*b*: 12 n. 33, 275–6).

the best didactic expertise. Rufinus has sent a letter of consolation, compared for its skill to the medical arts of Machaon (5).[58] Rufinus' efforts are described as *admonitus* (8) and *praecepta* (27). Ovid was far on the road to recovery, when he suffered a fatal relapse, 27–30:

> cum bene firmarunt animum praecepta iacentem,
> sumptaque sunt nobis pectoris arma tui,
> rursus amor patriae ratione ualentior omni,
> quod tua fecerunt scripta, retexit opus.

(After your teaching had given strength to my prostrate spirit and I had taken up the weapons offered by your wisdom, love of my fatherland, stronger than all reason, undid the work performed by your writing.)

In the exile poetry Rome takes the place of the elegiac *puella* as the object of an irresistible desire. In *Ex Ponto* 1. 3 the disease is aggravated by the fact that those who offer advice are themselves loved; cf. 45–6 *effice uos ipsi ne tam mihi sitis amandi, | talibus ut leuius sit caruisse malum* ('see to it that you yourselves are not such objects of love to me, so that your absence is easier to bear'). *Omnia uincit amor.*

---

[58] For the art of Machaon, cf. *Rem.* 545–6, *Ars* 2. 491.

Part III

Politics

10

Erotic Aetiology: Romulus, Augustus, and the Rape of the Sabine Women

Mario Labate

The proem of the *Ars Amatoria* undertakes the task of demonstrating that 'love is an art'. As this prefatory assertion implies, the amorous relations of Latin elegy are a subject capable of being taught—in the same way as any other subject of a technical or scientific nature—and are therefore susceptible to becoming the subject of a didactic poem. The difficulty of such a demonstration is reflected in the radical overturning not only of common sense (where love is understood as a disorientation of the mind, a unique individual experience which by its very nature resists submission to any form of instruction) but also, above all, of the fundamental principles of the elegiac genre (where sincere expression is replaced in the *Ars* by the rhetoric of simulation, and the ideology of passion by the ideology of reason). The implicit syllogism embedded in the poem's priamel-like second couplet—*Ars* 1. 3–4 *arte citae veloque rates remoque moventur,* | *arte leves currus: arte regendus amor,* supported by the authority of Homer (*Iliad* 23. 315–18 μήτι... μήτι... μήτι)—takes on a burden of explanation that will clearly require the deployment of all the persuasive resources of the poet.[1]

---

[1] See Citroni (1984). Greek and Latin translations are taken or adapted from the relevant volume of the Loeb Classical Library: Ovid (G. P. Goold), Dionysius of Halicarnassus (E. Cary), Homer (W. F. Wyatt), Livy (B. O. Foster), Lucretius (M. F. Smith), Propertius (G. P. Goold). Many thanks to Roberto Chiappiniello for translating this chapter.

The necessity of viewing love as an art is not confined to the skilful rhetoric of the proem, but pervades the whole work, strengthening the comparison between the *Ars Amatoria* and other *artes*. This sustained comparison, together with the display of a rich didactic terminology, suggests that the inclusion of the *Ars* within the didactic genre is a battle continuously won but never-ending:[2] a type of challenge to the skill of the rhetorician that resembles, in certain respects, the challenge to be undertaken by Lucian in demonstrating ὅτι... τέχνη ἐστὶν ἡ παρασιτική (*Paras.* 13, 'that being a parasite is an art').

The skilful alternation between technical expository sections and narrative excursus is a distinctive mark of didactic discourse. The more difficult and 'unpoetic' the material over which this genre had extended its influence became, the greater the need to guarantee to the reader the relief of *uariatio*.[3] The digressions constitute, therefore, at the level of artistic strategy, clear 'indications of genre', essential components of the Ovidian poem. Furthermore, since the corpus of Latin literature already included ideologically and artistically ambitious works such as the *de Rerum Natura* and the *Georgics*, readers of Ovid's didactic-erotic poetry (which seeks legitimacy in the literary world) ought to expect to encounter these excursuses which the poet will inevitably insert, not simply for entertainment but as a fundamental part of the poem's purpose (in accordance with the prestigious and overwhelming models of Lucretius and Vergil). Indeed, these excursuses contain messages, messages of important truth—a feature consistent with the dominant ideological-cultural model within which the poet-*magister* writes his teachings (a model his teachings also help to create).[4]

The first of the sections in which the subject of the *Ars Amatoria* is articulated—the section dedicated to *inuentio* (1. 35 *principio quod amare uelis reperire labora*)—presents a relationship between exposition and excursus in which the digressions dominate. Out of a total

---

[2] Labate (1984: 167 ff.). On the characteristics of Greek and Latin didactic poetry, see Effe (1977), Toohey (1996); on the issue of inclusion of the *Ars Amatoria* in the didactic genre, see now Volk (2002: 157 ff., 187–8) (with further bibliography).
[3] See Pöhlmann (1973: 885), Steudel (1992: 166) (with a useful further bibliography).
[4] See Barchiesi (1982: 43 ff.).

of 222 verses, 32 contain an excursus proper (the story of the rape of the Sabine women: 1. 101–32), whilst the opportunity suddenly offered to amorous young men by civil ceremonies celebrating political and military power, takes up a good 52 verses (177–228) in the imagined chronicle of the triumphal procession which will inevitably follow the heralded expedition of Gaius Caesar against the Parthians.

The first excursus has a clear aetiological framework and recounts one of the most well-known legends of the origin of Rome, the Sabine rape, in which, according to historians and antiquarians, important aspects of national institutions, as well as private customs and Roman social life, are rooted.[5] The Ovidian excursus contains the main distinguishing marks of Roman aetiological poetry, such as the recalling of Roman sites in their primitive aspect (with the contrast between the simplicity and rustic poverty of the past and the urban splendour of the Augustan present),[6] and the quasi-formulaic underlining of persistent characteristics of the remote past that suggest the 'causes' of the present (1. 133–4 *scilicet ex illo sollemni more*... |*nunc quoque*). These characteristics accord with the model first set out in the *Aeneid* and later laid out as a poetic manifesto by Propertius in the proem to his fourth book.

As with other legends that tradition connects to important aspects of Roman cultural identity, the story of the Sabine women (the series of events in historical legend that culminate in the rape of women organized by Romulus) would be better suited to that strand of elegiac poetry which ambitiously invokes the model of the *Aitia* of Callimachus. The climb up the slopes of Helicon proposed by Vergil to Cornelius Gallus and then attempted in a more sustained manner by Propertius, was not really achieved in Rome before Ovid himself essayed this type of poetry in his poem on the Roman calendar.

It is surely not an arbitrary interpretation, from the historical and literary point of view, to consider the excursus on the Sabine women as anticipating the *Fasti*. We can legitimately imagine that an author

---

[5] For a brief survey of the sources and the principal problems of interpretation, see Ogilvie (1965: 64 ff., 777).

[6] La Penna (1977: 187 ff.); Labate (1991: 167–84); Fantham (1997: 122 ff.); Gazich (1997: 289 ff., esp. 306 ff.).

such as Ovid, who undertook to experiment with new possibilities in the sphere of Latin literature, deliberately involved his public both in the spectacle of his untiring development of one project from another, and in the study of possible zones of overlap, as well as the exploration of boundaries that mark out poetic differences and peculiarities. It has been noted, and I myself have looked at this point recently,[7] that Ovid, more than any other ancient author, keeps open a dialogue with his readers, in order to update them on the development of his poetic interests. Ovid concerns himself with addressing a multiplicity of forms and with poetic experimentalism, and his declarations, summaries, proposals, and *specimina* weave, throughout all his texts, a rich pattern of cross-references. In particular, his work on the aetiological poetry of the nation is flagged to readers of elegy and didactic love poetry in the festival of Juno Falisca in *Amores* 3. 13 (which is likely to belong to the second edition of the *Amores*) and in the excursus on the rape of the Sabine women in the first book of the *Ars Amatoria*.[8]

However, this point of view loses legitimacy if one considers these episodes as independent from the work in which they are placed and from which they take their meaning. Even the elegy of Juno Falisca, which strikes the reader with its extraneousness with respect to the world of elegiac love, obtains its sense precisely because it is a negation of this world and an indication of the anticipated desertion of a known genre by a poet capable of *polyeideia*.

I will undertake, above all, to illustrate the specific function of the excursus within the context of the poem and its complex relationship with the cultural model offered by the didactic love poetry of Ovid, although I remain aware here of those poetic features which look forward to peculiarities in the Ovidian approach to the poetry of the past.

In a recent study dedicated to the mythological narratives of the *Ars*, Konrad Heldmann speaks of an 'anti-*exemplum*':[9] instead of a mythological tale which sets out a positive and authoritative

---

[7] Citroni (1995: 431 ff.), Labate (1999).
[8] Labate (1999: 141 ff.).
[9] See Heldmann (2001: esp. 24 ff. for the excursus of the Sabine women); also Steudel (1992: 167 ff.), with a good bibliographical survey of previous work.

example, the didactic project conceived by the *praeceptor amoris* for the Sabine women episode is in effect a 'back to front' example, which contradicts the dynamics of his work. This is a good starting point, and it is from here that we will begin our analysis, drawing an 'ideological' map of the episode in question.

The excursus of the Sabine women, both in the description of the scene and in the events narrated, presents in an almost obsessive fashion a kind of leitmotiv, that of 'the absence of *ars*'.[10] The scene of the primitive theatre, which hosts the performance organized by Romulus, is a *scaena sine arte*, made of Palatine leaves *simpliciter positae* (1. 105). This spectacle corresponds to the model, reconstructed by scholars in Roman antiquity, of dramatic art in ancient Rome.[11] A dancer who strikes his foot on the floor three times accompanied by the rustic music of an Etruscan flautist is enough to sustain the enthusiasm of the public: the triple-rhythm dance, the dance of the Salii, evokes archaic and martial associations (1. 111–12 *rudem praebente modum tibicine Tusco | ludius aequatam ter pede pulsat humum*). The signal to commence the assault is given amid applause, although the poet feels the need to clarify that, in those times, the technique of applause did not yet exist (1. 113 *plausus tunc arte carebant*). When the young Romans yell as they pounce on the Sabine virgins, the women flee, terrified in the face of violent and uncontrolled virility (1. 119 *illae timuere uiros sine lege ruentes*).

Ars is not only the title of the poem: consistent with the title of the poem, it is also the dominant word (almost sixty occurrences) and lends support to the rich and varied semantic category that constitutes the cornerstone of the poem's ideology. This verbal constellation comprises, in addition to its own derivatives (*artifex, iners*), terms such as *sapere* (*sapientia, sapienter*), *cauere* (*cautus, caute*), *prudentia, doctrina* (*doctus, docte*), *calliditas* (*callidus*), *inuenta*. The master of love, *uates peritus*, thanks to the skills obtained through his experience, takes on the duty of *docere* and *erudire*, of transforming his *rudes* disciples into perfect *artifices*—capable of obtaining, through rules and technical procedures, the main object of this art. In the case of the

---

[10] See Myerowitz (1985: 64–5).
[11] See Brink (1962: 175 ff.), (1982: 179 ff.) (with bibliography).

Ars Amatoria, there is just one objective, which can be divided into three progressive stages: *reperire, exorare, ut duret amor.*

The technique that permits one to control and benefit from amorous relations between the sexes is presented as one of the fundamental elements of human 'civilization'.[12] The need to please and to conquer the other sex is for Ovid one of the many needs which (according to a rational and scientific concept of human progress) humanity has satisfied with the invention of arts. These arts progressively free humankind from the hard conditions of a primordial life exposed to the assaults of hostile Nature and to the violence of human intercourse based on misanthropy and the law of the jungle. The refinement of customs and lifestyles is made to appear a general and coherent process, which involves as much the spiritual aspects of life as the material ones.

With Ovidian *humanitas*, the gentleness of customs, respect for others, the courtesy and pleasantness of human relations, and the advantages of an organized and peaceful social life are inseparable not only from a corresponding development in education and culture, but also from the comforts that concern one's way of living and dressing, the care of one's person, and participation in social life, entertainment, and amusements.[13] The civilized world of the *Ars* presupposes the backdrop and resources of an affluent, modern capital city, with its inexhaustible supply of people and things, with its urban splendours, free from every basic need of an economic and political nature, open to the pleasure and elegance of *otium*. There is no need to recall the most famous passage of the poem, that eulogy to modernity which sets against the archaism of Augustan orthodoxy the ideals of *cultus*—a refinement inseparable from *ars*, because it is created with skill and care, with the exercise of choice, and a sense of opportunity and moderation.[14]

In the moment in which it finds its most complete achievement, in the book dedicated to women, the Ovidian ideal of *urbanitas* concerns itself with explicitly rejecting and disregarding, once and for all, the ideological model linked to the recollection of ancestral Rome, a

---

[12] Solodow (1977: 106 ff.).
[13] See Labate (1984).
[14] Watson (1982: 237 ff.), Myerowitz (1985: 56 ff.) On the presence of 'moderation' in Ovidian didactic poetry, see Gibson, Ch. 7 in this volume.

Rome of mud-huts, of animals, of primitive men, of natural spaces, and roughly hewn buildings. The comparison of ancient and modern Rome, stressed by the artfully mirror-like arrangement (appearing after approximately one hundred lines in both *Ars* 1, addressed to men, and *Ars* 3, addressed to women), appears as an explicit denial, if one still needs a denial, that the bellicose and peasant-like Rome of Romulus' time could provide a worthy model for the graceful Rome of Augustus:

> tunc neque marmoreo pendebant uela theatro,
>   nec fuerant liquido pulpita rubra croco,
> illic quas tulerant nemorosa Palatia frondes
>   simpliciter positae, scaena sine arte fuit;
> in gradibus sedit populus de caespite factis,
>   qualibet hirsutas fronde tegente comas. (*Ars* 1. 103–8)

(No awnings then hung over a marble theatre, nor was the platform ruddy with crocus-spray; there, artlessly arranged, were garlands which the leafy Palatine had borne, the stage was unadorned; the people sat on steps of turf, any chance leaves covering their unkempt hair.)

> simplicitas rudis ante fuit, nunc aurea Roma est
>   et domiti magnas possidet orbis opes.
> aspice, quae nunc sunt, Capitolia, quaeque fuerunt:
>   alterius dices illa fuisse Iouis.
> Curia consilio nunc est dignissima tanto,
>   de stipula Tatio regna tenente fuit;
> quae nunc sub Phoebo ducibusque Palatia fulgent,
>   quid nisi araturis pascua bubus erant? (*Ars* 3. 113–20)

(Formerly rustic simplicity existed, but now Rome is golden, and possesses the vast wealth of the conquered world. See what the Capitol is now, and what it was: you would say they belonged to different Jupiters. The senate-house is now most worthy of so great a council, but was, when Tatius held sway, made of wattles. The Palatine, where now Phoebus and our leaders are set in splendour, what was it except pasture for oxen destined for the plough?)

The idea of using one of the most venerable national legends as the origin and authority for the practices of elegant and sophisticated Rome presents itself, however, as a paradoxical and disconcerting oxymoron. Of the numerous reasons put forward for Ovid's choice of myth here—an inclination for amazing and disorientating the reader, a *reductio ad amorem* which provocatively affirms the right of the new cultural ideal to absorb all the consolidated cultural ideals of the Roman community,[15] parody of the forms and intentions of serious aetiological-didactic poetry,[16] irreverent revisiting of Augustan themes, pastoral Rome, and the Palatine hill,[17] demystification of the supposed moral soundness of our ancestors as a model for Augustan restoration of customs (and, in particular, the matrimonial customs of which the Sabine women were a symbol)[18]—none can be rejected as unjustified. But, in my opinion, none of them is fully satisfying.

One must reconsider one of the sources for Ovid's ideas, which can be traced back to a passage of Propertius (2. 6. 15–22):

> his olim, ut fama est, uitiis ad proelia uentum est:
>   his Troiana uides funera principiis.
> aspera Centauros eadem dementia iussit
>   frangere in aduersum pocula Pirithoum.
> cur exempla petam Graium? tu criminis auctor,
>   nutritus duro, Romule, lacte lupae.
> tu rapere intactas docuisti impune Sabinas,
>   per te nunc Romae quidlibet audet Amor.

(Those vices of old, the story goes, led to wars: from those origins arose the slaughter at Troy. The same frenzy bade the Centaurs hurl embossed goblets against Pirithous and break them upon his head. Why seek I precedents from Greece? You, Romulus, nursed on the harsh milk of a she-wolf, were the instigator of the crime: you taught us to rape the Sabine virgins with impunity: through your fault Cupid dares any outrage at Rome.)

According to the contradictory rhetoric of Propertian elegy, the elegiac lover assumes in his jealousy the role of moralist and longs for a golden age of feminine chastity in which faithfulness to a single lover is not compromised by the boldness of male suitors or by the fickleness of women. If the chastity of wives has its classical exemplars in Alcestis and Penelope, the audacity and effrontery of men is open to inspiration by the deceitfulness of Paris or the brutal violence of the Centaurs who assaulted Pirithous' wife on her wedding day. The

---

[15] See Solodow (1977: 112 ff.).
[16] See Durling (1958: 160); Effe (1977: 247); see also Pianezzola (1991) on *Ars* 1. 101–34.
[17] Hollis (1977: 52–3).
[18] Myerowitz (1985: 61 ff.).

affinity of this last *exemplum* with the national episode of the Sabine rape suggests the idea (topical in Roman morality) that the evils of the present have their genesis in the very foundation of the city. Just as ancestral fratricide forms the tragic *aition* of civil war, so the Sabine rape might be considered the origin of the sexual freedom within which elegiac love finds its home and its fulfilment—but the contradictions of which the poet-lover suffers, in his continuously frustrated hope of a stable, exclusive relationship based on *fides*.

It is clear that the Ovidian solution to this elegiac contradiction,[19] with his systematization of libertine love in which *fides* is not an unachievable ideal but is considered shameful (1. 644 *hac minus est una fraude pudenda fides*) and in which each person must play their part (1. 645 *fallite fallentes*), discourages every condemnation of Romulus as the *heuretes* of licentiousness and sexual freedom. However, notwithstanding the fact that the Ovidian excursus ends with clear praise for the founder, the *aition* of the Sabine women cannot be reused by the *praeceptor amoris* with a simple, provocative change to transform Propertian reproof into Ovidian approval. If the example set by Romulus is no longer liable to objection, then equally, in fact even more so, it becomes inappropriate for (as it were) technical and artistic reasons, since this *exemplum* profoundly contradicts the aim of his didactic poem. Paradoxically, Romulus can indeed be seen as *auctor* of the libertine behaviour deeply rooted in the modern city but, at the same time, he embodies a primitive world incapable of that cultural sophistication that the teacher of love presents to his pupils as the only form of civilization suited to the Augustan present.

Paraphrasing a Stoic maxim, mentioned by Lucian, Quintilian, and other ancient authors, τέχνη can be defined as 'a complex of knowledges exercised in combination for a purpose useful in life'.[20] It is not so much the achievement of the aim, but the way in which the aim is achieved—that is to say, the use of a procedure based on knowledge and, therefore, attainable by anyone who is able to understand the

---

[19] Labate (1984: 28 ff., 37 ff.).
[20] Lucian *Paras.* 4 τέχνη ἐστιν, ὡς ἐγὼ διαμνημονεύω σοφοῦ τινος ἀκούσας, σύστημα ἐκ καταλήψεων συγγεγυμνασμένων πρός τι τέλος εὔχρηστον τῷ βίῳ; Quint. 2. 17. 41 *siue ille ab omnibus fere probatus finis obseruatur, artem constare ex perceptionibus consentientibus et coexercitatis ad finem utilem uitae* (for more quotations, cf. *SVF* 1. 73).

instructions of the teacher—which characterizes τέχνη. Romulus does achieve his pragmatic objective of finding women for his soldiers, but his method is not 'artistic', and his means are too simplistic and direct. His methods are suitable perhaps for the pre-civilized world to which he belongs as a man 'nourished by the harsh milk of a she-wolf', a world utterly characterized by coarseness and an absence of *ars* (the leitmotiv of the Ovidian excursus), but not for the cultured, orderly, and refined world of Augustan Rome,[21] and even less so for a poem which aims to teach love as *ars*.

It is significant that Ovid repeatedly excludes from the ambit of his subject the means that might achieve the goal too easily—particularly those which depend on the possession of qualities not available to everyone, such as wealth and natural beauty:

> non ego diuitibus uenio praeceptor amandi,
>   nil opus est illi, qui dabit, arte mea.
> secum habet ingenium qui, cum libet, 'accipe' dicit,
>   cedimus, inuentis plus placet ille meis.   (*Ars* 2. 161–4)

(I come not to teach the rich to love: he who will give has no need of my art. He who when he pleases says 'accept' has a talent of his own, I give way, my devices will not please so much as he.)

> forma dei munus, forma quota quaeque superbit?
>   pars uestrum tali munere magna caret.
> cura dabit faciem...   (*Ars* 3. 103–5)

(Beauty is heaven's gift: how few can boast of beauty! A great part of you lack a gift so precious. Care will give good looks...)

> non mihi uenistis, Semele Ledeue, docendae,
>   perque fretum falso, Sidoni, uecta boue,
> aut Helene, quam non stulte, Menelae, reposcis,
>   tu quoque non stulte, Troice raptor, habes.
> turba docenda uenit, pulchrae turpesque puellae:
>   pluraque sunt semper deteriora bonis.
> formosae non artis opem praeceptaque quaerunt:
>   est illis sua dos, forma sine arte potens[22]   (*Ars* 3. 251–8)

---

[21] On the role of love as an idiosyncratic Roman cultural construction in Ovidian didactic poetry, see Volk, Ch. 12 in this volume.

[22] On this aspect, see Gibson (2003a: 25 n. 64) (see also nn. on 3. 253–4 and 258), who aptly underlines the distance between the 'normal' *puellae* of the *Ars* and the elegiac *domina*, whose beauty can compete with the heroines of the myth.

(You have not come to be taught by me, Semele and Leda, or you, Sidonian girl, borne on the false bull over the sea; or Helen, whom not foolishly, Menelaus, you demand back, and whom not foolishly, Trojan abductor, you keep. It is the crowd that come to be taught, women both fair and plain; and ever are the plain more numerous than the fair. The beautiful care not for precepts and the help of art; they have their dowry, beauty that is powerful without art.)

Furthermore, Ovid's instructions on love exclude even the possibility of using the methods of other *artes* (above all, the art of magic, not particularly elegant and also socially questionable[23]), methods that in the context of love might turn out to be ineffective, or perhaps, on the contrary, too effective. In other words, the objective is achieved through a short cut, which avoids the proper path of *sapientia*:[24]

> sunt quae praecipiant herbas, satureia, nocentes
>   sumere, iudiciis ista uenena meis.
> aut piper urticae mordacis semine miscent
>   tritaque in annoso flaua pyrethra mero.
> sed dea non patitur sic ad sua gaudia cogi,
>   colle sub umbroso quam tenet altus Eryx.
> docta, quid ad magicas, Erato, deuerteris artes?
>   interior curru meta terenda meo est.   (*Ars* 2. 415–20, 425–6)

(Some counsel the taking of savoury, noxious herb; it is poison, in my judgement. Or they mingle pepper with the seed of biting nettle, and yellow camomile ground up in old wine. But the goddess whom lofty Eryx holds upon his shady hill will not thus be driven to her joys.... Why turn, learned Erato, to magical arts? My chariot must graze the inner side of the turning point.)

> sic potius †tuos urget amor† quam fortibus herbis,
>   quas maga terribili subsecat arte manus:
> nec uos graminibus nec mixto credite suco
>   nec temptate nocens uirus amantis equae.   (*Medic.* 35–8)

(Thus rather [...] than by strong herbs, which the hand of the sorceress gathers as she plies her terrible craft. Do not trust grasses nor a mixture of juices, nor attempt the noxious venom of an infatuated mare.)

---

[23] Cf. *Ars* 2. 99 ff., 2. 415 ff.; *Rem.* 249 ff.
[24] Labate (1984: 119, 221).

I cannot say whether Francis Goodrich, Albert Hackett, and Dorothy Kingsley, authors of the screenplay for the musical *Seven Brides for Seven Brothers* (of which the film adaptation was a world-wide success in the 1950s and 1960s), ever read the *Ars Amatoria*.[25] I believe Ovid would have been amused to see in the plot of a musical the same contradiction between the excursus of the Sabine women and the subject of his didactic poem.

Seven brothers, lumberjacks by trade, live a solitary and primitive existence in a valley in Oregon. The eldest, Adam Pontipee, goes to the city and convinces Milly to marry him and to come with him back to the ranch. Only when she arrives does Milly find out that she has to make house for not just one man but seven—unless, of course, she can find wives for the other brothers. To solve this problem, Milly assumes the role of *praeceptor amoris* and decides to 'civilize' her uncultured brothers-in-law and to instruct them in the all-important art of pleasing women. Milly's *Ars Amatoria* ('knowing how to speak to girls', 'giving compliments', 'being a gentleman', 'demonstrating good manners', 'offering your arm', 'being gallant', 'learning to say "my sweetheart", "my darling", "my precious", "my love" ') culminates in a song significantly titled *Goin' courtin'*. Her pupils seem to benefit from these lessons and, at a barn-dance, could have been successful if they had not got into a fight with some suitors from the city, following which the Pontipees are outlawed and return home to their ranch utterly despondent. At this point, the 'feminine' solution of Milly, based on culture and a taught technique, is replaced by Adam's masculine and violent approach, which he devised after hearing the story of Romulus and the Sabine rape from his wife (who inherited from her father two books, the Bible and the *Lives* of Plutarch). On Adam's initiative and under his guidance, the brothers 'do as Romulus did with the Sabine women': they carry women off by force and are severely rebuked by an unwitting Milly ('aren't you ashamed of your behaviour? Don't you see, you're behaving like animals?'). The story then continues along the lines of the myth until the inevitable happy ending.

[25] The screenplay is an adaptation of a short story by Stephen Vincent Benét (written towards the end of the 1920s), playfully entitled *Sobbin' Women*, which, in turn, was based upon the story of the Sabine women as it is described in Plutarch's *Life of Romulus*.

Just as the logic of Milly, teacher of courtship and author of an *Ars Amatoria*, is opposed to the approach of Adam, or the new Romulus, so the method of Ovid's *Ars Amatoria* is clearly opposed to that of the *exemplum* that the poem aetiologically presents in its first excursus.

This is not the only puzzle that the reader of the *Ars* has to resolve. The ancient tradition of the Sabine rape is always associated with the *Consualia*,[26] the festival of the god Consus who oversees the storing of the harvest, and which was celebrated on two different dates in the religious calendar of the Romans (21 August and 15 December).[27] A subterranean altar in the Circus Maximus (*ad primas metas*), which remained underground all year and was only brought out for the *Consualia*, was dedicated to this god. The festivities comprised horseracing, which led people to identify Consus with *Poseidon hippios* (*Neptunus equestris*). Ovid himself, when he recalls in his *Fasti* the heroism of the Sabine women (who interpose themselves between their husbands and their armed parents) as the *aition* of the *Matronalia*, confirms this established view and indicates to the reader that the rape of the Sabine women will be examined in the part of his poem that deals with the festival of the *Consualia*.[28]

---

[26] Var. *L*. 6. 20. 5 *Consualia dicta a Conso, quod tum feriae publicae ei deo et in circo ad aram eius ab sacerdotibus ludi illi, quibus uirgines Sabinae raptae*; Liv. 1. 9. 6 ... *ad uim spectare res coepit. cui tempus locumque aptum ut daret Romulus ... ludos ex industria parat Neptuno equestri sollemnis, Consualia uocat*; Dion. Hal. 2. 30. 3 'After he had taken this resolution, he first made a vow to the god who presides over secret counsels to celebrate sacrifices and festivals every year if his enterprise should succeed. Then, having laid his plan before the senate and gaining their approval, he announced that he would hold a festival and general assemblage in honour of Neptune, and he sent word round about to the nearest cities, inviting all who wished to do so to be present at the assemblage and to take part in the contests'; 2. 31. 2 'And the Romans even to my day continued to celebrate the festival then instituted by Romulus, calling it the Consualia, in the course of which a subterranean altar, erected near the Circus Maximus, is uncovered by the removal of the soil round about it and honoured with sacrifices and burnt-offerings of first-fruits and a course is run both by horses yoked to chariots and by single horses. The god to whom these honours are paid is called Consus by the Romans, being the same, according to some who render the name into our tongue, as Poseidon Seisicthon or the "Earth-shaker" '; Plu. *Rom*. 14. 3; Tert. *Spect*. 5. 92; Serv. Dan. *ad Aen*. 8. 635; 8. 636.

[27] See Wissowa (1912: 201 ff.).

[28] Ov. *Fast*. 3. 199–200 *festa parat Conso. Consus tibi cetera dicet*, | *illa facta die dum sua sacra canet*.

The reader of the *Ars*, therefore, must have known that the rape of the Sabine women took place during the festival of Consus, that the spectacle staged by Romulus was *ludi circenses*, and that the location was in all likelihood the same *uallis Murcia* where the Circus Maximus was eventually situated. Just as many modern scholars have done, so must the ancient reader have questioned the reason for the novel changes introduced (and probably devised) by Ovid in the *Ars*: no mention of Consus, *ludi scaenici* instead of horseracing, and a primitive and rustic theatre as the setting instead of the Circus Maximus (even though his mention of *nemorosa Palatia* might have been intended to evoke the traditional *uallis Murcia*).

The answers to these inevitable questions have been found (starting with the article by Wardman and subsequently reworked a number of times[29]) in Ovid's intentional exposure of the moralizing pretensions of Augustan ideology and politics and, in particular, critique of the decree that consigned the female public to the back rows of the *cauea*. The Sabine Rape perhaps demonstrates that the theatre and its corrupting influence was not a Greek importation (the view of the traditionalists), but was rooted in the genetic make-up of Rome and that, therefore, the segregation of the sexes was an utterly ineffectual measure. This provocative attitude seems to be clearly confirmed in the final line which praises Romulus as the only person capable of giving *praemia* to his soldiers, and assuring them of 'fringe benefits'—in order to convince even the most reluctant recruits (such as the poet of the *Amores*). This is a jest that would have amused many people, even if it would probably not have been greatly appreciated by a leader who had in fact to deal with the thorny problem of keeping veterans and recruits happy.[30]

I am not convinced by this point (or many others), not only because this type of explanation seems rather strained, as in the example of Wardman, but, above all, because this interpretation fails to delve beneath the surface of the text (a text whose *urbanitas* undoubtedly does offer a series of pungent witticisms at the expense

---

[29] Wardman (1965: 101 ff.), cf. Myerowitz (1985: 64); Steudel (1992: 169 n. 268).

[30] Cf. Petersen (1961: 446); Pianezzola (1999: 24); according to Withehorn (1979: 157–8), the polemical reference would be quite clear for it evokes the prohibition of marriage for soldiers (introduced by Augustus?). See also Hollis and Pianezzola ad loc.

of contemporary social and political events).³¹ Likewise, finding the key to Ovid's intent in parody (of didactic poems or of aetiological poetry) fails to penetrate the surface. Rather, I believe one must look for answers that link Ovidian innovation to the deeper structure of the poem.

One must observe, first of all, that by taking the decision to offer a witty episode about Roman antiquities which recalls a legend staged in the context of a spectacle, the theatre stakes its claim to being the means par excellence by which to represent the world of primitive Rome. This is either because, from the urban perspective, the theatre was the most representative marvel of the splendour and luxury of contemporary times and this invited recollection of its primitive counterpart,³² or because antiquarians concentrated their research on ancient forms of dramatic art and entertainment. It is significant that Ovid manages to condense the *locus classicus* of Livy on the origin of theatre, which in its turn was based on the writings of Varro, and that he exhibits other antiquarian skills including a probable allusion to the etymology (perhaps Varronian?) of *scaena* from the Greek σκία: *illic qua tulerant nemorosa Palatia frondes | simpliciter positae scaena sine arte fuit.*³³

More relevant, in my view, is the different organization of seating in the *circus* (where promiscuity was allowed) and theatre (where the female public had a reserved area). As elegy 3. 2 of the *Amores* had already shown, the *lex loci* of the *circus*, which allowed a man to sit next to an unknown woman, was an almost unique occasion for paying a wide range of flattering attentions to the beloved, but also for the most powerful and time-honoured means of persuasion: the spoken word (cf. *Ars.* 1. 459 ff. *disce bonas artes, moneo, Romana iuuentus...*).

In the structure of the first book of the *Ars*, the arrangement of the material reflects the two phases of *reperire* (1. 41–262) and *exorare*

---

[31] One can find an example of this approach (less superficial, but, in my view, still unsatisfactory) in Casali's subversive interpretation, in Ch. 11 of this volume, of the passage of 'propaganda' in *Ars* 1 for the triumph of Gaius Caesar.

[32] *Ars* 1. 103–4 *tunc neque marmoreo pendebant uela theatro, | nec fuerant liquido pulpita rubra croco*, Prop. 4. 1. 15–16 *nec sinuosa cauo pendebant uela theatro, | pulpita sollemnes non oluere croco*; cf. Lucr. 4. 75 ff.

[33] Cf. Serv. ad *Aen.* 1. 164 *et dicta scena* ἀπὸ τῆς σκιᾶς: *apud antiquos enim theatralis scena parietem non habebat, sed de frondibus umbracula quaerebant*; see Merkel (1841: CLXII); but see also Cardauns (1976: 179).

puellam (1. 263–770), a distinction that is clear from a logical and theoretical point of view, but in practice is not easily maintained, as the period of courting is inevitably intertwined with a period of persuasion.[34] A suitor frequents those places where he is most likely to find a *puella* and, once he finds her, he starts to put into operation his seduction strategies. The *praeceptor amoris*, for his part, shows his pupils those places suitable for *inuentio*, but at the same time as pointing out the places in Rome best for courting, he starts to provide the first hints on seduction techniques. If an obstacle makes the suitor's approaches difficult, then smooth progress from *inuenire* to *exorare* is impeded and the suitor must find a more subtle and elaborate method of courting for that occasion.

If one looks at the thematic structure of the section on *inuentio*, one notes that Ovid starts with subsections in which the women can be merely seen and singled out (promenades, temples, and forum: 1. 67–88, theatre: 1. 89–134). These are followed by subsections devoted to approaching and, at the same time, courting the beloved (in the *circus*, during the gladiatorial shows or triumphs), which act as a 'bridge' to the next section on *exorare*.

The *circus*, in which women are immediately accessible to men, is used by Ovid, therefore, to show how to begin the conquest of a woman from the moment you meet her, whilst the theatre is more suitable for illustrating a different process, in which an immediate approach is impossible and a more patient and complicated strategy is called for, made up of a gradual series of manoeuvres. It is only at the end of this skilful operation, which the teacher will illustrate in detail in the sections focused on *exorare*, that the suitor will actually make contact with the woman and have the possibility of speaking to her directly (1. 607 ff. *conloquii iam tempus adest* etc.). The fortunate spectator at the *circus*, however, has the benefit of this contact at once.

By situating the Sabine Rape in the theatre, rather than in the *circus*, Ovid (in addition to safeguarding this peculiarity of the *circus* already brilliantly employed in the *Amores*) gives prominence— through the paradox of an 'anti-exemplum'—to this 'need for *ars*' to which his didactic poetry is systematically impelled to respond.

---

[34] On the differentiation and overlapping of structural themes in Ovidian didactic poetry, see the excellent observations in Gibson (2003a: 3 ff.).

Romulus instructed his soldiers to conquer the women through straightforward violence. This epitomizes a *feritas* and *rusticitas* commensurate with the cultural level of Romulus' primitive Rome, but is quite unsuitable for the times of the new *pater patriae*. It is this same *feritas* which the teacher of love succeeds in domesticating and bringing firmly within the bounds of civilization (as Chiron did with Achilles, that symbol of warlike strength):

> Phillyrides puerum cithara perfecit Achillem
>   atque animos placida contudit arte feros.
>
> Aeacidae Chiron, ego sum praeceptor Amoris;
>   saeuus uterque puer, natus uterque dea   (*Ars* 1. 11–12, 17–18)

(The son of Philyra made the boy Achilles accomplished on the lyre, and by his peaceful art subdued those savage passions.... Chiron taught Aeacides, I am Love's teacher: a fierce lad each, and each born of a goddess.)

The *Ars Amatoria* portrays itself as the perfection of the process of civilization and refinement of customs that reaches its apex in the Augustan city and distances humankind from its origins, when the law of the jungle governed a world bound by its basic instincts (food, clothing, survival, reproduction). The Romulus of legend was too close to the brutality of the caveman, whom Lucretius imagined as little inclined to the complexities of courting (5. 962–5):

> et Venus in siluis iungebat corpora amantum,
> conciliabat enim uel mutua quamque cupido
> uel uiolenta uiri uis atque impensa libido
> uel pretium, glandes atque arbita uel pira lecta.

(And Venus joined the bodies of lovers in the woods; for either the woman was attracted by mutual desire, or caught by the man's violent force and vehement lust, or by a bribe—acorns and arbute berries or choice pears.)

In the age of *humanitas*, the ancestral legend of the Sabine Rape could not be evoked without embarrassment, because the *subagreste consilium* of Romulus (Cic. *Rep.* 2, 12) seemed to link Roman identity with a model too coarse and unruly. In fact, almost all the versions that have come to us (before this myth was used by Christian writers in their indictments of pagan culture and religion) are marked, to varying degrees, by an apologetic tone.

There is no suggestion of this in Ovid. The *praeceptor amoris* is silent about all the motivations and political strategies that influenced Romulus to choose violence (therefore obscuring any mitigating circumstances for actions).[35] The assault by the Romans is described as an ambush by barbarian-like warriors. When the king suddenly gives the signal,[36] the soldiers spring up howling and rush towards their prey (it is no coincidence that Ovid, alongside his starting point in Propertius, echoes these scenes in the *Metamorphoses* when describing the assault by the Centaurs of the Lapith women):

> protinus exiliunt animum clamore fatentes
> uirginibus cupidas iniciuntque manus   (*Ars* 1. 115–16)

(Straightway they leap forth, by their shouts betraying their eagerness, and lay lustful hands upon the maidens.)

> protinus euersae turbant conuiuia mensae,
> raptaturque comis per uim noua nupta prehensis.
> Euritus Hippodamen, alii quam quisque probabant
> aut poterant, rapiunt, captaeque erat urbis imago.   (*Met.* 12. 222–5)

(Straightway the tables were overturned and the banquet in an uproar, and the bride was caught by her hair and dragged violently away. Euritus caught up Hippodame, and others—each took one for himself as he fancied or as he could, and the scene looked like the sacking of a town.)

The brutality of the soldiers is slightly mitigated by the words of comfort uttered to their victims after the attack:

---

[35] Cf. e.g. Liv. 1. 9. 1–5; Dion. Hal. 2. 30. 1–2; Plut. *Rom.* 14. 1–2; Serv. Dan. ad *Aen.* 8. 635. A brief mention in Myerowitz (1985: 65–6, 71).

[36] *Ars* 1. 114 *rex populo praedae signa* †*petenda*† *dedit*. Kenney (1959: 242–3) discusses the text and the different corrections, although he prefers to print *petenda* with the cruces of *locus desperatus*. The conjecture of *petita* suggested by Bentley and Madvig is picked up and given new explanation by Goold (1965: 60–1). Avery (1974) suggests an unlikely *pudenda*. In my view, one should consider more carefully the emendation of *repente*—already pointed out by Burman and endorsed by Delz (1971: 52–3)—by observing a suggestive parallel with Verg. *A.* 5. 315–16 *haec ubi dicta, locum capiunt signoque repente | corripiunt spatia audito*. Just like the Vergilian athletes, so for the soldiers of Romulus the expected signal arrives suddenly, for they know it must arrive but do not know when. One might have expected the latter to act during the applause when the spectators are distracted, but in that 'primitive' time the reaction of the public was not regulated by the technique of clapping (*plausus tunc arte carebant*), and therefore the applause took place unexpectedly and unpredictably.

atque ita 'quid teneros lacrimis corrumpis ocellos?
quod matri pater est, hoc tibi' dixit 'ero'. (*Ars* 1. 129–30)

(And said 'Why do you spoil those tender eyes with tears? What your father is to your mother, that will I be to you.')

After this almost promising start, perhaps not unworthy of Catullus and his preoccupation with the eyes of Lesbia (3. 17–18 *tua nunc opera meae puellae | flendo turgiduli rubent ocelli*), the erotic eloquence of the abductors reveals its shortcomings. 'I will be to you what your father is to your mother' is the expression, within the limits of a rudimentary rhetoric, of a reassurance in respect of the women's future matrimonial status which is found in various versions of the episode.[37] However, the readers of Livy were acquainted with Romans who were more capable not only of speaking good sense, but also of appealing to the feelings and vanity of the women whom they had conquered by force, in order to win them over with words. The Romulus of Livy seeks to recall the pathos of one of the archetypes of matrimonial love, the dialogue between Hector and Andromache at the Scaean Gates:[38]

mollirent modo iras et, quibus fors corpora dedisset, darent animos. saepe ex iniuria postmodum gratiam ortam, eoque melioribus usuras uiris, quod adnisurus pro se quisque sit, ut, cum suam uicem functus officio sit, parentium etiam patriaeque expleat desiderium (Liv. 1. 9. 15)

(Only let them moderate their anger and give their hearts to those whom fortune had given their persons. A sense of injury had often given place to affection, and they would find their husbands the kinder for this reason, that every man would earnestly endeavour not only to be a good husband, but also to console his wife for the home and parents she had lost.)

Ἕκτορ ἀτὰρ σύ μοί ἐσσι πατὴρ καὶ πότνια μήτηρ
ἠδὲ κασίγνητος, σὺ δέ μοι θαλερὸς παρακοίτης (*Iliad* 6. 429–30)

(Hector, you are to me father and queenly mother, you are brother and you are my vigorous husband.)

---

[37] Dion Hal. 2. 30. 5 'The next day, when the virgins were brought before Romulus, he comforted them in their despair with the assurance that they had been seized, not out of wantonness, but for the purpose of marriage'; Liv. 1. 9. 14 *illas tamen in matrimonio, in societate fortunarum omnium ciuitatisque et quo nihil carius humano generi sit liberum fore.*

[38] See Ogilvie (1965: 70 ad loc.).

Romulus' soldiers, meanwhile, know how to flatter women speaking to them of love and desire:

accedebant blanditiae uirorum factum purgantium cupiditate atque amore, quae maxime ad muliebre ingenium efficaces preces sunt. (Liv. 1.9.16)
(His arguments were seconded by the wooing of the men, who excused their act on the score of passion and love, the most moving of all pleas to a woman's heart.)

Ovid has deliberately portrayed Romulus and his soldiers as falling far short of this standard in order to highlight the distance between the coarse ancestors and their descendants, the Augustan youth whom only the *praeceptor amoris* will perfect in the art of conquering women. I believe that this intention fits with a further inference, which can be drawn from the moving of the episode from the *circus* to the theatre, and from the consequent elimination of all mention of the *Consualia*. The ancient tradition connected the name of Consus with the idea of *consilium* (in particular, *consilia* which were kept hidden, like the altar of the god) and, in this case, with the secret plan concocted and then put into practice.[39] Ovid, on the contrary, wanted to describe the event as an act of force, setting aside the aspects of astuteness, shrewdness, and strategy, which rendered the *consilium* of Romulus too close to the idea of rationality and technique.

In conclusion: the *aition* of the Sabine Rape presents an *exemplum* which acts, in reality, as an anti-*exemplum*. Heldmann has noted that something similar occurs in *Am.* 1. 3, at the beginning of the

---

[39] Paul. Fest. 36 L. *Consualia: ludi dicebantur, quos in honorem Consi faciebant, quem deum consilii putabant*; Aug. *C.D.* 4. 11 *et deus Consus praebendo consilia*; Arnob. 3. 23 *salutaria et fida consilia nostris suggerit Consus*; Serv. Dan. *ad Aen.* 8. 636 *Consus autem deus est consiliorum, qui ideo templum sub circo habet, ut ostendatur tectum esse debere consilium... ideo autem dicato Consi simulacro rapuerunt Sabinas, ut tegeretur initum de rapto consilium*; Dion Hal. 2. 31. 2–3 'The god to whom these honours are paid is called Consus by the Romans, being the same, according to some who render the name into our tongue, as Poseidon Seisichthon or the "Earth-shaker"; and they say that this god was honoured with a subterranean altar because he holds the earth. I know also from hearsay another tradition, to the effect that the festival is indeed celebrated in honour of Neptune and the horse-races are held in his honour, but that the subterranean altar was erected later to a certain divinity whose name may not be uttered, who presides over and is guardian of hidden counsels'; Plu. *Rom.* 14. 3–4; Tert. *Spect.* 5. 92.

collection, where the poet presents his credentials as a passionate, elegiac lover, servant of love, and champion of *fides*, whilst the exempla which identify him with the *desultor amoris* of myth—Jupiter the capricious lover of Juno, Leda, and Europa—plainly cast doubt on his trustworthiness.[40]

However, the example of the Sabine Rape is exactly the reverse. The exempla in *Am.* 1. 3 contradict the immediate context, but fit with the overall intention of the collection. The *exemplum* of the Sabine Rape is congruous with the immediate context (Ovid focuses on the time and place of the conquest of women rather than on the means employed), but presents a cultural model contrary to that which forms the basis of erotic didactics. The contrast of the anti-*exemplum*, therefore, serves to highlight the instructions of the teacher.

Just like the soldiers of Romulus, the pupils of Ovid will frequent the theatres and other places of entertainment as propitious venues for finding women and for singling out the most attractive ones. The city of the emperor, with its three splendid theatres and with ceremonies and spectacles that attract people from all over the globe, has no need to envy the city of the founder. However, faced with difficulties of access to their prey, Ovid's pupils will become acquainted with the 'artistic' or 'civil' procedures of *exorare* (*Ars* 1. 266 *praecipuae... artis opus*). In addition to a number of preliminary methods (mediation by maidservant, epistolary approaches), refined manoeuvres of courtship are possible through a language made up of looks, gestures, and significant signals, even in those places of the *inuentio* where direct approaches are not permitted. In particular, in 1. 497–504, the *praeceptor amoris* 'revisits' the place of the Sabine Rape to show how one ought to act in the age of *cultus* and *urbanitas*:

> nec sine te curuo sedeat speciosa theatro:
> quod spectes, umeris adferet illa suis.
> illam respicias, illam mirere licebit,
> multa supercilio, multa loquare notis,
> et plaudas aliquam mimo saltante puellam,
> et faueas illi, quisquis agatur amans.
> cum surgit, surges, donec sedet illa, sedebis:
> arbitrio dominae tempora perde tuae.

---

[40] Heldmann (2001: 12 ff.).

(Nor let her sit in the round theatre, her fair looks by you unheeded; something worth looking at she will bring on her shoulders. On her you may turn your looks, her you may admire; much let your eyebrows, much let your gestures say. Applaud when an actor portrays some woman in his dance, and favour whoever be the lover that is played. When she rises you will rise; while she sits you will sit too; waste time at your mistress' will.)

In the process of civilization, which must free love from all trace of coarseness and primitiveness, the acts that lead to the possession of the desired object are ritualized and seen metaphorically.[41] The women will continue to be *praeda*, courting will remain a hunt or conquest, the theatres will continue to be places of *insidiae*. However, through *ars*, these words will loose the brutality of their proper sense and gain the refinement of metaphor. As the crowning achievement of this didactic project, even violence will be redeemed (at least from a tenaciously masculine point of view) as a kind of ritual between the sexes. After having carried out all the instructions of the teacher, the suitor will be able to, in fact will have to, overcome (but with a violence that is always controlled by *ars*) a feminine resistance that is portrayed as a necessary part of the game:[42]

> quis sapiens blandis non misceat oscula uerbis?
>   illa licet non det, non data sume tamen.
> pugnabit primo fortassis et 'improbe' dicet;
>   pugnando uinci se tamen illa uolet.
> tantum, ne noceant teneris male rapta labellis
>   neue queri possit dura fuisse, caue.
> oscula qui sumpsit, si non et cetera sumit,
>   haec quoque, quae data sunt, perdere dignus erit.
> quantum defuerat pleno post oscula uoto?
>   ei mihi, rusticitas, non pudor ille fuit.
> uim licet appelles: grata est uis ista puellis;
>   quod iuuat, inuitae saepe dedisse uolunt.   (*Ars* 1. 663–74)

(Who that is wise would not mingle kisses with coaxing words? Though she give them not, yet take the kisses she does not give. Perhaps she will struggle at first, and cry 'you villain!', yet she will wish to be beaten in the struggle. Only beware lest snatching them rudely you hurt her tender lips, and she be

---

[41] In Sharrock, Ch. 2 in this volume, the 'romanticization of force' is recognized as the leitmotiv of the first book of the *Ars*.
[42] Myerowitz (1985: 67 ff.).

able to complain of your roughness. He who has taken kisses, if he take not the rest beside, will deserve to lose even what was granted. After kisses how much was lacking to your vow's fulfilment? Ah, that was awkwardness, not modesty. You may use force; women like you to use it; they often wish to give unwillingly what they are willing to give.)

The *exemplum* that confirms and seals this 'artistic' use of violence is found in Greek myths rather than Roman legends. Achilles takes by force the hardly reluctant Deidameia.[43] The positive model for the Ovidian lover will not be, therefore, a hairy and primitive soldier of Romulus, but Achilles, the warrior hero who, dressed as a woman, found himself handling wool, baskets, and spindles, instead of the Pelian spear, the boy who, domesticated and civilized by Chiron, learnt to play the lyre.

---

[43] Sharrock, Ch. 2 in this volume, draws attention to the 'narrative' continuity of the digressions in Ovidian didactic poetry.

11

The Art of Making Oneself Hated: Rethinking (Anti-)Augustanism in Ovid's *Ars Amatoria*

Sergio Casali

My subtitle implies that I want to strike a balance, or to discuss the question of the Augustanism/anti-Augustanism of the *Ars* from a theoretical point of view. In fact, I won't be doing that. The 'Augustan' side of the question has been treated in the best possible way by Mario Labate in his book *L'arte di farsi amare*,[1] the 'anti-Augustan' side by Alison Sharrock, particularly in her article on 'Ovid and the Politics of Reading',[2] and the 'aporetic' side by Duncan Kennedy and Alessandro Barchiesi.[3] I couldn't do it better. So, the first part of my title is more relevant for my chapter. It makes fairly clear, I think, my predilection for a good old anti-Augustan approach to Ovid. 'The Art of Making Oneself Hated' naively alludes to the irony of a book that, proposing to teach Romans how to love and be loved, in fact achieved the result of winning for its author the implacable hatred of the most important Roman of all—at least according to

---

I wish to thank Roy Gibson, Steven Green, and Alison Sharrock, for many valuable comments and criticisms. Thanks also to Alessandro Barchiesi, Niklas Holzberg, Mario Labate, Costanza Mastroiacovo, and Fabio Stok.

[1] Labate (1984). His approach is restated in his contribution to the present volume. Gibson (2003a: 22–3, 33–5) is an interesting revision of Ovidian 'moderation' as an anti-Augustan (not a label he uses) attitude (Labate: Augustus and Ovid *share* moderation; Gibson: Ovid's sexual moderation *contrasts* with Augustan rigidity).

[2] Sharrock (1994b).

[3] Kennedy (1992); Barchiesi (1994 = 1997) and (1993 = 2001).

Ovid's construction of his own relationship with the imperial power. Obviously it also alludes to Mario Labate's fundamental study: I hope that my irreverence will not have the same effect as Ovid's.

THE OBSESSION WITH 'HIDDEN MEANING' AND AUGUSTUS AS AN ANTI-AUGUSTAN READER

'Now you're really getting paranoid.'
'The question is not whether I am paranoid, but whether I am paranoid *enough*.'[4]

'Augustan' readings of the *Ars* tend to deplore above all two interpretative attitudes that are usually closely related with each other. On the one hand, that it is wrong to have that 'almost neurotic suspiciousness', that 'obsession with hidden meaning' which pervades anti-Augustan readings. On the other hand, it is equally wrong that 'the later events—which are for the most part obscure—in the poet's life should interfere so heavily in the attempt to decipher the cultural expectations, proposals, and literary practice of Ovidian elegy'.[5]

The results of this 'almost neurotic suspiciousness' on the part of the interpreter and of the interference from what is known of Ovid's life in his relationship with imperial power are a straining of the text—reading in more than is written, over-interpreting, and misunderstanding.[6] In the case of Ovid, however, things are a bit complicated. Duncan Kennedy, in his article on 'Augustanism' and 'anti-Augustanism', rightly says that: 'The degree to which a voice is heard as conflicting or supportive is a function of the audience's—or critic's—ideology, a function, therefore, of reception.'[7] So, what happens when it is the author himself who gives us information about the qualities of 'conflict' and 'support' in his own work? If we say that the poet's life ought not to interfere in the interpretation

---

[4] *Strange Days* (1995), directed by Kathryn Bigelow, screenplay by James Cameron and Jay Cocks.
[5] Labate (1984: 14–15 and 36).
[6] On the practice of a 'suspicious reading' see Eco (1990: esp. 86–99).
[7] Kennedy (1992: 41).

of his work, it seems that we are acting sensibly; we need to read texts, not the biographies of authors. But in Ovid's case it is *other texts* by the same author which tells us quite explicitly about the reception of his earlier texts. Ovid *tells us* about the anti-Augustan reception of his work—by Augustus himself—and so he himself shapes his own reception.[8] When we allow his conflict with Augustus (which is biographical only in so far as Ovid *tells us* it is biographical)[9] to interfere with our reading, and when we take up an attitude of almost neurotic suspiciousness in reading the *Ars*, we are displaying docile obedience to the reception of the *Ars* in the terms prescribed by Ovid.

Now, it is by no means clear that we should display such docile obedience. What I mean is that we ought to be aware that if, under the influence of a laudable desire not to betray the 'author's intention', we abstain from 'forcing' the *Ars*, we will find ourselves in the position of having to 'force' the interpretative response that the author himself has constructed for us. Ovid wrote the *Ars*, and then he devoted the rest of his poetic career, starting from the sequel itself of the *Ars*, the *Remedia* (see below), to constructing that poem as a poem that has excited Augustus' anger. Looking for the anti-Augustan elements in the *Ars* is the strategy of reading that the poet prescribes to his Model Reader.[10] The reader can find anti-Augustan elements in the *Ars*, if s/he wants, but in a sense, paradoxically, Ovid's textual/political strategy might be seen as even more interesting if the reader does *not* find (chooses not to find) anti-Augustan elements in the *Ars*. For what happens if the *Ars* appears to be a loyal and collaborative Augustan work, but the poet himself says that, on the contrary, a very special reader such as Augustus himself finds it anti-Augustan enough to exile Ovid for having written it? An 'Augustan' reader of the *Ars* must read it in a way opposite to that which (Ovid says that) Augustus read it; an anti-Augustan reader, conversely, has to identify himself with Augustus when s/he finds Ovid's poem

---

[8] The point is nicely made by B. Gibson (1999: 19).

[9] In other words, the biographical or historical 'fact' of Augustus' negative reaction to the *Ars*, and the issue of how much the *Ars* actually contributed to Ovid's banishment (itself not a 'fact', but a discourse constructed by the poet: a textual fact, not a historical one—something true even if we do believe that Ovid really was banished to Tomi) are not really relevant.

[10] Cf. Nugent (1990: 240–1).

outrageous. Ovid constructs Augustus as the first anti-Augustan reader of the *Ars*.[11]

When people speak of 'later events in Ovid's life', they are usually thinking of his exile, and the exilic works, especially *Tristia* 2, as testimony to these events. In fact, however, as regards the *Ars*, we do not have to go so far, chronologically and otherwise, in order to get some information from Ovid on how we might be justified in imagining an 'Augustan' reception of the *Ars*.

Ovid's representation of an Augustan attack on the *Ars* does not wait until AD 8. It is absolutely immediate, almost contemporaneous with the publication of the *Ars*. In fact Ovid describes an 'Augustan' attack in the central digression of the *Remedia*, the work which is an integral part of the amatory cycle, and which is usually dated to AD 2, more or less contemporaneous with the publication of the final version of the *Ars* in three books. In *Rem.* 361–96, Ovid makes a violent attack on the detractors of his *Ars*. They are not named: in 361 he speaks of 'some people' (*quidam*), according to whom Ovid's work is *proterua*. In 364 it is 'one or two people' (*unus et alter*) who attack his work. A little later, however, the detractor becomes a single individual, who is offended, or hurt, by the poet's *licentia* (371–2). Finally, Ovid addresses *Livor edax*, that is, obviously, his jealous detractor: *rumpere, Liuor edax*... (389–92). Even Augustan readings willingly concede to the poet of the *Ars* a tone here of 'playful aggression' towards Augustan power; I think that it can be taken for granted that addressing the *princeps* in these terms ('burst, envious one') is a mode of joking that is decidedly over the top. These lines expose with impressive lucidity Ovid's project of constructing his poetic career as a constant pain in Augustus' neck. It has been rightly noticed that in this digression Ovid is creating an intertextual parallel to the proem of *Georgics* 3.[12] Just as Vergil there announced his future Augustan poetic career, so here Ovid both starts the construction of his past poetic production as anti-Augustan, and announces his future anti-Augustan career: Vergil, *modo uita supersit* (*Georg.* 3. 10), will erect a temple on the banks of the Mincius, and

---

[11] On Augustus as the ideal anti-Augustan reader in *Tristia* 2, see Barchiesi (1993 = 2001), to which I am much indebted.

[12] See Woytek (2000: 192–9); also Holzberg, Ch. 3 in this volume.

Caesar will be in the middle of it; Ovid's poetic projects do include Caesar as well, but in a very different way: *uiuam modo, plura dolebis*.[13]

When Ovid says *uiuam modo*, it is as if he were challenging Augustus to have him murdered: 'if only I continue to live', if no one murders me.[14] One might wonder whether Ovid is not alluding to this prophetic passage in the *Remedia* when he closes his *Metamorphoses* by making anew the promise (or the menace) of continuing to live: *siquid habent ueri uatum praesagia, uiuam* (*Met.* 15. 879).[15]

I have taken it for granted that the unnamed detractor is Augustus. But naturally, he is *not* Augustus. He is not named. They are 'some people', they are 'one or two people', it is someone unknown. *uiuam modo* is a topos of the promise of future glory, etc. I would like to consider this attitude for a moment. These 'some people' who ferociously criticize the *libelli* of Ovid are the 'censors': *quidam...,* | *quorum censura Musa proterua mea est*. Everything encourages us to see here a reference to the anger of Augustus; the thunderbolt of Jupiter is the standard image in the exile poetry for Augustus' anger (we are talking about sixty occurrences in fifty elegies in the *Tristia*), and in any case 'Jupiter with thunderbolts' *is* Augustus in Augustan poetry. It was not invented by Ovid in the *Tristia*.[16] Geisler is right and honest to note on *Rem.* 370: '*fulmina... Iouis:* testimony first of

---

[13] The *Remedia* digression does not affect only the reception of the *Ars*. By representing *Liuor edax* as attacking his previous work on moral and political grounds (*Rem.* 385–6 is explicit on this: it is not a matter of literary tastes), Ovid extends the revision of his poetic production as under imperial attack even to the *Amores*: *Rem.* 389 continues a dialogue with *Liuor edax* started in *Amores* 1. 15. 1. Ovid wants to construct himself as a victim of political persecution since the very beginning of his career.

[14] The phrase *uiuam modo* recurs for the second (and last) time in Ovid's work at *Tristia* 4. 4. 47 in explicit connection with Augustus' hatred of him. In the exilic works, Ovid connects the continuation of his life, expressed by *uiuam*, to Augustus' mercy: *Tr.* 1. 1. 20. Ovid's careful construction of the image of himself as constantly threatened with death by the emperor is underlined by the thread connecting *uiuam* at the close of *Am.* 1. 15, with *uiuam* in the middle of *Remedia*, and with *uiuam* at the end of *Metamorphoses*.

[15] Notice that a few lines earlier, immediately after having lingered on the idea of Augustus' death and apotheosis (*Met.* 15. 868–70), Ovid has claimed that his work *nec Iouis ira nec ignis* | *nec poterit ferrum nec edax abolere uetustas* (15. 871–2). The 'wrath and fire' of Jupiter suggest imperial persecution; a 'sword' (*ferrum*) is quite a strange weapon to be used against a book (more appropriately against a poet); and *edax* recalls *Liuor edax* of *Am.* 1. 15. 1 and *Rem.* 389.

[16] References e.g. in Nisbet and Hubbard (1970: 164–6); Galasso (1995: 152–3).

the jealousy of the gods, this is however at the same time a cautious allusion to the anger of Augustus'.[17]

Holzberg's chapter in this volume mounts a very detailed case for *not* reading Augustus as the unnamed critic. Furthermore, he argues that the passage is a staged reader response to Ovid's poetry, rather like the response of Furius and Aurelius to Catullus' poetry, and that, in both cases, an opportunity for self-promotion (and further obscenity) follows. I totally agree that the passage is 'a staged reader response, designed by Ovid as a marketing strategy'—but the point is that the reader whose response is staged by Ovid is Augustus. Saying that the detractor is Augustus does not necessarily mean that Ovid is answering 'to concrete criticism brought forward against him in real life'. Ovid is staging the response of a particular reader, Augustus.

By staging the response of Augustus-the-reader, Ovid is at the same time constructing another figure of reader, his suspicious and paranoid reader. Immediately before addressing Augustus-the-reader, Ovid has addressed his Model Reader. In the verse immediately preceding the polemical digression, Ovid has advised as a remedy for love going to visit the woman while she is putting on make-up: the disgusting smells will turn the lover's stomach (351–6). After this, Ovid announces another cure: 'attitudes to maintain while making love' (357–8). At this point Ovid asserts: 'many of these things I am ashamed to say, but you, with your understanding, will take away more than I say' (*ingenio uerbis concipe plura meis*, 359–60). As Alessandro Barchiesi (1993: 175 = 2001: 97) says, when the subject is sex, the reader is invited to invent for himself more than is said; ergo, construction of a lascivious reader. Right. But I would say that there is also another implication of the greatest importance. The 'precept' *ingenio uerbis concipe plura meis* does not in fact introduce the licentious and lascivious discussion of sex, but rather the polemical digression in which Ovid attacks unnamed detractors, censors, thunderbolt-hurlers, who look suspiciously like Augustus; but in order to say that they are Augustus we would need precisely

---

[17] Geisler (1969: ad loc.) Cf. also Henderson (1979: 88). On the identification of the unnamed detractor with Augustus see now especially Woytek (2000: 201–9).

something that is not in the text, a name, an addition, a supplement—it would involve *ingenio plura concipere*.[18] Not just the construction of a lascivious reader, then, but the construction of a suspicious reader, who is obsessed with hidden meaning, a reader of a *Musa proterua*—not only 'lascivious', but 'aggressive towards authority'[19]—in the only way one can do that under a tyrant, namely in a very disguised manner.

THE PARTHIAN EXPEDITION OF GAIUS CAESAR

I would now like to take a look at the most literally 'Augustan' part of the *Ars*, to which Ovid, it seems, draws attention in *Tristia* 2. 61–2, when, in addressing the *princeps*, he makes claims about the importance of the directly panegyric elements even in the work which constitutes his crime: even the *Ars* is 'filled with your name in a thousand places'. Now, the Ovidian reader who reads this can do only one thing: straightaway go and count up the number of times Augustus' name appears in the *Ars*, to see if it really is a myriad of places. You do not need to use the PHI CD-Rom to find out: not a thousand places, but four places, all in one context, the panegyric on the Parthian expedition of Gaius Caesar, in *Ars* 1. 171–228. Twice Caesar is certainly Augustus (171, 203), once it is plural, 'the Caesars' (184), and once it might be either Gaius or Augustus (177). Four occurrences, in the space of thirty-two lines. So let's see what it is that ought to assure Augustus of the panegyrical nature of the *Ars*. And naturally we will look at it with a certain suspicion, as perhaps one is invited to do, when, on looking for the thousand Augustuses we in fact find a mere handful of Caesars.

The one truly propagandistic piece in the *Ars*, which ought to make Augustus happy, is concerned with the expedition of Gaius

---

[18] Cf. Casali (1997: 80–2) on *Trist*. 1. 1. 21–2 *quaerenti plura legendum*.
[19] Just like the speeches of Thersites in *Met*. 13. 233. On Thersites as a figure for Ovid's aggressiveness against Augustus in the exile poetry, see Casali (1997: 96–102). Similarly, the *licentia* which 'hurts' Ovid's detractors is both sexual 'licentiousness' and excessive 'freedom of speech' (*OLD* s.v. 3, and *Rhet. ad Her.* 4. 48).

Caesar against the Parthians.[20] When faced with this passage, what is a suspicious reader led to do? S/he is led, first of all, to see in the 'excesses' of the praise an ironic, demystifying intention, and perhaps to look in the text for implicit meanings, hidden purposes, and polemical allusions.[21] In the second place, this suspicious reader can look at the particular context of the passage: the triumph of the young *princeps*, the eulogy of his august parent, the national and patriotic motifs, in the midst of advice that an erotic poet addresses to a frivolous audience of lovers. So let's do that, first implied meanings and hidden purposes in praise, and then the context.

Ovid says: look, here is Caesar (Gaius or perhaps better Augustus himself) who is preparing to add to Roman dominion whatever in the world is still missing from it, who is preparing to conquer Parthia. Let the two Crassi, killed at Carrhae in 53 BC, rejoice, and the standards which had fallen into barbarian hands: the avenger is at hand. The panegyric is divided into various sections. First, Ovid pauses to defend the young age of Gaius, who *primis... in annis* is appointed as *dux*. In fact, to the Caesars valour comes before the normal age (181–94). After this, Ovid moves on to justifying the expedition to the East and to affirming the righteousness of the Roman cause against the Parthians, justification based on family values (195–202). Then we have the promise from Ovid of a future poetic celebration of Gaius' Parthian war (203–12), and finally a description of Gaius' future triumph, which will be an occasion for the *amator* to make a impression on the *puella* (213–28).

Each of these sections would merit a full treatment, but I'll limit myself to focus on three problematic points in Ovid's Gaius passage: (1) the justification of Gaius' expedition as a defence of family values; (2) the presentation of the aims of the expedition as (*a*) the revenge for the defeat of Carrhae, and (*b*) the conquest of Parthia; and (3) Ovid's implicit discourse on the 'theatricality' of Augustus' Parthian policy.

---

[20] On the extremely complex background to Gaius' Eastern expedition, see esp. Pani (1972: 17–55); Chaumont (1976: 73–84); Hollis (1977: 65–73); Syme (1978: 8–13); Bowersock (1984); Sherwin-White (1984: 322–41); Gruen (1990: 396–9); Brunt (1990: 456–64); Campbell (1993: esp. 220–8).

[21] Galinsky (1969: 98–103) underlines the ironic tone and the 'mocking flattery' of Ovid's passage. For treatments of it as 'serious' panegyric, see e.g. Meyer (1961: 82–6); Williams (1978: 74–80); Wildberger (1998: 60–76); and Schmitzer (2002: esp. 287–304). See also Hollis (1977: 73); Steudel (1992: 175–83); Heyworth (1995: 145–9).

A FAMILY MATTER

Let us pause a while over the justification for the expedition to the East, and the assertion of the justice of the Roman cause that we see in 195–202. As Pianezzola (1991: 212) says, this justification 'is based on family values, on the moral obligation to defend the rights of persons in accordance with their roles within the family'.

The poet says: *cum tibi sint fratres* ('since you have brothers', that is Lucius and Agrippa Postumus, and Tiberius),[22] *fratres ulciscere laesos* ('avenge the wrongs which brothers have undergone', namely the four Parthian hostage-princes, legitimate sons of Phraates IV, who had been supplanted and sent to Rome owing to the machinations of Thesmusa, or Thea Musa, an Italian maidservant who became first Phraates IV's concubine and then his wife, and the mother of Phraataces): naturally this is not a matter of wrongs suffered by the brothers of Gaius, but of the wrongs suffered by the brothers— actually half-brothers—of Phraataces (or Phraates V, king from 2 BC to AD 4), who were cheated of the throne. Ovid continues: *cumque tibi pater sit* (that is, Augustus, the adopted father of Gaius), *iura tuere patris*, 'defend the rights of a father', that is, the right of Phraates IV to choose which of his sons should succeed him—even if Josephus (*Ant. Iud.* 18. 42) says that Phraates himself voluntarily sent his four legitimate sons to Rome, albeit under Thesmusa's pressure;[23] after that, he was murdered by Phraataces, with the assistance of Thesmusa.

Lines 195–6 firm up a very close parallel between the family situation of Gaius, that is to say, the family of Augustus, and that of Phraataces. The couplet is extremely vague (see Hollis (1977: 77–8) for earlier misinterpretations of it), and suggestive. The parallel between the healthy 'royal' family of Rome and the perverted royal family of Parthia 'must' naturally be a form of opposition: 'Gaius,

---

[22] Cf. the candid comment by Brandt (1902: 20): '*fratres*. Gaius hatte zwei Brüder, Lucius und Agrippa Postumus. (...) Von ihm [i.e. Agrippa Postumus] wird wenig rühmliches berichtet (...), daher ist vielleicht hier nicht an ihn, sondern an Tiberius zu denken, der ebenfalls von Augustus adoptiert, mithin des Gaius Halbbruder war.'

[23] Not at all an unlikely explanation of Phraates IV's behaviour: cf. Strabo 16. 1. 28 (748–9); Tac. *Ann.* 2. 1. 2, and see Sherwin-White (1984: 325).

who exemplifies family loyalty, concord, and dutifulness, should punish Phraataces for his flagrant lack of these qualities' (ibid. 77). But let's read the couplet with a bit less Augustan devotion. 'Since Gaius has brothers, he ought to go and avenge the wrongs of brothers (who were excluded from the right of succession). Since he has a father, he ought to defend the rights of a father (to choose his own successor)'. It seems clear to me that Ovid leaves a fair bit for the reader to do. The reader must fill in several holes in this line of reasoning, and it is hard to imagine that a reader who has in him even a drop of demystification about the dynastic issue of the succession to Augustus would not fill these gaps in the most natural way. What exactly does it mean that 'since Gaius has brothers, he ought to go and sort out the dynastic quarrels of other brothers'? Augustan reading (Hollis): Gaius, that shining example of 'family loyalty, concord, and dutifulness', cannot not feel personally touched on seeing brotherly concord violated in Parthia. Okay. A slightly less loyalist reading, and surely a not less natural one: Gaius Caesar, as heir designate, obviously has every interest in ensuring the integrity of the rights of a father to choose who he wants as his successor, and could not but feel himself touched to see the laws of succession violated in Parthia, since he too has brothers who are, or could be, just as disloyal and treacherous as those who liven up the dynastic succession to the Parthian throne.

Gaius Caesar has two brothers, Lucius Caesar and Agrippa Postumus; the second of these, poor boy, has always been a bit unnecessary in the family, and we know that he will come to a bad end; but Gaius has also a stepbrother, by the name of Tiberius. The line immediately previous to 195–6 refers to the conferring of the title of *princeps iuuentutis* on Gaius, an event of 5 BC.[24] To designate Gaius (and Lucius) as successors naturally implies the setting aside of the previous aspirant to the succession, Tiberius, who in the previous year (6 BC) was in fact sent to Rhodes for an educational trip that looked suspiciously like exile.[25]

I even wonder whether a Roman suspicious reader might not find it more natural to see *Tiberius* rather than Phraataces as the 'bad

[24] Cf. *RG* 14. 2; Dio 55. 9. 9; Tac. *Ann.* 1. 3. 2; Wolters (2002).
[25] See Dio 55. 9. 5–8 with Swan (2004: 86–8).

brother', the 'enemy' of Gaius, who 'wants to take away the kingdom from his father', in lines 197–200. Both the Roman prince and the Parthian king are under threat from dangerous brothers who are in exile (Tiberius retired in Rhodes, the four hostage-princes confined in Rome); dangerous mothers (Livia and Thesmusa) work behind the scenes in both royal families;[26] and after all, Gaius, before he meets the Parthian 'bad brother' Phraataces, takes care of meeting his own 'bad brother'. When Gaius leaves for the East, his first important 'victory' is the one he wins over the retired Tiberius.[27]

Later, Gaius will meet the Parthian king Phraataces 'in perfect amity'[28] (see below). His meeting with Tiberius apparently must have been much less friendly.[29]

GAIUS ULTOR

But let us say only that, to insist on the contrast between the bad royal family of Parthia (because it has brothers against brothers) and the good family of Augustus (because it has brothers who are filled with love and harmony), is something that ought to rankle a bit for a reader who has the slightest knowledge of what has been going on at court. Ovid touches a sore point.

---

[26] For Thesmusa's plots in favour of her son Phraataces, see esp. Ios. Flau. *Ant. Iud.* 18. 42. Not surprisingly, Livia will be suspected of being involved in the immature deaths of both Gaius and Lucius: Dio 55. 10a. 10; Plin. *Nat.* 7. 46. 147–50; Tac. *Ann.* 1. 3. 3 (cf. Levick (1976: 271 n. 32)). Interestingly, the prodigiously precocious Gaius is compared by Ovid to Hercules and Bacchus (187–90): apart from the panegyrical implications of these parallels (Hollis (1977: 75)), a reader might also note that Hercules and Bacchus, both sons of Jupiter (cf. 1. 188; compare Gaius in Antipater, *AP* 9. 297. 1), demonstrated their precocity by facing the threats of their stepmother Juno (Juno sent the snakes against Hercules; Bacchus' Eastern wanderings were caused by Juno's persecution). For Livia as a dangerous stepmother for Gaius, cf. Tac. *Ann.* 1. 3. 3. On the image of Livia in the *Ars* see Barchiesi, Ch. 6 in the present volume. Thesmusa was Augustus' own gift to Phraates IV (Ios. Flau. *Ant. Iud.* 18. 40): the perversion of the harmony of the Parthian royal family was caused by Augustus' persistent attitude of interference in family matters.

[27] For an instructive treatment see Dio 55. 10. 19 with Swan (2004: 116–7).

[28] Syme (1978: 11).

[29] Cf. Levick (1976: 31–46, and esp. 44–5).

Actually it is in general more the very choice of the expedition of Gaius Caesar against Parthia as the motive for the one truly encomiastic passage in Ovid's erotic work which is, at least, an extremely unhappy choice. It is the expedition itself which is one big sore point. The fact is that Gaius' expedition, at least as far as regards the conquest of the Parthian kingdom announced by Ovid, will be something of a farce.[30]

The character of the *mise-en-scène* of this Parthian expedition of Gaius Caesar is perfectly in keeping with the whole nature of the 'military' initiations of Augustus against the Parthians, beginning with the famous return of the standards of Crassus. The return of the standards of Carrhae was achieved by diplomatic means in 20 BC, but of course Augustus had passed it off as a great military success.[31] On the occasion of the inauguration of the temple of Mars Ultor in the Forum Augusti in 2 BC, Augustus had placed the returned standards in the inner sanctum of the temple (*RG* 29. 2), giving to the temple the clear symbolic significance of celebrating his own *ultio* of the defeat of Carrhae.[32]

Ovid has just recorded the celebrations for the temple of Mars Ultor in the section on the Naumachia of 2 BC (1. 171–6), which comes just before the section on the Parthian expedition of Gaius. But he does not say that the Naumachia was part of the celebrations for the dedication of the temple of Mars Ultor; he does not mention Mars Ultor at all. The Naumachia is presented in total isolation. But of course everybody knew that the Naumachia was associated with the temple of Mars Ultor, and so with Augustus' revenge against the Parthians. In 1. 180 Ovid mentions the returned standards; but again with no explicit connection with their final dislocation into the temple of Mars Ultor.

---

[30] Cf. Hollis (1977: 72). Line 1. 182 *bellaque non puero tractat agenda puer* might have a double meaning: 'a boy manages a war which ought not to be waged by a boy', but also 'a war not to be actually waged by a boy', nor by anybody else. In *Ars* 2. 175 *proelia cum Parthis, cum culta pax sit amica* there might be a similar point (after all, a 'Parthian' approach to the *amica* would not be so warlike as one might think).

[31] Cf. e.g. Gabba (1991: 438); Cresci Marrone (1993: 210–11); Rich (1998: esp. 71–9).

[32] On the dedication of the temple of Mars Ultor, see Hannah (1998); Rich (1998); Spannagel (1999) with Rich (2002); Barchiesi (2002b).

Immediately after (181), *ultor adest*—that is, Gaius: we suddenly discover that, well, the revenge against the Parthians is still to be done. This is clearly a problem. It is difficult to see why one should say *ultor adest* with regard to the *present* expedition, seeing that the *ultio*, according to Augustan propaganda, would have to have happened already. It is one thing to herald triumphs over the Parthians in the 20s BC (Propertius 3. 4, above all),[33] but it is quite another matter to redo Propertius 3. 4 after the restoration of the standards—as if there had not been an *ultio*: no mention of the standards on the occasion of the Naumachia of 2 BC, and the *ultor* becomes Gaius.[34]

In sum, presenting Gaius as the 'avenger' of Crassus and Roman honour immediately after having alluded to the dedication of the temple of Mars Ultor in 2 BC seems to imply in the clearest way that Augustus' earlier campaign was not proper 'vengeance'.[35]

Readers have reacted variously to this problem. The point is whether Ovid in presenting Gaius' departure for the East as an imperialistic venture, and especially as the vengeance for the defeat of Carrhae, is developing Augustan propaganda, or whether on the contrary he is advancing an embarrassing, and even offensive, over-interpretation of Gaius' campaign.

The first position is maintained by Herbert-Brown, in her discussion of the section on the temple of Mars Ultor in *Fast.* 5. 545–98, where Ovid explains that Augustus earned the title 'Ultor' for Mars on two counts: first, his vengeance for the murder of Julius Caesar (569–78); second, the vengeance he took on the Parthians in 20 BC with the restorations of the standards (579–94). Herbert-Brown suggests that Augustus may have always had a problem in characterizing his Parthian 'campaign' as 'vengeance'. She thinks that this may

---

[33] On Ovid and Prop. 3. 4 see Wildberger (1998: 66–76). Obviously, 'The clamour for vengeance on the Parthians is a familiar theme in poetry *predating* 20 BC' (Herbert-Brown (1994: 100); my emphasis): Verg. *Georg.* 3. 31; 4. 560–1; Hor. *Sat.* 2. 5. 62; *Od.* 1. 2. 21–2, 51–2; 3. 3. 43–4; 3. 5. 3–12; Prop. 3. 4. 9–10.

[34] At the beginning of his panegyric Ovid clearly alludes to the close of Propertius 4. 6 (written in 16 BC): cf. esp. 1. 179 ~ Prop. 4. 6. 83. In my view, Ovid alludes to a passage that is dramatically polemical against Augustan mystifications about the 'winning back' of the standards of Carrhae. On Prop. 4. 6 see Sidari (1977–8: 39–40) (difficult to reconcile with Sidari (1979–80: 300)). But differently Sherwin-White (1984: 324–5); Campbell (1993: 227).

[35] See also Meyer (1961: 82–5); *contra*, unconvincingly, Wissemann (1982: 114–16).

account for the long delay in building the temple; and that it may also account for the timing of the dedication in 2 BC—Gaius' imminent campaign against the Parthians provided (at last) justification for dedication of a temple to Mars the Avenger in which the standards were housed.[36] In this case, we would need other, official evidence to support the idea that Ovid's depiction of Gaius as the 'avenger' of Crassus does reflect Augustan propaganda. It does not seem that there is any sure evidence for that.[37] It is indeed probable that Gaius' departure for the East was sold to the Roman audience as an important military enterprise, and so with some connections with the dedication of the temple of Mars Ultor, but probably the emphasis was more on the 'realistic' Armenian side of the expedition[38] than on fantastic projects of conquest of the Parthian kingdom.[39]

[36] Herbert-Brown (1994: 100–8).

[37] Ibid. 104 refers to 'a series of coins celebrating the mounted and armed *C. Caes Augus f* depicting an aquila between two standards behind him', that according to Romer (1978: 198–9) were issued to mark Gaius' departure for the East. But Romer's own explanation of those coins (the standards depicted on them are those recovered in 20 BC and installed in the temple of Mars in 2 BC) is perfectly sound (also Bowersock (1984: 173)). According to Herbert-Brown 'they were also celebrating Gaius' forthcoming revenge on Parthia', but this idea is based, in a circular way, on the testimony of Ovid. Potentially more interesting is the decorative programme on the cuirass of a statue found in Cherchel in Algeria (Herbert-Brown (1994: 106–7)). But the identification with Gaius (Zanker (1988: 223–4)) is not certain. Herbert-Brown could have also considered the Messenian inscription *SEG* 23 [1968] no. 206; note esp. the reference there to Gaius as 'having avenged himself upon the barbarians'. This strongly suggests the campaign of Artagira as the best reference for the inscription: Gaius was wounded during the siege of Artagira, but afterwards he succeeded in capturing the city (cf. Dio 55. 10a. 6–7). It is difficult to think, *pace* Zetzel (1970: 264), that the phrase ὑγιαίνειν τε καὶ κινδύνους ἐκφυγόντα does not refer, at least in a vague way, to the fact of Gaius' wounding at Artagira and to his apparent recovery after that (Florus 2. 32. 45). So, this inscription is not evidence for a public image of Gaius as 'avenger' of Crassus and Roman honour. On Plut. *Mor.* (*Reg. et imp. apophth.*) 207 E, cf. Cresci Marrone (1993: 47).

[38] Cf. after all Augustus' own record of Gaius' Eastern enterprises in *RG* 27. 2 (with Campbell (1993: 227–8)). Ovid alludes to the Armenian side of Gaius' expedition only at 1.225 *hos facito Armenios* (cf. Wissemann (1982: 114)).

[39] Gaius' rather modest achievements did not prevent his Pisan fans from celebrating his enterprises after his death; see the Pisan decree of AD 4 (*CIL* 11. 1421 = *ILS* 140 = Ehrenberg-Jones 69); cf. e.g. Cresci Marrone (1993: 166–7). This may suggest that Ovid's total silence about Gaius in the *Fasti* might be seen as a rather embarrassed silence: after his ludicrous eulogy in the *Ars*, of all the Empire's subjects, *he* was the only one who could not have possibly afforded any posthumous celebration of Gaius.

That the presentation of Gaius as the 'real' avenger of Carrhae implies an opposition to Augustus on the part of Ovid is maintained by Braccesi and other scholars influenced by him.[40] They see Ovid as supporting the Gaian party against the Tiberian one in the struggles for Augustus' succession. Ovid would be critical of Augustus, but he could count on Gaius' favour and protection. So, Ovid's panegyric would be anti-Augustan, but still a sincere panegyric, of Gaius.

In fact, I find it difficult to believe on the one hand, that something good for Gaius could have been bad for Augustus; and on the other, that Ovid's encomium could have really been appreciated by Gaius. Ovid's Parthian extravaganza is an embarrassment both for Augustus and for Gaius.[41] In the light of the disastrous precedents of Roman military expeditions against the Parthians, rushing to write about a future Parthian triumph in such an emphatic and premature way cannot be seen as a wise move. True, Ovid could not foresee the future outcome of Gaius' expedition. But in any case he decided to run an extremely high risk. By frantically exaggerating the tones of his encomium Ovid obtains the effect (1) of demystifying Augustan propaganda about the recovering of the standards in 20 BC (we still need an *ultio*); and (2) of creating embarrassingly high and unrealistic expectations for an expedition that it was just too easy to see in its real, modest dimensions as an action of 'military diplomacy', and as a way of promoting Gaius' public image as the designate successor.[42]

By ludicrously exaggerating the importance of Gaius' Eastern expedition (and even *before* the very departure of Gaius), Ovid is ironically parodying Augustus' typical attitude towards foreign policy on the Eastern front.[43]

---

[40] See Braccesi (1976: 191–4); (1986: 56–9); Cresci Marrone (1993: 261–3). Sidari's (1977–8: 35–54; 1979–80: 298–9) position is similar, but according to her, Ovid's treatment of Gaius conformed to Augustus' wishes.

[41] For a more aporetic but stimulating evaluation, cf. Campbell (1993: 227 n. 3). Similarly Sherwin-White (1984: 324 n. 3) speaks of Ovid as 'misinterpreting the intentions of Augustus' in the *Ars*.

[42] Antipater's *propemticon* for Gaius (*AP* 9. 297 = 47 Gow-Page) interestingly does not make any explicit reference to proper warlike activity against the Parthians on the part of Gaius, revealing either a more sober adherence to Augustan propaganda about Gaius' enterprise (cf. Cresci Marrone (1993: 262–3)), or a slightly malicious attitude (the extension of Roman power to the extreme East announced in 6–7 is meant to be achieved, rather ingloriously, by taking advantage of the Parthians' internal divisions)—or both things.

[43] For a similar approach see Beard (2003: 36 n. 58).

IMAGINES BELLI

'We can't afford a war.'
'We ain't gonna have a war. We're gonna have the *appearance* of a war.'[44]

Historians of the Augustan period are agreed on one point: Augustus' foreign policy on the Eastern front (Armenia and Parthia) was a politics of making spectacles: diplomatic actions were presented to Rome as great military endeavours. The terminology which modern historians use to describe this politics is one of simulation ('Presentation of the event in Rome (. . .) endeavoured to *simulate* military victory'),[45] and of an almost theatrical show. This is what Gruen says on the Gaius expedition: 'The *princeps staged* a public demonstration to reassure the citizenry...', and with regard to the reconciliation between Gaius and Phraataces (there was a dinner in the Roman camp, followed by one in the Parthian camp):[46] 'The whole *scene* had been carefully orchestrated in advance.'[47] What Augustus was doing with the Parthians was to make a show of an invented war, which brought invented triumphs, as in the case of the restoration of the standards.

In fact, selecting only the Naumachia—a mock battle against an Eastern people—among the various public events that celebrated the dedication of the temple of Mars Ultor in 2 BC is highly significant: what better celebration of a false military victory over the Parthians than a staged battle? And what better introduction to the new expedition projected by Gaius?[48]

---

[44] *Wag the Dog* (1997), directed by Barry Levinson, screenplay by Hilary Henkin and David Mamet.

[45] Gruen (1992: 397), on the delivery of Tigranes to the vacant throne of Armenia in 20 BC.

[46] Vell. 2. 102. Cf. Dio 55. 10a. 4; Syme (1978: 11 n. 6). Afterwards Gaius died ingloriously in Lycia on 21 February AD 4; on Gaius' death, see Zetzel (1970: 261); on his killer 'Addon', see Pani (1972: 53–5); Chaumont (1976: 81–2). For rumours about Livia's involvement in Gaius' death, see above, n. 26.

[47] Gruen (1990: 398). But see already Velleius (quoted below). Cf. also the reference to 'dramatization' in Romer (1979: 203).

[48] The Naumachia had in itself political implications, and a connection between the staged battle of Salamis and the Parthian associations of the temple of Mars Ultor is highly probable; see Bowersock (1984: 174–5); Scheid (1992: 127); Hannah (1998: 424 and n. 12); Swan (2004: 101). See also Coleman (1993: 68–74, esp. 72). Ovid shifts the emphasis from a parallelism in content (protection of the Greeks, conquest of the Eastern enemies) to a parallelism in representation.

Ovid's 'encomiastic' passage on the expedition of Gaius speaks of this also. Let's consider the context in which it is placed. Even the most pro-Augustan interpreters are disposed to admit that it is not completely silly to say that the insertion of 'the triumph of the young prince, the eulogy of his august father, the national and patriotic motives in the middle of advice which an erotic poet addresses to his frivolous audience of lovers' could be 'daring, with little regard for such solemnity'.[49] No doubt. But this is not the context to which I refer here. I want to look at the more immediate context into which the passage is inserted. It is part of the section which goes from 1. 171 to 228. Ovid puts together, without any interruption, the representation of the battle of Salamis staged by Augustus in 2 BC, and the 'staging' of the Parthian expedition of Gaius. The juxtaposition creates a 'syntagmatic effect' which causes the theatricality and the simulatedness of the Augustan Naumachia to reverberate on the Parthian expedition and on the 'invented' triumph of Gaius. The mock sea-battle and the mock Parthian war.

The Naumachia is introduced as *belli naualis imago* (171), the 'representation of an naval battle'—although perhaps the poetic usage *bellum = proelium*[50] is not by chance: Augustus provides his subjects not only with 'battles', but also with real and proper imaginary wars. Appropriately, a war between East and West, and in particular a war with its ending already written: the Naumachia of 2 BC was particularly difficult to carry out because there was the further problem that the 'Athenians' were of course meant to be the winners—and Dio (55. 10. 7–8) attests that this was in fact the outcome of the feigned battle:[51] evidently, 'The whole scheme had been carefully orchestrated in advance' (to repeat the phrase that Gruen applies to Gaius' Parthian campaign).[52]

In fact, if we read the two sections on the Naumachia and on Gaius' expedition, forgetting for a moment that they are, in fact, two

---

[49] Labate (1984: 73).
[50] *OLD* s.v. 3.
[51] See Coleman (1993: 72).
[52] Velleius calls the meeting of Gaius and Phraataces a *spectaculum* (Vell. 2. 101. 2–3). Interestingly, *spectaculum* is a word the anti-Gaian Velleius has just used to refer to the Naumachia of 2 BC (the same word used in *RG* 23): Vell. 2. 100. 2.

The Art of Making Oneself Hated

(fairly) distinct sections, the Ovidian discourse seems really very fluid between the *mise-en-scène* of Salamis and the preparation of the Parthian expedition. In 171–6: Caesar (first mention of Augustus in the *Ars*) has staged the battle between the Persians and the Athenians; a huge crowd swarmed to Rome for the occasion, young men and young women: who has not found someone to love in such a mêlée? Ah, how many were tormented by Love on that occasion! And now Caesar prepares to add whatever is still missing from the world to his dominion: now, far East, you will be ours. What does this future event which is about to unfold in the East refer to? Is Ovid opening a new section, with a different subject, or is he beginning a commentary on the Naumachia?—as if the Augustan way of conquering the Persian East which was still lacking to Roman dominion was the Naumachia itself. Okay, gradually the reader comes to understand that no, Ovid is talking about something else, about this great Parthian expedition, a real expedition, not a circus-show, nothing to do with gladiatorial games, theatrical shows, and the like—or perhaps, everything to do with them.

The parallel between the *mise-en-scène* of the Naumachia and that of the Parthian expedition is naturally underlined by the way Ovid goes on to describe the future triumph of Gaius as absolutely 'fictional'. Just as the outcome of the feigned battle of Salamis has already been written, so too is that of the *belli Parthi imago*. The playboy who, to court a girl, makes up the names of conquered cities and enemy leaders led in triumph, is doing something really very 'Augustan'. Parthian triumphs, like that celebrated for the 'winning back' of the standards of Carrhae, are 'fictional' triumphs, inventions. This is how Ovid closes the section which had opened with the description of the feigned battle of Salamis: *ille uel ille duces, et erunt quae nomina dicas,* | *si poteris, uere, si minus, apta tamen,* 'This or that enemy leader is there, and there are names which you can say, if you can, truly, if not, at least appropriately' (1. 227–8). The advice of the *praeceptor* to his would-be lover sounds remarkably similar to the Augustan programme in preparing for the theatre of war on the Eastern front; what we could have here is a spin-doctor for Augustus who would advise on how to prepare for the war in perfect 'Wag the Dog' style. The important thing is to go, leave, make a bit of noise, then you'll always find a way to sell a grand triumph to the Roman audience.[53]

The propaganda machine that knew how to bring to the right-hand bank of the Tiber a whole flotilla of *Persides... rates*, 'Persian ships' (1. 172), for the circus pseudo-battle of 2 BC, would have no problems in bringing to Rome the Euphrates, the Tigris, Armenians, *Daneia Persis*, 'the Persian land of Danae', and a city that rose up, note, actually *in Achaemeniis uallibus*, in Achaemenian valleys. For the Achaemenids, a welcome return to Rome, after the battle of the Achaemenid Xerxes against the Athenians at Salamis, on the banks of the Tiber.

---

[53] On Ovid as spinning 'the problem of belief and interpretation' in the *Ars* passage see Beard (2003: 35–7).

12

Ars Amatoria Romana: Ovid on Love as a Cultural Construct

Katharina Volk

Early in Jane Alison's recent 'Ovid novel' *The Love-Artist*, the poet is somewhat improbably taking a vacation in a remote corner of the Black Sea, a place uncannily similar to that of his ultimate exile. However uncivilized this area may be, it turns out that the Roman poet's works have already preceded him and that the *Ars Amatoria* especially has made quite an impression on the female population:

[T]hey'd been transformed, a new consciousness like light falling upon them, their clothes worn differently, several desperate efforts made to control their snaky hair. Within weeks there wasn't a Phasian girl who hadn't crouched over a pool of water and turned herself this way and that with newly quizzical eyes. *Goat girls*, Ovid would call them, *Don't be a goat girl from the Caucasus—be sure to shave your legs!* (Alison (2001: 20–1))

The Phasian girls' efforts at beautification are clearly pathetic, and however much they may try, the teachings imparted in the *Ars Amatoria* simply do not work for them. As Ovid himself says, in the passage to which Alison is clearly alluding, he is not in the business of instructing girls from such barbarian locations:

Versions of this chapter were presented as papers at the conference 'Ars Amatoria 2000' in Manchester (September 2002), at Dartmouth College (November 2003), and at Rutgers University (March 2004). My thanks for comments and suggestions go to the audiences at these events and especially to Roy Gibson, Steven Green, and Alison Sharrock, the organizers of the Manchester conference and editors of this volume.

> quam paene admonui, ne trux caper iret in alas
>   neue forent duris aspera crura pilis!
> sed non Caucasea doceo de rupe puellas
>   quaeque bibant undas, Myse Caice, tuas. (*Ars* 3. 193–6)

(How close I came to admonishing you that the wild he-goat should not settle in your armpits and your legs should not be rough with hard hair! But I am not teaching girls from the Caucasian rock or those who drink your waters, Mysian Caicus.)

What the *praeceptor amoris* is up to is teaching the art of love specifically to the men and women of Rome. In this chapter, I examine the 'Romanness' of the *Ars Amatoria* and argue that the explicit restriction of Ovid's audience to certain members of the Roman people attests to an underlying awareness that *amor*—'love', as taught in the poem—is a practice defined by its historical, geographical, and social context or, to use a fashionable term, that it is a 'cultural construct' rather than a universal experience.[1]

That the *Ars Amatoria* is geared exclusively to Romans is clear from the famous first distich of the poem:

> si quis in hoc artem populo non nouit amandi,
>   hoc legat et lecto carmine doctus amet. (*Ars* 1. 1–2)

(If anybody in this people does not know the art of love, let him read this and, having read the poem, love as an expert.)

Ovid's teaching is meant for 'this people' (cf. *in hoc... populo*, 1)—clearly the *populus Romanus*—and, we infer, for no one else. Within the tradition of didactic poetry, this exclusive attitude is next to unique. It is true that didactic poems often have individual addressees, such as Hesiod's Perses, Empedocles' Pausanias, and Lucretius' Memmius, while Ovid offers to instruct 'anyone' (cf. *si quis*, 1) in his targeted audience.[2] Still, even when there is a specific student figure, the usual implication is that the poem imparts universally valid teaching. For example, it would be absurd to assume that Lucretius

---

[1] The focus of this chapter is thus the opposite of that of Molly Myerowitz Levine ('Ovid's Evolution', Ch. 13), who maintains the universality of Ovid's amatory instructions (see also below).

[2] On the addressee in ancient didactic poetry, see the papers in Schiesaro, Mitsis, and Clay (eds.) (1993) and Volk (2002: 37–9 and Index s.v. 'teacher-student constellation').

regards Epicureanism as useful only for Memmius; on the contrary, it is generally recognized that intra-textual didactic addressees (such as Memmius) function as foils or dummies for the larger extra-textual readership that is actually envisaged. This is not to say that didactic poems and their characters lack individual features altogether: Memmius clearly is a Roman aristocrat, and the *Works and Days*, to take another example, shows plenty of local colour, however historically accurate, or not, we believe Hesiod's depiction of Ascra to be.

Even Vergil's *Georgics*, a didactic poem with a national theme and an envisaged audience of specifically Italian farmers, does not stress its 'Italianness' except in a few distinct passages, most notably the *laudes Italiae* in Book 2, where the poet grandly addresses the *Saturnia tellus* ('land of Saturn', 173), to which his poetry is dedicated (173–6). On the whole, though, the *Georgics* reads just like a general textbook of agriculture, in the tradition of the *Works and Days*, and if its instructions are, at least in theory, such as to apply in particular to the conditions—climatic, geological, and otherwise—of the Italian peninsula, this does make a lot of sense: in agriculture, after all, geography makes a difference. It is not immediately obvious that the same holds true for love also, and the pronounced *Romanitas* of the *Ars Amatoria* is thus worthy of closer investigation.

In spite of the generalizing *si quis*, it is clear that Ovid does not intend his teaching for the entirety of the Roman people: while the group of his male students remains largely undefined, except for the frequent implication that they are *iuuenes* ('young men'), the poet severely restricts his female audience. Already in the proem to Book 1, he excludes married women (31–4), a stricture that is repeated again and again throughout the work (see 2. 599–600, 3. 57–8, 483, and 613–16) and that is, of course, occasioned by Augustus' marriage laws that made adultery a crime.[3] The poet's generic description of his female pupil as *modo quam uindicta redemit* ('she whom the rod recently set free', 3. 615) appears to indicate that he particularly envisages freedwomen as the audience of his amatory instructions, and it has therefore often been assumed that the imagined student body of the *Ars Amatoria* is thus more or less identical with the

---

[3] Ovid clearly alludes to this legislation in 1. 34 (cf. *crimen*), 2. 599 (cf. *lege*), and 3. 58 (cf. *leges et sua iura*) and 614 (cf. *leges duxque*).

typical personnel of Roman love elegy, that is, young, presumably upper-class, male citizens[4] and young women of lower status, especially freedwomen.[5] This picture is somewhat complicated by the fact that there is no evidence that freedwomen were exempted from the strictures of the *lex Iulia*[6]—which does raise the question of what women Ovid really thinks he is teaching and whether he can possibly be sincere in his avowed adherence to the Augustan laws.[7]

However, in this chapter I am interested not in the actual intention of the historical author Publius Ovidius Naso (who may have wanted his *Ars Amatoria* to be read by women of all social strata and any marital status—or who may have been writing primarily for men) or in the many possible ways in which the text can be read (and, obviously, it could and can be read as a manual for adultery), but solely in the rhetoric employed by the poem's speaker, the persona of the *praeceptor amoris*, to whom I refer, throughout the chapter, in a kind of critical shorthand, simply as 'Ovid' (or, occasionally, 'the *praeceptor amoris*' or 'the poet'). This distinction is important. To take another example, I venture the guess that the historical Ovid would have been pleased enough to know that his work was being studied among non-Romans, be they girls from the Caucasus or modern European and American critics. It can also not be denied that amatory behaviour remarkably similar to that described in the *Ars Amatoria* could and can be observed at places other than Augustan Rome and that numerous and diverse people, from

---

[4] The social status of the *Ars Amatoria*'s young men is never made explicit, but passages such as 1. 459–68 (discussed below), where Ovid appears to assume a high level of education on the part of the *iuuenes*, clearly point to their belonging to the elite (cf. Gibson (1998: 302 and n. 23)).

[5] See Stroh (1979*b*: 325–36). Of course, inquiring about the social status of the protagonists of elegy (and the *Ars Amatoria*) makes sense only up to a point: after all, these literary characters may not reflect actual contemporary social categories, living in a poetic world that works according to its own laws (cf. James (2003: 35–68)).

[6] McGinn (1998: 194–202) discusses the categories of women who did not fall under the law; as far as we can tell (unless we want to use *Ars* 3. 615 as evidence; cf. Stroh (1979*b*: 325–6)), freedwomen were not among them.

[7] On Ovid's female students and all issues surrounding the *lex Iulia*, see Gibson (2003*a*: 25–37, 334–5 (specifically on the problematic passage 3. 611–16), and Index s.v. 'freedwomen (*libertinae*)'); cf. also *idem* (1998) and his contribution to this volume, Ch. 7.

Alison's Phasians to contemporary Westerners, may over the centuries have been attempting to implement Ovid's erotic instructions, whether successfully or not.[8] My sole focus in what follows, though, is on the ways in which the persona (not the author) presents his amatory teaching as targeted to a very specific audience in a very specific historical and geographical situation. Thus, however we are to understand Ovid's restrictions of his female audience in detail, we can nevertheless conclude that in these passages, the poet shows himself to be aware of writing at a particular moment in time (during the reign of Augustus) and that he explicitly aims his instructions exclusively at specific sections of contemporary Roman society, a fact that is in itself remarkable and largely unparalleled.

Love, as taught by Ovid, is an activity that takes place exclusively in the city of Rome and its environs. The extensive description of where to find a *puella*, which takes up the first half of *Ars Amatoria* 1 (67–262), is a gold mine of topographical and historical detail, enumerating such venues as porticoes, temples, fora, theatres, and the circus and such urban events as gladiatorial games, re-enactments of naval battles, triumphs, and banquets, in addition to fashionable spots just outside town, such as Baiae and Nemi. As the *praeceptor amoris* assures his students in 1. 51–60, there is no reason for them to leave town to pursue their amatory interests (note that it is naturally assumed that the young men are in Rome and nowhere else):

> tot tibi tamque dabit formosas Roma puellas,
>   'haec habet' ut dicas 'quicquid in orbe fuit.'   (1. 55–6)

(Rome will give you so many and such beautiful girls that you will say: 'It contains whatever there is in the world.')

A more explicit instance of wordplay with *urbs* (∼*Roma*) and *orbis* occurs a little later when Ovid mentions the mock naval battle staged by Augustus in 2 BC, which was attended by visitors from all over the world (*ingens orbis in Vrbe fuit*, 'the whole world was there in the City', 1. 174) and thus presented an especially good opportunity for

---

[8] An undergraduate student once told me that he considers the *Ars Amatoria* his 'bible' *in eroticis*. On the continuing appeal of the *Ars Amatoria* to modern readers, see also Myerowitz Levine, Ch. 13 in this volume; on creative engagement with the poem through the centuries, see Genevieve Liveley's paper, Ch. 16 in this volume.

picking up girls.[9] In addition to such explicit references to Roman places and events, there are also throughout the poem a number of passing allusions to things unmistakably Roman that add local colour: for example, the fruit basket that the lover is advised to present to his mistress with the claim that it comes from his suburban estate was really bought in a cheap shop in the Via Sacra (2. 263–6), and it would be very bad form to ask a girl under which consul she was born, a task better left to the stern censor (2. 663–4).

If the Roman audience and locale are thus quite obvious, there is also another way in which the *Ars Amatoria*, especially in the first two books, presents itself as uniquely Roman. In his course for the young men, Ovid humorously avails himself of the discourse of Roman education, that is, the entirety of practices designed to shape a *iuuenis* into a true Roman man. The most prominent of these practices is instruction in the art of public speaking, and scholars have noted that the title of Ovid's poem constitutes a play with *ars oratoria* and that the *praeceptor*'s amatory teaching is modelled on, and of course parodies, typical Roman rhetorical teaching (see Stroh (1979a)). The parallels between the two are clearest in the passage where Ovid explicitly points to the uses of rhetoric in seduction:

> disce bonas artes, moneo, Romana iuuentus,
>   non tantum trepidos ut tueare reos:
> quam populus iudexque grauis lectusque senatus,
>   tam dabit eloquio uicta puella manus. (1. 459–62)

(Roman youth, I admonish you, learn the good arts, not only in order to help trembling defendants: just like the people and the stern judge and the assembled senate, thus also the girl will submit to you, conquered by your eloquence.)

Note especially the exaggerated exhortion, *disce bonas artes, moneo, Romana iuuentus* (1. 459): the *praeceptor amoris* here pompously

---

[9] A large number of the pick-up places and opportunities listed by Ovid are not only particularly Roman, but specifically associated with Augustus and his family (witness the Porticus of Octavia and Theatre of Marcellus, 69–70; the Porticus of Livia, 71–2; the Temple of Palatine Apollo, 73–4; the Forum Iulium, 81–2; the mock naval battle, 171–6; and the anticipated Parthian triumph, 177–228). The *Ars Amatoria* thus teaches the young men not just how to practise *amor* in Rome, but how to avail themselves of the opportunities afforded by the Augustan regime and adapt their amatory pursuits to both the place and the historical circumstances.

adopts the morally charged role of teacher of the Roman youth, appropriately quoting a favourite line-ending of Ennius (*Ann.* 499, 550, and 563 Skutsch; cf. Hollis (1977) on *Ars* 1. 459). In what follows, he proceeds to give detailed instructions as to the right style to be employed when wooing the *puella* (1. 463–8).

Ovid's concern for the properly Roman education and behaviour of his pupils is evident also elsewhere. He stresses the importance of studying the liberal arts and learning Greek as well as Latin (2. 121–2; cf. Janka (1997 ad loc.)) and, crucially, gives detailed advice concerning men's outer appearance (1. 505–24).[10] There, a narrow course has to be steered between grubbiness and effeminacy in order to realize the goal of cultivated manliness, an ideal achieved through such specifically Roman practices as acquiring a tan on the Campus Martius and sporting a spotless toga (1. 513–14).[11] Recent work by Maud Gleason (1995), Erik Gunderson (2000), and others has focused on the Roman obsession with the proper construction of masculinity, a discourse with which Ovid was clearly familiar and which he uses, tongue in cheek, for his own purposes.

I have been surveying some of the prominent 'Roman' features of the *Ars Amatoria*, features that make Ovid's work stand out among didactic poems, which usually tend to stress, or at least imply, the universality of their teaching. This specificity of Ovid's didacticism is, I believe, intrinsically connected to the poet's understanding of his poem's subject matter and to the question of what it is that the *Ars Amatoria* purports to teach.[12] There is in the scholarly literature a certain confusion over what Ovid's 'art of love' is actually about, a confusion that is, I would argue, deliberately engineered by the poet himself. While the Latin word *amor* typically connotes a strong feeling of desire and affection, Ovid for most of the *Ars Amatoria* uses it instead to refer to the social practice of establishing and

---

[10] The traditional nature of Ovid's instructions on the latter topic is apparent from the fact that they closely resemble those given in Cic. *Off.* 1. 130 (see Labate (1984: 135)).

[11] Exercising on the Campus Martius was meant to prepare a Roman man for his military duties, while wearing the toga was associated with his civic activities. In Ovid, the practices designed to make a young man a Roman soldier and citizen are thus wittily reinterpreted as making him a Roman lover.

[12] For a fuller discussion of the argument put forth in this paragraph, see Volk (2002: 168–73).

participating in sexual relationships. The *Ars Amatoria* is thus really something like the art of dating, the art of the love affair, and *not* the art of love. This, of course, is the reason why it is teachable in the first place: *amor* is for Ovid not a feeling but a mode of behaviour, and thus can be mastered by following the simple steps laid out in his didactic poem.

Being a social practice, the love taught in the *Ars Amatoria* is not something universal, experienced equally by all people everywhere, but a phenomenon that is shaped by place, time, and circumstances. In other words, it is a cultural construct: any culture, any society will define and practise 'love' differently. My argument is that Ovid is well aware of the cultural constructedness of *amor* and that this is one of the reasons for the Romanness of his poem: love as practised in Rome, in the age of Augustus, by certain social groups is simply *not* the same as love practised by other people, at another time, elsewhere—and the *Ars Amatoria* is therefore of necessity a predominantly Roman poem.

The discovery that sexual activities, as well as the very concept of 'sexuality', are not unchanging facts of human life but very much a product of a given society's concepts and values is typically associated with the work of Michel Foucault and has informed much recent scholarship on Greek and Roman sexuality;[13] however, at least some of the ancients themselves came to the same conclusion. In Plato's *Symposium*, for example, Pausanias surveys differing amatory practices in a number of places and even provides sociological explanations for the discrepancies among them (182a7–c4). Thus, in societies where eloquence does not play a large role (as is supposedly the case in such backwaters as Elis and Boeotia), homosexual relationships are formed without much ado and without the complicated wooing ritual in place in Athens. By contrast, in the tyrannical Persian empire, such relationships, which are deemed a possible danger to the state, do not exist at all.[14]

If Plato could be aware that love is not the same the world over, so surely could Ovid. Note, though, that while the practice of 'love' as

---

[13] See Foucault (1976–84), vol. 1 and the papers in Halperin, Winkler, and Zeitlin (eds.) (1990) on Greek sexuality, and Hallett and Skinner (eds.) (1997) on Roman sexuality.

[14] For a similar discussion, see Xen. *Lac.* 2. 12–14.

described in the *Ars* is clearly culturally determined, Ovid appears to regard the very act of sex as something natural that is the same for all people and that thus, interestingly, need not be taught. Witness his description of how primitive man and woman were perfectly adept at having intercourse, without a *magister* and without any *ars*:

> blanda truces animos fertur mollisse uoluptas:
>   constiterant uno femina uirque loco.
> quid facerent, ipsi nullo didicere magistro;
>   arte Venus nulla dulce peregit opus.   (2. 477–80; cf. also 2. 703–8)

(It is said that seductive pleasure softened the harsh minds [of early human beings]: man and woman had come together in one place; without a teacher, they learned themselves what to do; Venus accomplished her sweet work without any art.)

Sex, to put it simply, is nature; love is culture.[15]

Before looking in greater detail at the 'cultural constructedness' of love in the *Ars Amatoria*, I would like to stress once again that I am concerned here solely with the 'official rhetoric' of the poem, that is, the attitude of the persona as it is explicitly stated or can be reasonably inferred. Thus, contrary to appearances, my argument is not in fact in direct contradiction to that of Myerowitz Levine in Ch. 13, who argues that the courtship techniques recommended by Ovid reflect universal amatory behaviour that transcends time and space. In my opinion, this may well be true, but it is not how Ovid himself presents his instructions, which is all I am interested in. While Myerowitz Levine is a universalist, Ovid is a constructionist, as I hope is becoming clear (and note that, as always, I am speaking about 'Ovid', the poetic persona). Myerowitz Levine and I are thus really talking about different things.

To clarify further my approach in this chapter and to place it in the context of Ovidian scholarship, I would like to point to a number of other interpretative paths that I am not adopting. The observation of the *Ars Amatoria*'s Romanness can be, and has been, taken in a

---

[15] It should be pointed out, though, that while Ovid appears to regard the basic sexual act as natural and not something to be taught, sexual technique (cf. 2. 717–32 and 3. 789–808) and in particular sexual positions (3. 771–88) are subjects of his amatory instruction and thus appear to fall on the other side of the nature–culture divide.

number of directions. Thus, most prominently, Mario Labate has examined the 'rhetoric of the city', showing that while all Latin love elegy typically takes place in Rome, it is only Ovid who puts a positive spin on the genre's urbanism.[16] In what follows, though, I am not in the first place interested in Ovid's ideology of city life and his contribution to the creation of an ideal of 'urbanity', a concept that has been traced through the ages by Edwin S. Ramage in his monograph (1973). I will likewise largely ignore the topic of Ovid's attitude to the Roman Empire (on which see now Habinek (2002)) and the much-debated question of the poet's relationship to Augustus (taken up once again by Sergio Casali in Ch. 11 of this volume). While the issues just enumerated are all closely related to the topic of this chapter and will occasionally come up in passing, I have deliberately narrowed my object of inquiry to the idea of love as a cultural construct. What I am trying to demonstrate is that the striking Romanness of the *Ars Amatoria* reflects an awareness on Ovid's part that the practice of *amor* is indeed determined by its time and place—nothing less and nothing more.

In itself, the fact that the *Ars Amatoria* has, as we have seen, a distinctly Roman flavour does not yet prove that Ovid thought that 'Roman love' was in any way different from love practised elsewhere. Strikingly, though, throughout the poem, the *praeceptor amoris* explicitly contrasts his own brand of *amor* with love that is taking place in other contexts. In doing so, he constructs a negative foil of what 'love here and now' is not like and thus, of course, helps define the positive image of the particular incarnation of *amor* that he is teaching. The first contrast is that between love now and love in the past, particularly in the hallowed age of early Rome. This is most prominent in the famous passage from the beginning of Book 3 where Ovid so amusingly rejects the 'good old days' in favour of the present age (3. 107–28, esp. 121–2; cf. Gibson (2003*a*): ad loc.). Critics have wondered how this attitude relates to Augustan ideology: the poet's sentiment is surely far removed from the idealization of early Rome found in such authors as Vergil. However, as especially Karl Galinsky has shown (1981/3; 1996: 97–100), the whole Augustan ideal of an earlier Golden Age is intrinsically ambivalent

---

[16] See Labate (1984) and cf. also the author's contribution to this volume, Ch. 10.

from the beginning, for how can you boast (as Augustus did; see Suet. *Aug.* 28. 3) about 'having found a city of brick and left a city of marble' and at the same time maintain that things were better in a more primitive age? This same ambivalence is found in Ovid, who, despite his enthusiastic allegiance to the present, is still aware of its moral shortcomings (cf. 3. 123–6).

What interests me is the context of Ovid's celebration of contemporary Rome. It is part of a large section at the beginning of Book 3 where the *praeceptor amoris*, in instructing the women, stresses the importance of *cultus*. He is well aware, though, that beautification did not always play a role in amatory relationships:

> corpora si ueteres non sic coluere puellae,
>   nec ueteres cultos sic habuere uiros.
> si fuit Andromache tunicas induta ualentes,
>   quid mirum? duri militis uxor erat.
> scilicet Aiaci coniunx ornata uenires,
>   cui tegumen septem terga fuere boum!
> simplicitas rudis ante fuit; nunc aurea Roma est
>   et domiti magnas possidet orbis opes.   (3. 107–14)

(If the girls of old did not take care of their bodies in the same way, the girls of old also did not have similarly groomed men. If Andromache was dressed in bulky tunics, no wonder: she was the wife of a rough soldier. Surely his wife would come all made-up to Ajax, who was covered by seven cow-hides! Rough simplicity was there before; now Rome is golden and possesses the great riches of the conquered world.)

The women of old were less sophisticated, and so were the men they were trying to seduce. Life and thus love were different in the olden days, which were characterized by *simplicitas*. In the reign of Titus Tatius (mentioned a few lines later in 3. 118), people just did not behave the way they do today.[17] While there is certainly a value judgement (the women of old are made fun of, and the poet explicitly approves of modernity), the main point is that different circumstances call for different practices, and that here and now, in Augustan

---

[17] Cf. also *Med. Fac. Fem.* 11–12: *forsitan antiquae Tatio sub rege Sabinae | maluerint quam se rura paterna coli* ('perhaps the ancient Sabine women in the reign of Tatius preferred the fields to be cultivated rather than themselves').

Rome, women have to pay attention to *cultus* if they want to succeed in love.[18]

The *simplicitas* which was appropriate in an earlier age but no longer is today calls to mind that other negative buzzword, *rusticitas*. You cannot successfully practise the art of love in the urban environment of Rome if you behave like a country bumpkin, for example, if you walk with the *rusticus... motus* ('rustic motion', 3. 305–6) exhibited by the wife of an Umbrian farmer:

> illa uelut coniunx Vmbri rubicunda mariti
>   ambulat, ingentes uarica fertque gradus.   (3. 303–4)

(That one walks like the sunburned wife of an Umbrian husband, and, broad-legged, takes immense strides.)

Again there is, of course, an element of derision, but the implication is that it is appropriate for an Umbrian wife to walk this way—but it is not appropriate for the young women of Rome.[19]

If already in the Italian countryside different rules of behaviour apply, the same is even more true for far-away peoples. As we have seen (in 3. 193–6, quoted above), if Ovid were teaching women from the Caucasus, he would have to go about his task differently and talk about such basics as the avoidance of body odour and the importance of shaving one's legs. However, he is instructing Roman *puellae*, who already know how to brush their teeth and apply make-up.

In this passage, Ovid implicitly contrasts foreign practice (as he constructs it) with the way things are in Rome: it is simply assumed that if you live on the Caucasian rock, you don't know about deodorants. There is clear ethnic stereotyping here, but there is not a lot of aggression. At other places, though, namely when talking about those Roman archenemies, the Parthians, the poet reverses his

---

[18] The same contrast between the past and the present also underlies the story of the rape of the Sabine women in *Ars Amatoria* 1, which Mario Labate discusses in Ch. 10 of this volume.

[19] Note, though, that the *puellae* are also cautioned against a way of walking that is too lascivious (3. 301–2, 306). As Roy Gibson in his contribution to this volume, ch. 7, discusses in detail (see also Gibson (2003*a*: ad loc.)), Ovid's treatment of the proper gait is a prime example of his general insistence on the 'middle way', a moderate kind of amatory behaviour that avoids extremes (cf. Gibson (forthcoming)).

strategy. Instead of claiming that the eastern people practise *amor* in a way unacceptable at Rome, he—patriotically and, of course, humorously—actively wishes on them those amatory mishaps that his Roman pupils are told to avoid. Thus, a Roman woman must never let herself be caught putting on her wig—that kind of embarrassment is fit for a Parthian girl:

> dictus eram subito cuidam uenisse puellae:
>   turbida peruersas induit illa comas.
> hostibus eueniat tam foedi causa pudoris
>   inque nurus Parthas dedecus illud eat!   (3. 245–8)

(My sudden arrival had been announced to some girl: in her haste, she put on her hair the wrong way around. May a cause for such awful shame befall our enemies and may that infamy afflict the Parthian girls!)[20]

Somewhat differently, the men are advised to keep peace with their 'cultured' (*culta*) Roman girlfriends and to save their fighting spirit for the barbarian Parthians (2. 175–6).

Perhaps the most interesting negative foil that Ovid uses to define love in contemporary Rome is mythology (and note that, as is typical in ancient literature, the poet presents his mythological stories simply as events of some undefined past, history in the widest sense). Normally, of course, Latin poets, and especially the elegists, use mythological exempla to point to the similarity of the mundane present and the fabled past, creating strong and often deeply meaningful parallels between situations and characters in the two different realms. For the most part, the mythological stories in the *Ars Amatoria* work along these same lines. Thus, for example, the young men are advised to judge women's beauty under good lighting conditions, just as the Judgement of Paris, too, took place in plain daylight (1. 245–52), and women are crazy about sex today, just like Pasiphae and others were in the past (1. 269–344). However, on more than one occasion, Ovid uses mythology as a negative example, pointing out that nowadays things are not as they were in the old stories and that

---

[20] The 'hair turned around' (cf. *peruersas... comas*, 246) constitutes a witty allusion to the notorious Parthian battle manoeuvre of the feigned turn-around (see Green (1982: 388)).

the rules that apply to mythological characters do not apply to his own pupils.[21]

This negative contrast of the present age to the mythological past can work in a number of different ways. First, Ovid cannot resist the temptation to point out that the reason why so many mythological love stories have a tragic ending is simply that the likes of Medea, Ariadne, Phyllis, and Dido were not familar with the art of love (*quid uos perdiderit, dicam: nescistis amare*, 'I will say what ruined you: you did not know how to love', 3. 41). His own students, of course, will not make the same mistake.[22]

Second, though (and this is actually a bit of a contradiction), mythological heroines are not, in fact, in need of the teacher's instructions:

> non mihi uenistis, Semele Ledeue, docendae,
>   perque fretum falso, Sidoni, uecta boue
> aut Helene, quam non stulte, Menelae, reposcis,
>   tu quoque non stulte, Troice raptor, habes.
> turba docenda uenit pulchrae turpesque puellae,
>   pluraque sunt semper deteriora bonis.
> formosae non artis opem praeceptaque quaerunt;
>   est illis sua dos, forma sine arte potens. (3. 251–8)

(You did not come to be taught by me, Semele and Leda, and you, woman of Sidon, riding over the sea on a false bull, or Helen, whom you, Menelaus, are not stupid to demand back and you, Trojan abductor, are not stupid to keep. The crowd that comes to be taught consists of pretty and ugly girls, and there are always more faults than virtues. Beautiful women do not need the help of art and instructions; they have their dowry, beauty powerful without art.)

A woman in the league of Semele, Leda, Europa, and Helen, one who is perfectly beautiful, will succeed in attracting a lover no matter what. Real women, however, are hardly ever perfectly beautiful; in fact, as Ovid realistically observes, unsightliness is rather more common than beauty. No wonder, then, that the Roman *puellae* have to

---

[21] Cf. the remarks of Mario Labate on Ovid's use of 'anti-exempla' (specifically the story of the rape of the Sabines): 'The contrast of the anti-exemplum...serves to highlight the instructions of the teacher.' (Ch. 10 of this volume).

[22] On mythological heroines as (negative) role models in the *Ars Amatoria*, see also the contribution of Duncan Kennedy to this volume, Ch. 4.

approach the practice of *amor* in a way entirely different from their mythological counterparts.

However, it is not as though Ovid generally regards the women of mythology as too good to be true, model females too perfect to be emulated by contemporary *puellae*. As a matter of fact, the behaviour of these heroines would all too often be entirely inappropriate for a practitioner of Ovid's specific brand of *ars amatoria Romana*. Thus, in 3. 109–12 (quoted above), the poet presents Andromache and Tecmessa as negative exempla, pointing out that their unattractive clothing and lack of adornment was indeed fitting for their own situations, given the lack of sophistication on the part of their husbands, but that it is not at all fitting *hic et nunc*, for the sophisticated women of *aurea Roma*.

The tragic heroines Andromache and Tecmessa appear once more later in Book 3, again as examples of how Ovid's female students ought not to behave:[23]

> odimus et maestas; Tecmessam diligat Aiax,
>   nos, hilarem populum, femina laeta capit.
> numquam ego te, Andromache, nec te, Tecmessa, rogarem
>   ut mea de uobis altera amica foret.
> credere uix uideor, cum cogar credere partu,
>   uos ego cum uestris concubuisse uiris.
> scilicet Aiaci mulier maestissima dixit
>   'lux mea' quaeque solent uerba iuuare uiros!   (3. 517–24)

(We also dislike glum women. Let Ajax love Tecmessa; a cheerful woman captivates us, fun-loving people that we are. I'd never ask you, Andromache, or you, Tecmessa, that the one or the other might be my girlfriend. I can hardly believe—though I am forced to believe it because of your offspring—that you had sex with your men. As if his depressive woman ever said to Ajax, 'my light', and whatever other words are accustomed to pleasure men!)

In the opinion of the *praeceptor amoris*, the sadness and earnestness of these women (they are *maestae*) is a turn-off: he himself certainly would not be interested in them and can hardly believe that they ever

---

[23] Note, however, that, as Alessandro Barchiesi discusses in his contribution to this volume, Ch. 6, Andromache is also on occasion (*Ars* 2. 709–10, 3. 777–8) shown engaging in types of behaviour that are deemed commendable; see also Gibson (2003*a*) *on* 3. 519–20.

'did it' at all. By pointing out how absurd it is to imagine that Tecmessa would have addressed Ajax as *lux mea*, Ovid stresses the profound difference between the world of tragedy and mythology and that of his Roman contemporaries: the amatory relationships of today's women just do not work along the same lines as those of the heroines of old.

As these examples show, Ovid defines Roman love implicitly by contrasting it with examples of how love is practised elsewhere or was in the past. In nearly all these cases, the poet makes it clear that he regards his own place and time as preferable and frequently mocks or denigrates the 'other' that he has set up. However, the main point of these passages is not, in my opinion, to hit away at the smelly Caucasian girls and Andromache with her bulky tunics, or chauvinistically to glory in the greatness of the Roman Empire. Attesting to an awareness on Ovid's part that love is not the same the world over—that it is, indeed, a cultural construct—these negative examples enforce the importance of the poet's own *Ars Amatoria*. If love (as opposed to sex) is not natural, but requires cultural and social expertise, then it is indeed something one needs to study, and if one happens to be in Augustan Rome, *in hoc populo*, then the best way to study it is by perusing Ovid's exclusively Roman Art of Love.

One thing is striking about the negative examples just discussed. They nearly all come from Book 3, the part of the *Ars Amatoria* addressed to the women. Why is this? Are women somehow more in need of being told what true Roman amatory behaviour is like, while the men already know? Indeed, in some of the passages the women are explicitly asked to adjust their own approach to fit a mode of behaviour that the men already exhibit anyway. Thus, in 3. 107–12, the *puellae* are instructed to practise *cultus* for the very reason that they have such 'cultivated' (*cultos*, 108) men;[24] similarly, in 3. 517–24, women are warned against being *maestae* because today's men are a *hilaris populus* (cf. 3. 518) and do not like glum women.

To a certain extent, this discrepancy can be explained by the fact that Book 3 comes after Books 1 and 2 and that at this stage in the

---

[24] As Roy Gibson points out to me, the same idea that female *cultus* responds to an already extant level of male refinement is found in *Med. Fac. Fem.* 23–6 (cf. Rosati (1985 ad loc.)).

game, Ovid's male students are imagined as being already well-versed in the practice of Roman *amor*: they themselves have been taught to be *culti* and always in a good mood, and now the women have to reach that same stage.[25] While the use of explicit counterexamples is less prevalent in the first two books, there still is a strong indication that the *iuuenes* are supposed to be shaped into specifically Roman men, as is clear from the rhetoric of education employed in *Ars Amatoria* 1 and 2.

Still, there seems to be a certain gender imbalance that calls for an explanation. One might maintain that Ovid is here adhering to that typical line of thought by which 'male' equals 'Roman' and 'cultured', while 'female' equals 'foreign' and 'barbarian'. Is it because of their very femininity that women are more prone to social malapropisms and therefore need to be continually admonished? To put this same idea into its socio-historical context, it is probable that Ovid's envisaged male students are born and bred Roman citizens (members of the upper classes, who, as we have seen, receive training in the liberal arts and in rhetoric), while his female students (whatever their exact social status may be; cf. the discussion above) belong to a lower level of society and—especially if we take seriously the poet's insistence that he is writing for freedwomen—may very well be predominantly foreigners. Perhaps these former slaves are more in need of being cued in to the sophisticated mores of the capital of the world—or at least, this may be the patronizing attitude of the *praeceptor amoris*.[26]

---

[25] One of the underlying conceits of the *Ars Amatoria* is the supposed simultaneity of teaching and learning: thus, in the course of Books 1 and 2, the young men are imagined as putting into practice the teacher's instructions at the same moment as they are imparted (cf. Volk (2002: 173–88)). On the 'narrative' of the *Ars Amatoria*, see also Alison Sharrock's contribution to this volume, Ch. 2.

[26] See Gibson (1998) (also (2003a: 35–6)) for a discussion of other ways in which Ovid on occasion alludes to the low social status of his female pupils.

13

Ovid's Evolution

Molly Myerowitz Levine

Acknowledging human nature does not mean overturning our personal world views, and I would have nothing to suggest as a replacement if it did. It means only taking intellectual life out of its parallel universe and reuniting it with science and, when it is borne out by science, with common sense. The alternative is to make intellectual life increasingly irrelevant to human affairs, to turn intellectuals into hypocrites, and to turn everyone else into anti-intellectuals.

Stephen Pinker, *The Blank Slate: The Modern Denial of Human Nature* (2002: 422)

Just as human nature is the same everywhere, so it is recognizably the same as it was in the past. A Shakespeare play is about motives and predicaments and feelings and personalities that are instantly familiar.... When I watch *Anthony and Cleopatra*, I am seeing a four-hundred-year-old interpretation of a two-thousand-year-old history. Yet it never occurs to me that love was any different then from what it is now. It is not necessary to explain to me why Anthony falls under the spell of a beautiful woman. Across time just as much as across space, the fundamentals of our nature are universally and idiosyncratically human.

Matt Ridley, *The Red Queen* (1993: 10–11)

Does Ovid's enduring ART OF LOVE have any relevance now... 2,000 years after it was written? Considering how little human nature seems to have changed over the years, this guide to courtship and romance is much more than a fascinating document of history—it is a manual to be heard and then put into practice. Join accomplished lovers throughout the ages who have boasted, 'Ovid was my teacher!'

Internet advertisement for Martin Jarvis' reading of Jack Shapiro's translation of Ovid's *Art of Love*, ISBN #1-57270-050-5, 2 cassette. 3 hour. $17.95, sold by Audio Editions, <http://www.audiopartners.com>.

Advertised as 'Perfect for Valentine's Day, 2000-Year Old "Rules of Love"', Ovid's *Art of Love* is the sole ancient work currently listed under the category of 'Classics & Poetry' by Audio Partners, a seller of books on tape. The choice of Ovid's infamous treatise on seduction is not serendipitous. What other Roman poem can rival Ovid's *Ars Amatoria* for content that is universally relevant? The fact that sooner or later most of us find ourselves in pursuit of a mate makes Ovid's poem of intrinsic interest even to readers with no knowledge of its literary pedigree or historical context. The purpose of this chapter is to attempt to explain the poem's persistently popular appeal by enlisting the old idea of 'Human Nature', as newly understood by modern evolutionary science. Today, the popular notion of human culture as an arbitrary, specific construct superimposed upon a mental *tabula rasa* is fast yielding place to the idea that innate, universal 'deeper mechanisms of mental computation' both generate and limit culturally specific behaviours. For students of the humanities, this deeper knowledge about how the human mind works opens a meaningful way to re-examine literature from a truly humanist perspective.[1]

Taken together, the many striking parallels between the prescriptions of Ovid's *praeceptor* and the descriptions of modern evolutionary scientists 'prove' only that both tap into a universal substratum that deeply influences how humans think and behave. Although since Fränkel (1945) and Wilkinson (1955), we should need no reminder of Ovid's humanity, the poet's interest in human nature means that our readings of Ovid as a 'strict constructionist' really miss the main point of his *Ars*.[2] More generally, I argue that for Classics, a field that,

---

[1] 'The Blank Slate' is the title of Pinker (2002), the phrase 'deeper mechanisms of mental computation' is from ibid. 39, 'how the mind works' is an allusion to the title of Pinker (1997). On implications for the humanities, see Pinker (2002: 400–20), Wilson (1998: 210–37).

[2] For the opposite position, see Volk's contribution in this volume, Ch. 12.

by definition, deals with artistic works of time-tested and cross-cultural appeal, a revised universalist approach can provide a productive counterweight to the particularism of recent scholarship on cultural constructs and contexts. This approach works especially well and with good reason for erotic literature and, as I hope to demonstrate below, deepens our understanding of Ovid's *Ars Amatoria*.

A recent work from the social sciences reveals the contemporary and cross-cultural persistence of the content of the *praeceptor's* instructions: David Buss's *The Evolution of Desire* (1994) is a study of universal human mating strategies based on reports from 'fifty collaborators from thirty-seven cultures located on six continents and five islands, from Australia to Zambia, urban and rural, old and young, rich and poor with representation across the entire range of political systems and from all major racial, religious, and ethnic groups—10,047 people worldwide'.[3] In Buss's work, Ovid's keen observations on human nature are borne out by recent science using methods and with explanations that the Roman poet could never have anticipated. Although they surely will miss Ovid's humour and parody, students of Ovid's erotodidaxis will feel on familiar terrain in the following selection of generalizations on human mating behaviour culled mainly from Buss with line references to their striking Ovidian parallels (sometimes, even in structure or metaphor):

It is possible to come up with 'a unified theory of human mating, based not on romantic notions or outdated scientific theories but on current scientific evidence'.[4] The process of mating consists of three stages: 'selecting a mate', 'attracting a mate' and 'keeping a mate'.[5] 'People do not always desire the commitment required of long-term mating. Men and women sometimes deliberately seek a short-term fling, a temporary liaison, or a brief affair.'[6] 'One impressive advantage humans have over many other species is that our repertoire of mating strategies is large and highly sensitive to context... *Just as the successful fisherman* uses the lure that most closely

---

[3] Buss (1994: 4).
[4] Ibid. 5; cf. *Ars* 1. 1–30.
[5] In his outline, Buss (1994: 6, 8, 10) follows the tripartite division of topics in *Ars* 1. 35–8. These three topics are fully treated in *Ars* 1. 41–262 (selection), *Ars* 1. 263–772 (attraction), *Ars* 2 (keeping).
[6] Buss (1994: 8); cf. *Ars* 1. 91–2, discussed below.

resembles food that fits the fish's evolved preferences, so the successful competitor employs psychological tactics that most closely fit the evolved desires of the opposite sex.'[7] 'It may seem odd to view human mating, romance, sex, and love as inherently strategic but...strategies are essential for survival on *the mating battlefield*.'[8] 'Success at attracting a mate...also hinges on besting the competition.'[9] 'Timing plays a key role [in mating strategy]...'[10] 'The female preference for males who offer resources may be the most ancient and pervasive basis for female choice.'[11] 'In psychology experiments, women strongly prefer ugly men wearing Rolexes to handsome men wearing Burger King uniforms.'[12] 'Members of one sex generally favor a common set of strategies which differs from the typical strategies pursued by members of the other sex...if women bait with sex, men bait with investment.'[13] 'Displays of love, commitment, and devotion are powerful attractions to a woman. They signal that a man is willing to channel his time, energy, and effort to her over the long run.'[14] 'One strong signal of commitment is a man's persistence in courtship.'[15] 'Displays of kindness, which also signal commitment, figure prominently in successful attraction techniques.'[16] 'A man can attract a woman by doing special things for her, showing a loving devotion to her.'[17] 'The simulation of commitment can be effective in attracting and seducing a woman...for females, this strategy poses the problem of detecting deception, discovering insincerity, and

---

[7] Buss (1994: 15, 97) (italics mine); cf. *Ars* 1. 755–70 with Myerowitz (1985: 129–34). Ovid also uses the fish/fisherman metaphor in *Ars* 1. 47–8, 393, 763–4, 3. 425–6. On the persistence of mating metaphors, Victoria Pedrick (personal communication) makes the interesting observation that 'the scientists quoted "sound" like Ovid with their talk of strategies, hunting, fishing, and gaming for a mate, etc., not merely because Ovid tapped into a substratum of human nature, but also because moderns cannot escape that substratum either. Their very descriptions are redolent with the essence of their theory.'

[8] Buss (1994: 5) (italics mine); cf. *Ars* 2. 233–7 (*militiae species amor est*, 'love is a form of military service').

[9] Ibid. 121, cf. e.g. *Ars* 1. 579–89, 601–2, 739–54; 2. 335 on male rivalry.

[10] Ibid. 100, cf. *Ars* 1. 399–404 (*tempora*).

[11] Ibid. 22, cf. *Ars* 1. 420–36 and Buss (1994: 47): 'Men strive to control resources and to exclude other men from resources to fulfill women's mating preferences. In human evolutionary history, men who failed to accumulate resources failed to attract mates.'

[12] Burnham and Phelan (2001: 167), cf. *Ars* 2. 161–8, 275–8.

[13] Buss (1994: 220, 121), cf. *Ars* 1. 399–436, 443–54, on competing strategies and goals.

[14] Ibid. 102, cf. *Ars* 1. 619–30, 2. 157–60 (*amor, blanditiae*).

[15] Ibid., cf. *Ars* 2. 177 (*perfer et obdura*).

[16] Ibid. 103, cf. *Ars* 2. 315–36 (*amor et pietas*).

[17] Ibid. 104, cf. *Ars* 2. 209–32 (*obsequium*).

penetrating disguise.'[18] 'Improvements in appearance that are designed for attracting a mate are twice as effective for women as for men. In contrast, men who devote a lot of attention to enhancing their appearance can hurt their competitive chances. People sometimes infer that they are homosexual or narcissistic.'[19] 'Submission or self-abasement is another tactic of emotional manipulation. For example, people may go along with everything a mate says, let a mate have his or her way... men submit to and abase themselves before their mates roughly 25% more than women in order to keep their mates.'[20] 'Another emotional manipulation is intentionally trying to provoke sexual jealousy with the goal of keeping a mate.'[21] 'Jealousy is not a rigid, invariant instinct that drives robot-like, mechanical action. It is highly sensitive to context and environment. Many other behavior options are available to serve the strategy of jealousy, giving humans a flexibility in tailoring their responses to the subtle nuances of a situation.'[22]

Like Ovid, Buss reminds us of the apparent paradox of human mating—at the same time instinctual yet subject to elaborate, outwardly recognizable patterns of behaviour and appearance; as the *praeceptor* puts it, Ars 1. 737–8 *ut uoto potiare tuo, miserabilis esto,* | *ut qui te uideat, dicere possit 'amas'* ('To get your wish, appear lovesick, so that anyone who sees you can say "you're in love"'). For the Roman poet, this very human paradox invites a didactic jeu d'esprit; for the modern scientist, a sober scientific explanation. Underlying this seeming contradiction between nature and nurture, argues Buss, is 'our evolutionary

---

[18] Buss (1994: 105; cf. Ars 1. 611–19 (*simulator*, with aside for females), 631–58, 2. 311–14 (*simulator*), 641–2 (*dissimulasse*).

[19] Ibid. 111; cf. Ars 1. 505–24, 3. 433–52, on male dress codes; by contrast nearly a quarter of Book 3 addressed to women covers strategies for enhancing female physical appearance and deportment; see Ars 3. 129–352 (on female hair, dress, make-up, concealment of physical flaws, deportment, voice and elocution, dance).

[20] Ibid. 134, Ars 1. 659–62 (*lacrimae*), 2. 179–232 (*obsequium*).

[21] Ibid., Ars 2. 435–66, for men, 3. 577–610, 667–82, for women.

[22] Ibid. 11 and Buss (2000). Ovid's *praeceptor* gives jealousy special attention and treats it in a highly nuanced fashion (Ars 2. 357–492, 3. 576–746). The *praeceptor* advises men to forestall a rival by not staying away too long (2. 357–72). Citing Medea, the *praeceptor* characterizes female jealousy as intense and violent (2. 373–89) and while allowing men to philander (*ludite*), he gives them specific instructions on avoiding detection (2. 389–408). If a man does get caught, he should expect retribution in kind and use sex to appease his mistress (2. 410–24; cf. the *praeceptor*'s advice to the would-be lover to approach his love interest when she, piqued by jealousy, wants to repay her current mate in kind (1. 365–74). It is as prudent for men to learn to control their jealousy (2. 539–600) as it is for women (3. 683–746). For a discussion of Ovid on jealousy, see Myerowitz (1985: 53–4, 93–4, 100).

past—a past that has grooved and scored our minds as much as our bodies, our strategies for mating as much as our strategies for survival'[23]

'Works of art that prove enduring', observes E. O. Wilson, the grand old man of sociobiology and consilience, 'are intensely humanistic. Born in the imagination of individuals, they nevertheless touch upon what was universally endowed by human evolution.'[24] No one would claim that Ovid was an evolutionary psychologist, but he clearly does belong in the company of those poets who 'without the benefit of credentials, are great psychologists', who 'create "just representations of general nature"'.[25] Ovid's keen psychological instinct provides the only possible explanation for the striking parallels between his *Ars Amatoria* and modern evolutionary science in respect not only to the content of the poem's many specific observations on erotic behaviour, but also in its representation of human sexual strategies as operating on a field of dynamic interaction between nature and nurture. For Ovid's *praeceptor amoris*, as I hope to show in this chapter, 'culture can determine itself, but it cannot determine human nature'[26] and human nature is itself not 'a formless lump pounded into shape by culture'[27] but includes 'culture' in the form of an innate template of evolved behaviour patterns and mental mechanisms that are common to all human beings. According to today's theorists, this inherited universal 'mental software' limits superficial variations across cultures, operating on the

---

[23] Buss (1994: 2).
[24] Wilson (1998: 219). Wilson (8) explains his choice of the term 'consilience' for the title and theme of his 1998 book as follows: 'Consilience is the key to unification. I prefer this word over 'coherence' because its rarity has preserved its precision, whereas coherence has several possible meanings, only one of which is consilience. William Whewell, in his 1840 synthesis *The Philosophy of the Inductive Sciences*, was the first to speak of consilience, literally a 'jumping together' of knowledge by the linking of facts and fact-based theory across disciplines to create a common groundwork of explanation. He said, 'The Consilience of Inductions takes place when an Induction, obtained from one class of facts, coincides with an Induction, obtained from another different class. This Consilience is a test of the truth of the Theory in which it occurs.'
[25] Pinker (2002: 422) quoting Samuel Johnson.
[26] Ridley (2003: 207).
[27] Pinker (2002: 55). Cf. Ridley (2003: 208): 'Genes are at the root of nurture as well as nature.'

analogy of a universal generative grammar that determines variations between individual languages.[28] Or, to take another familiar example, 'people may dress differently, but they may all strive to flaunt their status via their appearance'.[29]

While Ovid writes for his specific Roman audience and invokes the alterity of people of other times and places,[30] his underlying grammar is a universal one. Generations of readers who with no specialist knowledge have found little difficulty in performing a virtually automatic translation of Ovid's erotic instruction from its very Roman context into their own experience have known this all along.[31] The explanation for the poem's instant relevance to readers of all eras, I suggest, is to be found by re-examining Ovid's *Ars Amatoria* from the perspective of universal human nature as redefined by recent decades of work in the sciences.

Human nature, in today's understanding, occupies a space best thought of as intermediary between full-blown, highly differentiated 'culture' and unmediated instinct common to all animal life. While human beings exist on a continuum with other animal species, 'human acts are not selected from a repertoire of knee-jerk reactions like a fish attacking a red spot or a hen sitting on eggs'.[32] Rather, human nature manifests itself on a field of reciprocity between Nature (universal) and Nurture (culturally specific but limited by our genetic inheritance to a relatively narrow range of expressions). Aspects of this nature–nurture dynamic have increasingly come under scrutiny by scientists in fields such as cognitive neuroscience, behavioural genetics, evolutionary psychology (the current euphemism for 1970s sociobiology), and environmental science. These

---

[28] Pinker (2002: 37); Pinker (1994).

[29] Pinker (2002: 39).

[30] Both mythological characters from the past (such as Andromache, Tecmessa (*Ars* 3. 109–12, 517–24), Hephaestus (*Ars* 2. 461–94) and Procris (*Ars* 3. 687–746)) and foreigners (e.g. *Ars* 3. 193–96) are often adduced as examples of uncultivated erotic behaviour, as emphasized by Volk in her contribution to this volume, Ch. 12. On Ovid's *cultus-rusticitas* contrast, see Myerowitz (1985: 41–72, 181–2). On the specifically urban colouring of the *Ars*, see D'Elia (1959: 186–97), Scivoletto (1976: 70–1), Labate (1979: 48–67). For an hitherto unnoticed allusion to the recently discovered Augustan *horologium* in *Ars* 1. 68 and 3. 388, see Simpson (1992).

[31] Or as one of my students recently put it: 'Ovid is a player!' Cf. Volk, Ch. 12 n. 8.

[32] Pinker (2002: 36).

so-called 'borderline disciplines' bridge scientific and humanistic studies and, according to Wilson, each approach contributes from its own perspective to the search for 'epigenetic rules': the hereditary bases common to all humans that bias our cultural choices, interpretations, and perceptions, thus giving new substance to the old idea of 'Human Nature'.[33] This 'borderline area' where biology and culture meet also happens to be the setting of Ovid's erotodidaxis in the *Ars Amatoria*.

As all readers know, Ovid's subject is not love, however defined, nor, for the most part, lovemaking, however much bed beckons to the student-lover as the coveted prize. Certainly, as the *praeceptor* repeatedly abjures, the *Ars Amatoria* is not about self-consciously 'procreative sex', within the context of marriage, institutionalized in Roman society as *liberorum procreandorum gratia* ('for the purpose of producing children').[34] But neither can its contents be limited unambiguously to 'recreational' or extramarital sex, as Ovid learned to his ultimate sorrow. For us as for Ovid or Augustus, all such distinctions are red herrings, as beside the point to the content of the *praeceptor*'s instructions as they are to nature itself. Mating strategy is the poet's subject, behaviour patterns which, it has been observed, 'survive remarkably intact... apparently... actually hardier than such details as, for instance, which sex a man should pursue'[35] or, I would add, whatever conscious goal is in mind. In other words, Ovid is writing about sexual selection.

Although Darwin recognized the distinction, since the 1930s biologists have lumped 'sexual selection' under the general term 'natural selection'. For our purposes it is important to restore the distinction. Differential reproduction is the motor of evolution, but in order to reproduce organisms must survive challenges of two different types.

---

[33] I have taken terms 'borderline disciplines', 'epigenetic rules', and much of the summary that follows from Wilson (1998: 164–80, 192). See Pinker (2002: 30–58) for an excellent summary of the last fifty years' advances in our understanding of human nature.

[34] Married women are explicitly excluded from the *praeceptor*'s audience in *Ars* 1. 31–4, 2. 599–600, implicitly in 2. 151–8, 3. 27, 57–8, 483–4, 585–6, 613–14 (cf. *Rem.* 385–6), and vociferously, by the exiled poet, e.g. *Tr.* 2. 243–53, 303–4, 347; *Pont.* 3. 3. 49–58. On procreation as the primary purpose of traditional Roman marriage, see Rawson (1986: 9).

[35] T. Goold (1963: 28).

'Natural selection' refers to the competition for survival against the challenges set by any given ecological niche. It depends on the selective advantage offered by random mutations and leaves little room for initiative or choice on the part of the animal. 'Sexual selection' refers directly to the competition for reproduction. The difference between the two modes of selection was instantiated in the paradox of the peacock's tail that to Darwin's keen eye posed an obvious threat to the animal's survival and that could only be explained as conferring a reproductive advantage in the competition for a desirable mate and continuation of the peacock's genetic line. For it is not enough for an organism to survive to sexual maturity through natural selection. In order to reproduce, it still must be selected over its rivals as a sexual partner by a member of the opposite sex. To return to an earlier point, sexual selection to a great extent turns on choice and the exercise of will. As Miller explains it:

One of the main reasons why mate choice evolves is to help animals choose sexual partners who carry good genes. Sexual selection is the professional at sifting between genes. By comparison, natural selection is a rank amateur. The evolutionary pressures that result from mate choice can therefore be much more consistent, accurate, efficient, and creative than natural selection pressures.[36]

One need not invoke the scientific distinction between 'proximate' and 'ultimate' causes, which in the case of sex would be respectively 'sensory pleasure' and 'reproduction', when experience suffices to teach us that procreation is not usually the conscious goal of individuals intent on sex. 'Ultimately people crave sex in order to reproduce (because the goal of sex is reproduction), but proximately they may do everything they can not to reproduce (because the proximate cause of sex is pleasure).'[37] In the same way, Ovid's *Ars* treats sexual selection as a goal in itself, with fine distinctions between sex and 'love' or transience and permanence largely irrelevant. The point is not lost on Ovid's *praeceptor* who claims (*Ars* 1. 91–2):

[36] Miller (2001: 8); for discussion, see Miller (2001) and Ridley (1993: 129–69). It is a curious historical coincidence that the *praeceptor*, too, invokes the peacock's tail as an analogy for human courtship behaviour in *Ars* 1. 627–8.

[37] Pinker (2002: 54).

illic inuenies quod ames, quod ludere possis, | *quodque semel tangas, quodque tenere uelis,* in a couplet that nicely mingles the specifically Roman setting (*illic*) with a universally human process: 'There [in the theatres] you will find love, flirtation, "a one-night stand" or a "keeper".'

The process of sexual selection occurs on the perilous road (the metaphor is Ovid's), between physical instinct and fulfilment, that borderline area where nature (sexual instinct) and nurture (cultural codes and their rationalizations) intersect, precisely where Wilson's 'epigenetic rules' should kick in.[38] Ovid's interest in this abstract 'place', I would argue, moves the *Ars* far beyond the specificity of its Roman context to a level best accessed by invoking the human universals of evolutionary theory.[39]

Indeed, the broadest humour of Ovid's *Ars Amatoria* relies on the assumption of an innate basis for human erotic behaviour, the *cultus* of sex. There is nothing intrinsically funny about sex (neither the instinct, nor its fulfilment). What humans do on the long road *between* instinct and fulfilment is the stuff of humour. This voyage is the poem's setting and subject, as directed by the *persona* of the pompous instructor, Ovid's *praeceptor amoris,* instructing an untutored student on 'what everybody knows'. As the poet himself later put it in the *Tristia* (1. 1. 112), his *Ars* taught loving (*amare*), a subject of which nobody is ignorant (*quod nemo nescit*).

The opening call to class sets up the running joke of the poem: *si quis in hoc artem populo non nouit amandi,* | *hoc legat et lecto carmine doctus amet* (*Ars* 1. 1–2, with its nice juxtaposition of the specific *hoc populo* and universal *quis*, 'If there's *anybody* in *this nation* who doesn't know the art of loving, let him read this poem and love as a learned lover'). In reality, there is no one to come forward and take the course. Both the *praeceptor* with his assumption that he has something 'new' to teach and the hypothetical student, a fictionalized construct of the naïf, are funny precisely because the reader already knows the rules, or, more likely, realizes that he has been acting upon

---

[38] For Ovid's pervasive use of the metaphor of a chariot or sea voyage in the *Ars,* see Myerowitz (1985: 73–103).
[39] For this reason I cannot agree with Volk's characterization of the poet as a blank slate constructionist, Ch. 12.

them all the time, as he hears the *praeceptor*'s theoretical instruction. The fact that never in 'real life' was there such a student or such a teacher is what makes this very funny poem so universally funny. For the running joke to work as well as it does, the poem must assume the reality of some type of 'epigenetic rules' already operative in the audience. Specialized studies of the Roman context can and do uncover less universally accessible, more culturally specific aspects of the poem's humour: these include Ovid's political 'irreverence' in casting seduction as a suitable subject for didactic poetry, while lifting language and form from *inter alia* Hesiod, Lucretius, and Vergil; Ovid's deflation of the Augustan claim to have restored the pristine virtue of the Roman family by his marriage legislation and propaganda, or the poet's general reluctance to subscribe to the Augustan myth of a restored golden age.[40] All add to the poem's richly textured humour and all would be cross-culturally incomprehensible to untutored twenty-first century readers.[41] But these approaches to the poem should not obscure the fact that for Ovid, as for today's evolutionary scientists, when it comes to sex, we humans all operate in pretty much the same way.

For moderns, however, Ovid's didactic poem may have resonances transcending the literary play that entertained his Roman audience. Along with determining the witty 'scientific' tone of his *Ars Amatoria*, the didactic genre draws attention to an evolved characteristic that is seen by contemporary science as uniquely human. In and of itself, the didactic genre instantiates the human 'ability to accumulate culture and transmit information' across generations and distances.[42] According to Ridley, it is this one highly evolved quality that sets human beings apart from other species, which have also been shown to be capable of culture, such as the use of tools.[43] Furthermore, not

---

[40] In this volume, see Chs. 11 and 7, by Casali and Gibson; more generally, see Rudd (1976).

[41] Most notably, moderns raised on a diet of sober 'self-help' manuals on every conceivable aspect of the erotic would probably miss the humour of Ovid's use of the didactic form for erotic instruction. Ovid's ancient audience would have appreciated the literary play as in the tradition of witty Hellenistic didactic poems on every conceivable topic including seduction and sex; see Parker (1992), Gibson (2003a: 13–21).

[42] Ridley (2003: 201).

[43] Ibid. 209 on chimpanzees etc.; see 201–30.

only does the didactic poet traditionally claim to offer content of universal application,[44] but the poetic genre also anticipates the analytic approach of the natural sciences, breaking down the object of study into its smallest unit, in the hope of reconstituting a whole, now better understood.

While the *praeceptor* proudly acknowledges real changes in Roman sexual culture over time (for example, his laudatory aside contrasting the cultivation of his own day with the brute simplicity of early Rome, *Ars* 3. 113–28), he also sets human sexual behaviour on an evolutionary continuum that acknowledges both discontinuity and continuity with other animals and that accords with the poet's general belief in change over time. The specifically literary and political implications of the poem's frequent analogies from the natural world have often been noted and studied.[45] But the *praeceptor*'s many analogies from nature also counterpoint his specifically Roman urban allusions and have the effect of universalizing the work. These allusions to the natural world evoke the full sweep of the human evolutionary journey by introducing both continuities and discontinuities with other forms of animal life. In the Lucretian anthropology of Book 2 (*Ars* 2. 467–92), sex (*voluptas*) is presented as a primordial agent of socialization for all animals, including brutish humanity.[46] Continuity between humans and other animals is further emphasized by likening the love object to fish, fowl, animals, and fields. Discontinuity is introduced by metaphors that liken the lover to hunter, fisherman, and farmer.[47] Thus for the poet, as for today's evolutionary scientists, humans are part of a natural continuum while at the same time a species in some respects set apart.

The universality of the poem's content has been confirmed by contemporary ethnographic research that goes beyond the strictly

---

[44] As noted by Volk in this volume, Ch. 12.
[45] See especially Kenney (1958) and Leach (1964).
[46] The passage is discussed extensively in Myerowitz (1985: 48–57).
[47] For flora and fauna see *Ars* 1. 45–8, 57–8, 93–6, 117–18, 271–2, 279–80, 391–3, 451, 471–2, 627–30, 757–66, 2. 147–50, 179–84, 363–4, 373–6, 3. 67–8, 77–80, 101–2, 249–50, 419–20; for hunters, trappers, etc., see *Ars* 1. 45–8, 89, 253, 263–6, 269–70, 391–3, 450, 763–6, 2. 513, 668, 671–2, 3. 425–8, 554–6. On the poem's relatively consistent association of the female with untamed nature and the male with tamer, trapper, and master of nature, see Leach (1964), Myerowitz (1981–2), Myerowitz (1985: 104–28).

erotic to cover the full range of human behaviours. A list of observed 'surface' universals (as opposed to deep mental structures theorized on the basis of experiment) has been compiled by Donald Brown.[48] Ovid's *praeceptor* not only covers most of Brown's 'universals' with either direct or indirect application to mating behaviour: sexual jealousy, modesty, attractiveness, attraction, coyness display. He also invokes more general patterns of human behaviour and cognition such as gift-giving, various uses and effects of language, manipulation of self-image, cultural variability, and even the perceived culture–nature distinction. For example, the *praeceptor* is excruciatingly sensitive to assumed oppositions between nature and culture in his claim that female passivity in courtship is a purely conventional cover for a *libido* fiercer than the male's (*Ars* 1. 275–82).[49] More pervasive is Ovid's application of cross-cultural characteristics of human social relations to specifically erotic ends. The *praeceptor*'s instructions include the human universals of 'risk taking' (*Ars* 1. 389–98, 608–10), 'manipulation of self image' (*Ars* 1. 505–24, 595–600, 723–38) and 'self-control' (*Ars* 2. 167–74, 529–32, 547–60). 'Triangular awareness (assessing relationships among the self and two other people', is a mainstay of his advice on manipulating a rival as well as the lady's maid and other servants (*Ars* 1. 350–98, 579–88, 739–54, 2. 251–660, 287–94, 335–6, 593–6). Language is surely the most powerful weapon in the *praeceptor*'s arsenal (*Ars* 2. 121–4). His recommended strategies for outwitting rivals and winning a mate resonate with every audience because they wittily invoke the full range of universal uses of language: notably, 'language employed to manipulate others' (*Ars* 1. 143–6, 421–86, 597–602, 609–10, 631–2, 2. 151–2, 641–2, 3. 675–8, 795–8), 'language employed to misinform and mislead' (*Ars* 1. 489–90, 2. 295–314,

---

[48] Brown's list is more inclusive than Buss's (1994) which is limited to sexual behaviour and has been referenced to the *Ars* earlier in this essay. Brown's 1989 list together with post-1989 additions forms the Appendix of Pinker (2002: 435–9). For discussion and references, see Brown (1991, 1999).

[49] 'Humanity shares this profile of ardent, polygamist males and coy, faithful females with about 99 percent of all animal species, including our closest relatives, the apes', remarks Ridley (1993: 178). Thus, the *praeceptor*'s observation on universal gender differences in human mating behaviour is true as far as it goes, but the pattern itself is an evolved behaviour with a good biological basis, rather than the purely arbitrary convention that he seems to assume.

327–8, 410, 3. 467–82, 607–8), and 'language [as] not a simple reflection of reality' *(Ars* 1. 219–28, 601–2, 2. 657–62, 3. 685–746).

We can discern yet another of Brown's 'Human Universals'— 'copulation usually conducted in private'[50]—in the *praeceptor*'s spirited condemnation of lovers who kiss and tell (*Ars* 2. 613–24):

> ipsa Venus pubem, quotiens uelamina ponit,
>   protegitur laeua semireducta manu.
> in medio passimque coit pecus: hoc quoque uiso
>   auertit uultus nempe puella suos.
> conueniunt thalami furtis et ianua nostris,
>   parsque sub iniecta ueste pudenda latet
> et, si non tenebras, ad quiddam nubis opacae
>   quaerimus atque aliquid luce patente minus.
> tunc quoque, cum solem nondum prohibebat et imbrem
>   tegula sed quercus tecta cibumque dabat,
> in nemore atque antris, non sub Ioue, iuncta uoluptas:
>   tanta rudi populo cura pudoris erat.
>
> (However often she lays aside her garments, Venus herself
>   covers her private parts, half bent, with her left hand.
> Beasts mate openly and everywhere: and at the sight of this,
>   a girl surely looks away.
> Bedrooms and a door suit our secret joys,
>   covers hide our private parts,
> and we seek, if not darkness, some dimness,
>   some shadier spot.
> Then too, when still no roof tile blocked out sun and rain
>   but only oaks provided food and shelter
> folks made love in woods and caves, not beneath the open air.
>   So great the care for modesty among primeval folk.)

When it comes to lovemaking, *pudor* or a desire for concealment from view is instinctive, goes back to primordial times, and sets humanity apart from even domesticated animals, (*pecus*), asserts the *praeceptor*. '[Humans, universally] have standards of sexual modesty—even though they might customarily go about naked. People, adults in particular, do not normally copulate in public, nor do they relieve themselves without some attempt to do it modestly,' writes the evolutionary scientist, confirming the *praeceptor*'s claim with

---

[50] See Pinker (2002: 436).

contemporary research.[51] The Ovidian passage playfully subsumes post-coital bragging under the logographic topos of public lovemaking in the way of cattle, a custom earlier attributed by Herodotus to distant peoples from India and the Caucasus region; cf. Hdt. 3. 101, 1. 203.14 with How and Wells ad loc. Together with word play (*pudor/pudenda*), the *praeceptor* invokes a generalized erotic representation in support of his association of *pudor* with coitus: the pose of Praxiteles' nude Aphrodite instantiates human *pudor*, as does any real-life *puella*'s aversion from the sight of animals in open copulation. In fact, the rhetoric of the passage quoted above extends the notion of a universal human *pudor* from reality to representation: to talk about love is as much a violation of the human instinct for concealment as to make love in the open. Taken together, the allusion both to the Praxitelean statue (whose coy poise assumes a human gaze) and to the *puella* (who shrinks from gazing) suggest that *pudor* is operative not only when we humans make love, but also when we view (or talk about, or hear about) others making love. In other words, the passage seems to imply that our 'human nature' may explain why we look at others making love with heightened sensibility of ourselves as voyeurs and transgressors.[52]

For the *praeceptor*, the voyeur translated into the 'player' who brags of his sexual conquests has transgressed a certain 'natural' universally human behaviour pattern and is to be deplored.[53] The acknowledgement that violations exist in no way suggests the absence of the norm in the poet's own day, since a universal taboo obviously implies the existence of its real or potential violation. 'Rape' together with 'Rape Proscribed'—both listed as 'Human Universals' by Brown[54]—offers a particularly striking example of the cross-cultural coexistence of a universal taboo together with its universal violation.

---

[51] See Brown (1991: 139), Diamond (1997: 3). The most obvious evolutionary advantage of concealment during sex would be a lesser likelihood of interruption.

[52] Although probably a natural extension, Ovid's observation is, to the best of my knowledge, as yet unsubstantiated in research on human universals. It is all the more remarkable coming from one whose work contains sexually explicit passages and who in his post-exilic defence of the *Ars* claimed that no connection exists between art and life and observed that sexually explicit paintings were present even in the imperial residences; cf. *Tr.* 2. 521–8 with Myerowitz (1992).

[53] On the voyeur as a transgressive figure in Roman art, see Clarke (1998: 103).

[54] See Brown (1991: 138), Pinker (2002: 438).

Ovid's Evolution

Not surprisingly, this complex situation elicits some highly nuanced observations on rape from the Ovidian *praeceptor*.

Ovid raises the possibility of sexual violence in the *Ars Amatoria* only to reject it. His excursus on the rape of the Sabine women (*Ars* 1. 101–34), *inter alia*, affords the *praeceptor* the opportunity to contrast the brutality of mating in Romulus' day with the cultivated courting of the poet's own age.[55] Later in the same book (*Ars* 1. 663–80), Ovid's *praeceptor* counsels his student to use *vis* (force), but this *vis*, as illustrated by mythological precedents (*Ars* 1. 679–704), turns out to be more of an act of male initiative against feigned female coyness than genuine rape. Ovid's is a mating game where both parties are playing by the same rules (*Ars* 1. 665–7, 673–8), where, as Miller puts it, 'Males Court, Females Choose'.[56] Indeed, in the same passage on *vis* the *praeceptor* warns his student against inflicting any real hurt (1. 667–8): *tantum, ne noceant teneris male rapta labellis/ neue queri possit dura fuisse, cave* ('But take care to be gentle when you're stealing kisses. Don't give her tender lips cause to complain').[57] The *praeceptor*'s repeated insistence on an ideal of mutuality in sex (*Ars* 2. 681–9, 725–8) also strongly argues for his condemnation of rape. Moreover, the *praeceptor*'s advocacy of female volition in the first two books of the *Ars* is the obvious *raison d'être* for his teaching, as is his assumption of actively interested women in Book 3 of the poem. After all, what would be the point of an elaborate treatise on seduction, if violent rape were considered a legitimate option?

According to recent scientific studies, female volition is as essential to evolution as it is to the *praeceptor*'s students. In the calculus of sexual selection, 'rape subverts female choice, the core of the ubiquitous mechanism of sexual selection. By choosing the male and the circumstances for sex, a female can maximize the chances that her offspring will be fathered by a male with good genes, a willingness

---

[55] The passage is treated by Labate, Ch. 10 in this volume; see also Myerowitz (1985: 62–7).

[56] See Miller (2001: 39), who attributes early opposition to Darwin's hypothesis of sexual selection to a Victorian ideological bias against the important role of female choice in the process.

[57] The *praeceptor* also condemns acts of jealous violence in *Ars* 2. 551–4.

and ability to share the responsibility of rearing the offspring, or both.'[58]

The poet's characterization of deep gender differences also accords with evolutionary theory: 'Unlike other human divisions such as race and ethnicity, where any biological divisions are minor at most and scientifically uninteresting, gender cannot possibly be ignored in the science of human beings', writes Pinker.[59] 'With respect to human sexuality', explains Donald Symons, 'there is a female human nature and a male human nature and these natures are extraordinarily different... Men and women differ in their sexual natures because throughout the immensely long hunting and gathering phase of human evolutionary history the sexual desires and dispositions that were adaptive for either sex were for the other tickets to reproductive oblivion.'[60] So, too, in the mating games of the *Ars Amatoria*, females dramatically differ from males in respect to their desires and dispositions: Ovid's females seek material security, his males seek sex. The *praeceptor* tutors his male audience on how best to evade giving gifts (1. 399–436, 2. 260–72).[61] He instructs females on how best to extract them (*Ars* 3. 529–32). In ringing Vergilian tones, the *praeceptor* defines the challenge for the male (*Ars* 2. 453): '*hoc opus, hic labor est*', *primo sine munere iungi* ('"his the task, this the toil": to bed her with no overheads').

This assymetrical characterization of the genders is not unique to any particular class or culture and has a clear evolutionary rationale. 'The gender that invests the most in creating and rearing the offspring, and so forgoes most opportunities for creating and rearing other offspring is the gender that has the least to gain from each extra mating.'[62] Because of their greater investment of time and energy in

---

[58] See Pinker (2002: 365). In their recent book, Thornhill and Palmer (2000) explain rape as an 'opportunistic' tactic for males who would not otherwise be selected; the authors document female resistance to rape throughout the animal kingdom.

[59] See Pinker (2002: 340).

[60] Symons quoted in Pinker (1997: 461). See also Symons (1992).

[61] On conflicting goals and competing strategies, cf. n. 13 and Myerowitz (1985: 118–26). Alison Sharrock has directed me to Sharon James's 2003 book on amatory persuasion in which the author argues that elegiac women cannot afford to love the lover for his own sake, though they would like to. Neither the *praeceptor* nor evolution allows this luxury to females.

[62] See Ridley (1993: 178); see also Buss (1994: 20), Pinker (1997: 460–91), Diamond (1997: 18–39).

rearing offspring, females have evolved to be more selective in choosing a mate, while males generally are less discriminating. Interestingly, neither the *praeceptor* nor evolution equates female selectivity with strict monogamy; the reverse is often the case.[63]

Ovid's *Ars Amatoria* treats *Ars* as well as *Amor*. The poem's *prooemium* pre-empts the question of the utility of his own *Ars* with its confident assertion that art is indeed useful and necessary and its 'proofs' by analogy from other areas of human experience. Scientists today are attempting to answer the same question in evolutionary terms. Evidence for the existence of art is as old as the human record, yet the reason for its existence still confounds us. Or, in evolutionary terms, the human impulse to create art is universal and inherited, but its adaptive functions are still subject to debate.[64] In his introduction, Ovid's *praeceptor* defines *ars* broadly as a technical skill and claims that it is a means of control. Love, like speeding ships and chariots, yields to the *artifex*, the practitioner of *ars (Ars* 1. 3–22). Later in the work, he narrows his definition of art to the 'fine arts': art is seductive, gives pleasure, and marks status. To attract a mate, we must know how to speak, to write, to sing, to dance, to recite poetry, including of course, the poems of a fellow named Ovid (*Ars* 1. 595–6, 3. 311–52).

The *praeceptor*'s observations are framed in a poem. In this sense, the *Ars Amatoria* is a meditation upon its own reason for being, with *ars* understood as poetry and song. If we were able to interview Ovid, he would probably respond that at the time he wrote the poem because he wanted to, because it gave him pleasure and status. This is reason enough for any individual artist. (Understandably, in exile he said that the 'stupid poem' wasn't worth it.)[65] If we were to ask the

---

[63] While a desire for multiple sexual partners is assumed for Ovid's males (*Ars* 2. 387–90), the possibility is also not excluded for his females (*Ars* 3. 611–66). According to evolutionary theory, female 'adultery' among humans and other animals is much more common than once believed and probably confers an evolutionary advantage; see Ridley (1993: 209–44), Hrdy (1981/1999).

[64] Under 'Human Universals', Brown lists, *inter alia*, aesthetics, poetry/rhetoric, polysemy, metaphor, metonym, narrative, music seen as art, onomatopoeia, rhythm, and symbolic speech. Pinker (2002: 403–8), citing Dennis Dutton, enumerates seven 'universal signatures' of art, but considers art itself a by-product of other adaptations: desire for status, aesthetic pleasure, technological ability. So, too, Wilson (1998: 224–6) sees art as an ancillary consequence of the human 'big brain.'

[65] On Ovid's impulse for writing the *Ars*, see e.g. *Tr.* 1. 153–4, 2. 354–8; cf. *Tr.* 5. 59–60 on writing in general. On the poet's regrets, see e.g. *Tr.* 2. 316, 341–4, 5. 12. 67–8, *Pont.* 2. 9. 73, 3. 3. 37.

poet for a transpersonal explanation for the human impulse to create art, he would probably generalize on the *praeceptor*'s observations on the utility of the arts for courtship, recalling by way of example, his commendation of the arts of eloquence (*bonas artes... eloquio*) as critical for success in seduction.[66] Or, he might send us to the following passage from his *Fasti* (4. 107–14):

> prima feros habitus homini detraxit: ab illa
>   uenerunt cultus mundaque cura sui.
> primus amans carmen uigilatum nocte negata
>   dicitur ad clausas concinuisse fores,
> eloquiumque fuit duram exorare puellam
>   proque sua causa quisque disertus erat.
> mille per hanc [Venus] artes motae; studioque placendi
>   quae latuere prius, multa reperta ferunt.

> (She [Venus] first lured men to shed their savage dress;
>   She brought refinement and self-conscious elegance.
> The first lover (so they say) sang his locked-out love song,
>   Keeping vigil in the lonely night.
> It took eloquence to win a stubborn girl; each lover
>   learned to speak for his own plight.
> Venus bore a thousand arts; men wished to please and
>   what formerly was hidden came to light.)

In this aetiology, Ovid explicitly ascribes a biological origin to human art: the first locked-out lover (*primus amans*) invented poetry to gain access to his lady love, eloquence was born in the desire to attract a mate.[67] Sexual selection gave rise to 'a thousand arts' (*mille artes*), including such highly literary genres as *peitho* poetry, praise poetry, and the *paraklausithyron*, all with cross-cultural shelf-lives documented from Egyptian love poetry of the second millennium BC to the lyrics of today's pop music.

---

[66] Cf. *Ars* 1. 459–62: *disce bonas artes, moneo, Romana iuuentus, | non tantum trepidos ut tueare reos, | quam populus iudexque grauis lectusque senatus, | tam dabit eloquio uicta puella manus*. For the specific '*Romanitas*' of the observation, see Volk's contribution to this volume, Ch. 12.

[67] See Fisher (1992: 35–6). Traditionally, Ovid is seen here to apply the Stoic notion of necessity as the mother of invention to the realm of courtship; the Stoic concept, in fact, inverts the evolutionary understanding of random mutations (= 'inventions') that are transmitted because they happen to serve some adaptive function (= 'necessity').

This Ovidian explanation for the origins of human art has recently been recast in evolutionist terms. As it turns out, the *praeceptor* may have been overly cynical in his claim that were the great Homer himself to come courting empty-handed in the poet's own day, he would have been summarily shown the door *(Ars* 2. 279–80). In his compelling book, Geoffrey Miller maintains that the arts (e.g. storytelling, poetry, art, music, dance, sports, humour, etc.) are among the many indicators of the fitness of a potential mate that have evolved through sexual selection. Furthermore, argues Miller, the uniquely human 'big brain' with its surplus of intelligence is itself the end result of the evolutionary pressures of courtship and mating.[68] Whether a by-product or cause of human intelligence, when seen in this light the 'useless' arts, like Darwin's peacock's tail (apparently useless, wasteful, and downright dangerous), turn out to be as critical for human survival as the *praeceptor*'s hyperbolic *prooemium* claimed. Certainly, Miller's argument gives new meaning to the exiled poet's words in *Pont.* 1. 5. 53–4: *magis utile nil est | artibus his, quae nil utilitatis habent* ('nothing is more useful than these arts which have no use').

The striking 'relevance' of the poem as seen through the prism of evolutionary theory on human nature makes Ovid's *Ars Amatoria* a good place to reflect upon how we read and teach the 'Classics' today. From the very outset, our readings of ancient texts have moved between the poles of the universal and particular. In other words, we read the ancient texts for their relevance to our own experience or we try to understand these texts within their own cultural context. In reality, usually a bit of both is what happens when we read any work from a time or place that is different from our own.

Because of its charged subject matter, Ovid's *Ars* has always been read in these two ways, even while these two reading modalities were subjected to extreme dissociation. As Ralph Hexter demonstrates in this volume, it was possible for medieval schoolmasters to contextualize Ovid's *Ars* as so peculiarly Roman that they could use the work as a reader for instructing their pupils in Latin grammar and Roman culture.[69] To specify the poem's content as belonging to an 'Other'

---

[68] See Miller (2001). Dissanayake (1988), (1992), (2000) also analyses art as an evolutionary adaptation.
[69] See Hexter, Ch. 15 below.

and thus irrelevant Roman world was presumably thought to ensure the desired effect of distancing student readers from the erotic content. But the exaggerated historicization that posited total experiential discontinuity between reader and text demands a fiction that must have been difficult for any reader to maintain. Over time, medieval responses to Ovid's erotodidactic poetry, Hexter writes, moved from emphasis on taking the poem as peculiarly Roman to taking its instruction literally as applicable beyond the Roman context to the reader's own world. For individual medieval readers, the tension between these two ways of reading must always have been felt. So, too, in our own age and perhaps with greater immediacy than in the case of most ancient literature, people inevitably read Ovid's *Ars Amatoria* in two ways.

The dynamic tension between these two ways of reading the Classics has yielded centuries of literary discourse resonant in such contemporary critical categories as 'Same' versus 'Other' and, more broadly, 'Nature' versus 'Culture' or 'Nurture'. Underlying all such antitheses is the notion of 'Universal' versus 'Specific'. In the mid-twentieth century, a time of ever-increasing prestige of the sciences and the demotion of the humanities to the status of 'luxury' items, the academic literary pendulum swung toward specialized 'scientific' readings that privileged the scholar-critic and consequently widened the breach between the specialist and the lay person. Indeed, perhaps the most dramatic shift in classical scholarship during the twentieth century was a swing towards culturally specific readings of ancient texts, best marked by the appearance of E. R. Dodd's, *Greeks and the Irrational* (1951), a watershed work that argued that Greek culture was markedly different from our own. This shift countered the then prevailing tendency to read classical texts as repositories of eternal truths, perhaps best exemplified by the enormous and enduring popularity of Edith Hamilton's *The Greek Way* throughout the first half of the twentieth century.[70] Not surprisingly, the scholarly sea change coincided with the rising professionalism and specialization of university humanities departments on the model of the natural and social sciences.[71]

[70] On Edith Hamilton's popularity, see Hallett (1996–7).

[71] For analysis and critiques of the phenomenon, but with conclusions different from my own, see Hanson and Heath (1998) and Hanson, Heath, and Thornton (2001).

The new emphasis was welcome and necessary, especially in the field of Classics. Ancient Greeks and Romans, together or in turn, had long been taken as progenitors of Western high culture, and as such even the most illiterate European or American could and often did assume that he was connected to classical culture in a direct line of descent. Paradoxically, by widening the gap between expert and lay person, the specialization of classical scholarship enabled the democratization of the profession. No longer did one inherit the Classics by virtue of birth; one acquired ownership of the ancient texts by study, with the option of hard work open to all, irrespective of gender or ethnicity. Besides, the classical texts themselves proved fascinating, well worth studying in their own right, not necessarily because their cultural contexts mirrored our own, but precisely because they were different and difference is interesting. Moreover, to clarify the nature of the discontinuities often enabled a clearer understanding of one's own cultures and world-views. The many late twentieth-century studies that contextualized classical texts within their particular historical and cultural settings yielded far richer and historically accurate readings, as they plumbed beneath the old, usually flawed, universalist generalizations. At the same time, they posed a forceful challenge to the 'old view' of the timelessness and transcendence of decontextualized classical culture that had long monopolized exclusive rights to top billing on any Western hierarchy of cultures.

This insistence on the radical 'Otherness' of ancient culture has been particularly pronounced in recent scholarship on ancient sexualities, generally characterized by the perspective that 'sexuality' as opposed to sex is a purely cultural construct emerging from a specific social and historical situation.[72] Indeed, scholarship on ancient sexualities offers what is perhaps the best access to a rich table of putative opposites: categories such as Universal/ Specific; Transcendent/ Historical; Nature/ Nurture; Nature/ Culture. As much political as academic, this approach proved a generally healthy corrective to the earlier tendency to lump all human sexualities under a monolithic,

---

[72] *Locus classicus* for the notion of human sexuality as a cultural construct or 'invention' is Foucault (1976–84); see also Halperin, Winkler, and Zeitlin (1989) with Clarke (1998), for a recent treatment of Roman erotic art using this approach.

transcendent Platonic Ideal inscribed by Nature or God. These readings, while not wrong, now seem to me to be incomplete.

After all, the old Nature/Nurture debate in its myriad permutations has perhaps finally outlived any usefulness, laid to eternal rest by recent work showing interdependence, i.e. *Nature via Nurture*.[73] In the case of sex, it may be not only sex that is universal, but also to a great extent 'sexualities': those putative 'cultural games', 'constructions', or 'inventions' may themselves bear study from a universalist perspective, *but* with a difference. On this go round, the universals of 'Human Nature' are to be sought not in transcendence—banal generalizations on ancients refashioned in our own image—but in immanence, the traditional realm of the natural sciences.

For classicists, this means reading those many ancient 'sexualities' on a relatively limited spectrum of expressions of a common human heritage carried in our genes and transmitted by sexual selection. Rather than yield universals so general as to be reductive, trivial, and useless, these supra- and transcultural readings may enrich our contextualized readings of many ancient literary works, precisely because of the importance of sexual selection both as the site of the evolutionary process and as the focus of enormous human cultural and educational effort.[74] As we have seen, Ovid's erotodidaxis offers generalizations on activities that each of us performs instinctively; his *praeceptor* quite remarkably *prescribes* many of the same rules that recent scientific studies of sexual selection and courtship patterns *describe*. The time now seems ripe to turn our attention to uncovering the 'tracks of evolution' in our study of ancient sexualities, on the model of Walter Burkert's sociobiological studies of ancient religion.[75]

---

[73] 'Nature via Nurture' is the title and thesis of Ridley (2003), as it is of most natural and social scientists today although popular debates are still usually framed around what Ridley (277–80) playfully terms '*homo stramineus*'. The 'new' synthetic approach has classical antecedents, for example, Cicero, *Arch.* 15 (relying on earlier traditions).

[74] On objections to evolutionary psychology as reductive, etc., as formulated by Clifford Geertz ('there is no mind for all cultures') and cited in Ridley (2003: 206), see Ridley's comments on the 'fallacy of determinism: set rules need not produce a set result. Within the sparse rules of chess, you can produce trillions of different games with just a few moves.' Cultural differences seen against this background emerge more sharply as fascinating variations on a universal theme; see Tooby and Cosmides (1992).

[75] See e.g. Burkert (1996) or more broadly Wilson (1998).

Such studies would reconcile spurious oppositions between nature and culture, integrating the past several decades' work on ancient sexualities within the wider context of evolutionary theory. Nor does the validity of one approach imply the delegitimization of the other. Culturally specific readings of Ovid's *Ars Amatoria* that explicate the Roman context of the poem remain important, indeed essential, for universalist readings, precisely because they demark the true cultural discontinuities and thus mark out the space for legitimate generalization.

Left to itself, in the very process of situating a work within its proper cultural milieu, contextualization can deracinate the classical texts from their universal human substrate. Paradoxically, the inclusion of 'science' forges readings more deeply 'humanistic', more inclusive than narrowly literary typologies, for the 'intertextuality' of evolution is inscribed in generations of human DNA. So, to approach literature and other cultural forms from an evolutionary perspective enlarges significantly our understanding of their place, function, and significance in human experience. This approach may make the humanities 'relevant' in the profoundest possible way.

With this in mind, I offer my reading of Ovid's *Ars Amatoria* as an example of a 'revised' universalist approach to an ancient erotodidactic text. Let us not altogether ignore the simple reality that most classical texts became classics because they can and do speak to any reader directly. As the advertisement for Ovid's *Ars* on tape reminds us, no text does so more than Ovid's *Ars Amatoria*.

Part IV

Reception

14

Paelignus, puto, dixerat poeta (Mart. 2. 41. 2): Martial's Intertextual Dialogue with Ovid's Erotodidactic Poems

Markus Janka

Martial and Ovid deserve further and more thorough comparison. The affinity between these two most influential Latin poets of their times is much closer than one may be willing to concede at first sight. Over the chronological and generic boundaries, which are of course undeniable, strong links tie them together.[1]

They are both brilliant masters of their main form of poetic articulation, the dactylic verse. As *poetae crypto-docti*, they combine intellectual humour based on literary allusions, innuendos, and double or even multiple entendres with at times shocking simplicity. The astonishing degree of self-referentiality with which they comment on their books, works, and œuvres distinguishes them from their less reflective colleagues as 'meta-poets' par excellence. Recently, Niklas Holzberg has shown that the structure of Martial's 'dodecalogue' with its poetological pieces as landmarks resembles the editorial technique applied in the series of books that constitute Ovid's exile poetry (five 'annuals', *Tristia*, plus four 'yearbooks', *Ex Ponto*).[2] Furthermore, the interrelation with their readers is integral to Ovid's

---

[1] For rather conventional catalogues of links between the two poets see Friedländer (1886: i. 25); Sullivan (1991: 105–7); Pitcher (1998: 59).

[2] See Holzberg (2002*b*: 130–2). At the end of his contribution to this volume, Ch. 3, Holzberg briefly treats the interrelation of the staged reader response in Mart. 1. 35 with Catullan and Ovidian pretexts.

as well as Martial's understanding of 'interactive' poetry and is, therefore, far more than accidental. The poems of both reflect their rather dialectical discourse with their *principes* and the political systems the Caesars represent. Moreover, their views on worldwide popularity and eternal afterlife achievable through the survival of their books tend to be quite similar, even up to the (virtually) comical implications of these claims of superiority.[3] Above all, they are both in a sense 'amatorians', since their use of motifs, phrases, and imagery shows overt as well as hidden features of a rather obsessive 'erotography', that is to say, a mode of literature in which sexuality dominates as a recurrent poetic theme and structural pattern.

1. HISTORY: FORMER SCHOLARSHIP ON THE (INTER)RELATIONS BETWEEN MARTIAL AND OVID

Despite this wide range of promising approaches towards a comparative poetology of Martial and Ovid, previous scholarship has mainly concentrated on details about biography, prosody, and antagonistic parameters such as dependence/independence, source/user, or innovation/imitation, leaving the more subtle problems open for investigation.[4]

The younger poet still finds himself reduced to his role as a kind of student of the elder and more famous Ovid, who according to the philological interpreters exerted great 'influence' on him. This

---

[3] For the amusing features of the poetological *ego Martialis*, see Holzberg (2002b: 124–6).

[4] There has been only slight progression from the positivistic collections and categorizations of 'allusions', 'resemblances/similarities' and phenomena of (quasi-) formulaic repetitions of phrases and verses—a tradition of research exemplified by Zingerle (1877), Wagner (1880), and Siedschlag (1972)—to a more recent focus on the complexity of Martial's Ovidian borrowings favoured by such scholars as Sullivan and Pitcher. Sullivan (1991: 107) summarizes the thematic scale of these reminiscences: 'Metaphors, similes and images on the composition of poetry, female colouring, old age, drinking from fountains of inspiration, even topographical references are freely borrowed by Martial (from Ovid) in the full expectation that the reader will at least vaguely recognise their source.'

picture of the relationship between a *praeceptor poeticus* and his admiring successor seems to fit well with Martial's frequent references to Ovid as a symbol of poetic fame through elegy; cf. e.g. Mart. 1. 61. 6 *Nasone Paeligni sonant* ('with Naso resound the Paelignians'). A striking example is the highly ironic utterance of Martial's *poeta*-speaker in 5. 10. 10: *norat Nasonem sola Corinna suum* ('the only one who knew her Naso was Corinna').[5] This might well be a bit of erotic/poetic jealousy on the speaker's part, if one understands *norat* as sexual, and the whole sentiment as poetological, i.e. about being a good reader. Be that as it may, the line is inverting *Am.* 3. 12 in a very amusing way. Who knows who Corinna is? Who knows who Ovid is?

In the nineteenth century Anton Zingerle argued that Martial studied Ovid carefully in order to become a more skilful versifier. That may be right, but it is certainly not enough. More than one hundred years after Zingerle, Roger Pitcher again focused on 'Martial's Debt to Ovid'. With scrutiny, but not without errors,[6] he explores the 'use' that Martial made of Ovidian features when he adapted them to his epigrammatic style. According to Pitcher, Martial borrowed particularly from Ovid's apologetic disclaimers in his addresses to his book(s) and to the emperor and overcame Ovidian love-poetry by eliminating subjectivity.[7]

2. TOWARDS A NEW APPROACH: INTERTEXTUAL DIALOGUE

In this chapter, I suggest a different approach. Instead of collecting and compiling new parallels to underscore the extent of Martial's 'debt to Ovid', I would like rather to shed new light on the intensity and depth of Martial's references to his ancestor within a process of congenial reception. It is not simply the case that he reminded his readers of his great predecessor by sporadically inserting Ovidian

---

[5] See Zingerle (1877: 3–4); Sullivan (1991: 106).

[6] For example, Ovid's comment about 'participating' in his own love poetry, which Pitcher seems to interpret as part of the autobiography of the real author, rather than as a literary construct.

[7] See Pitcher (1998: 75).

phrases.[8] By interpreting paradigmatic intertexts, I shall argue that Martial engaged in a creative dialogue with Ovid's erotic didactic poetry, especially the *Ars Amatoria*.

Adequate methodological instruments for analysing the interrelations between particular texts are provided by the theory of intertextuality. For me it seems to be most fruitful to adopt the variants of this Protean theory modified for the classicists' purposes by Don Fowler, Stephen Hinds, Richard Thomas, and Lowell Edmunds.[9] When applied to our two poets, these methodological premises should lead us to a new insight into the relationship between erotodidaxis and satirical epigram. The intertextual signals Martial so eagerly makes must no longer be restricted to their extratextual implications, namely, as homages to the great paradigm of witty Latin love poetry; they ought rather to be understood as creative responses to a classic revived through this dialogue by being interpreted, reaffirmed, questioned, debased, stained, or parodied.[10]

3. INSTANCES OF INTERTEXTUALITY BETWEEN (MOCK-)DIDACTIC AND EPIGRAM

(a) *libelli ludentes* as *theatra scripta?*

Let me begin with an example which has by now escaped the attention of comparative philologists. In the final part of his proemial

---

[8] Cases are numerous, but to take a specific allusion to the *Ars*: the line *puero liquidas aptantem Daedalon alas* (Mart. 4. 49. 5) is modelled on Ovid's *aptat opus puero* (*Ars* 2. 65) and *cera deo propiore liquescit* (*Ars* 2. 85). See Janka (1997: 86–7, 97 ad loc.). As well as isolated echoes, Martial quoted, picked up and parodied even whole passages and patterns in order to incorporate these mock-didactic features in the satirical cosmos of his epigrams.

[9] See Fowler and Hinds (1997); Fowler (2000*a*: 115–37); Thomas (1998); Edmunds (2001).

[10] In a forthcoming paper about 'Martial's Ovid', Stephen Hinds sketches the macrostructural outlines of Martial's continuous interplay with Ovidian genres, motifs, and individual pretexts which, according to Hinds, are transformed into 'Martial's *Tristia* (at home and abroad)', 'Martial's *Metamorphoses* (on myth)', 'Martial's *Remedia* (sex in the city)'.

epistle[11] introducing 'Book One' and thus the whole collection of his epigrams, Martial advises prudish and moralistic readers with old-fashioned disdain for frivolous language to read no further than the present opening comment: *si quis tamen tam ambitiose tristis est ut apud illum in nulla pagina latine loqui fas sit, potest epistula uel potius titulo contentus esse* ('but if anybody is so eager to be unhappy that he will tolerate Latin frankness not on one page, then let him be content with the letter or even the title', Mart. 1 *epist*. 12–14). Adding a more blatant definition of his desired audience, the poet/speaker compares his *epigrammata* with the *ludi Florales* (the games of Flora celebrated with licentious mimes) and consequently uses the metaphor 'my theatre' (*theatrum meum*) for his book(s). As soon as the books and verses have become a place, access can be allowed or denied: Martial puts it most trenchantly by remodelling a well-known anecdote about Cato Uticensis watching Flora's games and leaving the theatre when informed that his presence interferes with the custom of *nudatio mimarum*[12]: *non intret Cato theatrum meum, aut si intrauerit, spectet* ('do not let Cato enter my theatre, but if he should have entered, let him watch', Mart. 1 *epist*. 15–16). 'Cato' here is the type of Stoic master of morality[13] representative of groups of readers[14] whom 'Martial' or his auctorial *ego* purports to warn. So this is a paradigmatic instance of the programmatic addresses to readers who are either invited to read or excluded from the intended audience. Ovid (above all in his *Ars*) is particularly fond of this didactic device. Already at the very beginning of the *Ars* he brings together in close proximity an invitation to inexperienced individuals and a reproach to chaste women.[15] He thus differentiates

---

[11] For the latest scholarly debate surrounding the political implications of the introductory epistle, see Beck (2002) and Grewing (2003).

[12] Citroni (1975: 11) refers to Val. Max. 2. 10. 8 and Sen. *Ep.* 97. 8, and compares also Mart. 9. 28. 3 *spectatorem potui fecisse Catonem*.

[13] On Cato Uticensis as an *exemplum* in Martial's epigrams, see Lorenz (2002: 138–41).

[14] See Citroni (1975: 11 ad loc.).

[15] Cf. Ov. *Ars* 1. 1–2 *si quis in hoc artem populo non nouit amandi, | hoc legat et lecto carmine doctus amet* ('if anybody amongst this people does not know the art of love, he should read this, and having read the poem be a learned lover'); *Ars* 1. 31 *este procul, uittae tenues, insigne pudoris* ('stay far away, fine hair-bands, signs of chastity'). See also Hollis (1977: 38): '... both Vestal Virgins and unmarried free-born girls wore *uittae*... the important point is that they were denied to *meretrices*'.

between welcome and unwelcome audiences. Martial modifies these Ovidian traits. At the end of the choliambs sealing the proemial epistle, the speaker directly addresses his 'Cato' with two questions: *cur in theatrum, Cato seuere, uenisti? | an ideo tantum ueneras, ut exires?* (Mart. 1 *epist.* 20–1). In my own paraphrase: 'For what purpose, rigid Cato, have you come to the theatre? Was this the one and only reason for you to come that you can go out again with the air of indignation about the scandalous show?'

The Martial proem and the opening of *Ars* 1 are specifically linked by the use of the didactic formula, *si quis.* Ovid's *si quis* invites us to read on; Martial's *si quis* (1 *epist.* 12) does not. Then Martial's next word, *tamen*, points to the way it is copying and modifying Ovid's opening. The term *tristis* probably evokes the anti-eroticism of tragedy/sadness. In each case, the author is using the implications of his *si quis* to construct a reader.[16] Martial is cleverly mixing up the Ovidian (pseudo-)injunction to polite women not to read, with the Ovidian construction of a staged critic who enables programmatic statements (and also political ones). This also effectively blurs distinctions between the pupil and the reader. Martial's apotropaic move, like Ovid's, could be interpreted as an enticement to read: he warns us about this when he says that if Cato took a peep into the book/theatre, he would be caught.

Furthermore Martial's combination of 'coming' (*uenire*) and 'watching' (*spectare*), i.e. of entering a show for individual reasons, refers specifically to one of Ovid's most celebrated hexameters; cf. Ov. *Ars* 1. 99 *spectatum ueniunt, ueniunt spectentur ut ipsae* ('They come to watch the show, they come to be watched as a show themselves'). A stark contrast is created between the 'usual' behaviour of the Ovidian girls (*puellae*), who come both to watch and to be watched in the 'shameless' location ideal for finding a girl-friend, and 'stern Cato', who sets himself up against such shamelessness. Martial uses the fact that the Ovidian quasi-proverb describes 'normal' people with commonsense attitudes to underline the 'perversion' of his moralist 'Cato'. In response to Ovid, Martial here quotes the spectacles of the *Ars* with affirmation to mark Cato's ridiculously deviant manners.

But we must not forget that Martial's *theatrum* (and *spectaculum*) is a metaphor for his satirical epigrams. Could this possibly be read as an

---

[16] See Holzberg and Casali in this volume, Chs. 3 and 11, on the reader as critic.

interpretative signal capable of enriching our understanding of the Ovidian source? What do we gain, if Ovid's *theatrum* is, on one level, a metaphor too, i.e. a metaphor for his own book, the *Ars* (1)? If we regard the *Ars* as a theatre staging spectacles of the legendary past[17] as well as future triumphs, which give way to new liaisons between spectators,[18] the effect of this reading on Ovid's internal Readers (with capital R),[19] the Roman youngsters eager to study love, is double-edged. On the one hand they are once again encouraged to read the book, because it is—like the Roman theatres, as depicted by the *praeceptor*—full of pretty girls and empty of moral restraints.[20] On the other hand, however, they are painfully disillusioned, as soon as they recognize that all the beautiful and willing objects of their desire that according to their teacher can be found and caught everywhere in Rome[21] are nothing but *scriptae puellae* and products of Ovid's imagination. Metapoetical intertext of this kind may well contribute to the 'dynamics' of reading the poems of both Ovid and Martial.

(b) Martial's School of Laughing and Crying (2. 41) and Its Ovidian Background

Creative intertext becomes more apparent in Martial's most pointedly 'Ovidian' epigram. It is the forty-first piece of the second book:

---

[17] Cf. Ov. *Ars* 1. 101–34, where the *ludi Romuli* provide an unsophisticated trap to catch the Sabine women for the 'primitive' Romans. For the complex messages of this 'anti-exemplum' that shows 'a lack of art', see Labate's contribution in this volume, Ch. 10. A different interpretation is suggested by Wildberger (1998: 50–5), but see also the review article of Janka (2004).

[18] Cf. *Ars* 1. 177–228, the prophesied scenario of celebration after the desired victory of young Gaius Caesar, esp. 217–18: *spectabunt laeti iuuenes mixtaeque puellae,* | *diffundetque animos omnibus ista dies.* The political implications of this quasi-*propempticon* and its exploitation for erotodidactic ends are the subjects of Casali's chapter, Ch. 11 above. See also Wildberger (1998: 60–76) with Janka (2004).

[19] The differentiation between internal addressees (Readers) and external readers is discussed *in extenso* by Sharrock (1994*a*: 10–17).

[20] Cf. Ov. *Ars* 1. 89–90 *sed tu praecipue curuis uenare theatris;* | *haec loca sunt voto fertiliora tuo*; *Ars* 1. 100 *ille locus casti damna pudoris habet.* Romulus is declared *aitios* and henceforth patron of this theatrical permissiveness: *Ars* 1. 131–4, esp. 133–4: *scilicet ex illo sollemni more theatra* | *nunc quoque formosis insidiosa manent.*

[21] Cf. e.g. *Ars* 1. 55–60, esp. 59 *quot caelum stellas, tot habet tua Roma puellas.*

'Ride si sapis, o puella, ride'
Paelignus, puto, dixerat poeta.   2
sed non dixerat omnibus puellis.
uerum ut dixerit omnibus puellis,   4
non dixit tibi: tu puella non es,
et tres sunt tibi, Maximina, dentes,   6
sed plane piceique buxeique.
quare si speculo mihique credis,   8
debes non aliter timere risum,
quam uentum Spanius manumque Priscus,   10
quam cretata timet Fabulla nimbum,
cerussata timet Sabella solem.   12
uoltus indue tu magis seueros,
quam coniunx Priami nurusque maior.   14
mimos ridiculi Philistionis
et conuiuia nequiora uita   16
et quidquid lepida procacitate
laxat perspicuo labella risu.   18
te maestae decet adsidere matri
lugentiue uirum piumue fratrem,   20
et tantum tragicis uacare Musis.
at tu iudicium secuta nostrum   22
plora, si sapis, o puella, plora.

('Laugh, if you are clever, my girl, just laugh!'
The Paelignian poet, I guess, said something like that.
However, he did not say that to all girls.
And even if he had said that to all girls,
he did not say it to you. You are no girl,
and three is the number, Maximina, of your teeth,
but they are plainly pitch-black or yellowish like boxwood.
Therefore, if you trust your mirror and me,
you have to be afraid of laughter just as
('thin-haired') Spanius is afraid of wind and ('old-fashioned') Priscus of hands,
just like Fabulla made up with chalk-powder fears the rain
and Sabella made up with face cream fears the sun.
Make yourself up with a facial expression darker
than that of Priam's wife and his major daughter-in-law.
The mimes of ridiculous Philistion
and parties of the happier kind are no-go areas for you
as well as anything humorous and cheeky

that opens the lips in visible laughter.
It suits you to sit by a *mater dolorosa*
or by someone who mourns her husband or her dear brother,
and spend your time but for the tragic Muses.
Nay, you should follow my advice and
cry, if you are clever, my girl, just cry!)

The opening line of this poem, framed like a jingle by its amusing imperatives *ride... ride*, gives the impression of a verbatim quotation from the 'Paelignian poet', i.e. Ovid. But already in line 2 the quoting *persona* qualifies this with *puto*, declaring that (s)he delivers the dictum loosely according to the capacity of his/her own memory. No wonder 'the passage is not found in his (i.e. Ovid's) extant works, which do not include hendecasyllables', as Shackleton-Bailey emphasizes in a note accompanying his translation.[22] Lucio Cristante correctly proved this line to be 'un verso fantasma di Ovidio' rather than an Ovidian fragment.[23] But this ambiguity turns out to be programmatic for the whole poem: the authority of Ovid and his *Ars* is not referred to as a canonical classic. It merely provides the flexible material for the poetic interplay which the epigrammatic *ego* has arranged. The general reference, however, is clear after the second verse. Martial's thematic scope is the third book of Ovid's *Ars*. 'Girls' in singular (*o puella*, 1) and plural (*puellis*, 3–4) are instructed about 'clever laughing', a notorious topic in Ovid's love-lessons for women (esp. *Ars* 3. 279–92, 509–18). But more specific points of reference still remain to be collected within Ovid's *Ars*. Most tricky is the seemingly harmless reservation *si sapis* (1), which in my view condenses Ovid's and his Apollo's concept of *sapienter amare* (loving wisely/cleverly) in *Ars* 2.[24] This quality of the erotic 'conqueror' is essentially based on proper self-knowledge;

---

[22] See Shackleton Bailey (1993: i. 163).

[23] See Cristante (1990: esp. 181–3) (with ample bibliography on the 'quotation' in the light of fragmentary philology) and his own interpretation of the reference 183–4: 'Si tratta evidentemente di un rifacimento degli intenti ovidiani, ed è il gioco fra la contiguità e la distanza nei confronti del modello a nutrire l'ironia scommatica: grazie al rovesciamento in clausola del precetto "ovidiano"... lo statuto del genere epigrammatico rivendica la propria assolutezza.'

[24] See Sharrock (1994a: 197–8, 248–56, esp. 248): '... *loving* wisely [is] an oxymoron, a contradiction in terms which epitomizes the essential paradox (which is not a paradox) of the *Ars*, that love is a skill which can be learned, and done well'.

cf. *Ars* 2. 501 *qui sibi notus erit, solus sapienter amabit* ('Only he who knows himself, will be a clever/skilful lover'); 511–12 *quisquis sapienter amabit, | uincet* ('whoever will be a clever/skilful lover, will emerge victorious').[25]

I would like to suggest that we can best interpret the verses of Martial 2. 41 as variations on an Ovidian theme, staged as a dialogue between two characters who both try hard to use the 'doctrines' of the *Ars* for their own ends. One could well imagine a hypothetical prelude in which the female part, named Maximina, made approaches to the male speaker of the epigram ('Martialis') by charmingly laughing at him. He in turn gave her a rebuff and simply said: 'Please do not laugh at me, Maximina.' The woman, as an apology for her own laughter to signal erotic appeal, could then have spoken vv. 1–2 of 2. 41 referring to Ovid's alleged advice that girls should laugh if they want to be clever lovers.

The twenty-one verses that follow (2. 41. 3–23) would thus be a detailed refutation of these impertinent remarks. The male *ego* 'Martialis' first argues that Ovid had a strictly defined group of female addressees in mind in which Maximina could not possibly belong. On the metatextual level, v. 3 points to the well-known general restrictions on the internal Readers of the *Ars*. The speaker holds that the *praeceptor*'s advice to laugh is by no means addressed to *all* girls. His counterpart could now make an attempt to prove this wrong. This attempt is strongly implicit in the concession of v. 4, with *uerum* marking a reply to an interlocutor. The speaker here refers to an argument from *Ars* 3 where 'Ovid' takes 'beautiful' as well as 'ugly' girls under his patronage and recommends the latter (who are the majority) to disguise their physical defects; cf. *Ars* 3. 255 *turba docenda uenit pulchrae turpesque puellae* ('Here comes the crowd to be taught by me, pretty and ugly girls alike'); 3. 261 *rara tamen menda facies caret: occule mendas* ('Yet rare is a face without blemish; disguise your blemishes').

As a consequence of his concession in v. 4 the male part sets forth to deny that the category 'girl' could ever be applicable to Maximina who is so old that she has only three teeth left which are totally

[25] See Janka (1997: 372–3, 379).

ruined and will probably soon fall out (vv. 5–7). This feature stigmatizes her as *uetula*, beyond both youth and any amatory qualities. His statement *tu puella non es* (5) turns out to be even more witty. At one level, it could mean 'you are not elegiac', or even 'you are not a woman of dubious morals'; it is only with the continuation that it means, quite simply, 'you are not young'. Interestingly, though, that particular form of slander is not one utilized by Ovid, who positively advocates the older and more experienced woman. The attack on the aged libertine (if female) belongs more to the discourse of satire (diatribe and iambic, in which epigram partakes) rather than that of elegy (which is more likely to talk about old age as a threat in the future)—so the whole thing becomes a generic statement. Martial appears at first to be using *puella* in a simple generic sense, but is in fact using the term in its very ordinary sense to relate to age and, in the process, make a complex generic point. This fits well with the exaggeration of the addressee's age compared with Ovid's 'imperfect *puellae*' (see below).

Which of the two antagonists has Ovid on his/her side here? In *Ars* 3 laughing belongs to the strategy of showing female *cultus* in order to gain male sympathies. On the one hand, Ovid warns girls not to laugh, if their teeth are ugly; cf. esp. 3. 279–80 *si niger aut ingens aut non erit ordine natus | dens tibi, ridendo maxima damna feres* ('If you have a black tooth or a huge one or one that has no proper position, then you will do yourself horrific harm by laughing'). On the other hand, he advises laughter as a sign of pleasant and joyful behaviour which renders girls lovable; cf. esp. 3. 513 *spectantem specta; ridenti mollia ride* ('If one looks at you, look at him; if one gives you a lovely smile, return the smile').[26] For coping with widespread imperfection, Ovid presents his 'school of moderate[27] and sophisticated laughing' which teaches *decor/decus* (3. 291 *decenter*) to avoid unattractive excesses in vehemence, loudness, and tone (3. 281–92). In 2. 41. 8, however, 'Martial' adopts the role of a trustworthy and mirror-like *doctor*

---

[26] This rule is complementary to the instruction given to young men at *Ars* 2. 201: *riserit: arride*. See Janka (1997: 179–80 ad loc.). Similarly, Ovid's Narcissus pretends to be loved, because he gets his smiles back from his 'beloved' reflected in the water (*Met.* 3. 459–60).

[27] For Ovid's 'doctrines' of moderation in *Ars* 3, see Gibson, Ch. 7 in this volume.

amoris (reinforced by the splendid zeugma *speculo mihique credis*)[28] just to state that in Maximina's case any 'school of laughing' would be out of place. Her set of teeth does not simply suffer from one of the defects listed by Ovid at *Ars* 3. 279–80; in fact, all three of her teeth are repulsive (Mart. 2. 41. 6–7 *tres... plane piceique buxeique*). So she suffers from a monstrously exaggerated defect of beauty in comparison with Ovid's imperfect *puellae*. Consequently her 'teacher' or therapist counsels her to be afraid of any situation that could possibly arouse her laughter. This could also serve as armour against Ovid's 'cures of love' (*Remedia*). There the teacher instructs his students to provoke the unattractive laughter of women with ugly teeth; cf. *Rem.* 339 *si male dentata est, narra, quod rideat, illi* ('If one has ugly teeth, tell her stories she will laugh at').

By striking analogies in the centre of the poem, Martial equates Maximina with individuals who necessarily have to fear (natural) forces strong enough to uncover their physical defects (2. 41. 8–12).[29] Consequently, Maximina's only way of showing *decor/decus*—a key theme of the *Ars Amatoria* and especially *Ars* 3[30]—is the exact opposite of laughing, i.e. the sort of extreme mourning and weeping that might surpass even the paradigms of wailing in literature (2. 41. 19–21). And these manners are normally—again according to Ovid—*eis ipsis* incompatible with erotic attractiveness; cf. esp. *Ars* 3. 517–18 *odimus et maestas; Tecmessam diligat Aiax, | nos, hilarem populum, femina laeta capit* ('We are also disgusted at weepers; may Ajax love Tecmessa; we as a funny folk, are caught by happy women'). 'Martial's' conclusion is thus inescapable: 'Maximina, you are too old, totally unlovable and inevitably alien to me and my poetry!' But

---

[28] This is a variation of the *praeceptor*'s appeal for trust in him and his experience which is so familiar in erotodidactic poetry, see e.g. *Ars* 1. 66, 2. 259, 464, 717 commented on by Janka (1997: 493); 3. 439, 511 *experto credite*, 653, 664, 792. Martial's zeugma here combines this claim of teaching authority with Ovid's amusing apostrophe advising his love-crazed mythical heroine Pasiphaë to trust her mirror which shows her that she is no heifer; cf. *Ars* 1. 307 *crede tamen speculo, quod te negat esse iuvencam*.

[29] *creta* (cf. Mart. 2. 41. 11) is the subject of *Ars* 3. 199, although Ovid there treats it very guardedly. Cosmetics which run through heat or sweat (cf. Mart. 2. 41. 12) are the subject of *Ars* 3. 211–12—and Ovid there is quite definitely sarcastic.

[30] See Gibson (2003*a*: 22–3 n. 57), also his notes on *Ars* 3 (ibid. 135–68, 169–92, 769–808, with further references).

this is not merely an invective against a lascivious older woman pretending to be young, charming, and attractive, all of which would be rather conventional a topic in the realm of satire or scoptic epigram.[31] The second half of the poem in particular has a strong metapoetic touch. The splitting of Martial's poem into two antithetic halves of roughly equal length—1–12 (ban on laughter), 13–23 (instructions to mourn and cry)—mirrored by the ring composition of the opening and closing lines, may also modify Ovid's idea of the confusion between laughter and crying that certain women produce. The structure of Martial's poem perhaps reflects the antithetic phrasing in *Ars* 3. 288 *risu concussa est altera, flere putes* ('Another woman shakes with *laughter* so that you think she is *weeping*').[32] The intertextual joke would then run like this: unlike Ovid's warning against weeping-like laughter, 'Martial' recommends excessive weeping instead of laughter. Furthermore, it is remarkable that Martial takes his examples of 'decorous' mourning, again an Ovidian invention,[33] from totally different genres of poetry: heroic epic[34] and 'tragic Muse' in more general terms (2. 41. 21) are opposed to mimes, parties (cf. the *conuiuium* as erotic scenery in *Ars* 1. 565–602), and 'licentious verses' (2. 41. 16–18). Since mimes,[35] *nequitiae* (dissoluteness)[36] and *procacitas* (naughtiness) are typical *chiffres* of Martial's own poetry (cf. 5. 2. 3–4 *tu, quem nequitiae procaciores | delectant nimium salesque nudi* ('he who is delighted about lasciviousness of the naughtier

---

[31] See Hoffmann (1955–6: 445) with the following list of Martial's epigrams against lecherous *uetulae* (category 'Lüsternheit von Frauen'): Mart. 2. 34; 3. 32; 3. 93; 9. 37; 10. 67; 10. 90; 11. 29.

[32] For the textual problems see the apparatus criticus in Kenney's edition. I adopt Alton's conjecture.

[33] With the 'decorous mourning' in Mart. 2. 41. 19, cf. esp. *Ars* 3. 291–2 *quo non ars penetrat? discunt lacrimare decenter | quoque uolunt plorant tempore quoque modo.* This parallel demonstrates among others the continuation of Ovidian themes into the second half of the poem.

[34] Cf. Hecuba and Andromache in Mart. 2. 41. 14, which makes us think readily of *Iliad* 24, where both of them are mourning Hector; cf. *Iliad* 24. 723–45, 747–59. Andromache (cf. Mart. 2. 41. 14) is both a negative and a positive role model in the *Ars*: 3. 107–10, 3. 517–20 (negative), 2. 709–10, 3. 777–8 (positive).

[35] Cf. Mart. 1 *epist.* 16–19 (discussed above); 1. 35. 8 *quis Floralia uestit*; 8 *epist.* 11–12 *mimicam uerborum licentiam*, there referred to with a gesture of distance.

[36] See also Mart. 6. 82. 5 *cuius nequitias iocosque novit*; 11. 16. 7–8 *tu quoque nequitias nostri lususque libelli | uda, puella, leges, sis Patauina licet.*

kind and spicy frivolity')), the female type Maximina represents is excluded from not only the speaker's erotic horizon, but also the inner circle of Martial's ideal readers.

(c) *Martial 11. 104: An Anti-Ars?*

Even without explicit reference to Ovid, this epigram is presumably Martial's most 'Ovidian' piece:[37]

Uxor, uade foras aut moribus utere nostris:
   non sum ego nec Curius nec Numa nec Tatius.   2
me iucunda iuuant tractae per pocula noctes:
   tu properas pota surgere tristis aqua.   4
tu tenebris gaudes: me ludere teste lucerna
   et iuuat admissa rumpere luce latus.   6
fascia te tunicaeque obscuraque pallia celant:
   at mihi nulla satis nuda puella iacet.   8
basia me capiunt blandas imitata columbas:
   tu mihi das, auiae qualia mane soles.   10
nec motu dignaris opus nec uoce iuuare
   nec digitis, tamquam tura merumque pares: 12
masturbabantur Phrygii post ostia serui,
   Hectoreo quotiens sederat uxor equo,   14
et quamuis Ithaco stertente pudica solebat
   Illic Penelope semper habere manum.   16
pedicare negas: dabat hoc Cornelia Graccho,
   Iulia Pompeio, Porcia, Brute, tibi;   18
dulcia Dardanio nondum miscente ministro
   pocula Iuno fuit pro Ganymede Iovi.   20
si te delectat grauitas, Lucretia toto
   sis licet usque die: Laida nocte volo.   22

(Wife, get out of the front door or fit in with my morals.
I am not a Curius, no Numa and no Tatius.
I am pleased by nights drawn out with cheering cups:
You hasten to get up sad when you have drunk water.
Darkness makes you happy. I get pleasure from playing games with the lamp as witness

---

[37] Also the preceding distich (11. 103) is a short variation on a topic familiar from Ovid's *Ars* ('incredible that this innocent person is a father/mother'); see Kay (1985: 275).

and from exhausting my loins with the daylight let in.
You are covered with a brassiere and tunics and obscuring robes.
But for my taste no girl lies naked enough.
Kisses that equate those of sexy doves thrill me:
You give me such as you give your grandmother in the morning.
You do not deign to help the job along with movement, voice
or fingers, as if you were preparing incense and wine:
Phrygian slaves used to masturbate behind the door
whenever his wife [Andromache] rode Hector's horse,
and although the Ithacan [Ulysses] was snoring, modest
Penelope always used to keep her hand *at that part*.
You forbid me sodomy: It was allowed by Cornelia to Gracchus
as well as by Julia to Pompey, and by Porcia to you, Brutus.
When the Dardanian (Trojan) servant did not yet mix the sweet
drinks, Juno was Jupiter's Ganymede.
If you are pleased by austere morals, you may be (a) Lucretia the whole
day: at night I want (a) Lais.)[38]

The most interesting feature of this neatly elegiac epigram is its consistent use of words, phrases, and motifs drawn from Ovid's erotodidactic works. As I shall argue, the poem astutely combines elements of allusion to and pointed opposition to Ovid in order to characterize the speaker as a wholly failing amatorian artist and a poor pupil of Ovid. The crucial question emerges, 'is Martial 11. 104 an *Ars* or an anti-*Ars*?'

On the surface of this complex poem, the *maritus* 'Martialis' teaches his wife mutual desire (*mutua uoluptas*) so that she may become a frivolous Lais at night, even if she remains a chaste Lucretia during the day. Like the *praeceptor amoris*, the husband 'Martialis' starts with what looks like a ban on matrons (in order to achieve more lustful sexual intercourse); cf. Mart. 11. 104. 1 *uxor, uade foras*... with *Ars* 1. 31–2 *este procul, uittae tenues*...| *quaeque tegis medios instita longa pedes* ('stay far away, fine hair-bands...| and you trailing robes which even cover half of the feet'). But whereas Ovid proclaims that marriage and matrons are totally alien to his *Ars*,[39] which stages 'free' and 'safer' love with libertines called *amicae*

---

[38] My translation here has been particularly influenced by the versions of Kay (1985: 276) and Shackleton-Bailey (1993: iii. 85).

[39] Cf. also *Ars* 2. 683–6 against sexual intercourse as conjugal duty which the *praeceptor* judges to be naturally unpleasant. For Ovid's consistently negative view of marriage in the *Ars*, see Gibson (2003a) on *Ars* 3. 303, 585–6, 587–8.

or *puellae*,[40] Martial's speaker tries to apply the *Ars* to the 'unartistic' realm of marriage (*uxor*) by exerting pressure on his wife and threatening her with divorce.[41] Thus the husband 'Martialis' abuses an Ovidian formula intended to define circles of readers in order to make his wife yield to his demands.

Both texts are linked by the attitude that favourable sexual intercourse requires mutual desire between the two lovers. The lack of this reciprocity marks the absence of emotional and erotic harmony. The diagnosis of 'Martial's' unhappy sex-life in marriage (Mart. 11. 104. 3–12 with a broad catalogue of contradictory preferences of both partners about drinking, light, clothing, kissing, stimulation, and sodomy)[42] reads like a case study of 'Ovid's' disdain for unequal intercourse; cf. esp. *Ars* 2. 683 *odi concubitus qui non utrumque resoluunt* ('I dislike intercourse which does not exhaust both partners'); 3. 794 *ex aequo res iuuet illa duos* ('the two partners should enjoy this act equally'). Yet both speakers praise the 'modern times' in which they live as an ideal playground for lascivious sex, thus exploiting only the sexual side of historical progress. Martial's speaker somewhat disingenuously contrasts his 'morals' (*mores*) with those of legendary forefathers such as Curius, Numa, and Tatius (11. 104. 1–2), who are presented as exemplars of chastity; Ovid's *praeceptor* appreciates his own (and thus Augustus') period only because it provides refined pleasures and opportunities for sophisticated lovemaking; cf. esp. *Ars* 3. 122 *haec aetas moribus apta meis* ('This age fits my morals'). Both speakers plead for dirty talk[43] and manual stimulation[44], and they both embed these techniques quite anachronistically within the sober tradition of epic literature.[45] The 'seriousness' (*grauitas*) 'Martial's' wife indulges in (11. 104. 21)

[40] Cf. e.g. *Ars* 1. 31–4, 2. 600 *in nostris instita nulla iocis* with Janka (1997: 423); 3. 483.

[41] See Kay (1985: 277): '*uade foras*: this would suggest divorce to Roman ears'.

[42] This catalogue gives the impression of a miniature *Ars Amatoria*, leading from 'meeting' a partner at a party, and 'winning' him/her by erotic clothing, to the final 'union' in bed.

[43] With Mart. 11. 104. 11 (*voce*), cf. *Ars* 2. 705 *sponte sua sine te celeberrima uerba loquentur*; 3. 795 *nec blandae uoces iucundaque murmura cessent*; 3. 803 *quid iuuet, et uoces et anhelitus arguat oris*.

[44] Mart. 11. 104. 12–16 is a typically more pungent and elaborate form than *Ars* 2. 706–7 *nec manus in lecto laeua iacebit iners*; | *inuenient digiti quod agant in partibus illis*.

[45] Cf. Mart. 11. 104. 13–16: Hector/Andromache: *Iliad*; Penelope/Ulysses: *Odyssey*; *Ars* 2. 716–17 Briseis/Achilles: *Iliad*.

emphasizes her outmoded character, since Ovid judges such manners as 'crude simplicity' (*simplicitas rudis*, *Ars* 3. 113) typical of a bygone age.

But these allusions and modified quotations are undermined by striking divergences. Martial's rhetoric of excess systematically exaggerates the Ovidian pedagogy of erotic 'moderation'.[46] 'Martial' prefers lovemaking with full light (11. 104. 5–6) and in complete nudity (11. 104. 7–8);[47] 'Ovid' on the contrary recommends faint half-light (*Ars* 2. 619–20) so that unattractive details of the (female) body can be hidden (*Ars* 3. 807–8). Sex without any dress is consequently part of Ovid's therapy against love; cf. *Rem*. 337–8 *omne papillae | pectus habent, uitium fascia nulla tegat* ('If the nipples of her bust cover all her breast, let no brassiere conceal the defect'). Next, 'Ovid' advises his female pupils to simulate orgasm as some kind of last resort; cf. *Ars* 3. 802 *effice per motum luminaque ipsa fidem* ('Be credible by your movements and even by your glances'). 'Martial's' *uxor*, however, was evidently not instructed by Ovid, since she is not at all willing to simulate anything; cf. 11. 104. 11 *nec motu dignaris opus nec uoce iuuare*. She behaves like Ovid's absolutely anti-erotic 'dry/frigid woman' (*sicca femina*, *Ars* 2. 686) whose sexual life is reduced to a marital duty tolerated as a passive object without ardour.[48]

Another amusing 'anti-text' to Ovid's *Ars* deals with the (horse)-riding position during sexual intercourse: 'Ovid' plainly denied that Hector and Andromache ever did it that way because of Andromache's extraordinary size; cf. *Ars* 3. 777–8 *quod erat longissima, numquam | Thebais Hectoreo nupta resedit equo* ('Because she was horribly tall, his Theban wife (i.e. Andromache) never rode Hector's horse'). 'Martial' by contrast proclaims that this was their usual *figura Veneris* (11. 104. 14 *quotiens*) with which they used to stimulate not only one another, but also indirectly their slaves. Of course, no one is able to

---

[46] For Ovid's coping with excess by implementing a rhetoric of restraint and self-control in *Ars* 3 generally, see Gibson, Ch. 7 in this volume.

[47] His strange phrase *nulla satis nuda puella* (11. 104. 8) skilfully echoes the Propertian *uni si qua placet, culta puella sat est* (Prop. 1. 2. 26). Also Martial's point about visible nudity as stimulus during intercourse could be derived from Propertius, cf. Prop. 2. 15. 5–6, 11–24.

[48] Her thinking of 'wool' (i.e. ordinary female housework) during sexual intercourse is intensified by 'Martial' whose 'wife' works against his lust by her sexual manners which resemble the chaste religious attendant (11. 104. 12).

prove or refute these insinuations. Martial thus prepares the way for more obscene and absurd details about alleged sodomy (*pedicare*) with most revered matrons in early Roman history (Cornelia), in more recent times (Julia and Porcia)[49] and even on Olympus (Juno as temporary solution before the rape of Ganymede). Ovid's *Ars*, which is far less explicit, eschews such fantastical excesses.

To sum up, within this 'husband', Martial deliberately confuses two Ovidian roles (*personae*). The speaker pretends to be a *praeceptor amoris* addressing his frigid wife for therapeutical reasons. In fact he acts like a recklessly egoistic pupil of the *doctor amoris* who longs for 'perfect voluptuousness' (*plena uoluptas*) and plunders the *Ars* for excessive and therefore un-artistic purposes. Seen against this backdrop, one can subtly appreciate the complete failure of the speaker. Because he is a criminally interested party, he lacks any erotodidactic appeal. He therefore not only fails as lover (misinterpreting sensual pleasure as a matter of will), but also as historian (maltreating Roman history), mythologist (fantastical and nonsensical *exempla*), and psychologist (fighting to produce pleasure by force and ignoring that a character can hardly be split up into 'day' and 'night'). 'Ovid' could rebuke this inattentive pupil: 'You want too much at once and hence you get nothing at all!' In addition to this, Martial's ingenious play with his Ovidian pretext(s) could also bring into question the role of male lovers and female 'objects' of their desire in Ovid's rather naively formulated cultural construct of *mutua uoluptas*. Martial perhaps points out the idealistic touch of this concept which provokes abuse by a speaker who declares that his own morals rule the sexual pleasures of both partners. In this respect, Martial wrote an Anti-*Ars* by exploiting the *Ars*.

4. CONCLUSION

I hope to have demonstrated the ways in which Martial's reception of Ovid's erotodidactic poems is much more complex than even

---

[49] Cf. Kay (1985: 281–2) rightly judging the historical examples as 'irreverently humorous', since 'these ladies are cited as exemplars of *pudicitia* by Seneca (frag. 79 Haase)'.

modern scholars assume. Martial's textual interplay is not restricted to the symbolic or paradigmatic value of Ovid and his œuvre. Rather, he takes the *Ars* (and *Remedia*) as texts with which to negotiate. As well as offering isolated signals to the reader of his debt to Ovid's erotodidactic corpus, Martial designs whole epigrammatic tableaux out of Ovidian amatory motifs. From a generic point of view, the disjunction we have seen between Martial and Ovid's *Ars*, especially with regards to Mart. 2. 41 and 11. 104 (above), might indicate that Ovid's teaching is suitable for elegiac men and women, but not for the more extreme amatory world of epigram—Ovid's discourse on moderation and sophistication is of no use in a world of the extreme, the crude, and the animalistic. When faced with the grotesque Maximina in Mart. 2. 41, for example, Ovid's teaching falls flat: as both 'Martial' and the girl attempt to apply Ovid's teachings, all that emerges is contradiction—his teachings were never meant for someone this ugly! Ultimately, Martial has to 'retune' Ovid's advice such that it is appropriate for women/love situations of epigram. Such intertextual dialogue might, in turn, invite us to reassess the Ovidian source itself. Their openness for inventive modification, already at an early stage of their afterlife, should alert us to the slippery nature of Ovid's erotodidactic poems, and the notoriously polyphonic atmosphere that pervades Ovid's ART.

15

Sex Education: Ovidian Erotodidactic in the Classroom

Ralph Hexter

> omnis scientia est a deo, sed
> ars amandi est scientia. ergo
> est a deo. ergo est bona.[1]
>
> it was easier [for the humanist educator]
> to curse the Middle Ages in theory
> than to replace it in practice.[2]

The Florentine preacher Giovanni Dominici, in his *Regola del governo di cura familiare* (1401–3), worried that 'now children were reading Ovid's *Metamorphoses, Heroides, Ars Amatoria,* and other lascivious texts [presumably the *Amores* and *Remedia Amoris*], Vergil, and [Seneca's] tragedies'.[3] However precisely this situation fits Florence in the first decade of the fifteenth century, parts of the picture seem more than a little familiar. If we are no longer surprised to find Ovid in Latin class, we should remind ourselves that he has not been thought fit for students in all times and places, and even when he was admitted, would-be pedagogical directors took pains to distinguish

---

[1] Munich, *codex latinus monacensis* (henceforth 'clm') 5426, fo. 163ʳ; cited from Baldwin (1992: 26).

[2] R. Sabbadini, 'il medio evo era più facile biasimarlo nella teoria che sostituirlo nella practica', 'Versi grammaticali di Lorenzo Valla', *La biblioteca delle scuole italiane* ser. 2, 8 (1899: 134–5), cited in Black (2001: 172).

[3] Cited from Black (2001: 247). Black refers to the edition of Garin (1958: 72) and to a partial translation by Gehl (1993: 198).

among works in the Ovidian canon. In the twelfth century, Conrad of Hirsau (via the *magister* in his dialogue) recommends the *Fasti*, *Epistulae ex Ponto*, and (the pseudo-Ovidian) *Nux* while steering students away from the amatory works and, it appears, the *Heroides*.[4] Alexander of Neckham likewise would keep the amatory (and satirical) works out of students' hands.[5]

The scandal of the *Ars Amatoria* goes back to Ovid's own (auto) biography and was not, of course, limited to the classroom. The *Ars* was, Ovid famously claims, one of the two reasons—*carmen et error* (*Tr.* 2. 207)—for his banishment from Rome. The recognition that the offending book was the *Ars Amatoria* was universal in medieval accounts, as one reads, for example, in many dozens of *accessus* and biographies.[6] The *Remedia Amoris* is presented in sequence directly following on the *Ars Amatoria* and the most common scenario either simply takes Ovid's stated intentions at face value—he wishes to provide the youths he has taught to love a 'remedy'—or with the additional elaboration that the youths have transgressed the barrier he himself set up and are now entering into illicit relationships with virgins and married ladies.[7] The reception of the *Remedia Amoris* is, then, both intimately bound up with but none the less potentially separable from that of the *Ars Amatoria*;[8] it is the latter that will be

---

[4] Huygens (1970: 114). The *Nux* will later have the distinction of a commentary by Erasmus himself.

[5] He positively commends Ovid's 'elegias' (likely the *Tristia* as well as the *Epistulae ex Ponto*), the *Metamorphoses*, and, above all, the *Remedia Amoris*: 'sed et precipue libellum de remedio amoris familiarem habeat'; cited in Hexter (1986: 18).

[6] To pick one nearly at random, 'Offenderat enim Augustum Cesarem per Artem Amatoriam' (Coulson (1991: 28); also referenced by Dimmick (2002: 273)). This is the 'Vulgate' commentary on the *Metamorphoses*. There is no mention of the *error* here. The standard medieval introductions to *auctores* known as *accessus* have been presented and described so often now that there is no need to include a complete list of references here; readers seeking discussion and earlier bibliography can turn, *inter alia*, to Minnis (1984) or (2001), or to Reynolds (1996).

[7] Cf. e.g. William of Orléans (Engelbrecht 2003: ad 1. 77) or the *accessus* at clm 19475, fo. 6ʳ (Huygens 1970: 34).

[8] Dimmick (2002: 273) well describes '[t]he acutely unstable relationship between *Ars* and *Remedia* in medieval readings'; valuable in this regard are ibid. 267–73 in their entirety. Christine de Pizan in 1399 and the slightly earlier anonymous author of the *Anti-Ovidianus* before her disparage both poems together (Dimmick (2002: 267–8); Hexter (1986: 96); Stroh (1969: 33)), but in the twelfth century (and not only then) there was an equally strong tradition that not only took the 'retractive' gesture of the *Remedia Amoris* at face value but for that very reason privileged it in the school

the primary focus of the present study, with a particular eye to its utilization in classrooms in the Middle Ages. Even that is too large a topic for thorough treatment in a brief space; the following is intended as basic orientation that will offer readers avenues for further exploration.[9]

While not yet anticipating the need for a formal 'remedy', there is already a sense of danger present from the beginning of *Ars* 1. For one thing, Ovid expects he will receive *further* wounds and burns at Love's hands (1. 21–4). Another sort of danger looms, ominously in retrospect, when Ovid, invoking Venus (1. 30), warns a subset of potential readers away from his text:

> este procul, uittae tenues, insigne pudoris,
>   quaeque tegis medios instita longa pedes:
> nos Venerem tutam concessaque furta canemus
>   inque meo nullum carmine crimen erit.   (1. 31–4)
>
> (Keep your distance, you narrow fillets, of chastity the sign,
>   and you, long dress with matronly hem, that falls mid-foot—
> safe sex we will sing and permissible escapades:
>   there will be no actionable offence in my song).

---

curriculum, e.g. William of Saint-Thierry; see Hexter (1986: 17). See also Hexter (ibid. 19). Since I conducted the first phase of my research in the late 1970s and early 1980s, vastly more and vastly more reliable information has become available. The appearance of the second volume of Munk Olsen's survey (that included Ovid), for example, appeared too late (1985) for me to make effective use of it in a book published in 1986. On my claim that 'all evidence seems to support the view that the *Ars Amatoria* was the most popular as teaching text first; only in the twelfth century did the *Remedia Amoris* catch up with the *Ars Amatoria*' (1986: 15) I stand happily corrected by Wilken Engelbrecht (2003: 2. 71 and 223 n. 3), whom I am pleased to thank for sharing his work on medieval Ovid commentary over now several years. (Dr Engelbrecht is now undertaking to publish his findings in English; his edition of the Latin is of course fully accessible even to the Dutchless.) His table on p. 71 strongly supports Black's own findings (based on Italian material) that, as Black (2001: 8) writes, 'confirms the hypothesis originally put forward by Louis Paetow in 1910 of the downfall of the classics in thirteenth-century Europe and Italy as a result of the rise of the universities'.

[9] Still less can the present study include an account of the long history of speculation on Ovid's '*error*' that compounded the 'pretext' of the *Ars* and led to his relegation to the Black Sea. For a brief overview of some of the more inventive medieval hypotheses, see Hexter (1999a: 334–6).

Of course, whether all Roman matrons immediately put down the scroll one may well wonder.[10] But Ovid himself includes within the *Ars* virtually from the get-go the problematic of who should be reading the text. From a certain perspective, the gesture of prohibiting some readers implies (and perhaps even seeks to guarantee) that it remain permitted to all others. But perhaps this was intended as mock solemnity from the start, even if Ovid may already have sensed that it was politic to make such a gesture.[11] Precautionary prudence and mockery can exist simultaneously. 'No one under 17 admitted without parental permission.' Then as now an exclusionary boundary can serve as enticement.

While this may be the most prominent instance of setting prohibition against permission, through its three books the *Ars Amatoria* plays various, and often competing, readerships against one another. *Ars* 1–2 ostensibly offer instruction specifically to men; yet women— at least unmarried women—are admitted to the readership of those books. *Ars* 3, meant to level the playing field, is explicitly directed to women: *arma dedi Danais in Amazonas; arma supersunt,* | *quae tibi dem et turmae, Penthesilea, tuae* (3. 1–2). Yet men were reading along. This is not just an assumption; Ovid sees to it that it is inscribed, for in vv. 7–8 he has one of them object, and responds to the objection in vv. 9–10 and for some lines beyond. The opening of *Ars* 3 is one of several points where the rapid change of addressees is dizzying.[12]

The *Ars Amatoria* in this regard anticipates its complex and contested placement in the classroom, where competing purposes and intentions coexist. Ovid's *Ars Amatoria* achieves a variety of didactic purposes in medieval classrooms, but rarely if ever is the aim of educators to provide their pupils instruction in loving (which is not

---

[10] The danger that can be involved in reading a particular text is a topos Ovid relishes exploring, for example, in the extreme situation Cydippe finds herself in after reading out the text Acontius had inscribed on an apple (*Her.* 20–1). Even more apt to the present situation may be the words of one very notable married lady, Helen, at (or near) the opening of her response to Paris's letter: *nunc oculos tua cum violarit epistula nostros,* | *non rescribendi gloria visa levis!* (*Her.* 17. 3–4 Dörrie).

[11] Ovid will subsequently adduce these lines in self-defence: Hollis (1977: 38) compares *Tr.* 2. 305–6. On the Augustan context, see the contribution of Casali, Ch. 11 in this volume.

[12] On the 'staginess' of these shifts, at both the micro- and macro-levels, see the contribution of Holzberg, Ch. 3 in this volume.

to say that pupils didn't learn a thing or two from their study of the poem *magistro nolente*).[13] Again, the poem at its start questions whether love is something that can be taught systematically. Ovid does not actually pose the question quite so baldly. He opens with a very clear claim: *si quis in hoc artem populo non nouit amandi, | hoc legat et lecto carmine doctus amet* (1. 1–2). No scepticism there, in the words themselves of course. But the very boldness of the claim belies, and is meant to belie (and to be seen to belie) its highly dubious nature. The bland over-confidence of the preceptorial voice carries through the next couplet: *arte citae ueloque rates remoque mouentur, | arte leues currus: arte regendus Amor* (1. 3–4). As if love (or Love) were no different from ships and chariots!

Ovid sprinkles objecting or questioning voices throughout his poetry and constantly provokes his readers to register objections or questions, inscribing them even when not 'scribing' them in so many words. This is the case here, as the twelfth-century commentator fully grasped who created a hypothetical questioner to make explicit the gap between the first and second couplets.

diceret aliquis, estne amor regendus arte? r. ita. et quod regendus sit arte ostendit per induxionem q. d. quaecumque reguntur, arte reguntur. ergo et amor. et exemplificat de quibusdam dicens, *arte*.[14]

---

[13] Abelard and Héloïse are the most famous example, though the texts they studied were not exclusively Ovidian by any means. (Abelard, though, specifically cites the *Ars Amatoria* as describing 'convivia' offering 'fornicationis occasionem'; see Stroh (1969: 16). On Abelard and Héloïse's knowledge of and references to the *Ars* and *Remedia*, see Baldwin (1992: 20–1).)

[14] Copenhagen, Kongelige Bibliotek, Gl. Kgl. Saml. 1905 4° (saec. XII/XIII), fo. 15ᵛ; see Hexter (1986: 58). (For issues of expansion and translation, see the following note.) This commentary, which I discuss at some length (ibid. 42–82), runs from fo. 15ᵛ to 24ʳ and is listed as no. 56 in Coulson and Roy (2000: 40–1). It overlaps to some extent—the degree of overlap is too involved a matter for discussion here—with the commentary of Fulco of Orléans on the *Ars Amatoria* identified by Hugues-V. Shooner (1981: 409–11), and is known from four other manuscripts (no. 173 in Coulson and Roy (2000: 66–7)). There can be no question about the attribution, though the Copenhagen manuscript (at least) also involves significant material that is not Fulco's. ('Si le début du commentaire est différent ... et cela jusqu'au vers 1.171, à ce point [fo. 17ʳ], sans que rien ne signale le fait, les gloses reprennent à 1.89 et coïncident avec celles des autres manuscrits [of Fulco's commentary], à part quelques variantes': Shooner (1981: 411 n. 17); cf. Hexter (1986: 44). Where Coulson and Roy (2000: 67) describe the material of Fulco in this manuscript as covering the Ovidian text 'to 1.89', they actually mean 'from 1.89'.) The *accessus* in the Copenhagen

(Were someone to ask, 'but is love governed by art?' he responds [or 'would respond'] thus. And that it is governable by art he shows by induction because he says 'whatever is governed, is governed by art. And thus also love'. And he provides various examples, saying 'by art'.)[15]

Further comments[16] turn the medieval student's experience of the opening movement of the *Ars Amatoria* into a truly dialogic one. In my view, this is not only a clever medieval way of reading and understanding Ovid. It reveals deep insight into the rhetorical manner by which Ovid proceeds: direct and often bravura argumentation, frequent changes of addressee, and deceptively suppressed terms or elided intermediate steps that need to be made explicit before one can follow the speaking voice. This Ovid himself does near the beginning of *Ars Amatoria* 3 where he presents a male objecting to his stated intention to 'arm' the ladies: *dixerit e multis aliquis* (3. 7). As so often, Ovid anticipates the very manoeuvres his much later commentators, and all readers for that matter, devise. It is as if there is no role, not even an oppositional one, that he has not already scripted for us.

---

manuscript is in fact 'contaminated' with material from William of Orléans' *Bursarii* (Engelbrecht (2003: 224 n. 5)). The material cited above comes from the section before the Fulconian text begins. One cannot sufficiently emphasize the value of studying each manuscript exemplar, for whether it is a 'pure' or 'contaminated' witness of an identifiable named commentary or, to go to the other end of the spectrum, an anonymous amalgam of glosses from here, there, and elsewhere combined with new material, each exemplar testifies to at least one authentic pedagogic approach. The work of the past twenty-five years, culminating (for Ovid) in Coulson and Roy (2000) and Engelbrecht (2003), permits us to link many unnamed texts with the named commentaries as well as explore affiliation between commentators. For analysing function, however, each text is significant completely apart from the affiliations it might have. Identifying the work and 'establishing the text' of a particular commentator to the degree possible is one of the tasks of the student of medieval commentary and education; it is not the only one. (See Hexter 1986: 9.)

[15] 'r' is usually 'respondet' but could also be 'respondeat'; 'q.d.' 'quod dicit' or 'quasi diceret'. I initially printed the final word of this section as 'rate' (Hexter (1986: 58)), and indeed, the word 'rates' occurs in that very line. But the practice of this commentator in this section (and most commentators in such a discussion) would be to cite the first word of the line or couple, so that 'arte' is more likely what was intended.

[16] E.g., 'possit obici' ('it might be objected') on vv. 6–7; 'diceret aliquis, tu dicis te esse doctorem amoris. sed hoc est impossibile, quod tu eum r<e>gas, quia ferus est' ('you say you're love's teacher, but it is impossible that you govern him, for he is wild) on vv. 9–10; see Hexter (1986: 58).

Ovid's claim to have mastered the material of his topic merges, via his allegory, with a fantasy that he has actually been made Love's instructor. Ovid leaves it to his audience to register the absurdity of the ratio Ovid: Amor: Chiron : Achilles (1. 17), rendered more absurd still by the patently lame argument that 'both are fierce boys, both goddess-born' (1. 18).[17] With the image of *praeceptor Amoris*— the very tutor of Love with a capital L—he conjures up an unruly student who, as sceptical readers (the kind he has called into existence) already know, will eventually exceed his would-be preceptor's control (the poet's brave confidence notwithstanding). When one looks at the history of the *Ars Amatoria* in the classroom, one finds an interesting reflex of the *amor/Amor* doublet. Ovid's image-producing mind permits an almost surreal and self-reflexive blend of topic and student: one has mastered Love (and even taught him ... love?) so that now one can teach love to others; likewise, in the classroom, what is taught is not so much love but the 'Art of Love' and, indeed, the very medium in which the 'Art of Love' teaches love, namely, language and rhetoric. We shall see this borne out in the *utilitas* the *Ars Amatoria* has for its medieval students.

In Horace and Ovid's day, it was still a relatively recent innovation that masters would use contemporary texts—Vergil first—for instruction in language and literature. Neither Horace nor Ovid, for all their projections of future literary survival (*Odes* 3. 30. 109; Ovid, *Met.* 15. 871–9), could imagine quite the ways their books would be used by Carolingian masters and their successors, even if Horace comes close in the witty final poem of the first book of his *Epistles*.[18] One of the earliest and most celebrated textual witnesses to

---

[17] Latin obviously blurs any imaginable boundary between *amor* and *Amor*. Ovid, when he refers to the boy and compares him to Achilles, Chiron's tutee, forces the divine personification to emerge, but earlier, the more natural sense is to understand 'love' as the entire practice and culture of loving, and there he is quite clear that the intended student is anyone *in hoc populo* (1. 1). As I have shown elsewhere, with few exceptions, the sense of *praeceptor Amoris* of 'Cupid's instructor' faded before the more obvious sense that, in the *Ars Amatoria*, Ovid is his readers' teacher in matters of love—the *praeceptor amoris* to all (Hexter (1986: 21–3)).

[18] There Horace, addressing the book he is now sending forth into the world, foresees a surprising and probably dismaying future for the young city-bound book: instead of the high life, in old age he'll end up 'teaching the boys their abc's in a far-flung township' (1. 20. 17–18).

the *Ars Amatoria*—Heinsius' Oxoniensis—is Bodleian Library Auct. F.4.32, known also as 'St Dunstan's Classbook' (and to Celticists as 'Oxoniensis Prior'). The fourth and last part (now fos. 37ʳ–47ʳ) contains a text of *Ars Amatoria* 1 with Latin and Welsh glosses. The text is dated on paleographic grounds to the ninth century, although, significantly, the final folio (fo. 47) was added by none other than the tenth-century Dunstan himself in whose hands we have 1. 747–72.[19] The glosses on the *Ars Amatoria* are concentrated on the first half of the book and are in a contemporary—in other words ninth-century—hand.[20] There are in addition syntactical (i.e. word order) marks.

What we have then is a book that indicates not only that the *Ars Amatoria*, or at least half of its first book, was used for educational purposes in the ninth century, when it was first written and glossed, but that its use in this fashion continued at least deep into the tenth century. In a text with scattered interlinear and marginal glosses, we have none of the more elaborate and formal headnotes (known as *accessus*) or potted biographies that later appear in so many Ovidian manuscripts, whether glossed manuscripts or independent commentaries. It is, nonetheless, possible to infer the type and level of instruction the user of this manuscript was involved in offering to his students.[21] What emerges is that the primary function of the glosses was to facilitate the reading and comprehension of Ovid's text. The particular form and focus of many of the glosses lead to the conclusion that the master was keen to improve students' Latin, especially their grasp of grammar and command of vocabulary. So the master glosses *sedeto* of 1. 139 with *sede*—yes, pupils, it is strange but is nevertheless an imperative. Sometimes such grammatical

---

[19] He was probably recopying what had been worn beyond usability in the original. See Hunt (1961); Hollis (1977: p. xix); Bodden (1979); Hexter (1986: 26–8).

[20] Glossed are vv. 1–389 and 620–52, with Old Welsh glosses appearing on vv. 31–370 and then on vv. 628 and 633; see Hexter (1986: 32 n. 56) and Hunt (1961: p. xiii). Although approximately 85 per cent of the glosses are in Latin, until my own study in 1986, almost all scholarship on the glossing had been by Celticists concentrating on the vernacular glosses.

[21] I am assuming that the primary user was a master rather than a student or mere casual reader. All we know of early medieval education, as well as of books and their uses, points in this direction. See also Hexter (1986: 28–9).

lessons involve the names of parts of speech (e.g. *labora* in 1. 35 is glossed 'imperatiuus'). Other expressions are expanded with words that would ease understanding. While the vernacular glosses served multiple functions, the greatest proportion simultaneously offer a lexical equivalent and grammatical reinforcement. Recurrence to vernacular was particularly helpful in explaining institutions that must have been unfamiliar to ninth-century insular students, such as *circus*, *theatra*, and *scena*, but Latin glosses, too, were used for the same purpose (e.g. those with the 'mos erat Romanorum' formula).

There is little 'art of love' left in an *Ars Amatoria* studied in this fashion, though, granted, one can never recover the remarks masters may have offered in passing to students that left no interlinear or marginal precipitate. What lay behind the decision to put this text to work teaching Latin to British students in the ninth century must also remain mysterious, the subject of speculation only. One cannot exclude the possibility that the master would have used any text of one of the *auctores* that came to hand. Still, at the very least it is worth observing that *Ars Amatoria* 1 was not considered out of bounds for either his purpose or his students who, to judge from their Latinity, could not have been very advanced. Even if in this particular spot, the *Ars* was the most convenient (non-Christian) 'auctorial' text available—or rather, given the near ubiquity of Vergil manuscripts, the most convenient non-Vergilian text—it may illustrate the infrequently recognized principle that always serves as a counterbalance to pedagogic traditionalism: in every generation there are teachers who want to try out something new, something that their own masters hadn't done.[22]

By the twelfth century, masters were happily introducing their students to virtually the full range of Ovid's œuvre. Teaching—and mastering—Ovid appears to have become a 'field' to which noted

---

[22] At the height of the *aetas vergiliana*, echoes of Ovid are far less frequent, but it is perhaps of some significance that when Theodulf (*c.*760–821) does echo the *Ars Amatoria*, it is from Book 1 and even the portion 'set' for ninth-century students by the master of Dunstan's classbook. Portions of Theodulf's 'Pillory of a judge with a hangover' (Godman (1985: 13)) are printed in Godman's anthology as no. 16; in v. 193 Theodulf echoes *Ars Amatoria* 1. 187 (ibid. 164 and n. 193). (The poem is Schaller-Könsgen no. 8493 and is printed in full in *MGH, Poetae* 1. 493–517.) Theodulf is an extraordinary figure for many reasons, including his unusually extensive familiarity with Ovid; for a recent summary, see Engelbrecht (2003: 2. 9–13).

scholars would apply themselves.[23] The productive industry of the modern scholars to whom I have referred above (see n. 14) makes it possible to compare commentaries on the *Ars Amatoria* that represent the teaching of three consecutive generations of Orléans' masters: Fulco, Arnulf, and William.[24]

I have mentioned Fulco above in connection with the commentary in the Copenhagen manuscript, which itself offers additional material.[25] Fulco of Orléans was active in the 1170s.[26] Arnulf of Orléans—nicknamed 'Rufus' and ridiculed relentlessly by Matthew of Vendôme[27]—was actually more or less simultaneous with Fulco, but one thinks of Arnulf as succeeding or surpassing Fulco primarily because Arnulf more than once criticizes various interpretations of Fulco while there is no extant example of the reverse. We have identifiable Arnulfian commentaries, some edited in full, on the *Metamorphoses, Amores, Ars Amatoria, Remedia Amoris, Ex Ponto,* and *Fasti.*[28]

[23] This is not to say that a scholar would necessarily devote himself exclusively to Ovid; Arnulf of Orléans, who has left us notes on much of Ovid, was if anything more famous for his glosses on Lucan and may also have commented on Horace; see immediately below.

[24] By 'generation' I mean here scholarly generations: the brief compass of elapsed time underscores the intensity of activity and even debate about the *auctores* that Ovidian scholarship inspired in this noted centre of learning at the end of the twelfth century.

[25] See n. 14, above, for basic references.

[26] 'we know that Fulco...wrote commentaries on the *Ars Amatoria* and the *Remedia*. In the meantime both these commentaries have been identified thanks to the work of Hugues-Victor Shooner, Bruno Roy and Frank Coulson, as is also the case with his commentaries on Ovid's *Amores, Heroides* and *Tristia*': Engelbrecht (2003: 2. 17), on whom I depend as the latest and fullest survey of the sequence. (What I cite is my own English translation of his Dutch original.) Fulco was not actually the first in the extraordinary line of Orléans Ovidians: a good many years earlier came Hilary the Englishman (*c.*1075–*c.*1150), not, however, known as a commentator (Engelbrecht (2003: 2. 15)).

[27] Shooner and Roy (1985–6). Arnulf and the famous goliardic poet Hugh Primas also came into conflict; see Engelbrecht (2003: 2. 19–20), with further references.

[28] Attribution to Arnulf of commentaries on the *Heroides* and *Tristia* has been proposed, and he may well also have commented on Horace's *Satirae, Epistulae,* and *Ars Poetica* (Engelbrecht (2003: 2. 21)). Engelbrecht further notes that his Lucan commentary (noted above) is not only his 'best known' but also the only one we are able to date with reasonable certitude. The most reliable route to accessing all Arnulf's texts is Coulson and Roy (2000), with some addenda in Coulson (2002). Hexter (1988) explores one dimension of Arnulf's treatment of the *Metamorphoses*—narrative segmentation—a topic taken up for the later Pierre Bersuire in Hexter (1989).

Relatively little is known about William. Engelbrecht concludes that he must have compiled and circulated his *Bursarii* very close to the year 1200. Engelbrecht devotes the bulk of the second volume of his dissertation to analysis of William of Orléans' interpretative modes in the *Bursarii*, which he edits in the first volume. It would be absurd to attempt any kind of condensation here, but let me note in the present context two salient features of the *Bursarii*: (1) William is much more selective in the number of lines (and thus passages) in any given work of Ovid's that he subjects to analysis than is Arnulf, say, or most other twelfth-century commentators, and (2) considerably more frequently than even his most immediate predecessors William confronts head-on variant readings he meets in the passages he chooses.[29] William's unusual attention to variant readings is part of the reason Engelbrecht entitles his work 'Philology in the thirteenth century'; of course William does not base his judgements on any kind of systematic study of manuscript traditions à la Lachmann.

Scholars such as Engelbrecht are at pains to differentiate the object of their study from their immediate forebears, but all these commentaries display substantial family resemblances. All of them, and the many other anonymous masters who copy them more or less verbatim or use them as the basis for their own customized teaching texts, still aim first and foremost to make sure that students understand Ovid's Latin. Even as advanced a commentary as William's will in certain places simply unravel the text via paraphrase.[30] Some years ago I tried to characterize the advance that the commentary in the Copenhagen manuscript (which represents over much of its extent Fulco's work) constitutes over the ninth-century Oxford manuscript, and—more significantly—what one might infer from that advance about the students in the later era and about the more advanced educational formation an encounter with a text such as the *Ars Amatoria* then supported. In ninth-century Britain 'the (presumably elementary) students read only a portion of one book of the *Ars Amatoria*. They were often hard pressed to understand the

---

[29] To cite (after Engelbrecht (2003: 2. 238)) one example from the *Ars Amatoria*: discussing 1. 587–8, Arnulf explains only the reading *inde procurator* of Berlin SBPK Diez B Sant 1 (thirteenth century) and some *deteriores*; William explicates that reading as well as the older *inde propinator*.

[30] These are often introduced by 'construe', 'continua', 'continuacio'.

vocabulary, and their master had to provide vernacular equivalents in many cases'. In marked contrast, the twelfth-century students reading the *Ars Amatoria* in classrooms whose practices are represented in the Copenhagen commentary must have had a firmer command of Latin, permitting the master to focus more on Ovid's modes of argumentation, on rhetoric, in other words. The relatively advanced standing of the pupils for which the commentary was compiled becomes clear when one notes what the commentator omits. He explains some customs and institutions of Ovid's Rome but skips others that he expects users of the commentary to know already with the tag 'fabula satis nota est'. In such a commentary, I conclude, 'we see the fruits of the three centuries of study and scholarship that intervened between it and St. Dunstan's Classbook'.[31]

Broadly speaking, much of the above applies not only to Fulco but to Fulco's immediate successors, even if, as Engelbrecht's careful analysis shows, there are significantly different centres of gravity and emphases in the work of Arnulf and William, respectively.[32] Given the fact that all three commentaries arose within a space of at most thirty-five years, it is remarkable that such different tendencies can be so clearly noted. William's more 'philological' tendencies are certainly significant and make sense in light of the shifting place of the *auctores* in Latin schooling as well as of trends in the academic study of grammar at the threshold of the thirteenth-century and the age of the universities. But the very energy with which these successive Orléans masters strove to create distinctive profiles for themselves as individual and unique explicators of Ovid's *Ars Amatoria* (and other works) itself bespeaks the cachet of Ovid at this time and the cultural capital to be accumulated if one could establish oneself as a master of Love's own master.

Vernacular glosses appear from time to time in the work of high-medieval commentators such as Arnulf though in no way as generously as they had in the ninth-century *Ars* glosses in the 'schoolbook

---

[31] Hexter (1986: 77).
[32] If 'in his commentary on the *Ars* William concentrates more than Arnulf did on historical realia' (Engelbrecht (2003: 2. 237)), Arnulf, in contrast, concentrates more than William (or Fulco, for that matter) on explicating the mythological background to references in Ovid.

of St Dunstan'.[33] The tradition of Latin school commentaries and, then, learned Latin commentaries on Ovid's works, the *Ars* included, continues unabated into the sixteenth century and even beyond. But a survey of the topic would not be complete without reference, however brief it must be due to restrictions of space, to the vernacular in later medieval and then Renaissance classrooms. This is a vast arena.[34] To do it justice one would have to trace the expanding opportunities—and demand—for education outside clerical milieux, nor could one simply give one account of vernacular learning or even translation, since the situation varied from region to region. France, for example, saw at least four distinct verse adaptations of the *Ars* between the thirteenth and fourteenth centuries, while the German-speaking countries saw none in the same period.[35] The French texts are not, however, in the least redolent of the schoolroom. At the risk of eliding important differences, one can say that they are to be read as belonging to (or distancing themselves from) the world of courtly love or *fin amors*.

Much more closely related to the classroom are several fourteenth-century Italian versions of the *Ars Amatoria*.[36] The direct overlap with Latin classrooms consists in the inclusion in these Italian *Ars* translations of explanatory material directly drawn from the Latin

---

[33] For another example: Old High German glosses in the Tegernsee commentary on the *Heroides* in clm 19475 I discuss in Hexter (1986: 205–9). (While not directly germane to the issue at hand here, some important additions and corrections to my initial work on this *Heroides* commentary have now been published by Gärtner (2000). In the meantime, I have presented some material from an unpublished *Heroides* commentary in Berkeley in Hexter (2002b).) Nor does this practice end with the Middle Ages; see Black (2001: 251) for a fifteenth-century manuscript of the *Remedia Amoris* from southern Italy (now Florence, Biblioteca Riccardiana 548) with extensive glossing, including vernacular, by more than one hand.

[34] Among recent works I can recommend for first orientation when trying to answer not only what was 'vernacular humanism' but how one even conceptualizes 'vernacular' are Copeland (1991); Wogan-Browne et al. (1999); Ferguson (2003); and Somerset and Watson (2003). Still valuable are earlier studies—some on rather more particular sectors of the field—by Monfrin (1972); Buck (1978); Guthmüller (1981); and Henkel (1988).

[35] See Minnis (2001) for a recent and excellent survey.

[36] Their recent editor presents three distinct Tuscan versions of both the *Ars* and the *Remedia Amoris* (A, B, and C) as well as a fourth Venetian version of the *Ars* alone (D): Lippi Bigazzi (1987), 1. 27–40.

school tradition.[37] Many of the extensive vernacular 'chiose' [glosses] are indebted to known Latin glosses. Like Latin glosses we have seen, these 'chiose' exhibit typical explanations of Ovid's mode of argumentation as well as mythological identifications and explanations, both long and short. While these Italian texts give access to the learning purveyed in Latin classrooms over several centuries, it is doubtful whether they directly represent contemporary vernacular classrooms. However much 'school' material appears, then, in the vernacular glosses, and however much the general cachet of Ovid had something to do with his place in the school curriculum, such vernacularization as the Italian *Ars* represents has clearly shifted the *Ars Amatoria* well into the realm of the 'illiterati', i.e. non-Latin users.

Despite the degree to which these fourteenth-century Italian translations suggest crossover between the Ovid of the Latin schools and the vernacular Ovid, for a time at least the two traditions moved further apart rather than closer. If some of the great early Italian poets whose appreciation for Ovid was well-nigh boundless—Dante, Boccaccio, Petrarch—themselves operated in both Latin and vernacular, only the first of the three really thought the vernacular fully fit for learned matters, and the 'high' Italian humanists of the fifteenth and early sixteenth century privileged Latin, at times even fanatically. There was a vernacular Ovid for the leisured class, but in the classroom the classical authors were studied for their ability to augment students' capacity in Latin rhetoric, style, and poetics.[38]

---

[37] In the Escorial manuscript of D, a long commentary precedes the bilingual *Ars Amatoria*; it explicitly claims not only that it was 'translate et vulgariçate' from a Latin commentary, but that the original commentary was by none other than Boccaccio (Lippi Bigazzi (1987: 473); cf. 476–8). Lippi Bigazzi (ibid. 10) raises the intriguing possibility that the 'scolaio rozzo' ('unfinished schoolboy') of the B tradition, who worked to compile the commentary and correct the translation itself, might have been Boccaccio.

[38] Even as I write the above I remind myself and readers of the explicit and implicit lesson of Black (2001) that in earlier studies of the *Quattrocento* and *Cinquecento* scholars have concentrated overmuch on a few exceptional figures at the 'top of the heap'; as noted above, Black's magisterial study of teaching texts from Italy gives a fuller picture and confirms continuity in practice along with innovations. Consider e.g. two fifteenth-century manuscripts of Ovidiana now in Florentine libraries, Biblioteca Medicea Laurenziana 37.12 and Biblioteca Nazionale Centrale Magl. VII.966. (For details, see Black (2001: 251–2)).

As I noted above, in anatomizing even one dimension of the reception of one of Ovid's works, one must attend to local variation. Generalizing about 'Italy' is already to paint with too broad a brush, and it would be equally careless to pick one English book to exemplify that very different tradition. A fitting book-end to a history of the *Ars Amatoria* in medieval classrooms that started in Britain with 'St Dunstan's Classbook' might well be a 1513 production of the noted London printer Wynkyn de Worde, *The flores of Ouide de arte amandi with theyre englysshe afore them: and two alphabete tablys. The fyrst begynneth with the englysshe hauyng the laten wordes folowynge, the other with the laten hauyging (the) englysshe wordes folowying.*[39] This book represents the first significant English rendering of an Ovidian text made directly from the Latin. De Worde seems not only to have effected or at least redacted the translation but also to have conceived the elements of the textbook and devised the attached tables that he calculated would promote its sale. It is the combination of all these elements that make this book so fascinating, for it is at once a translation and Latin primer. If, on the one hand, in 1513 we are in the world of print capitalism, seemingly post-medieval by definition, on the other hand, the use of Ovid to teach Latin, and a vernacular rendering subordinated to that end as well, was the standard medieval situation.[40] De Worde probably also aimed to capitalize on a market that was larger than traditional schools: individuals, whether parents of children they hoped would learn more Latin, or who themselves wished somehow to pick up a 'little Latine' and thus participate in a culture that carried with it no little prestige.[41]

[39] I have consulted a complete photo of the original in the British Library, STC 18934, at the Huntington Library (San Marino, Calif.).
[40] De Worde evokes the world of the traditional classroom situation by means of the sort of image readers would know from manuscripts, if now produced by printerly technology: the woodcut that appears on the title page and that is then repeated on the *verso* of (unnumbered) fo. a ii shows a schoolmaster teaching three boys; they sit on a bench and each has a text open before him. Presumably de Worde would hope that each copy had been purchased from his shop.
[41] The headnote to the English to Latin vocabulary includes remarks that bear on the translation and the non-traditional audience it wants to address: 'For we haue added moch englysh more than is laten fore in the versis to make the sentens playn: to whom we haue also added laten for chyldren: that they shuld lacke not laten wordis to make theyr englyshe in to laten worde by worde as nugh: as the dyuersite of the langages wol soffer' ((unnumbered) fo. a viii).

De Worde has selected couplets from all three books of the *Ars Amatoria* and presents each one as a separate opportunity for a Latin lesson. A very full and faithful English prose rendering precedes each Latin distich. So preceding *Ars* 1. 3–4, students read 'Swifte shipis be iouerned be craft | & with sele and oare & a light swyfte chare is gouerned by crafte: and lyke wyse loue most be gouerned by crafte'. *Ars* 1. 35–6 is glossed 'In the begining first of all labour to fynd it that thu may desyer to loue for thyn own profit the which commyst now first a neue soudier in to harnes.' These painstakingly complete renderings are generally reliable, even if the boar of *Ars* 1. 46 has become 'a fromyng wylde bere'. Book 1 is only slightly 'over-sampled': thirty-one distichs are selected from it, with twenty-nine from Book 2 and twenty-five from Book 3.[42] It does not appear that there is one easily formulated principle by which one can explain why de Worde selected precisely these distichs for translation. What emerges is a predilection for vivid images (e.g. the overhanging river bank eaten away by the flowing water (1. 620)) and a veritable menagerie of animals.[43] Perhaps the most surprising couplet to be highlighted is 2. 717–18: *crede mihi, non est Veneris properanda uoluptas | sed sensim tarda prolicienda mora*.[44]

[42] The 31 distichs selected from *Ars* 1 ([a ii]–a iiii) are: 1.3 f., 35 f., 45 f., 47 f., 51 f., 271 f., 279 f, 349 f., 379 f., 381 f., 391 f., 401 f.*, 435 f., 471 f., 473 f., 475 f., 513 f.*, 519 f., 583 f.*, 589 f., 591 f., 597 f., 599 f.*, 615 f.*, 619 f., 641 f.*, 645a + 655b/656*, 757 f.*, 759 f., and 765 f.*; the 29 from *Ars* 2 (aiiii - [a vi]) are 2.9 f., 13 f., 43 f., 107 f., 113 f., 115 f.*, 117 f., 119 f., 121 f., 145 f., 147 f., 151 f., 167 f.*, 179 f., 183 f.*, 263 f., 277 f., 317 f.*, 341 f., 343 f., 357 f.*, 363 f., 437 f., 513 f., 603 f.*, 633 f.*, 717 f., and 731 f.; the 25 from *Ars* 3 ([a vi – a vii verso]) are 3.63 f.*, 65 f., 73 f., 75 f., 93 f., 101 f.*, 105 f., 121 f., 257 f.*, 259 f., 261 f.*, 279 f., 419 f., 425 f., 427 f.*, 491 f., 493 f., 501 f., 503 f., 525 f.*, 583 f., 595 f., 667 f., 669 f., and 673 f.*. (I have marked with an asterisk the instances where the Latin De Worde prints departs from the current standard text.)

[43] Some phrases seem likely to have been chosen for their apophthegmatic qualities (e.g. 3. 63–6) or to exemplify certain constructions valuable for students to learn (e.g. *tot... quot* (1. 759)). The longest run of consecutive lines—2. 113–22—exemplifies the much-loved topos of age's effect on beauty. It took until the end of the sixteenth century for Thomas Heywood to produce the first complete translation of the *Ars Amatoria* into English (first printed in the seventeenth century, newly edited in Stapleton (2000)). The poem was not generally thought fare for English students until Hollis published his commentary on the first book of *Ars Amatoria* (1977).

[44] Could he have shared Voltaire's view 'du livre innocent de l' Art d'aimer, livre très-décemment écrit, et dans lequel il n'y a pas un mot obscène' (cited from Stroh (1969: 81))? Voltaire was writing tongue-in-cheek, I suspect; in any event, it was the arbitrary action of absolute imperial power he wished above all to castigate.

This intermittent review of several distinct points in a long history might be able to suggest a somewhat surprising thesis: for all the attempted explanations of *utilitas* in the medieval *accessus* that accompanied the *Ars Amatoria*, the *Ars* was able to be included in the curriculum because it was largely irrelevant. Put another way, the medieval relevance of the *Ars* was independent of its ostensible Roman aim of erotodidaxis.[45] Although there were certain figures, such as William of St-Thierry, Andreas Capellanus, or Peter Cantor, who did try—each in a different way—to relate Ovid and the erotodidactics of the *Ars Amatoria* to contemporary discourses about love (both sacred and secular), by and large, in texts such as the Munich manuscript from which the epigraph to this article is drawn, there is a disjunction between any gestures in this direction that are found in the *accessus* and the mass of commentary that follows.[46]

Without underrating the significant insights the *accessus* offer into medieval literary interpretation, I continue to maintain that this larger mass of more pedestrian commentary reflects in some way the real division of *pedagogic* labour: much more time and energy were invested in working through the text and dealing with the kinds of question the *glosulae* address. From this it seems clear to me that reading the *Ars Amatoria* (and other works of Ovid) in the schools was largely a means to an end: learning Latin and commanding the diction of Roman poetry that were clearly important constituents of high medieval Latin school culture and tools for acculturation and advancement. In commentaries such as the Copenhagen version of Fulco's commentary to which I have frequently referred—but the trend is evident earlier and is by no means restricted to commentaries on the *Ars* or *Remedia*—the frequent comments of the type 'mos erat romanorum' can be understood as a distancing device. Though of course the historical accuracy of these observations (as with many a

---

[45] 'Ostensible' or 'pretended'. Ovid's real aim was presumably to write brilliant poetry and to be recognized as a daring wit—to reveal our (or at least my own) modern prejudice. Is this something hinted at in William of Orléans' distinction under the standard *accessus*-category of *utilitas*: 'Utilitas quantum ad auctorem delectacio, quantum ad legentes amoris cognicio, unde habetur in secundo versus: "Et lecto carmine doctus amet"' (Engelbrecht (2003: 224–5))?

[46] Baldwin (1992) highlights some of these links and prints (p. 92) a brief if fascinating sequence of scholastic argument on 'ars amatoria' from clm 5426. On the disjunction between *accessus* and the bulk of commentary, see Hexter (1986: 212–14).

mythological explanation) is highly variable, it is an honest medieval attempt at historical understanding. One cannot compare the 'historicity' of these comments with the cumulative fruits of modern philology any more than one can judge William of Orléans' 'philology' by nineteenth- and twentieth-century standards. However, there is no doubt that the erotic games of the *Ars Amatoria* could be assimilated to a then/now rhetoric that runs back through (most famously) Augustine's *City of God* to the Christian apologists of the first centuries. I have elsewhere explored the ways in which this other 'Roman' world was accessed via the poetry of Roman *auctores*, and Ovid especially was evoked to authorize, to a certain limited extent, some spaces of licence and relative freedom.[47] But this was always a counter-discourse, however elegant and (in some circles) admired, and the conventional position certainly emphasized the otherness, not only merely temporally but in terms of the pagan/Christian succession, of Ovid's Roman world.

The distinct popularity of the *Remedia Amoris* and its inclusion in anthologies apart from the *Ars Amatoria* is one symptom of a different perspective that, with time, was expressed with increasing insistence. The *Remedia Amoris*—however speciously—seems as though it might be a helpful guide to steer youths away from the entanglements of dangerous love affairs and wild passion. While, on the one hand, it might appear a mistake to take this explanation any more seriously than so many other claims under the headings *intentio* or *utilitas* in the *accessus*, on the other hand, one can and, I believe, should understand it as marking a new form of relevance, one that does need to invoke the cultural distance of the *Romani* with their peculiar and different *mores*.

Might one align this (from the high medieval perspective) oddly 'ahistorical' attitude with the advent of humanism? I realize that this will sound like a highly counterintuitive, possibly even perverse claim, since humanist scholars' understanding of the ancient world, not only Rome but, as renewed study allowed, Greece as well, marked a real advance in depth, breadth, and accuracy.[48] The impulse,

[47] Hexter (1999: 338–44) and (2002a: 432–9).
[48] The idea that the Latin Middle Ages were entirely without Greek has long since been corrected. Both Black (2001) and Engelbrecht (2003) add new dimensions to the foundational study of Berschin (1980/1988).

however, to look to the ancients for usable models for contemporary behaviour and forms of society (as well as plastic and literary art) also has its ahistorical dimensions. Granted, contrary, even contradictory impulses exist in most periods, so this should surprise us no more than the fact that in high medieval Latin culture Ovidian erotics could be simultaneously held at a distance and yet admired and emulated.

The expanding opportunities for encountering Roman authors in various vernaculars also added momentum to this movement. As Ovidian material passed beyond the walls of monastery and cathedral schools and out of the control of masters who could guarantee that their students, still relatively few in number, still all clerics (however irregular some), still overwhelmingly male, would understand these texts in some sort of 'historical' context as bespeaking Roman mores (that were by definition not their own), concern about the possibility of misunderstanding yielded to fear of almost inevitable misapplication.[49] Even in Latin, the number of warnings and prohibitions rise; one thinks, for example, of the fourteenth-century *Anti-Ovidianus* mentioned above. The baleful effects of overly sympathetic reading are most clearly dramatized by Dante when he describes the fall of Paolo and Francesca into adulterous fornication, though it was not a classical text that lay open before them. But the *Metamorphoses in volgare* or any number of other texts could have the same effect, and one senses the ripe atmosphere of classically based erotics certainly as early as Gottfried's *Minnegrot* and even more in the *Roman de la Rose*, with Narcissus and his fountain. Boccaccio's Dioneo introduces one of Apuleius' naughtier tales to the *brigata* in the *Decameron* (5. 10), and the 'Chaucer' figure in *The House of Fame* well exemplifies the confused interpretative exuberance of the vernacular humanist who is by no means clear on the differences between Vergil's Dido and Ovid's Dido, and who seeks 'tidynges of love' from a pantheon of *auctores* now largely available, if not yet in English, then in at least one of the romance languages.

---

[49] One of the most telling episodes of the demand for moral accountability, even a certain 'political correctness', is inspired by a vernacular text, the *Roman de la rose*, though the *querelle* that ensues also involves ripostes in Latin. For a recent guide to the fascinating debate, see Minnis (2001).

It is against the background of such a shift in sensibilities that we must look at the increasingly fraught place of Ovid's erotodidactic poetry in the schoolroom. It is in some sense remarkable that the *Ars Amatoria* hung on as long as it did, whether in fourteenth- and fifteenth-century Italy or early sixteenth-century England. Then as now, masters—joined soon by printers—had enormous power to direct young minds to look to Ovid's Latinity, his mythological learning, his rhetorical craft. One should never underestimate the power either of tradition or the mind's capacity for cognitive dissonance.

16

Ovid in Defeat? On the reception of Ovid's *Ars Amatoria* and *Remedia Amoris*

Genevieve Liveley

> The grammar of Love's Art
> Ovid still teaches,
> Grotesque in Pontic snows
> And bearskin breeches.
>
> 'Let man be ploughshare,
> Woman his field;
> Flatter, beguile, assault,
> And she must yield.'
>
> 'Snatch the morning rose
> Fresh from the wayside,
> Deflower it in haste
> Ere the dew be dried.'
>
> Ovid instructs you how
> Neighbours' lands to plough;
> 'Love smacks the sweeter
> For a broken vow.'
>
> Follows his conclusion
> Of which the gist is

Thanks are due to Carcanet Press and the estate of Robert Graves for their permission to reproduce 'Ovid in Defeat' from *Poems (1914–26)* by Robert Graves, copyright 1927. I would also like to thank Roy Gibson, Steve Green, and Alison Sharrock in Manchester and Duncan Kennedy, Charles Martindale, and Vanda Zajko in Bristol for their generous help in shaping and improving this chapter. I am also grateful to Robert Knapp and Ellen Oliensis for inviting me to spend the 2002–3 academic year at University College, Berkeley, where work on this piece was begun.

Ovid in Defeat?

The cold 'post coitum
Homo tristis.'

Thereat despairing,
Other Ovids hallow
Ploughshare in rust
And field left fallow,

Or, since in Logic books
Proposed they find,
'Where two ride together,
One rides behind,'

This newer vision
Of love's revealed,
Woman as the ploughshare,
Man, her field.

Man as the plucked flower
Trampled in mire,
When his unfair fair
Has eased desire.

One sort of error
Being no worse than other,
O, hug this news awhile,
My amorous brother,

That the wheel of Fortune
May be turned complete,
Conflict, domination,
Due defeat.

Afterwards, when you weary
Of false analogy,
Offending both philosophy
And physiology,

You shall see in woman
Neither more nor less
Than you yourself demand
As your soul's dress.

Thought, though not man's thought,
Deeds, but her own,
Art, by no comparisons
Shaken or thrown.

Plough then salutes plough
And rose greets rose:
While Ovid in toothache goes
Stamping through old snows.
(Robert Graves, *Ovid in Defeat*)

Robert Graves, writing in 1925, offers a rare acknowledgement of Ovid's influence upon his own literary work in the short poem 'Ovid in Defeat'.[1] Explicitly correlating Ovid's *Ars Amatoria* and *Remedia Amoris* with the poet's banishment to Tomis, Graves's poem assesses the implications of Ovid's declared project to arm both the Greeks and the Amazons, both men and women, with the *ars* of love. The result is a tense piece of writing, formed in crisply rhyming stanzas that seem to mimic paired elegiac couplets, which engages combatively with Ovid's *Ars* and *Remedia* to comment not only upon the gendered dynamics of the sexual conflict and competition implied by the erotic precepts of these poems, but also the dynamics of their reading and reception. Thus, stanzas 1–5 deal with Ovid's erotodidactic and exilic works—*Ars* 1–2, the *Remedia*, *Tristia*, and *Ex Ponto*; stanzas 6–10 turn to their reading and literary reception, including *Ars* 3; and stanzas 11–15 turn to Graves's own 'teachings' as *praeceptor*.

Graves's piece is unusual, not just in its rare recognition of the poet's own literary indebtedness to Ovid or in its understatement of the erotic or pornographic potential of the *Ars* and *Remedia*, but in its creative response to Ovid's erotodidactic poetry.[2] Following

---

[1] First published under the title of 'Ovid's Breeches' in *Welchman's Hose*. Reprinted in his collected *Poems (1914–26)* of 1927, and included in the 1998 collection of *Ovid in English*.

[2] As Ralph Hexter hints in Ch. 15 of this volume, the reception of the *Ars* and *Remedia* from the early seventeenth century onwards was marked by a trend that positioned Ovid's erotodidactic works as scandalous works of 'drollery', titillation, and even pornography. From the first publication of Thomas Heywood's *Loues Schoole* around 1600; the 1662 publication of *Ovid De Arte Amandi and the Remedy of Love Englished: As Also the Lovs of Hero and Leander, a Mock-Poem: Together with Choice poems, and Rare Pieces of Drollery* by various authors (its popularity such that it ran to six editions); Henry Fielding's 1747 *Ovid's Art of Love Paraphrased, and Adapted to the Present Time* (reissued in 1760 as *The Lovers Assistant, or New Art of Love*); through numerous twentieth-century English translations which exploited the pornographic potential of the *Ars* (see Gibson (1996)) with 'erotic' illustrations and titillating 'blurbs'; to Walerian Borowczyk's 1983 film *Ars Amandi* or *Art of Love*, and the 1989 special 'Sexual Arts Issue' of *Forum* magazine—'196 pages (not to be missed!) on oral sex, masturbation, sm, massage, sexual surprises and more...'—featuring an illustrated free translation of the first two books of the *Ars* by Peter Jones.

almost six centuries in which translation provided the principal vehicle for the reception of Ovid's *Ars* and *Remedia*,[3] 'Ovid in Defeat' represents something of a return to an earlier tradition of contentious engagements and critical rereadings of Ovid's controversial erotodidactic works, such as those presented in Marie de France's twelfth-century *Guigemar*, Guillaume de Lorris and Jean de Meun's thirteenth-century *Roman de la rose*, or Chaucer's fifteenth-century 'The Wife of Bath's Prologue and Tale'. These texts, like Graves's poem, do not merely appropriate, reproduce, or critique the precepts outlined in the *Ars Amatoria* and *Remedia Amoris*, but engage in innovative re-enactments of the gendered conflict between the sexes—and for sex—outlined in Ovid's erotodidactic poetry.[4] In these medieval and early modern receptions, Ovid's *Ars* and *Remedia* are subjected to an aggressive mode of appropriation. They provide the weapons and the battleground for a series of eroticized conflicts and competitions and a series of concomitant victories and defeats. Authors and their characters, both male and female, contend with Ovid for authority in and over the arts of love—in education, seduction, manipulation, and interpretation.

In a contemporary reading of the *Ars* that has much to inform an analysis of this poem's historical reception, Alison Sharrock employs the discourse of reader-response criticism to configure the relationship between the author of the *Ars* and his/its readers and pupils explicitly in terms of such conflict. She sees the engagement between Ovid and his readers as a confrontation, a struggle for interpretative authority, in which 'Ovid contends as teacher, seducer, manipulator,

---

[3] Although allusions to Ovid's amatory works are regularly featured in early modern and Renaissance plays.

[4] In the *lai* of Marie de France, a wall painting decorating the bedchamber in which Guigemar's lady is imprisoned depicts Venus burning 'Ovid's book' (taken by some readers to be the *Remedia Amoris* and others to be the *Ars Amatoria*) in a destructive condemnation of the *praeceptor*'s teachings. The *Roman de la rose*, despite Guillaume de Lorris' unambiguous claim at the start of the poem to have written a new *Ars Amatoria* (*Roman* I. 37–9), offers a valorization of the principles of romantic 'courtly' love rather than a cynical exposé of love's conventions and tropes in its allegorical narrative. In it, Ovid's precepts are resolutely resisted and Love (*Amant*) ultimately triumphs over Art—and the *Ars*. Chaucer's 'Wife of Bath' challenges Ovid's erotodidactic precepts to question the benefits that the art of love can really offer her. See Stapleton (1996) on Marie de France, Dimmick (2002) on *Roman de la rose*, and Calabrese (1994) on Chaucer.

Author for supremacy over the reader/pupil' (1994*a*: 293). Within this conflict, she suggests, readings do not emerge through diplomatic negotiation and concord between author, text, and reader, but through a process of domination and defeat. Other stories of reading might emphasize the mutual 'coming together' of author and reader upon the site of the text to make meaning as one, but according to this reading of the combative relationship between author and reader of the *Ars* the author and text 'defeat' any reader who passively receives the poetry and precepts offered, but the reader defeats the author and text if he or she plays an active role in appropriating the text and determining its meaning. So (1994*a*: 293),

In so far as we see the reader (ourselves) as the passive recipient of advice, instruction, and poetry, the text wins. But if we see the reader as the constructor of the reading in which the poet is controller, the reader wins, for the reader has constructed the meaning.

This accent upon the competitive and combative relationship between author and reader, teacher and pupil, in Sharrock's reading of the *Ars* responds to a similar emphasis and association between conflict and reading evident in both the *Ars* and *Remedia*. As Philip Hardie notes in this volume, Ovid's prologue to the *Remedia* vigorously denies that he is making war on *Amor* (1–4):[5]

> legerat huius Amor titulum nomenque libelli:
> 'bella mihi, uideo, bella parantur' ait.
> 'parce tuum uatem sceleris damnare, Cupido,
> tradita qui toties te duce signa tuli.

(Love read the title and name on this little book. He said: 'I see war, war is being prepared against me'. 'Don't attack your poet for a crime, Cupid, he who has so often carried the standard you handed him, under your command.)

Yet this denial of intent, like so many other disclaimers in the *Ars* and *Remedia*, is far from straightforward—if not entirely disingenuous. It returns to the sustained military imagery invoked in the *Ars* and implies that, having armed the Amazons and Greeks with the tools to fight fairly against each other in the *Ars*, Ovid intends now to

---

[5] See Rosati and Hardie, Chs. 8 and 9 in this volume.

arm them both against *amor* in the *Remedia*.⁶ In the *Ars*, however, Ovid has already revealed that once he has armed his readers/pupils he cannot fully direct their use of such weapons—which may even be used against him. Indeed, he recognizes that having armed his (female) readers he himself may be betrayed by his own precepts and defeated by weapons which he has himself provided his enemy (*Ars* 3. 667–72):

> quo feror insanus? quid aperto pectore in hostem
>   mittor, et indicio prodor ab ipse meo?
> non auis aucupibus monstrat, qua parte petatur:
>   non docet infestos currere cerua canes.
> uiderit utilitas: ego coepta fideliter edam:
>   Lemniasin gladios in mea fata dabo.

(Where is my madness taking me? Why am I rushing with bared chest against the enemy, why am I betrayed by my own advice? The bird does not show the hunters the places where it may be hunted; The deer does not teach the enemy hounds to run. Let utility see to itself; I will faithfully complete my undertaking; I will give the Lemnian women weapons to kill me.)

In Ovid's self-conscious arming of his pupil/readers against himself, distinctions between recipient and controller of advice, instruction, and poetry, between pupil and *praeceptor*, reader and author, are blurred—and the battle-lines in a conflict for interpretative authority are drawn up. Ovid in the *Ars* and *Remedia* arms his pupils and readers with precepts that he acknowledges and even expects may be used against him. 'Ovid in Defeat' takes up those precepts and arms.

Significantly, *Welchman's Hose*, in which 'Ovid in Defeat' first appeared as 'Ovid's Breeches', is acknowledged as one of the most self-consciously 'Ovidian' examples of Graves's poetic works. According to Michael Kirkham's assessment of the pieces presented in this text (1969: 87):

More than anything else the reader is conscious of the mask of urbanity which these poems wear. Generally, the verse is 'classical'—the tone polished and glinting with irony, and most of the poems are either wittily presented allegories or lightly mocking discussions of ideas.

---

[6] See particularly Hollis (1977), Sharrock (1994*a*), and Gibson (2003*a*) on the military imagery employed in the *Ars*.

'Ovid in Defeat', he suggests, is representative of this collection's style and tone as Graves matches the cynicism of the *praeceptor amoris* with his own. Moreover, though Graves's resistance to Ovid's 'grammar' appears to be signalled from the opening stanza in which the Roman poet is configured as barbarian other, it is Ovid who arms Graves with the very weapons with which he may be seen to engage, ridicule, and defeat him here. Indeed, this aspect of the poem is underscored in the retitled version that appears in Graves's *Poems (1914–26)*, where the line placing Ovid in 'bearskin breeches' is glossed with a line (unattributed) from the *Tristia* (5. 7. 49)—*pellibus et sutis arcent mala frigora braccis*—revealing this poem to be informed by Graves's close reading of Ovid's exilic writing, just as close readings of the *Metamorphoses* and *Fasti* inform much of his other work.[7]

With Ovid's exile—or at least, the tropes of Ovid's exile—influencing the frame of Graves's poem, the first stanza of 'Ovid in Defeat' provides clues as to why Graves may have decided to change the title of the poem in its 1927 publication from 'Ovid's Breeches', and perhaps why the image of Ovid's 'defeat' has appeared as such a determining factor in the reception of the *Ars Amatoria* and *Remedia Amoris*.[8] In the first stanza, we see Ovid still teaching his Arts of Love, 'Grotesque in Pontic snows | And bearskin breeches', the incongruity of this image signalling an apparent resistance to Ovid and his *Ars* from the outset. But whom, in this 'barbarian' costume, does Graves imagine Ovid to be still teaching?

Ovid's own exile poetry describes another incongruous scene in which he claims to have given a public recitation of a poem composed in Latin metre but in the Getic language to an assembly of barbarian (*inhumanos*—22) locals who brandish their weapons (35) in appreciation of his work (*Pont.* 4. 13).[9] Elsewhere, though, he writes of his inability to communicate with the local Tomitians, to whom he—the *Romanus uates* (*Tr.* 5. 7. 55)—seems the unintelligible barbarian (*Tr.* 5. 10. 37).[10] The Getae then, ostensibly like Graves,

---

[7] For an annotated Graves bibliography, see Bryant (1986).
[8] The short stories inspired by Ovid's *Ars* and *Remedia* in Philip Terry's collection of modern responses to Ovid continue to reflect this trend.
[9] See Williams (2002: 239).
[10] See Volk, Ch. 12 in this volume on the *Romanitas* of the *Ars*.

appear to represent an unaccommodating and resistant audience for Ovid's 'grammar of Love's Art'. Yet, lest we are tempted to identify ourselves—or Graves—as among the barbarian Tomitians who do not understand or appreciate Ovid's poetry, Graves dresses Ovid himself in the animal-skin costume of the Getans—identifying the *Romanus uates* as the barbarian other, in outward appearance at least. Indeed, in his caricature of Ovid in Pontic snows and bearskin breeches, Graves seems to re-enact the censorious condemnation of the poet to a permanent exile. For in responding to Ovid in this way Graves initially positions himself alongside the Augustan readers whom Ovid represents as misreading his *Ars*, thus making himself vulnerable to similar charges of misreading and misinterpreting Ovid's poetry. For, as Gareth Williams observes of Ovid's banishment to Tomis (2002: 238):

> The penalty he pays in exile for the 'corrupting' *Ars Amatoria* is a form of solitary linguistic confinement, his Latin powerless to exercise any kind of influence among the uncomprehending Tomitians; and yet a more sympathetic reading of the *Ars Amatoria* suggests that Ovid's Latin is misunderstood not only in Tomis but also, in a different way, by that austere section of his Roman readership which originally found fault with the *Ars*.

However, Graves is better able to disprove these charges than Ovid's 'original' Augustan readership by offering strong evidence of his close—and even sympathetic—reading of the Roman poet's work. In a parodic abbreviation of the (parodic) Georgic imagery[11] employed in the *Ars*, Graves condenses Ovid's precepts in Books 1 and 2 of the *Ars* to three terse stanzas. His synthesis of the erotodidactic precepts of the *Ars* is disarmingly succinct. Three stanzas, highlighted as paraphrase by quotation marks, seem sufficient to express the substance of the poem's first two books. The elegant compression of ideas in epigrammatic style, the parodic use of metaphor and the play of wit, moreover, intimate a characteristic 'Ovidian' quality to Graves' poem.[12]

The exhortation in Graves' poem for the would-be lover to 'Flatter, beguile, assault,' the female object of his desire may be seen to represent a fair condensation of similar teachings in the *Ars*—particularly

---

[11] See Leach (1964).   [12] See Kirkham (1969: 87).

the precepts outlined in *Ars* 1. 619–78, in which Ovid advises the putative lover to employ flattery (*Ars* 1. 619–30), false promises (*Ars* 1. 631–63), and force (*Ars* 1. 664–78) in order to win the object of his affections. Indeed, the tension in the reworking of this last contentious precept subtly highlights the aggressive power-play implicit in the *praeceptor*'s recommendation that 'force' or *uis* may legitimately and successfully be used as a strategy for seduction. The forceful tenor of Graves' couplet—'Flatter, beguile, assault, | And she must yield'—reminds us that, in this context, the lover's application of such *uis* may imply rape, although *Ars* 2. 197—*cede repugnanti: cedendo uictor abibis* ('Yield to she who resists: by yielding, you will leave as the victor')—suggests that submission may itself be a strategy for victory in the battle for sex.

Some of the other rules presented here, however, are derived from conflicting Ovidian precepts and positions, and—lacking the playful ambiguity of the *Ars*—misrepresent the teachings of the *praeceptor*. In particular, the idea that the lover should 'Snatch the morning rose' has an obvious parallel in Book 3 of the *Ars*:[13]

> nostra sine auxilio fugiunt bona; carpite florem,
>   qui, nisi carptus erit, turpiter ipse cadet. (*Ars* 3. 79–80)

(Our charms flee without our help; pluck the flower, Which, if it is not plucked, will only fall rotting itself.)

Yet, the *praeceptor* also advises his pupils that it is not young virgins but older women who make the best lovers, endorsing this personal preference with an elaborate conceit (*Ars* 2. 695–700). Graves's version of the precept that, having plucked his rose, the lover should 'Deflower it in haste' similarly reflects an Ovidian instruction. For, although the *praeceptor* repeatedly recommends a gentle pace both for courtship and for sex itself (*Ars* 2. 717–18)— *crede mihi, non est ueneris properanda uoluptas,* | *sed sensim tarda prolicienda mora* ('Believe me, the pleasure of love should not be hurried, but gradually drawn out by slow delay')—he also advises, at 2. 727–32, *cum mora non tuta est, totis incumbere remis* | *utile, et*

---

[13] It is significant that this advice—clearly directed at a male audience—appears in Book 3. Compare Graves's advice in stanzas 13–14 which similarly assumes a male reader/pupil.

admisso subdere calcar equo ('When delay is not safe, it is useful to press on with all oars, and to spur on the galloping horse').

The precept highlighted in the poem's fourth stanza focuses upon the contentious view that Ovid advises his pupils how to commit adultery: 'Ovid instructs you how | Neighbours' lands to plough'. Here, Graves ignores Ovid's own emphatic (and emphatically disingenuous) disclaimer that the *Ars* does not teach or condone adultery:[14]

> este procul, uittae tenues, insigne pudoris,
>   quaeque tegis medios, instita longa, pedes.
> nos uenerem tutam concessaque furta canemus,
>   inque meo nullum carmine crimen erit.   (*Ars* 1. 31–4)

(Keep away, slender headbands, signs of chastity, And the long skirt which covers the feet in its folds. I tell of safe sex and permissible cheating, And in my poem there will be no crime.)

Graves uncompromisingly resists the playful import of such disclaimers (also offered at *Ars* 2. 599–600, 3. 57–8, 3. 483–4, 3. 613–16 and *Rem.* 3. 85–6), appearing to recognize the provocative ambiguity of their presentation but electing to offer an unequivocal reading of the 'immoral' teachings of the *praeceptor* on this subject. For although, as R. K. Gibson notes (2003*a*: 27), Ovid occasionally 'sails especially close to the wind' and even appears explicitly to challenge the *lex Iulia de adulteriis coercendis* at *Ars* 3. 611–58, the *praeceptor* does not explicitly give instruction on how to commit adultery nor 'how | Neighbours' lands to plough'—although he appears to suggest that adultery may enhance sexual desire and pleasure):

> sed cur fallaris, cum sit noua grata uoluptas
>   et capiant animos plus aliena suis?
> fertilior seges est alienis semper in agris,
>   uicinumque pecus grandius uber habet.   (*Ars* 1. 347–50)

---

[14] On adultery and related disclaimers in the *Ars*, see Gibson (2003*a*). He notes that: 'the disclaimers not only contain ambiguities of phrasing, but also are often playfully expressed, appear in contexts which provoke scepticism about their seriousness, and frequently draw attention to, rather than resolve, issues of social and marital status' (26).

(But why should you be mistaken, since it is new pleasures that are pleasing And since what is another's captivates us more than our own? The grass is always greener in another's fields, And the neighbour's herd has bigger udders.)

Ovid's tacit endorsement of infidelity, however, is perhaps less seriously expressed than Graves's synthesis allows. The provocative *praeceptor* may ostensibly be seen to argue the point that 'Love smacks the sweeter | For a broken vow' in Book 3 of the *Ars*, when he advises women (*puellae*) to encourage and excite their lovers with the pretence that they are committing adultery (*Ars* 3. 589–610), but the emphasis in this passage, as elsewhere, is upon the presentation of a convincing *imitation* of adultery, rather than a convincing invitation to commit it. The *praeceptor*'s version of Graves's maxim would be that 'Love smacks the sweeter | For *the appearance of* a broken vow'; his advice to his pupils is to feign an adulterous affair, rather than actually to commit any crime. Indeed, though it is possible that Graves is here influenced by another of Ovid's precepts in the *Ars*— 1. 615–16 *saepe tamen uere coepit simulator amare,* | *saepe, quod incipiens finxerat esse, fuit* ('But often the pretender begins to love truly, and often becomes what he has first pretended to be')— Graves's urbane abbreviation of the 'grammar of Love's Art' seems to lack something of the playful ambiguity characteristic of his subject's own poetic treatment of these themes.

Yet in Graves's refusal to accept at face value Ovid's poetic declarations of modesty and respectability for both his life and work, he might also be considered a sympathetic Ovidian reader, recognizing the disingenuous character of the poet and *praeceptor*. Moreover, in representing Ovid as an *obsceni doctor adulterii* (*Tr.* 2. 212), Graves employs internal evidence from the Roman poet's own texts, rereading the *Ars* and *Remedia* through a critical lens that is coloured by the autobiographical poems of the *Tristia* and *Epistulae ex Ponto*.[15] It is perhaps not surprising then that, having offered this concentrated reading of Books 1 and 2, Graves temporarily withholds his reading of Book 3 to map a direct correlation between what he represents as Ovid's provocative teachings on adultery and their immediate reception, referencing both the *Remedia Amoris* and *Tristia* in one allusive

---

[15] See Hardie, Ch. 9 in this volume.

stanza: 'Follows his conclusion | Of which the gist is | The cold "*post coitum* | *Homo tristis*".'

The 'conclusion' that Graves posits as following the first two books of the *Ars* is clearly not identifiable as anything resembling Book 3,[16] but appears to be the *Remedia*, the 'gist' of which might indeed be represented as, 'after sex, man is sad'. The Latin motto[17]—'*post coitum* | *Homo tristis*'—is implicitly paired with the Ovidian precept cited in the preceding stanza—'Love smacks the sweeter | For a broken vow'—also notionally distinguished from Graves's own text with quotation marks, and indicates that Graves's unequivocal representation of Ovid as *doctor adulterii* in his poem may owe as much to his reading of Ovid's *Remedia* as to his *Ars*. Indeed, Graves's text here seems to identify Ovid's exile as a direct consequence of the publication of the *Ars*, effectively eliding distinctions between the two events. Thus, the 'conclusion' to which Graves refers could also be recognized as an allusion to the 'Augustan' response to these texts and to Ovid's banishment to the cold of Tomis, and the '*Homo tristis*' could be identified as Ovid—author of the *Tristia*—himself.[18] As Graves's allusive references to the *Remedia* and *Tristia* remind us, one interpretative issue and one reading dominate receptions of the *Ars*.

Allegations of immorality against the *Ars* and its author direct interpretations of the text still, and Ovid's own accounts of this early response to his work have themselves become an integral part of—no less than an influence upon—the text's reception. The

---

[16] See Sharrock (1994*a*: 18–20) on Ovid's own playful presentation of the chronology of the three books of the *Ars*.

[17] See *Remedia* 15–42 and 397–440, in which the *praeceptor* gives advice to his male pupils on how to fall out of love during sex. The source of the Latin dictum cited here is unknown. Its more familiar form runs: *omne animal post coitum triste*—'every animal is sad after sex', and in a fuller form, *omne animal post coitum triste praeter gallum mulieremque*—'every animal is sad after sex, except a cock and a woman'. Although Duncan Kennedy points out to me the potential play on gallus/Gallus as 'eunuch', rendering: every animal is sad after sex, except a eunuch and a woman. For a discussion of the contentious attribution of this phrase to Latin translations of Aristotle and Galen see Glenn (1982).

[18] Indeed, *post*-publication of the *Ars* and *Remedia*, writing in the *Tristia* Ovid complains bitterly about the cold (*frigore*—Tr. 5. 13. 3–6) and bleak (*tristis*—Tr. 5. 7. 43–4) land to which he has been exiled. See Rosati and Hardie, Chs. 8 and 9 in this volume.

Remedia—arguably the first work directly to respond in a mode of creative reception to the *Ars*[19]—ostensibly offers an early reading of Ovid's erotodidactic project, establishing its role as the author's sequel to the *Ars* even as it asserts its independence (*Remedia* 9–12). Of particular significance to Graves's reading of the *Remedia* (and *Ars*) moreover, is the defensive excursus of the *Ars* that this poem appears to offer (*Remedia* 361–96), in which Ovid tells us that: *nuper enim nostros quidam carpsere libellos, | quorum censura Musa proterua mea est* ('Recently certain people have picked faults in my books, and complain that my Muse is immoral'). The excursus implies that this defence is presented as a 'real' response to 'real' readers and critics who have interpreted the *Ars* as Graves appears to have done in 'Ovid in Defeat'. However, as Niklas Holzberg suggests in this volume, parallels between this excursus and similar arguments in Ovid's *Tristia* may encourage readers to (mis)read the digression in the *Remedia* as a vindication of the *Ars* rather than as a 'staged reader response'—an effort to direct the readership and reception of both the *Ars* and *Remedia*, repeating those already made in the *Ars* (1. 31 ff., 3. 57–8, 3. 613–14). Graves may be seen to fall into a similar trap. His reading and interpretation of the *Ars* is controlled by his reading and interpretation of the *Remedia*, which is in turn controlled by his reading of the *Tristia*. As the passive recipient of the advice, instruction, and poetry outlined in each of these texts, Graves the reader and pupil appears to be seduced, manipulated, and controlled by Ovid, and from this view of the conflict between author and reader, he loses this battle for interpretative authority and Ovid wins. Or does he?

Before moving on to consider Ovid's precepts for women in *Ars* 3 and to the focus of his attack upon Ovid, Graves underscores the significance of the theme of reading and reception in his poem with a further concentrated but illuminating commentary upon the historical reception of the *Ars* and *Remedia*: 'Thereat despairing, | Other Ovids hallow | Ploughshare in rust | And field left fallow'. Here he develops his allusion to the *Remedia* and *Tristia* as works responding

---

[19] Direct references and allusions to the *Ars Amatoria* occur throughout the poem. See 9–12, 43, 71–2, 361–5, 385–8, 487, 512. On the *Remedia* as a response to the *Ars*, see Casali, Ch. 11, and Holzberg, Ch. 3 in this volume.

to the *Ars*, with a reference to the rejection of Ovid's erotodidactic precepts in the *Ars* and the valorization of the *Remedia* in later literary receptions. By implication here, 'despair' induced by following the precepts of *Ars* leads to the rejection both of the *Ars* and of sex.

The emphasis in this stanza is placed upon 'Other Ovids', some of whom, Graves reminds us, responded to Ovid's *Remedia* in particular by reading it as a guide to sexual abstinence and chastity.[20] However, the provocative introduction to the next stanza, 'Or, since in Logic books | Proposed they find, | "Where two ride together, | One rides behind"', points to an alternative, eroticized mode of reception. Indeed, as a fitting contrast to medieval appropriations of the *Remedia* as a chastity manual for those in holy orders, Graves may here be seen to allude to an alternative tradition in the medieval reception of the *Ars*, such as that epitomized in Chaucer's representation of the Wife of Bath. Chaucer's Wife, partially inspired by the character of La Vieille (the old woman) in the *Roman de la rose*, draws heavily from the *Ars* and from 'Logic Books' in her attack against scriptural authority and religious commandments—and in her efforts to assert *maistrye* over her husband, anticipating the reversal of gender roles envisaged by Graves's following stanzas.[21]

Indeed, although the 'Logic book' maxim, 'Where two ride together, | One rides behind', may also suggest an oblique reference to the later addition of the third Book of the *Ars*, its image of inequality negatively prefigures the image of sexual partnership and equality evoked in the poem's final stanza. Moreover, Graves's arrangement of his verse indicates that this 'proposal' of equality is still to be associated with 'Other Ovids', and that the subsequent 'vision | Of love' revealed may be attributed not to Ovid—or, at least, not only to Ovid—but to these 'Other' Ovidian readers, pupils, and poets. This equivocation, emerging in the central stanza of Graves's piece, is

---

[20] See Kirkham (1969: 87). The serious study of the *Remedia* in the early Middle Ages as a guide to chastity for those in holy orders may seem incongruous, yet, in *Ovid Recalled*, Wilkinson (1955: 383) describes 'Brother Bertrand Ginesse settling down to transcribe it at 5.00 am on the Vigil of the Conception and finishing his task at eleven o'clock that night "to the praise and glory of the Virgin Mary" '.

[21] See Calabrese (1994) on Chaucer's sources and Russell (1998) on Chaucer's uses and abuses of logic in the *Wife of Bath's Tale*.

significant. It opens up the potential for the remainder of the poem to be read as a literary attack upon Ovid's 'grammar of Love's Art', or as an attack upon its literary misappropriation. It offers the possibility of a reading of Graves's poem which emphasizes Ovid in defeat *and* Ovid in triumph—still teaching his vision of love, albeit in exile and in bearskin breeches.

Just as he condenses the primary precepts of *Ars* 1 and 2, Graves similarly abbreviates the precepts for women outlined in *Ars* 3, but here he overtly signals that the principles described represent neither a faithful version of Ovid's *Ars* 3 nor his own reading of this book by omitting the quotation marks that enclosed his synthesis of Books 1 and 2. Moreover, he distances himself further from the reading offered—soon to be exposed as an 'error'—by describing this re-presentation of the teachings of Book 3 as something 'revealed' to or by others. This reconfiguration of the precepts of *Ars* 3 suggests a reading of this book as a *re-reading* of *Ars* 1 and 2 and seems to assume that Book 3 offers a straightforward reinterpretation of Ovid's advice to men, reversed and restructured for a female audience. Graves seems to assume that the teachings of *Ars* 3 simply reverse the oppositional gender roles and the gendered precepts delineated in the *Ars* to re-present 'Woman as the ploughshare | Man, her field'.[22]

Graves presents Ovid's precepts for men and women in parallel stanzas, as if giving equal measure to each, yet there is a significant element of inequality in this highly negative representation of female sexuality and particularly the kind of female sexual empowerment advocated and taught by Ovid in *Ars* 3. Thus, although Georgic imagery of fields, flowers, and ploughshares is reflected in both sets of precepts, Graves's lines attribute a violence and vengeful aggression to women that is absent from corresponding descriptions of male behaviour: men 'snatch' and 'deflower', but women also 'trample' in the mire; man may be sad (*tristis*) in or after love, but fair woman is 'unfair'. Indeed, in this attitude of gender inequality concealed by a veneer of parity and fairness of treatment, Graves's response to Ovid's precepts for women is characteristically 'Ovidian'.

[22] For the parallels in organization between Books 1–2 and 3, see Gibson (2003*a*: 1–6).

For Ovid too typically reassures his female reader/pupils of the balanced equality of his teachings at the very moment in which he betrays their interests to his male readers (*Ars* 3. 1–6, 43–8, 453–67). And even in his identification of his female pupil/readers as Amazons (*Ars* 3. 1–4)—female warriors renowned not simply for their battles against Greek men, but for their emphatic *defeats* at their hands—the *praeceptor* betrays both his sympathies and his female audience.

The tension in this paired representation of Ovid's *praecepta* for men and women might be seen to reflect a similar anxiety evident in the erotodidactic poetry surrounding the authority of the *praeceptor* as an adviser both to men and to women. In particular, the absence of the quotation marks that framed the 'citations' of Ovid's instructions for men from the precepts for women in the poem marks a key difference and tension in the treatment of these two sets of projected pupils and readers. The absence of such punctuation may emphasize that the precepts for women represent only an *interpretation* of Ovid's teachings and are not intended to be read as direct textual references to Book 3, focusing attention upon the struggle for authority attendant upon any reading or work of reception. Significantly, however, this appropriation of Ovid's teachings—whether attributed to Graves or to Other Ovids—may also focus attention upon Ovid's own appropriation in *Ars* 3 of the *praecepta* and position more usually associated with a female *lena*, in a parallel struggle for authority. Like Ovid, Graves does not seek to disguise his recuperation of another's discourse but, also like Ovid, intimates a degree of anxiety surrounding this contentious act of usurpation. In Ovid's case, this tension appears to concern his erotodidactic authority as a male *praeceptor amoris* to a female audience, and is marked by his modification of many of the female *lena*'s traditional teachings better to suit the interests of the male lovers of his pupils (who are, of course, also his pupils).[23] In Graves's poem too, this equivocation appears to be an expression of an analogous struggle for interpretative authority, in which *praeceptor*, poet, pupil, and reader compete over the construction and possession of meaning in a chain of readings and receptions in which the poet is and is not controller or victor.

[23] See ibid. 19–21 on the *praeceptor* as *lena* in *Ars* 3.

Simultaneously conceding and defending this point, Graves identifies the reading and reworking of Ovid's erotodidactic precepts for the purposes of female sexual empowerment as an emphatic 'error'; an error, moreover, which is 'no worse'—and presumably no better—than that made by Ovid in his antifeminist teachings. However, Graves's careful use of this term reminds his reader again that from its earliest point of reception Ovid's *Ars* has been identified as provocative and *proterua*, as the poetic contribution to his notorious *carmen et error*, and as one of the principal grounds for his banishment from Rome.[24] While Graves is careful to hint in this stanza that the 'error' of belligerent antifeminist/feminist erotodidacticism may be attributed to both Ovid and Other Ovids, his apostrophe appears directly to invoke the author of the *Ars Amatoria* and *Amores*, addressed here as, 'O...My amorous brother'. Indeed, this stanza marks a second turning point in this tripartite poem in which, having dealt with Ovid's teaching of the grammar of Love's Art and its reception, Graves transforms himself from didactic reader to didactic author—this metamorphosis signalling continuity no less than change, and suggesting that the poet was *already* also a reader, and as a reader *already* an author. Thus, Graves offers his own set of precepts to guide the successful coming together of man and woman, Greek and Amazon, now for the first time addressing his Reader and reader(s) in the second person. But who is the didactic 'you' to whom Graves addresses his new grammar of Love? Is it Ovid 'himself'— Graves's amorous brother—or other 'Ovids', among whom we might number 'ourselves'—if not excluded by the projected masculine perspective of this second-person address? Perhaps, to paraphrase Alison Sharrock (1994a: 11): 'Simply by our involvement in the text we are—in some senses—all Ovids...Any reader is Graves' (and thus Ovid's) metaphorical brother.' With a deft turning of the didactic 'wheel' Graves appears to take Ovid's place as *praeceptor* and poet, addressing not only Ovid or Other Ovids but *all* Ovids. Yet, in seeming to turn author into reader and reader into author, Graves signals that the battle-lines between these ostensibly opposed positions were always blurred, that authors and readers both fight on the site of the text for the construal of meaning.[25]

[24] See ibid. and Hollis (1977) for speculation on Ovid's *'carmen et error'*.
[25] For more theoretical discussions of these views, see Iser (1978), Jauss (1982), and Martindale (1993).

Indeed, Graves argues that difference is not synonymous with inequality and need not inevitably involve a battle for authority and control. Drawing a gendered analogy between the combative relationship between author and reader and Ovid's (and others') representation of the contentious relationship between women and men, he maintains that a simple reversal of positions in the hierarchy of sex and gender in order to empower women to act as men does nothing to advance relations in the 'battle of the sexes' or in the battle for sex. In both cases, he suggests, the resulting struggle can never produce concord or negotiation but only result in 'Conflict, domination, | Due defeat'.

Critics are wrong then to argue that here Graves rejects Ovid's teachings and, 'engaging him with his own weapons, defeats him not with hot invective but on a point of logic—convicting him "Of false analogy, | Offending both philosophy | And psychology" ', so that 'The Roman is made to look in comparison clumsy and uncivilized—"Grotesque in Pontic snow | And bearskin breeches" ' (Kirkham (1969: 87–8)). Rather, in emphasizing the essential similarities between men and women, the mutability of the positions they hold, and the complementary roles they play in relation to one another, Graves maps out a comparable relationship between authors and readers. He declares that 'you' may see in woman 'Thought, though not man's thought, | Deeds, but her own, | Art, by no comparisons | Shaken or thrown'. Here, an ingenious and distinctive allusion to Ovid's *Ars*, prominently positioned in this proto-postmodern view of gender and sexuality, serves to underline a correlation between sexual and textual engagements, as Graves highlights and privileges difference as the key to establishing equality and mutuality in the battle of the sexes *and* in the conflict for authority between author and reader.

In a final reworking of Ovid's erotodidactic precepts, Graves proposes that having learnt this lesson, equality may be achieved: 'Plough then salutes plough | And rose greets rose: | While Ovid in toothache goes | Stamping through old snows.' Yet, the juxtaposition of Ovid, snowbound and alone, against the image of perfectly—if tritely—matched couples 'coming together' in this final stanza offers an incongruous conclusion to this work of reception. Here in the final stanza of 'Ovid in Defeat' we are presented with a pointed contrast: couples resist the teachings of Ovid's Art to come together in accord, while Ovid trudges on alone in snow and in pain. Having ostensibly distanced both his own position and that of the *praeceptor Amoris* from the possibility or desirability of true sexual equality, and having argued for difference and otherness as the key to establishing concord in the battle of the sexes, Graves now seems to celebrate the triumph of equal sexual union in an image of treaty between Greeks and Amazons, plough and rose. Yet, in the superficially romantic vision Graves offers of lovers in concord and Ovid in toothache, his perfect couples seem dully pedestrian, lacking the emotive power inspired by his image of Ovid resolutely stamping through old snows. Indeed, Graves's sympathetic representation of Ovid in defeat seems to hint that the poet and *praeceptor* is perhaps the true victor in this exchange; it is Ovid who walks away at the end of the poem, but leaves the impression that he goes as a victor, particularly in the light of one of his own precepts—*cedendo uictor abibis*.

Graves's use of the present tense and return to the snow imagery of the opening stanza constitute a strong sense of continuity and permanence in these final lines, marking the impression of Ovid's survival as *praeceptor Amoris*, still teaching 'The grammar of Love's Art' even 'in defeat'. The image that Graves presents of Ovid here, moreover, is fundamentally a 'newer vision' of the same image that Ovid presents of himself in his exile poetry. He not only complains repeatedly of the snow and extreme cold (*non modico frigore*—*Tr.* 5. 13. 3–6, *Pont.* 2. 7. 31), of the illnesses and minor pains that torment him (*Tr.* 3. 3. 3–14, 3. 8. 23–34, 4. 6. 39–44, *Pont.* 1. 10. 3–14, etc.), but he also reflects upon his loneliness and, in particular, his suffering in the absence of his wife (*Tristia* 3. 4b. 60–1). Graves's image reminds us that the cold and barren landscape and the poet's ill health also serve as potent metaphors for Ovid's lonely and loveless life in exile, distinguishing this as the ultimate humiliation in Ovid's 'defeat'. What the image in this concluding stanza obscures, however, is that behind Graves's rosy picture of man and woman 'coming together' in the face of Ovid's defeat, lies a key Ovidian precept (*Ars* 2. 682–3): *quod iuuet, ex aequo femina uirque ferant. | odi concubitus, qui non utrumque resoluunt* ('Let woman and man feel pleasure equally. I hate unions in which both are not satisfied'). With understated irony, Graves recasts Ovid's teachings as his own at the same moment in which he ostensibly casts the *praeceptor* out into the cold.

Thus, in the end as in the beginning of Graves's poem, we see Ovid *still* teaching his Arts of Love, 'Stamping through old snows'—alone, alien, and even 'grotesque' in his barbarian breeches—but stamping still: a representation that suggests resolution and resistance, continuity and movement. Ovid, still teaching his 'grammar of Love's Art'—to Graves if not to plough and rose—even in defeat, goes on.

Appendix: Timeline

Genevieve Liveley

Selected dates in the reception of Ovid's *Ars Amatoria* and *Remedia Amoris*. (*Some dates are necessarily approximate or speculative.*)

410	Augustine, *The City of God*
760–821	Bishop Theodulf of Orléans active
930–88	'St Dunstan's Classbook'
1100?	Anon, *Liebesconcil*
1100?	William St Thierry, *De natura et dignitate amoris*
1150	Conrad of Hirsau, *Dialogus super auctores*
1157–1217	Alexander of Neckham active
1160	Chrétien de Troyes, *Ars*
1170	Fulco, Arnulf, and William of Orléans active
1171	Peter Cantor active
1185	Andreas Capellanus, *De Amore*
1160–80	Marie de France, *Guigemar*
1200	William of Orléans, *Bursarii*
1200	Anon, *Art d'amours*
1200?	Anon, *Roman D'Eneas*
1200?	*Carmina Burana*
1225?	Gottfried, *Minnegrot*
1230–80	Guillaume de Lorris and Jean de Meun, *Roman de la rose*
1265–1321	Dante Alighieri active
1280	Anon, *La Clef d'amors*
1300?	Anon, *Pamphilus de Amore*
1304–74	Petrarch active
1313–75	Giovanni Boccaccio active
1330	Juan Ruiz, *Libro de Buen Amor*
1390?	Anon, *Anti-Ovidianus*
1401–3	Giovanni Dominici writes on the school curriculum
1405	Christine de Pizan, *Le Livre de la Cité de Dames*
1486–9	Geoffrey Chaucer, *The House of Fame*, 'The Wife of Bath's Prologue and Tale'
1497	The works of Ovid, Propertius, and Dante are destroyed in the bonfire of Savonarola as erotic, impious, and corrupting

Appendix: Timeline

1513	Wynkin de Worde, *The Flores of Ovide De Arte Amandi with Theyr Englysshe afore Them*
1528	Erasmus, *Ciceronianus*
1600	F.L., *The first booke of Ouidius Naso, entitled The Remedie of Loue*
1600	Thomas Heywood, *Loues Schoole*
1602	Thomas Heywood, *How a Man May Chuse a Good Wife from a Bad*
1620	Sir Thomas Overbury, *The First and Second Part of the Remedy of Love*
1636	John Carpenter, *Ovid's Remedy of Love*
1648	Robert Herrick, *Hesperides*
1661	Francis Wolferston, *The Three Books of Publius Ovidius Naso, De Arte Amandi: Translated, with Historical, Poetical, and Topographical Annotations: By Francis Wolferston, of the Inner-Temple, Gent.*
1662	Various authors, *Ovid De Arte Amandi and the Remedy of Love Englished: As Also the Lovs of Hero and Leander, a Mock-Poem: Together with Choice poems, and Rare Pieces of Drollery* (running to six editions: two in 1662, 1672, 1677, 1682, 1684)
1662	Thomas Hoy, *Ars Amatoria*
1692	Dryden, Tate and Congreve, *Ovid's Art of Love: In Three Books: Translated by Mr. Dryden, Mr. Congreve, &c: Together with the Remedy of Love: To Which Are Added, The Court of Love, A Tale from Chaucer, and The History of Love: Adorned with Cuts* (reprinted regularly)
1709	Nahum Tate, *Ovid's Remedy of Love*
1745	Mary Wortley Montagu, *Ars, The Art of Love*
1747	Henry Fielding, *Ovid's Art of Love Paraphrased, and Adapted to the Present Time* (reissued in 1760 as *The Lovers Assistant, or New Art of Love*)
1880	Wilkie Collins, *Heart and Science*
1925	Robert Graves, 'Ovid in Defeat'
1928	US Customs bar imports of the *Ars Amatoria*
1929	*Ars Amatoria* banned from public libraries and bookshops in San Francisco
1931	E. Phillips Barker, *The Lover's Manual of Ovid* (with illustrations by A. R. Thomson)
	Charles, D. Young, *The Art of Love*
1935	B. P. Moore, *The Art of Love: Ovid's Ars Amatoria*

1949	H. T. Riley and W. S. Keating (with illustrations by R. Farrugio), *The Art of Love*
1953	R. Seth (with illustrations by G. Nicholls), *Ovid's Art of Love—A New Prose Translation*
1957	Rolfe Humphries, *Ovid: The Art of Love* (becomes the first best-seller for the University of Indiana Press)
1959	Frederico Castellon, *The Art of Love and Other Love Books of Ovid*
1968	Paul Turner, *The Technique of Love and Remedies for Love*
1977	Adrian Hollis, *Ovid Ars Amatoria 1*
1982	Peter Green, *Ovid: The Erotic Poems*
1983	Walerian Borowczyk, *Ars Amandi* or *Art of Love* (film)
1989	'Sexual Arts Issue' of *Forum* magazine featuring an illustrated translation of *Ars Amatoria 1 and 2* by Peter Jones
1990	A. D. Melville, *Cures for Love*
2000	Philip Terry, 'Void'; Rosalind Belben, 'Disjecta membra'; Paul West, 'Nightfall on the Romanian Coast', in Philip Terry (ed.), *Ovid Metamorphosed*

References

ALISON, J. (2001), *The Love-Artist* (New York).
ARIEMMA, E. A. (2001), 'Il Punto sull'*Ars Amatoria* di Ovidio (1991–2000)', *BStudLat* 31: 579–99.
ARMSTRONG, R. (2004), 'Retiring Apollo: Ovid on the Politics and Poetics of Self-Sufficiency', *CQ* 54: 528–50.
AVERY, W. T. (1974) 'Ovid *Ars Amatoria* 1.114: an Emendation', *CPh* 69: 279–80.
BALDWIN, J. (1992), 'L'*Ars amatoria* au XIIe siècle en France: Ovide, Abélard, André le Chapelain et Pierre de Chantre', in *Historie et société. Mélanges offerts à Georges Duby*, i. *Le couple, l'ami et le prochain* (Aix-en Provence), 19–29.
BALSDON, J. P. V. D. (1962), *Roman Women: Their History and Habits* (London).
BARCHIESI, A. (1982), 'Lettura del secondo libro delle Georgiche', in M. Gigante, *Lecturae Vergilianae* (Naples).
—— (1986), 'Problemi d'interpretazione in Ovidio: continuità delle storie, continuazione dei testi', *MD* 16: 77–107.
—— (1991), 'Discordant Muses' *PCPhS* 37: 1–21.
—— (1992), *P. Ovidi Nasonis Epistulae Heroidum 1–3* (Florence).
—— (1993), 'Insegnare ad Augusto: Orazio, *Epistole* 2, 1 e Ovidio, *Tristia* II', *MD* 31: 149–84 (= idem (2001), 'Teaching Augustus through Allusion', in *Speaking Volumes: Narrative and Intertext in Ovid and Other Latin Poets* (London), 79–103).
—— (1994), *Il poeta e il principe: Ovidio e il discorso augusteo* (Rome-Bari) (= idem (1997), *The Poet and the Prince: Ovid and Augustan Discourse* (Berkeley)).
—— (2001), *Speaking Volumes. Narrative and Intertext in Ovid and Other Latin Poets* (London).
—— (2002a), 'Narrative Technique and Narratology in the *Metamorphoses*', in Hardie (2002a: 180–99).
—— (2002b), 'Martial Arts. Mars Ultor in the Forum Augustum: A Verbal Monument with a Vengeance', in Herbert-Brown (2002: 1–22).
—— (2005), *Ovidio, Metamorfosi I* (Milan).
BARSBY, J. (1978), *Ovid*, Greece & Rome New Surveys in the Classics 12 (Oxford), 19–24.

BARTMAN, E. (1999), *Portraits of Livia: Imaging the Imperial Woman in Augustan Rome* (Cambridge).
BEARD, M. (2003), 'The Triumph of the Absurd: Roman Street Theatre', in C. Edwards and G. Woolf (eds.), *Rome the Cosmopolis* (Cambridge), 21–43.
BECK, J.-W. (2002), *Quid nobis cum epistula? Zum Anfang von Martials erstem Epigrammbuch* (Göttingen) (= AAWGö, phil.-hist. Kl., Jg. 2002, Nr. 3, 171–202).
BERSCHIN, W. (1980/1988), *Griechisch-Lateinisches Mittelalter. Von Hieronymus zu Nicolaus von Kues* (Berne and Munich)/*Greek Letters and the Latin Middle Ages from Jerome to Nicholas of Cusa* (Washington, DC).
BETTINI, M. (1997), 'Ghosts of Exile: Doubles and Nostalgia in Vergil's *parva Troia* (*Aeneid* 3. 294 ff.)', *CA* 16: 8–33.
BLACK, R. (2001), *Humanism and Education in Medieval and Renaissance Italy. Tradition and Innovation in Latin Schools from the Twelfth to the Fifteenth Century* (Cambridge).
BODDEN, M.-C. (1979), 'A Study of the Anglo-Saxon Classbook Bodley Auct. F.4.32', diss. Toronto.
BÖMER, F. (1958), *P. Ovidius Naso. Die Fasten*, ii. *Kommentar* (Heidelberg).
BOWERSOCK, G. W. (1984), 'Augustus and the East: The Problem of the Succession', in F. Millar and E. Segal (eds.), *Caesar Augustus: Seven Aspects* (Oxford), 169–88.
BRACCESI, L. (1976), 'Livio e la tematica d'Alessandro in età augustea', *CISA* 4: 179–99.
—— (1986), *L'ultimo Alessandro (dagli antichi ai moderni)* (Padua).
BRANDT, P. (1902), *P. Ovidii Nasonis de arte amatoria libri tres* (Leipzig).
BRETZIGHEIMER, G. (1981), 'Ovids Ars amatoria', in *Europäische Lehrdichtung, Festschrift für W. Naumann zum 70. Geburtstag* (Darmstadt), 1–32.
—— (2001), *Ovids Amores: Poetik in der Erotik* (Tübingen).
BRINK, C. O. (1962), 'Horace and Varro', in *Varron* (Geneva), 175–206.
—— (1982), *Horace on Poetry. Epistles Book II: The Letters to Augustus and Florus* (Cambridge).
BROWN, D. E. (1991), *Human Universals* (New York).
—— (1999), 'Human Universals', in R. A. Wilson and F. C. Keil (eds.), *The MIT Encyclopedia of the Cognitive Sciences* (Cambridge, Mass.).
BRUNELLE, C. (2000–1), 'Form vs. Function in Ovid's *Remedia Amoris*', *CJ* 96: 123–40.
—— (2002), 'Pleasure, Failure and Danger: Reading Circe in the *Remedia*', *Helios* 29: 55–68.
BRUNT, P. A. (1990), *Roman Imperial Themes* (Oxford).
BRYANT, H. B. (1986), *Robert Graves: An Annotated Bibliography* (New York).

BUCK, A. (1978), 'Die Bedeutung der "volgarizzamenti" für die Geistes- und Literaturgeschichte', in A. Buck and M. Pfister (eds.), *Studien zu den 'Volgarizzamenti' römischer Autoren in der italienischen Literatur des 13. und 14. Jahrhunderts* (Munich).

BURKERT, W. (1996), *Creation of the Sacred: Tracks of Biology in Early Religions* (Cambridge, Mass.).

BURMANN, P. (1727), *Publii Ovidii Nasonis Opera Omnia*, i. (Amsterdam)

BURNHAM, T., and PHELAN, J. (2001), *Mean Genes* (New York).

BUSS, D. M. (1994), *The Evolution of Desire: Strategies of Human Mating* (New York).

—— (2000), *The Dangerous Passion* (New York).

CALABRESE, M. A. (1994), *Chaucer's Ovidian Arts of Love* (Gainesville, Fla.).

CAMPBELL, J. B. (1993), 'War and Diplomacy: Rome and Parthia, 31 B.C.–A.D. 235', in J. Rich and G. Shipley (eds.), *War and Society in the Roman World* (London), 213–40.

CARDAUNS, B. (1976), *M. Terentius Varro, Antiquitates Rerum Divinarum*, i. *Die Fragmente* (Wiesbaden).

CARY, E. (1917), *Dio's Roman History*, vi. (London and New York)

CASALI, S. (1997), '*Quaerenti plura legendum*: On the Necessity of "Reading More" in Ovid's Exile Poetry', *Ramus* 26: 80–112.

CHAUMONT, M. (1976), 'L'Arménie entre Rome et l'Iran I: de l'avènement d'Auguste à l'avènement de Dioclétien', *ANRW* 2. 9. 1: 71–194.

CITRONI, M. (1975), *M. Valerius Martialis. Epigrammaton Liber Primus* (Florence).

—— (1984), 'Ovidio, Ars 1, 3–4 e Omero, Iliade 23, 315–18: l'analogia tra le artes e la fondazione del discorso didascalico', *Sileno* 10: 157–67.

—— (1995), *Poesia e lettori in Roma antica. Forme della comunicazione letteraria* (Rome-Bari).

CLAES, P. (2002), *Concatenatio Catulliana: A New Reading of the Carmina* (Amsterdam).

CLARKE, J. R. (1998), *Looking at Lovemaking: Constructions of Sexuality in Roman Art 100 B.C.–A.D. 250* (Berkeley).

CLAUSEN, W. V., GOODYEAR, F. R. D., KENNEY, E. J., RICHMOND, J. A. (eds.) (1966), *Appendix Vergiliana* (Oxford).

COLEMAN, K. M. (1993), 'Launching into History: Aquatic Displays in the Early Empire', *JRS* 73: 48–74.

CONTE, G. B. (1986), *The Rhetoric of Imitation: Genre and Poetic Memory in Virgil and Other Latin Poets* (Ithaca, NY).

—— (1989), 'Love without Elegy: The *Remedia Amoris* and the Logic of a Genre', *Poetics Today* 10: 441–69 (= idem (1994), *Genres and Readers* (Baltimore), 35–65).

CONTE, G. B. (1994), *Genres and Readers: Lucretius, Love Elegy, Pliny's Encyclopaedia* (Baltimore).
COPELAND, R. (1991), *Rhetoric, Hermeneutics and Translation in the Middle Ages: Academic Traditions and Vernacular Texts* (Cambridge).
CORBEILL, A. (2004), *Nature Embodied: Gesture in Ancient Rome* (Princeton and Oxford).
COULSON, F. (1991), *The 'Vulgate' Commentary on Ovid's Metamorphoses. The Creation Myth and the Story of Orpheus* (Toronto).
—— (2002), 'Addenda and Corrigenda to *Incipitarium Ovidianum*', *Journal of Medieval Latin* 12: 154–80.
—— and ROY, B. (2000), *Incipitarium Ovidianum. A Finding Guide for Texts Related to the Study of Ovid in the Middle Ages and Renaissance* (Turnhout).
CRESCI MARRONE, G. (1993), *Ecumene augustea: una politica per il consenso* (Rome).
CRISTANTE, L. (1990), 'Un verso fantasma di Ovidio (*Inc.* 6, p. 143 Morel; 145 Büchner)', *Prometheus* 16: 181–6.
DALZELL, A. (1996), *The Criticism of Didactic Poetry: Essays on Lucretius, Virgil and Ovid* (Toronto).
DAVIDSON, J. (1997), *Courtesans and Fishcakes* (New York).
DAVIS, P. (1995), '*Praeceptor Amoris*: Ovid's Ars Amatoria and the Augustan Idea of Rome', *Ramus* 24: 181–95.
DAVISSON, M. H. T. (1996), 'The Search for an "alter orbis" in Ovid's "Remedia Amoris" ', *Phoenix* 50: 240–61.
D'ELIA, S. (1959), *Ovidio* (Naples).
DE WORDE, W. (1513), *The flores of Ouide de arte amandi with theyre englysshe afore them: and two alphabete tablys. The fyrst begynneth with the englysshe hauyng the laten wordes folowynge, the other with the laten hauyging (the) englysshe wordes folowying* (London).
DELLA CORTE, F. (1973), 'Perfidus hospes', *Opuscula* 4 (Genoa), 229–44 (= *idem* in J. Bibauw (ed.) (1969), *Hommages à M. Rénard* (Brussels), i. 312–21).
DELZ, J. (1971), 'Kritische Bemerkungen zu Tibull, Ovid und Martial', *MH* 28: 49–59.
DIAMOND, J. (1997), *Why is Sex Fun?* (New York).
DIMMICK, J. (2002), 'Ovid in the Middle Ages: Authority and Poetry', in P. Hardie (ed.), *The Cambridge Companion to Ovid* (Cambridge), 264–87.
DISSANAYAKE, E. (1988), *What Is Art For?* (Seattle).
—— (1992), *Homo Aestheticus: Where Art Comes From and Why?* (New York).
—— (2000), *Art and Intimacy: How the Arts Began* (Seattle).

DOWNING, E. (1990), 'Anti-Pygmalion: The *praeceptor* in *Ars Amatoria*, Book 3', *Helios* 17: 237–49 (= *idem* in J. I. Porter (ed.) (1999), *Constructions of the Classical Body* (Michigan) 235–51).
DURLING, R. M. (1958), 'Ovid as *praeceptor amoris*', *CJ* 53: 157–67.
ECO, U. (1990), *I limiti dell'interpretazione* (Milan).
EDMUNDS, L. (2001), *Intertextuality and the Reading of Roman Poetry* (Baltimore and London).
EDWARDS, C. (1993), *The Politics of Immorality in Ancient Rome* (Cambridge).
EFFE, B. (1977), *Dichtung und Lehre. Untersuchungen zur Typologie des antiken Lehrgedichts* (Munich).
ELLIOTT, J. M. (2003), 'A New Mime Fragment (P. Col. inv. 546 A)', *ZPE* 145: 60–6.
ENGELBRECHT, W. W. K. H. (1991), '*Bursarii Ovidianorum*—ein Ovid-Kommentar des Wilhelm von Orléans (um 1200)', *Mittellateinisches Jahrbuch* 26: 357–8.
—— (2003), 'Filologie in de Dertiende Eeuw: De *Bvrsarii svper Ovidios* van Magister Willem van Orléans (fl. 1200 AD). Inleiding, editie en commentaar', diss. Utrecht.
FANTHAM, E. (1997), 'Images of the City: Propertius' New-Old Rome', in T. Habinek and A. Schiesaro (eds.), *The Roman Cultural Revolution* (Cambridge), 122–35.
FERGUSON, M. W. (2003), *Dido's Daughters: Literacy, Gender, and Empire in Early Modern England and France* (Chicago and London).
FISHER, H. (1992), *Anatomy of Love* (New York).
FLORY, M. B. (1993), 'Livia and the History of Public Honorific Statues for Women in Rome', *TAPA* 123: 287–308.
FOLEY, H. P. (2001), *Female Acts in Greek Tragedy* (Princeton).
FOUCAULT, M. (1976–84), *Histoire de la sexualité*, 3 vols (Paris).
FOWLER, D. (2000*a*), *Roman Constructions. Readings in Postmodern Latin* (Oxford).
—— (2000*b*), 'The Didactic Plot', in M. Depew and D. Obbink (eds.), *Matrices of Genre* (Cambridge Mass), 205–20.
FOWLER, D., and HINDS, S. (eds.) (1997), *Memoria, arte allusiva, intertestualità/Memory, Allusion, Intertextuality, Materiali e Discussioni* 39.
FRÄNKEL, H. (1945), *Ovid: A Poet between Two Worlds* (California).
FRIEDLÄNDER, L. (1886), *Valerii Martialis Epigrammaton Libri. Mit erklärenden Anmerkungen*, 2 vols. (Leipzig).
FULKERSON, L. (2002), 'Writing Yourself to Death: Strategies of (Mis)reading in *Heroides* 2', *MD* 48: 145–65.

FULKERSON, L. (2004), 'Omnia vincit amor: why the Remedia fail', CQ 54: 211–23.

FYLER, J. M. (1971), 'Omnia vincit amor: Incongruity and the Limitations of Structure in Ovid's Elegiac Poetry', CJ 66: 196–203.

GABBA, E. (1991), 'I Parti', in Schiavone (1991: 433–42).

GALASSO, L. (1995), P. Ovidii Nasonis Epistularum ex Ponto Liber ii (Florence).

GALINSKY, G. K. (1969), 'The Triumph Theme in the Augustan Elegy', WS 3: 75–107.

—— (1975), Ovid's Metamorphoses: An Introduction to the Basic Aspects (Oxford).

—— (1981/3), 'Some Aspects of Ovid's Golden Age', GB 10: 193–205.

—— (1996), Augustan Culture: An Interpretive Introduction (Princeton).

GÄRTNER, T. (2000), 'Zur Rekonstruktion eines mittellateinischen Kommentars zu den Heroidenbriefen Ovids', Archivum Latinitatis Medii Aevi 58: 151–210.

GAZICH, R. (1997), 'Moenia disponere: Properzio, Callimaco e la città augustea', Aevum Antiquum 10: 289–336.

GEISLER, H. J. (1969), P. Ovidius Naso. Remedia Amoris mit Kommentar zu Vers 1–396, diss. Berlin.

GIBSON, B. (1999), 'Ovid on Reading: Reading Ovid. Reception in Ovid Tristia 2', JRS 89: 19–37.

GIBSON, R. K. (1996), 'Vade mecum in Wantonness: The Ars Amatoria and Its Translators', JACT Review NS 19: 3–5.

—— (1997), 'Didactic Poetry as "Popular" Form: A Study of Imperatival Expressions in Latin Didactic Verse and Prose', in C. Atherton (ed.), Form and Content in Didactic Poetry (Bari), 67–98.

—— (1998), 'Meretrix or Matrona? Stereotypes in Ovid Ars Amatoria 3', PLLS 10: 295–312.

—— (2000), 'Book Endings in Greek Poetry and Ars Amatoria 2 and 3', Mnemosyne 53: 588–92.

—— (2003a), Ovid Ars Amatoria Book 3 (Cambridge).

—— (2003b), 'Pliny and the Art of (In)offensive Self-Praise', Arethusa 36: 235–54.

—— (forthcoming), Excess and Restraint: Propertius, Horace and Ovid's Ars Amatoria (Bulletin of the Institute of Classical Studies, Supplement) (London).

GLEASON, M. W. (1995), Making Men: Sophists and Self-Presentation in Ancient Rome (Princeton).

GLENN, J. (1982), ' "Omne animal post coitum triste" a Note and a Query', American Notes and Queries 22: 49–51.

GODMAN, P. (1985), Poetry of the Carolingian Renaissance (Norman, Okla.).

GOOLD, G. P. (1965), 'Amatoria Critica', *HSCPh* 69: 1–107.
GOOLD, T. (1963), *Platonic Love* (London).
GRAHAM, E. L. (2002), *Representations of the Posthuman. Monsters, Aliens and Others in Popular Culture* (Manchester).
GRASSMANN, V. (1966), *Die erotischen Epoden des Horaz: Literarischer Hintergrund und sprachliche Tradition* (Munich).
GRAVES, R. (1927), *Poems: 1914–26* (London).
GRAY, C. (ed.) (1995), *The Cyborg Handbook* (London).
GREEN, C. M. C. (1996), 'Terms of Venery: Ars Amatoria 1', *TAPA* 126: 221–63.
GREEN, P. (1982), *Ovid: The Erotic Poems* (London).
GREEN, S. J. (2004), 'Contextualisation and Textual Criticism: Making Sense of Character in Propertius IV.4 and Ovid, *Heroides* 1', *CW* 97: 363–72.
GREWING, F. (2003), Review of Beck (2002) in *Göttinger Forum für Altertumswissenschaft* 6: 1023–8.
GRILLET, B. (1975), *Les Femmes et les fards dans l' antiquité grec* (Lyons).
GRUEN, E. S. (1990), 'The Imperial Policy of Augustus', in Raaflaub and Toher, (1990: 395–416).
GUNDERSON, E. (2000), *Staging Masculinity: The Rhetoric of Performance in the Roman World* (Michigan).
GUTHMÜLLER, B. (1981), *Ovidio Metamorphoseos Vulgare: Formen und Funktionen der volkssprachlichen Wiedergabe klassischer Dichtung in der italienischen Renaissance* (Boppard).
HABINEK, T. (2002), 'Ovid and Empire' in Hardie (2002*a*: 46–61).
HALLETT, J. P. (1996–7), 'Edith Hamilton (1867–1963)', *CW* 90: 107–47.
—— and SKINNER, M. P. (eds.) (1997), *Roman Sexualities* (Princeton).
HALPERIN, D. M., WINKLER, J. J., and ZEITLIN, F. (1990), *Before Sexuality: The Construction of Erotic Experience in the Ancient Greek World* (Princeton).
HANNAH, R. (1998), 'Games for Mars and the Temples of Mars Ultor', *Klio* 80: 422–33.
HANSON, V., and HEATH, J. (1998), *Who Killed Homer: The Demise of Classical Education and the Recovery of Greek Wisdom* (New York).
—— —— and THORNTON, B. (2001), *Bonfire of the Humanities: Rescuing the Classics in an Impoverished Age* (Wilmington, Del.).
HARAWAY, D. J. (1997), *Modest_Witness@Second_Millennium.FemaleMan ©_Meets_OncoMouse* ™ (London and New York).
HARDIE, P. (1986), *Virgil's Aeneid: Cosmos and Imperium* (Oxford).
—— (ed.) (2002*a*), *The Cambridge Companion to Ovid* (Cambridge).
—— (2002*b*), *Ovid's Poetics of Illusion* (Cambridge).
—— (2004*a*), 'Political Education in Virgil's *Georgics*', *SIFC* 97: 83–111.

—— (2004b), 'Ovidian Middles', in S. Kyriakidis (ed.), *Middles in Latin Poetry* (Bari), 151–82.

HEATH, J. R. (1986), 'The Supine Hero of Catullus 32', *CJ* 82: 28–36.

HEATH, M. F. (1985), 'Hesiod's Didactic Poetry, *CQ* 35: 245–63.

HELDMANN, K. (1981a), 'Ovidius amoris artifex, Ovidius praeceptor Amoris (zu *Ars am.* 1, 1–24)', *MH* 38: 162–6.

—— (1981b), 'Schönheitspflege und Charakterstärke in Ovids Liebeslehre', *WJA* 7: 153–76.

—— (2001), *Dichtkunst oder Liebeskunst? Die mythologischen Erzählungen in Ovid Ars Amatoria* (Göttingen).

HENDERSON, A. A. R. (1979), *P. Ovidi Nasonis Remedia Amoris* (Edinburgh).

HENDERSON, JEFFREY (1991), *The Maculate Muse: Obscene Language in Attic Comedy*, 2nd edn. (Oxford).

HENDERSON, JOHN (1991), 'Wrapping up the Case: Reading Ovid, *Amores* 2. 7 (+8), I', *MD* 27: 37–88.

—— (2002), 'A Doo-Dah-Doo-Dah-Dey at the Races: Ovid *Amores* 3. 2 and the Personal Politics of the *Circus Maximus*', *CA* 21: 41–66.

HENKEL, N. (1988), *Deutsche Übersetzungen lateinischer Schultexte. Ihre Verbreitung und Funktion im Mittelalter und in der frühen Neuzeit. Mit einem Verzeichnis der Texte* (Munich).

HERBERT-BROWN, G. (1994), *Ovid and the Fasti: A Historical Survey* (Oxford).

—— (ed.) (2002), *Ovid's Fasti: Historical Readings at Its Bimillennium* (Oxford).

HERTER, H. (1960), 'Die Soziologie der antiken Prostitution im Lichte des heidnischen und christlichen Schrifttums', *JAC* 3: 70–111.

HEXTER, R. (1986), *Ovid and Medieval Schooling. Studies in Medieval School Commentaries on Ovid's Ars Amatoria, Epistulae ex Ponto, and Epistulae Heroidum* (Munich).

—— (1988), 'Medieval Articulations of Ovid's *Metamorphoses*: From Lactantian Segmentation to Arnulfian Allegory', *Mediaevalia* 13: 63–82.

—— (1989), 'The Allegari of Pierre Bersuire: Interpretation and the Reductorium morale', *Allegorica* 10: 49–82.

—— (1999a), 'Ovid's Body', in J. I. Porter (ed.), *Constructions of the Classical Body* (Michigan), 327–54.

—— (1999b), 'Imitating Troy: A Reading of *Aeneid* 3', in C. Perkell (ed.), *Reading Vergil's Aeneid. An Interpretive Guide* (Norman, Okla.), 64–79.

—— (2002a), 'Ovid in the Middle Ages: Exile, Mythographer, and Lover', in B. W. Boyd (ed.), *Brill's Companion to Ovid* (Leiden), 413–42.

—— (2002b), 'Narrative and an Absolutely Fabulous Commentary on Ovid's *Heroides*', in C. Lanham (ed.), *Latin Grammar and Rhetoric: Classical Theory and Medieval Practice* (London and New York), 212–38.

HEYWORTH, S. J. (1992), 'Ars moratoria (Ovid, A.A. 1.681–704)', *LCM* 17: 59–61.
—— (1995), 'Notes on Ovid's *Tristia*', *PCPS* 41: 138–52.
HINDS, S. (1998), *Allusion and Intertext. Dynamics of Appropriation in Roman Poetry* (Cambridge).
—— (1999), 'First among Women: Ovid, *Tristia* 1.6 and the Traditions of "Exemplary" Catalogue', in S. Morton Braund and R. Mayer (eds.), *Amor: Roma: Love and Latin Literature: Essays for E. J. Kenney* (Cambridge), 123–42.
—— (2000), 'Essential Epic: Genre and Gender from Macer to Statius', in M. Depew and D. Obbink (eds.), *Matrices of Genre* (Cambridge Mass.), 221–44.
—— (forthcoming), 'Martial's Ovid'.
HOFFMANN, R. (1955–6), 'Aufgliederung der Themen Martials', *Wissenschaftliche Zeitschrift der Universität Leipzig, Gesellschafts- und sprachwis. Reihe* 6: 433–74.
HOLLANDER, J. (1981), *The Figure of Echo: A Mode of Allusion in Milton and After* (Berkeley).
HOLLEMAN, A. W. J. (1971), 'Ovid and Politics', *Historia* 20: 458–66.
HOLLIS, A. S. (1973), 'The *Ars Amatoria* and *Remedia Amoris*', in J. W. Binns (ed.), *Ovid* (London), 84–115.
—— (1977), *Ovid Ars Amatoria I* (Oxford).
HOLZBERG, N. (1981), 'Ovids erotische Lehrgedichte und die römische Liebeselegie', *WS* 15: 185–204.
—— (1997), *Ovid: Dichter und Werk* (Munich) (= idem (2002c)).
—— (2000a), 'Lesbia, the Poet, and the Two Faces of Sappho: "Womanufacture" in Catullus', *PCPhS* 46: 28–44.
—— (2000b), 'Naso Magister', *CR* 50: 50–2.
—— (2002a), *Catull: Der Dichter und sein erotisches Werk* (Munich).
—— (2002b), *Martial und das antike Epigramm* (Darmstadt).
—— (2002c), *Ovid: The Poet and his Work* (Ithaca, NY).
How, W. W., and WELLS, J. (1912), *A Commentary on Herodotus* (Oxford).
HRDY, S. B. (1981/1999), *The Woman That Never Evolved* (Cambridge, Mass.).
HUNT, R. W. (1961), *Saint Dunstan's Classbook from Glastonbury* (Leiden).
HUNT, T. (1991), *Teaching and Learning Latin in Thirteenth-Century England*, 3 vols. (Cambridge).
HUNTER, R. (2003), *Theocritus. Encomium of Ptolemy Philadelphus* (Berkeley, Los Angeles, London).
HUYGENS, R. B. C. (ed.) (1970), *Accessus ad auctores, Bernard d'Utrecht, Conrad d'Hirsau 'Dialogus super Auctores'* (Leiden).

ISER, W. (1978), *The Act of Reading: A Theory of Aesthetic Response* (Baltimore).
JACOBSON, H. (1974), *Ovid's Heroides* (Princeton).
JAMES, S. L. (2003), *Learned Girls and Male Persuasion: Gender and Reading in Roman Love Elegy* (Berkeley).
JANKA, M. (1997), *Ovid: Ars Amatoria—Buch 2: Kommentar* (Heidelberg).
—— (2004), Review of Wildberger (1998) in *Gnomon* 76: 215–23.
JAUSS, H. R. (1982), *Towards an Aesthetic of Reception* (Brighton).
JOHNSON, P. J. (1997), 'Ovid's Livia in Exile', *CW* 90: 403–20.
JONES, D. (1997), *Enjoinder and Argument in Ovid's Remedia Amoris* (Stuttgart).
KAY, N. M. (1985), *Martial Book XI. A Commentary* (London).
KELLUM, B. A. (1990), 'The City Adorned: Programmatic Display at the Aedes Concordiae Augustae', in Raaflaub and Toher (1990: 276–307).
KENNEDY, D. F. (1984), 'The Epistolary Mode and the First of Ovid's *Heroides*', *CQ* 34: 413–22.
—— (1992), ' "Augustan" and "Anti-Augustan": Reflections on Terms of Reference', in Powell (1992: 59–82).
—— (1993), *The Arts of Love: Five Studies in the Discourse of Roman Love Elegy* (Cambridge).
—— (2000), 'Bluff Your Way in Didactic: Ovid's *Ars Amatoria* and *Remedia Amoris*', *Arethusa* 33: 159–76.
—— (2002a), *Rethinking Reality: Lucretius and the Textualization of Nature* (Ann Arbor, Michi.).
—— (2002b), 'Epistolarity: the *Heroides*' in Hardie (2002a: 217–232).
KENNEY, E. J. (1958), '*Nequitiae Poeta*', in N. I. Herescu (ed.), *Ovidiana: recherches sur Ovide* (Paris), 201–9.
—— (1959), 'Notes on Ovid: II', *CQ* NS 9: 240–60.
—— (1961), *P. Ovidi Nasonis Amores, Medicamina Faciei Femineae, Ars Amatoria, Remedia Amoris* (Oxford).
—— (1965), 'The Poetry of Ovid's Exile', *PCPS* 191: 37–49.
—— (1995), *P. Ovidi Nasonis Amores, Medicamina Faciei Femineae, Ars Amatoria, Remedia Amoris, iteratis curis edidit* (corrected edition) (Oxford).
KIRKHAM, M. (1969), *The Poetry of Robert Graves* (London).
KNECHT, A. (1972), *Gregor von Nazianz: Gegen die Putzsucht der Frauen* (Heidelberg).
KORZENIEWSKI, D. (1964), 'Ovids elegische Proömium', *Hermes* 92: 182–213.
KOSTER, S. (1981), 'Catull beim Wort genommen (Zu c. 8; 83; 93)', *WJA* 7: 125–34.

KRAUS, C. S. (2002), 'Introduction: Reading Commentaries/Commentaries as Reading', in R. K. Gibson and C. S. Kraus (eds.), *The Classical Commentary: Histories, Practices, Theory* (Leiden), 1–27.

KÜPPERS, E. (1981), 'Ovids Ars Amatoria und Remedia Amoris als Lehrdichtungen', *ANRW* 2. 31. 4: 2507–51.

KURKE, L. (2002–3), 'Gender, Politics and Subversion in the *Chreiai* of Machon', *PCPS* 48: 36–65.

LA PENNA, A. (1977), *L'integrazione difficile. Un profilo di Properzio* (Turin).

—— (1979), 'Gusto modernizzante e modello arcaico nell'etica dell'eros di Ovidio', in idem, *Fra teatro, poesia e politica romana* (Turin), 181–205.

LABATE, M. (1979), 'Poetica ovidiana dell'elegia: la retorica della citta', *MD* 3: 9–67.

—— (1984), *L'arte di farsi amare: Modelli culturali e progetto didascalico nell'elegia ovidiana* (Pisa).

—— (1991), 'Città morte, città future: un tema della poesia augustea', *Maia* NS 43: 167–84.

—— (1999), 'La Poétique de l'élégie et la carrière poétique d'Ovide', in J. Fabre-Serris and A. Deremetz (eds.), *Élégie et épopée dans la poésie ovidienne (Héroïdes et Amours)* (Lille), 127–43.

LATOUR, B. (2002), 'Body, Cyborgs and the Politics of Incarnation', in S. Sweeney and I. Hodder (eds.), *The Body* (Cambridge), 127–41.

LATTE, K. (1960), *Römische Religionsgeschichte* (Munich).

LAZZARINI, C. (1986), *Ovidio. Rimedi contro l'amore* (Venice).

LEACH, E. W. (1964), 'Georgic Imagery in the *Ars Amatoria*', *TAPA* 95: 142–54.

LENZ, F. W. (1969), *P. Ovidi Nasonis Ars Amatoria* cum appendice ad *Remedia* pertinente (Berlin).

LEVICK, B. (1976), *Tiberius the Politician* (London).

LIPPI BIGAZZI, V. (1987), *I volgarizzamenti trecenteschi dell'Ars amandi e dei Remedia amoris: edizione critica* (Florence).

LODGE, D. (2001), *Thinks ...* (London).

LORENZ, S. (2002), *Erotik und Panegyrik. Martials epigrammatische Kaiser* (Tübingen).

LUCKE, C. (1982), *P. Ovidius Naso. Remedia Amoris: Kommentar zu Vers 397–814* (Bonn).

LYNE, R. (2002), 'Ovid in English Translation', in Hardie (2002a: 249–63).

MCCLURE, L. (1999), *Spoken Like a Woman: Speech and Gender in Athenian Drama* (Princeton).

MCGINN, T. A. J. (1998), *Prostitution, Sexuality, and the Law in Ancient Rome* (New York and Oxford).

McHALE, B. (2001), 'Weak Narrativity: The Case of Avant-Garde Narrative Poetry', *Narrative* 9: 161–7.
McKEOWN, J. C. (1989), *Ovid: Amores*, ii. *A Commentary on Book One* (Leeds).
—— (1998), *Ovid: Amores*, iii. *A Commentary on Book Two* (Leeds).
MACKIE, N. (1992), 'Ovid and the Birth of Maiestas', in Powell (1992: 83–97).
MADER, G. (1988), 'Ovid the Iconoclast: Argumentation and Design in *Ars*, 3.101–128', *Latomus* 47: 365–75.
MARTIN, C. (1998), *Ovid in English* (New York).
MARTINDALE, C. A. (1993), *Redeeming the Text: Latin Poetry and the Hermeneutics of Reception* (Cambridge).
MATTHEWS. V. J. (1996), *Antimachus of Colophon* (Leiden).
MERKEL, R. (1841), P. *Ovidius Naso Fastorum libri sex* (Berlin) (reprinted (1971), Hildesheim and New York).
MEYER, H. D. (1961), *Die Aussenpolitik des Augustus und die augusteische Dichtung* (Köln-Graz).
MILLAR, F. (2000), 'The First Revolution: Imperator Caesar, 36–28 B.C.', in A. Giovannini (ed.), *La Révolution romaine après Ronald Syme: Bilans et Perspectives*, Entretiens Hardt 46 (Geneva).
MILLER, G. (2001), *The Mating Mind: How Sexual Choice Shaped the Evolution of Human Nature* (New York).
MILLER, J. F. (1993), 'Apostrophe, Aside and the Didactic Addressee: Poetic Strategies in *Ars Amatoria* III', in A. Schiesaro, P. Mitsis, and J. Clay (eds.), *Mega Nepios: il destinatario nell' epos didascalisco* (*MD* 31) (Pisa), 231–41.
MINNIS, A. J. (1984), *Medieval Theory of Authorship: Scholastic Literary Attitudes in the Later Middle Ages* (London).
—— (2001), *Magister amoris: The Roman de la Rose and Vernacular Hermeneutics* (Oxford and New York).
MONFRIN, J. (1972), 'La Connaissance de l'antiquité et le problème de l'humanisme en langue vulgaire dans la France du XVe siècle', in G. Verbeke and J. Ijsewijn (eds.), *The Late Middle Ages and the Dawn of Humanism Outside Italy* (Leuven and The Hague), 131–70.
MOST, G. (1989), 'The Stranger's Stratagem: Self-Disclosure and Self-Sufficiency in Greek Culture', *JHS* 109: 114–33.
MUNK OLSEN, B. (1982–9), *L'Étude des auteur classiques latins aux XIe et XIIe siècles*. i. *Catalogue des manuscrits classiques latins copiés du IXe aux XIIe siècle. Apicius-Juvénal* (1982); ii. *Catalogue des manuscrits classiques latins copiés du IXe au XIIe siècle. Livius-Vitruvius; florilèges-essais de plume* (1985); iii/1. *Les classiques dans les bibliothèques médiévales* (1987); iii/2. *Addenda et corrigenda, tables* (1989) (Paris).

MURGATROYD, P. (1982), *Ovid With Love. Selections from Ars Amatoria I and II* (Chicago).

MURGIA, C. (1986), 'The Date of Ovid's Ars Amatoria 3', *AJPh* 107: 74–94.

MYEROWITZ, M. (1981–2), 'The Women of Ovid's *Ars Amatoria*: Nature or Culture?', *Scripta Classica Israelica* 6: 30–56.

—— (1985), *Ovid's Games of Love* (Detroit).

—— (1992), 'The Domestication of Desire: Ovid's *Parva Tabella* and the Theater of Love', in A. Richlin (ed.), *Pornography and Representation in Greece and Rome* (Oxford), 131–57.

MYERS, S. (1999), 'The Metamorphosis of a Poet: Recent Work on Ovid', *JRS* 89: 190–204.

NELIS, D. (2001), *Vergil's Aeneid and the Argonautica of Apollonius Rhodius* (Leeds).

NISBET, R. G. M., and HUBBARD, M. (1970), *A Commentary on Horace, Odes, Book I* (Oxford).

—— and RUDD, N. (2004), *A Commentary on Horace, Odes, Book III* (Oxford).

NUGENT, S. G. (1990), '*Tristia* 2: Ovid and Augustus', in Raaflaub and Toher (1990: 239–57).

OGILVIE, R. M. (1965), *A Commentary on Livy, Books 1–5* (Oxford).

O'GORMAN, E. (1997), 'Love and the Family: Augustus and Ovidian Elegy', *Arethusa* 30: 103–23.

O'HARA, J. J. (1990), 'The Significance of Vergil's *Acidalia mater* and *Venus Erycina* in Catullus and Ovid', *HSCP* 93: 335–42.

OLIENSIS, E. (1997), 'Return to Sender: the Rhetoric of *nomina* in Ovid's *Tristia*', *Ramus* 26: 172–93.

PANI, M. (1972), *Roma e i re d'Oriente da Augusto a Tiberio (Cappadocia, Media, Armenia, Media Atropatene)* (Bari).

PARKER, H. (1992), 'Love's Body Anatomized: The Ancient Erotic Handbooks and the Rhetoric of Sexuality', in A. Richlin (ed.), *Pornography and Representation in Greece and Rome* (Oxford), 90–111.

PELLEGRIN, E. (1957), 'Les *Remedia amoris* d'Ovide, texte scolaire médiéval', *Bibliothèque de l'École des Chartes* 115: 172–9 (= idem (1989), *Bibliothèques retrouvées. Manuscrits, bibliothèques et bibliophiles du moyen âge et de la renaissance* (Paris), 409–15).

PETERSEN, H. (1961), 'Livy and Augustus', *TAPA* 92: 440–52.

PIANEZZOLA, E. (ed.) (1991), *Ovidio: L'arte di amare*, comm. by E. Pianezzola (Bk. 1); G. Baldo (Bk. 2); L. Cristante (Bk. 3) (Milan).

PIANEZZOLA, E. (1999) 'Conformismo e anticonformismo politico nell'*Ars amatoria* di Ovidio', in *Ovidio: modelli retorici e forma narrativa* (Bologna), 9–27 (= idem (1972), *QIFL* (Padova) 2: 37–58).

354 References

PINK FLOYD (1972), *Obscured by Clouds*, Harvest, EMI Records.
PINKER, S. (1994), *The Language Instinct* (New York).
—— (1997), *How The Mind Works* (New York).
—— (2002), *The Blank Slate: The Modern Denial of Human Nature* (New York).
PINOTTI, P. (1988), *Publio Ovidio Nasone: Remedia Amoris* (Bologna).
PITCHER, R. A. (1998), 'Martial's Debt to Ovid', in F. Grewing (ed.), *Toto notus in orbe. Perspektiven der Martial-Interpretation* (Stuttgart), 59–76.
PÖHLMANN, E. (1973), 'Charakteristika des römischen Lehrgedichts', *ANRW* 1. 3: 813–901.
POWELL, A. (ed.) (1992), *Roman Poetry and Propaganda in the Age of Augustus* (London).
PRETAGOSTINI, R. (1997), 'L'omosessualità di Agatone nelle "Tesmoforiazuse" di Aristofane e la figura del keletizein (v. 153)', in *MOYSA: Scritti in onore di Giuseppe Morelli* (Bologna), 117–23.
PRINZ, K. (1914), 'Untersuchungen zu Ovids *Remedia amoris* i.', *WS* 36: 36–83.
—— (1917), 'Untersuchungen zu Ovids *Remedia amoris* ii.', *WS* 39: 91–121, 259–90.
PURCELL, N. (1986), 'Livia and the Womanhood of Rome', *PCPS* 32: 78–105.
QUINN, P. (ed.) (2000), *Robert Graves: Some Speculations on Literature, History and Religion* (Manchester).
RAAFLAUB, K. A., and TOHER, M. (eds.) (1990), *Between Republic and Empire: Interpretations of Augustus and His Principate* (Berkeley, Los Angeles, London).
RAMAGE, E. S. (1973), *Urbanitas: Ancient Sophistication and Refinement* (Norman, Okla.).
RAMÍREZ DE VERGER, A. (2003), *P. Ovidius Naso: Carmina amatoria: Ars amatoria, Remedia amoris, Medicamina faciei femineae, Amores* (Stuttgart).
RAWSON, B. (ed.) (1986), *The Family in Ancient Rome: New Perspectives* (Ithaca, NY).
REYNOLDS, S. (1996), *Medieval Reading. Grammar, Rhetoric and the Classical Text* (Cambridge).
RICH, J. W. (1998), 'Augustus' Parthian Honours, the Temple of Mars Ultor and the Arch in the Forum Romanum', *PBSR* 56: 71–128.
—— (2002), Review of Spannagel (1999), *BMCR* 2002.03.21.
RIDLEY, M. (1993), *The Red Queen: Sex and the Evolution of Human Nature* (New York).
—— (2003), *Nature Via Nurture* (New York).

ROMER, F. E. (1978), 'A Numismatic Date for the Departure of C. Caesar?', *TAPA* 108: 187.

—— (1979), 'Gaius Caesar's Military Diplomacy in the East', *TAPA* 109: 199–214.

ROSATI, G. (1985), *Ovidio: I cosmetici delle donne* (Venice).

ROY, B. (ed.) (1974), *L'Art d'amours: traduction et commentaire de l'Ars amatoria d'Ovide* (Leiden).

—— (1985–6), 'Querelles de maîtres au XIIe siècle: Arnoul d'Orléans et son milieu', *Sandalion* 8–9: 315–41 (= *idem* (1992), *Une culture de l'équivoque* (Montréal and Paris), 141–63).

—— and SHOONER, H. (1996), 'Arnulfi Aurelianensis *Glosule de Remediis amoris*', *The Journal of Medieval Latin* 6: 135–96.

RUDD, N. (1976), 'Ovid and the Augustan Myth', in *Lines of Inquiry: Studies in Latin Poetry* (Cambridge), 1–31.

RUSSELL, J. S. (1998), *Chaucer and the Trivium: The Mindsong of the Canterbury Tales* (Gainesville: Fla.).

SCALIGER, J. J. (ed.) (1573), *P. Virgilii Maronis Appendix* (Lyons).

SCHEID, J. (1992), 'Myth, Cult and Reality in Ovid's *Fasti*', *PCPS* 38: 118–31.

SCHEIDEL, W. (1999), 'Emperors, Aristocrats, and the Grim Reaper', *CQ* 1999: 279–80.

SCHIAVONE, A. (ed.) (1991), *Storia di Roma*, ii pt. 2. (Turin)

SCHIESARO, A., MITSIS, P., and CLAY, J. S. (eds.) (1993), *Mega Nepios: Il destinatario nell'epos didascalico/The Addressee in Didactic Epic* (= *MD* 31) (Pisa).

SCHILLING, R. (1954), *La Religion romaine de Vénus* (Paris).

SCHMITZER, U. (2002), 'Die Macht über die Imagination: Literatur und Politik unter den Bedingungen des frühen Prinzipats', *RhM* 145: 281–304.

SCIVOLETTO, N. (1976), *Musa Iocosa: Studio sulla poesia giovanile di Ovidio* (Rome).

SEAGER, R. (1980), '*Neu sinas Medos equitare inultos*: Horace, the Parthians and Augustan Foreign Policy', *Athenaeum* 68: 103–18.

SHACKLETON BAILEY, D. R. (1993), *Martial. Epigrams. Edited and Translated*, 3 vols. (Cambridge, Mass.).

SHARROCK, A. R. (1994*a*), *Seduction and Repetition in Ovid's* Ars Amatoria *II* (Oxford).

—— (1994*b*), 'Ovid and the Politics of Reading', *MD* 33: 97–122.

—— (2002), 'Ovid and the Discourses of Love: The Amatory Works', in Hardie (2002*a*: 150–62).

SHARROCK, A. R. and MORALES, H. (eds.) (2000), *Intratextuality: Greek and Roman Textual Relations* (Oxford).

SHERWIN-WHITE, A. N. (1984), *Roman Foreign Policy in the East, 168 BC. to AD 1* (London).
SHOONER, H.-V. (1981), 'Les *Bursarii Ovidianorum* de Guillaume d'Orléans', *Mediaeval Studies* 43: 405–24.
SHULMAN, J. (1981), '*Te Quoque Falle Tamen*: Ovid's Anti-Lucretian Didactics', *CJ* 76: 242–53.
SIDARI, D. (1977–8), 'Il problema partico nella poesia ovidiana', *AIV* 136: 35–54.
—— (1979–80), 'Studi su Gaio e Lucio Cesare', *AIV* 138: 275–302.
SIEDSCHLAG, E. (1972), 'Ovidisches bei Martial', *RFIC* 100: 156–61.
SIEMS, K. (1974), 'Aischrologia. Das Sexuell-Häßliche im antiken Epigramm', diss. Göttingen.
SIMPSON C. J. (1992), ' "Unexpected" references to the *Horologium Augusti* at Ovid *Ars Amatoria* 1, 68 and 3, 388', *Athenaeum* 80: 478–84.
SOLODOW, J. B. (1977), 'Ovid's *Ars Amatoria*: The Lover as Cultural Ideal', *WS* 11: 106–27.
SOMERSET, F., and WATSON, N. (2003), *The Vulgar Tongue: Medieval and Postmedieval Vernacularity* (University Park, Pa.).
SOMMARIVA, G. (1980), 'La Parodia di Lucrezio nell' *Ars* e nei *Remedia* ovidiani', *A&R* 25: 123–48.
SPANNAGEL, M. (1999), *Exemplaria Principis: Untersuchungen zu Entstehung und Ausstattung des Augustusforums* (Heidelberg).
STAPLETON, M. L. (1996), *Harmful Eloquence: Ovid's Amores from Antiquity to Shakespeare* (Ann Arbor, Mich.).
—— (2000), *Thomas Heywood's Art of Love. The First Complete English Translation of Ovid's Ars Amatoria* (Ann Arbor, Mich.).
STEUDEL, M. (1992), *Die Literaturparodie in Ovids Ars Amatoria* (Hildesheim).
STEVENSON, T. R. (1992), 'The Ideal Benefactor and the Father Analogy in Greek and Roman Thought', *CQ* 42: 421–36.
STEWART, A. (1996), 'Reflections', in N. B. Kampen (ed.), *Sexuality in Ancient Art* (Cambridge), 136–54.
STROH, W. (1969), *Ovid im Urteil der Nachwelt. Eine Testimoniensammlung* (Darmstadt).
—— (1979a), 'Rhetorik und Erotik: Eine Studie zu Ovids liebesdidaktischen Gedichten', *WJA* 5: 117–32.
—— (1979b), 'Ovids Liebeskunst und die Ehegesetze des Augustus', *Gymnasium* 86: 323–52.
SULLIVAN, J. P. (1991), *Martial: The Unexpected Classic. A Literary and Historical Study* (Cambridge).

SWAN, P. M. (2004), *The Augustan Succession: A Historical Commentary on Cassius Dio's Roman History Books 55–56 (9 B.C.–A.D. 14)* (Oxford).
SYME, R. (1978), *History in Ovid* (Oxford).
SYMONS, D. (1992), 'On the Use and Misuse of Darwinism in the Study of Human Behavior', in J. Barkow, L. Cosmides, and J. Tooby (eds.), *The Adapted Mind: Evolutionary Psychology and the Study of Culture* (New York), 137–59.
TAYLOR, R. (1997), 'Torrent or Trickle? The Aqua Alseatina, the Naumachia Augusti, and the Transtiberim', *AJA* 101: 465–92.
TERRY, P. (ed.) (2000), *Ovid Metamorphosed* (London).
THOMAS, R. (1998), *Reading Virgil and his Texts* (Ann Arbor, Mich.).
THORNHILL, R., and PALMER, C. T. (2000), *A Natural History of Rape: Biological Bases of Sexual Coercion* (Cambridge, Mass.).
TOOBY, J., and COSMIDES, L. (1992), 'The Psychological Foundations of Culture', in J. Barkow, L. Cosmides, and J. Tooby (eds.), *The Adapted Mind: Evolutionary Psychology and the Study of Culture* (New York), 19–136.
TOOHEY, P. (1996), *Epic Lessons: An Introduction to Ancient Didactic Poetry* (London).
TRAILL, A. (2001), 'Menander's Thais and the Roman Elegists', *Phoenix* 55: 284–303.
TRÄNKLE, H. (1960), *Die Sprachkunst des Properz und die Tradition der lateinischen Dichtersprache* (Wiesbaden).
TREGGIARI, S. (1991), *Roman Marriage: Iusti Coniuges from the Time of Cicero to the Time of Ulpian* (Oxford).
TRIMBLE, J. (2000), 'Replicating the Body Politic: The Herculaneum Woman Statue Types in Early Imperial Italy', *JRA* 13: 41–68.
VOLK, K. (2002), *The Poetics of Latin Didactic: Lucretius, Vergil, Ovid, Manilius* (Oxford).
WAGNER, E. (1880), 'De M. Valerio Martiale poetarum Augusteae aetatis imitatore', diss. Königsberg.
WARDMAN, A. E. (1965), 'The Rape of the Sabines (Ovid, *Ars Amatoria* 1.89 ff.)', *CQ* 15: 101–3.
WATSON, P. A. (1982), 'Ovid and *cultus*, *Ars Amatoria* 3.113–28', *TAPA* 112: 237–44.
—— (1983), 'Mythological Exempla in Ovid's *Ars Amatoria*', *CP* 78: 117–26.
—— (1984), 'Love as Civiliser: Ovid, *Ars Amatoria* 2,467–92', *Latomus* 43: 389–95.
WATSON, P. A. (2002), '*Praecepta amoris*: Ovid's Didactic Elegy', in B. W. Boyd (ed.), *Brill's Companion to Ovid* (Leiden), 141–65.
WEBER, G. E. (1832), *Corpus Poetarum Latinorum* (Frankfurt).

WEBER, M. (1983), *Die mythologische Erzählungen in Ovids Liebeskunst: Verankerung, Struktur und Funktion* (Frankfurt).
WELLMANN-BRETZIGHEIMER: see Bretzigheimer.
WHITTA, J. (2002), 'Ille ego Naso: Modoin of Autun's Eclogues and the *Renouatio* of Ovid', *Latomus* 61: 703–31.
WILDBERGER, J. (1998), *Ovids Schule der 'elegischen' Liebe: Erotodidaxe und Psychagogie in der Ars Amatoria* (Frankfurt).
WILKINSON, L. P. (1955), *Ovid Recalled* (Cambridge).
WILLIAMS, G. D. (1992), 'Ovid's Canace: Dramatic Irony in *Heroides* 11', *CQ* 42: 201–9.
—— (2002), 'Ovid's Exile Poetry: *Tristia, Epistulae ex Ponto* and *Ibis*', in Hardie (2002a: 233–45).
WILLIAMS, G. W. (1978), *Change and Decline: Roman Literature in the Early Empire* (Berkeley, and Los Angeles).
WILLIAMS, R. D. (1962), *Virgil Aeneid III, edited with a Commentary* (Oxford).
WILLIAMS, T. (1969), *The Tony Williams Lifetime. Emergency!*, Polydor Records, London.
WILLS, J. (1996), *Repetition in Latin Poetry. Figures of Allusion* (Oxford).
WILSON, E. O. (1998), *Consilience: The Unity of Knowledge* (New York).
WISSEMANN, M. (1982), *Die Parther in der augusteischen Dichtung* (Frankfurt).
WISSOWA, G. (1912), *Religion und Kultus der Römer* (Munich).
WITHEHORN, J. E. G. (1979), 'Ovid, *A.A.* 1.101–132 and Soldier's Marriage', *LCM* 4: 157–8.
WOLTERS, R. (2002), 'Gaius und Lucius Caesar als designierte Konsuln und *principes iuventutis.* Die *lex Valeria Cornelia* und *RIC* I 205 ff.', *Chiron* 32: 297–323.
WOODBURY, L. (1967), 'Helen and the Palinode', *Phoenix* 21: 157–76.
WOGAN-BROWNE, J., WATSON, N., TAYLOR, A., EVANS, R. (eds.) (1999), *The Idea of the Vernacular: An Anthology of Middle English Literary Theory, 1280–1520* (University Park, Pa.).
WOYTEK, E. (2000), '*In medio et mihi Caesar erit*... Vergilimitationen im Zentrum von Ovids *Remedia amoris*', *WS* 113: 181–213.
WYKE, M. (1989), 'Reading Female Flesh: *Amores* 3.1', in A. Cameron (ed.), *History as Text: The Writing of Ancient History* (London), 113–43 (revised form in *eadem* (2002), *The Roman Mistress: Ancient and Modern Representations* (Oxford), 115–54).
—— (1994), 'Woman in the Mirror: The Rhetoric of Adornment in the Roman World', in L. J. Archer, S. Fischler, M. Wyke (eds.), *Women in Ancient Societies: An Illusion of the Night* (London), 134–51.

ZANKER, P. (1988), *The Power of Images in the Age of Augustus* (Ann Arbor, Mich.).

ZETZEL, J. E. G. (1970), 'New Light on Gaius Caesar's Eastern Campaign', *GRBS* 11: 259–66.

—— (1996), 'Poetic Baldness and Its Cure', *MD* 36: 73–100.

ZINGERLE, A. (1877), *Martial's Ovidstudien* (Innsbruck).

ZINN, E. (ed.) (1970), *Ovids Ars Amatoria und Remedia Amoris: Untersuchungen zum Aufbau* (Stuttgart).

Index Locorum

Aetna
  21–2: 58
Consolatio Liviae
  349–51: 105
Culex
  131–3: 67
Dirae
  2–3: 60
  3: 61 n. 14
  47–51: 61
  80–1: 61
Rhetorica ad Herennium
  3. 17. 30: 189

APOLLODORUS
Epitome
  5. 1: 83 n. 15
APOLLONIUS
Argonautica
  1. 469 ff.: 27 n. 9
  1. 730 ff.: 27 n. 9
APULEIUS
Metamorphoses
  3. 23. 6–7: 149
  3. 25. 3: 150
  9. 18. 2: 150 n. 15
ARISTOPHANES
Wasps
  500–2: 110
ARISTOTLE
Poetics
  1448[b]: 23
[AURELIUS VICTOR]
Epit. Caes.
  1. 24: 140

BION
  fr. 10: 168

CALLIMACHUS
Aetia
  fr. 67. 1–3: 64
  fr. 556 Pf.: 63
Hymn to Delos
  233–4: 182
On the Bath of Pallas
  22: 125
CATULLUS
  3. 17–8: 211
  8. 11–2: 175
  16. 12–3: 43
  55. 18–20: 175
  64. 72: 181 n. 40
  64. 130–5: 59, 60
  64. 126–9: 71
  64. 143–4: 59
  64. 290–1: 67 n. 26
  76. 11–6: 175
  85: 175
  93: 44
  95. 10: 109 n. 23
CICERO
Ad Atticum
  6. 1. 25: 116
Brutus
  191: 109 n. 23
De Domo Sua
  92–3: 156
  96: 156

Ad Familiares
  7. 14. 1: 185 n. 51
De Re Publica
  2: 209
  12: 209

DIO
  54. 23. 6: 106 n. 16, 116
  55. 10. 7–8: 232
  58. 2. 4: 117

ENNIUS
Annals
  35: 182 n. 42
  499: 241
  550: 241
  563: 241
EURIPIDES
Andromache
  207–8: 117
  213–27: 117

GELLIUS
  1. 5. 3: 130

HERODOTUS
  1. 203. 14: 266
  3. 101: 266
HESIOD
Theogony
  53–5: 180
  98–103: 179
HOMER
Iliad
  6. 429–30: 211
  23. 315–18: 193
Odyssey
  10. 234 ff.: 149
  19. 392: 149 n. 13

HORACE
Carmen Saeculare
  57–60: 114 n. 34
Odes
  1. 5. 5: 126 n. 12
  1. 16: 150
  3. 6: 123 n. 4
  3. 30. 109: 304
Satires
  2. 3. 288: 181 n. 41
HYGINUS
Fabulae
  59: 69

LIVY
  1. 9. 14–15: 211
  1. 9. 16: 212
LUCIAN
De Parasito
  4: 201 n. 20
  13: 194
LUCRETIUS
  1. 35: 111
  4. 75 ff.: 207 n. 32
  5. 962–5: 100, 209
  5. 1011–23: 100

MARTIAL
  1 *Epist.* 1. 5: 53 n. 27
  1 *Epist.* 12: 284
  1 *Epist.* 12–14: 283
  1 *Epist.* 15–16: 283
  1 *Epist.* 20–2: 284
  1. 10: 53
  1. 35: 52
  1. 61. 6: 281
  2. 41: 285, 288–91
  2. 41. 2: 279
  4. 49. 5: 282 n. 8

5. 2. 3–4: 291
5. 10. 10: 281
11. 104: 109, 292–6

OVID
Amores
  1. 1: 171 n. 12, 172
  1. 1. 1–2: 145, 167, 173
  1. 1. 1–6: 144
  1. 1. 15: 146
  1. 1. 23–4: 155 n. 35
  1. 1. 26: 168
  1. 2. 9–10: 159
  1. 2. 31: 180
  1. 3: 212–13
  1. 5. 11:133
  1. 5: 36 n. 20, 52 n. 24
  2. 1: 83
  2. 9. 50: 181 n. 41
  2. 18. 32: 56 n. 5
  2. 19. 3: 157
  3. 1: 50, 141
  3. 1. 7–14: 138
  3. 2: 207
  3. 2. 27–9: 112
  3. 9. 30: 154
  3. 12: 281
  3. 13: 196
  3. 15: 141
Ars Amatoria
  1. 1: 134
  1. 1–2: 54–5, 98, 167, 236, 261, 283 n. 15, 302
  1. 3–4: 163, 193, 302, 313
  1. 3–22: 269
  1. 5–8: 183 n. 45
  1. 8: 163
  1. 9–10: 145
  1. 11: 83
  1. 11–12: 209
  1. 17–18: 209, 304
  1. 21: 159
  1. 21 ff.: 145
  1. 21–2: 176
  1. 21–4: 300
  1. 29: 66
  1. 30: 300
  1. 31: 49 n. 18, 156, 283 n. 15
  1. 31–2: 293
  1. 31–4: 237, 300, 327
  1. 35: 194, 306
  1. 35–6: 313
  1. 35–8: 93
  1. 35–40: 2, 40, 81
  1. 41–88: 31
  1. 41–262: 207
  1. 46: 313
  1. 49: 85
  1. 51: 31
  1. 51–4: 30
  1. 51–60: 239
  1. 55: 41 n. 3
  1. 55–60: 285 n. 21
  1. 65–6: 88
  1. 67–74: 101
  1. 67–134: 208
  1. 67–262: 239
  1. 69: 103
  1. 71: 114
  1. 71–2: 115
  1. 72: 104, 106
  1. 89: 30
  1. 89–90: 285 n. 20
  1. 100: 285 n. 20
  1. 101–30: 30, 195
  1. 101–34: 200 n. 16, 267
  1. 103–4: 207 n. 32
  1. 103–8: 199

Ars Amatoria (cont.)
1. 105: 197
1. 109–10: 30
1. 111–13: 197
1. 114: 210 n. 36
1. 115–6: 210
1. 118: 111
1. 119: 197
1. 129–30: 211
1. 133–4: 195, 285 n. 20
1. 139–40: 30
1. 140: 31
1. 142: 31
1. 143: 31
1. 149–52: 31
1. 156: 31
1. 163–70: 32
1. 171–6: 9, 32, 227, 233
1. 171–228: 10, 222–3, 232
1. 172: 234
1. 177–228: 32, 195, 285 n. 18
1. 180: 227
1. 181: 228
1. 182: 227 n. 30
1. 195–202: 224–226
1. 227–8: 233
1. 228: 32
1. 229: 33
1. 245–52: 33, 247
1. 259: 33
1. 277–80: 85 n. 16
1. 263–6: 93
1. 263–8: 33
1. 263–770: 208
1. 266: 213
1. 269: 43 n. 7
1. 269–70: 33
1. 269–344: 247
1. 275–82: 264
1. 289–326: 26
1. 347–50: 327
1. 351: 33
1. 357–8: 81 n. 7
1. 365: 34
1. 365–74: 33
1. 389–98: 264
1. 399–436: 268
1. 437: 33
1. 459: 241
1. 459 ff.: 207
1. 459–62: 240, 270 n. 66
1. 463–8: 241
1. 469: 34
1. 483: 34
1. 487–97: 34
1. 497–504: 213
1. 505: 34
1. 505–24: 241, 264
1. 525: 34
1. 565–602: 291
1. 569: 34
1. 595–6: 269
1. 595–600: 264
1. 607 ff.: 208
1. 608–10: 264
1. 611: 55, 63
1. 611–2: 54, 64
1. 613: 65
1. 615–6: 54, 158, 328
1. 617–8: 42 n. 6
1. 619–78: 326
1. 620: 313
1. 630–6: 68
1. 644–5: 201
1. 659–62: 65
1. 663: 34
1. 663–74: 214
1. 663–704: 267
1. 681–706: 35
1. 705–12: 85
1. 711: 35
1. 715–22: 35

Index Locorum 365

1. 723–38: 264
1. 737–8: 256
1. 739: 35
1. 771–2: 93
1. 772: 177 n. 25
2. 7–8: 33
2. 13–20: 94
2. 17–20: 160, 185
2. 65: 282 n. 8
2. 86: 282 n. 8
2. 98: 160 n. 57
2. 99 ff.: 68
2. 112: 81 n. 7
2. 119: 81 n. 7, 85
2. 120: 85
2. 121–4: 264
2. 121–2: 61 n. 14, 241
2. 125–42: 177
2. 133–8: 189
2. 145: 81 n. 7
2. 145 ff.: 35
2. 148: 111
2. 153–8: 35
2. 161–4: 202
2. 167–74: 264
2. 175: 227 n. 30
2. 175–6: 247
2. 177–8: 35
2. 185–94: 112
2. 197: 326
2. 197–202: 35
2. 233–7: 255 n. 8
2. 237: 35
2. 242: 85
2. 245: 35
2. 251: 35
2. 260–72: 268
2. 263–6: 240
2. 263–8: 114 n. 35
2. 279–80: 271
2. 287 ff.: 35

2. 307–8: 86
2. 315: 36
2. 339 ff.: 86
2. 358–72: 84
2. 364: 111
2. 387 ff.: 86
2. 410: 36
2. 413: 36
2. 413–4: 91 n. 30
2. 415–20: 203
2. 425–6: 203
2. 427 ff.: 36
2. 427–8: 87
2. 435 ff.: 86
2. 445: 28 n. 12
2. 447–8: 28 n. 12
2. 453: 268
2. 467–92: 263
2. 473–80: 100
2. 477–80: 243
2. 481–8: 85 n. 16
2. 493–510: 179
2. 501: 81 n. 7, 288
2. 511–2: 65 n. 20, 288
2. 551–4: 267 n. 57
2. 519 ff.: 86
2. 529–32: 264
2. 530: 86
2. 537–8: 86
2. 547–60: 264
2. 600: 294 n. 40
2. 607–8: 114 n. 34
2. 613–24: 265
2. 619–20: 295
2. 645–6: 108
2. 646: 185
2. 647: 86, 87
2. 653: 185
2. 663–4: 240
2. 669: 87
2. 679–80: 87

Ars Amatoria (*cont.*)
2. 681–9: 267
2. 682–3: 86, 87, 336
2. 683: 294
2. 685–96: 87
2. 686: 295
2. 695–700: 326
2. 702: 42, 86
2. 703 ff.: 86
2. 703–4: 36
2. 703–8: 243
2. 703–10: 81 n. 6
2. 703–33: 80
2. 705–7: 294 n. 43–4
2. 707–11: 108
2. 709–16: 107
2. 717–18: 186, 313, 326
2. 725–8: 267
2. 727–32: 326
2. 733–44: 40
2. 741–4: 109 n. 27
2. 743–744: 90
2. 744: 82, 94, 99
2. 745–6: 2, 40, 41 n. 3, 94
3. 1: 29 n. 13, 94
3. 1–2: 41 n. 3, 62, 83, 170 n. 8, 301
3. 3: 30 n. 13, 80
3. 5: 30 n. 13, 80
3. 5–10: 83 n. 12
3. 7: 303
3. 7–10: 301
3. 7–28: 173 n. 16
3. 8: 111
3. 25: 81
3. 29–42: 62–4
3. 38: 56 n. 5
3. 41: 248
3. 47–8: 94
3. 49–50: 82
3. 57: 81
3. 57–8: 134, 156 n. 40
3. 59: 70 n. 32
3. 59–82: 89
3. 69–70: 70 n. 32
3. 79–80: 326
3. 87–98: 127
3. 88–98: 122
3. 101–5: 94 n. 38
3. 101–34: 126
3. 103–5: 134, 202
3. 107–10: 108
3. 107–12: 250
3. 107–14: 245
3. 107–28: 244
3. 113: 295
3. 113–20: 199
3. 113–28: 263
3. 118: 245
3. 121: 114 n. 35
3. 121–8: 62
3. 122: 294
3. 123–6: 245
3. 128: 114 n. 35
3. 129–234: 123
3. 135–48: 124, 125
3. 137–40: 127
3. 145: 127
3. 149–52: 125
3. 169–80: 128–9
3. 187–9: 128
3. 191: 128
3. 193–6: 236, 246
3. 199–204: 131
3. 200: 132
3. 205–8: 94 n. 38, 152
3. 209: 38, 39
3. 210: 132
3. 245–8: 247
3. 251–8: 134, 202, 248
3. 255: 288
3. 279–80: 289, 290

3. 279–92: 287
3. 283: 136
3. 287: 39
3. 291–2: 66, 291 n. 33
3. 293: 39
3. 303–6: 246
3. 311–52: 269
3. 311–432: 123
3. 329 ff.: 152
3. 329–38: 55
3. 339–46: 49, 55
3. 341–5: 94 n. 38
3. 353–4: 168 n. 4
3. 391–2: 101, 103
3. 419: 111
3. 445–50: 39
3. 459–60: 58
3. 467–8: 38
3. 477: 28 n. 12, 70 n. 32
3. 479–80: 136
3. 509–18: 287
3. 513: 289
3. 517–18: 290
3. 517–23: 108
3. 517–24: 249–50
3. 529–32: 268
3. 555–76: 87 n. 22, 137 n. 27
3. 589–610: 328
3. 608: 39
3. 611–58: 327
3. 615: 237
3. 663–6: 91 n. 32
3. 667–72: 323
3. 669: 77
3. 673–4: 176 n. 23
3. 677: 70
3. 687–746: 28
3. 747: 79, 89
3. 747–68: 38 n. 23
3. 747–808: 123
3. 765–68: 89

3. 769–78: 81 n. 6
3. 770: 82
3. 772–80: 110
3. 775: 112
3. 777–8: 107–9, 295
3. 794: 294
3. 794–96: 90
3. 800: 90
3. 805–6: 97 n. 3
3. 807–8: 295
3. 811: 134
3. 811–12: 90
3. 842: 99
Ex Ponto
1. 3: 189–90
1. 5. 53–4: 271
3. 1. 113–17: 115
3. 1. 141–2: 115
3. 1. 145: 115 n. 37
3. 3. 2–3: 182 n. 43
4. 13: 324
Fasti
2. 771–4: 189
3. 28: 182 n. 42
3. 471–6: 59
4. 1–8: 171 n. 12
4. 7: 172
4. 8: 172
4. 16: 172
4. 107–14: 270
5. 23–30: 114 n. 34
5. 545–98: 228
6. 637–44: 106 n. 16
6. 639–48: 116
Heroides
1. 1: 70
1. 33–6: 189
1. 101 ff.: 62
2. 1–2: 68
2. 3–8: 69
2. 13: 68

Heroides (cont.)
2. 23: 69
2. 25–6: 64
2. 26: 68
2. 27: 65
2. 31–2: 68
2. 43–4: 68
2. 49–52: 65
2. 54: 65
2. 65: 65
2. 74: 65
2. 78: 67, 68, 71
2. 116: 56 n. 5
2. 121–2: 70
2. 127–8: 71
2. 133–6: 56 n. 5
2. 139–42: 56 n. 5
5. 150: 165
7. 167: 177, 187 n. 55
10. 19–20: 71 n. 34
10. 19–24: 58, 60–1
10. 25–8: 71
11. 33: 67 n. 25
13. 105: 182 n. 42
15. 215–16: 183 n. 45
16. 160: 152 n. 27
17. 3–4: 301 n. 10
20. 23 ff.: 64 n. 18
20–1: 301 n. 10
21. 53: 67 n. 25
Medicamina Faciei Femineae
1–100: 94 n. 38
11–2: 245 n. 17
23–6: 250 n. 24
35–8: 203
Metamorphoses
1. 1–2: 38
1. 456: 172
1. 469: 170
3. 466: 162 n. 60
7. 646: 182 n. 42
10. 161–4: 67 n. 24
10. 693–5: 115 n. 35
11. 712–3: 189
12. 222–5: 210
12. 614: 169
13. 233: 222 n. 19
14. 275: 149 n. 13
14. 277 ff.: 148
14. 278: 149 n. 13
14. 299–301: 149
15. 868–72: 220 n. 15
15. 871–9: 304
15. 879: 220
Remedia Amoris
1–2: 143
1–4: 166, 322
1–40: 171 n. 12
2–3: 145
4: 172
7: 145
7–8: 143
8: 82
9: 145, 152
9–11: 144
9–12: 330
11–12: 154, 166
12: 167
15–16: 176 n. 24
16: 155
17–22: 151
20: 145
24: 145
28: 145
29–38: 173
37: 145
37–8: 151
39: 160, 167
40: 166
41: 155, 166
41–2: 186 n. 53
41–4: 147

43: 166
43–4: 151, 178
45–6: 152
47–8: 170
49–50: 83
50: 170
55: 56, 64
55–6: 187
56: 188
70: 160, 177
71–2: 82, 152
73–4: 179 n. 32
75–8: 146, 167 n. 2, 178
108: 161 n. 58
119: 160
124: 168 n. 4
128: 168 n. 4
135: 168 n. 4
138: 67 n. 25
140: 172
143: 171
143–4: 159, 176
148: 160
150: 168 n. 3
153–66: 170
166: 168
168: 160
170: 179
197–200: 161
211: 148
213–24: 161
218: 175
233: 155
237–48: 161
245: 175
249 ff.: 68
251: 161
259: 150
259–60: 161
261–88: 29
263–88: 177

267–8: 161
273–4: 177
285: 186
285–6: 184
291–2: 161
296: 168 n. 4
297: 148 n. 8
337–8: 295
339: 290
339 ff.: 50 n. 21
351–60: 221
357–8: 161 n. 58
357–96: 45–47
359–60: 51 n. 22, 53 n. 27
361 ff.: 155
361–88: 108
361–96: 330
361–496: 219
362: 49, 156
370: 221 n. 17
371: 48, 49
381–6: 108
385: 53 n. 27
385–8: 48, 49
386: 156
387: 53 n. 27
391: 155
397–8: 160
397–440: 47
399: 87 n. 23
399–404: 91
411–12: 91
417–19: 52
429–432: 52, 91
431–2: 162
437–8: 52
439: 168
441: 91
441–488: 171
443: 91
462: 152

370 Index Locorum

Remedia Amoris (*cont.*)
487: 82 n. 9
487–8: 153
497: 55
501–2: 158 n. 45
503: 85 n. 17, 160
511: 153
517–24: 153
526: 67 n. 25
529–32: 161
539: 86
541: 162
545–6: 190 n. 58
547 ff.: 186
549–78: 167, 178–86
552: 183
555–6: 182
555–7: 178
557: 152, 170, 176, 179, 181, 184
559: 179
571: 186
575: 185, 186
575–6: 181, 184, 186
576: 182
577–8: 160, 182–3
578: 188
579–84: 162
584: 187
591–608: 187
597: 67, 187
599–600: 187
601: 188
602: 56 n. 5
606: 67 n. 26
607–8: 83 n. 12
609 ff.: 169, 185, 187
610: 160
613–22: 161
629: 169
629–30: 163

642: 175
646: 161
648: 164, 166
649–50: 175
653–4: 162
657–8: 175
661–2: 162, 169
676: 83
679–82: 158 n. 48
704: 146
704–6: 178
715–30: 188
719–22: 170 n. 8
729: 162, 169
731: 163
751–2: 176
752: 148, 161, 167
757–8: 164 n. 68
766: 164
767: 146
768: 67 n. 25
779–81: 152
787–8: 162 n. 59
789–90: 146
803–10: 179 n. 32
804: 168 n. 4
811: 91
811–12: 160, 163
811–14: 174
813–14: 83 n. 12
814: 91
Tristia
1. 1. 21–2: 222 n. 18
1. 1. 112: 261
1. 6. 21–3: 105
2. 12: v
2. 61–2: 222
2. 207: 299
2. 211 ff.: 48
2. 212: 49, 122, 155, 328

2. 246: 92
2. 253–6: 118
2. 278: 122
2. 287–8: 118
2. 301–2: 118
2. 305–6: 301 n. 11
2. 307–12: 118
2. 345–6: 49
2. 521–8: 118, 266 n. 52
5. 6. 7–8: 183 n. 45
5. 7. 49: 324
5. 7. 55: 324
5. 10. 37: 324

Persius
1. 34: 56 n. 5, 69
Plautus
Amphitruo
687–8: 157
Epidicus
229 ff.: 129 n. 16
Propertius
1. 1. 9–17: 112
1. 1. 17: 185 n. 50
1. 1. 17–18: 184
1. 1. 27: 170 n. 8
1. 2. 1–12: 133
1. 2. 26: 295 n. 47
1. 5. 28: 67 n. 25
1. 7. 14: 67 n. 25
1. 9. 18: 67 n. 25
1. 12. 18–19: 171
1. 12. 20: 170
2. 2. 13–14: 133
2. 6. 15–22: 200
2. 12: 181 n. 41, 185
2. 12. 13–15: 185
2. 24. 43–4: 62
3. 4: 228
3. 17. 3–6: 179 n. 32
3. 24. 15–20: 174
3. 24. 19: 178 n. 31, 180
4. 1. 15–6: 207 n. 32

Quintilian
2. 3. 2: 157
2. 17. 41: 201
10. 1. 88: 122
11. 1. 22: 156

Seneca the Elder
Controversiae
2. 2. 12: 122
2. 5. 7: 126 n. 10
2. 7. 3: 126 n. 10
9. 5. 17: 122
Seneca the Younger
De Clementia
1. 11. 1–2: 140
Epistulae
50. 8: 147 n. 7
Troades
633: 143
Suetonius
Augustus
13–5: 140
21. 2–3: 140
27. 3–4: 140
28. 3: 245
43–5: 140
51: 140
69: 140
72–7: 141
89.2: 140
Iulius
73: 45

Tacitus
Annals
1. 7: 57
13. 25: 57

Index Locorum

THEOCRITUS
Idylls
17.1: 170 n. 9
TIBULLUS
1. 2. 87: 67 n. 25
1. 8. 64: 67 n. 25
2. 6. 19: 67 n. 25
[TIBULLUS]
3. 6. 33–6: 57 n. 9
3. 13. 9–10: 57 n. 9
4. 11–12: 182 n. 42

VARRO
De Lingua Latina
6. 20. 5: 205 n. 26
VIRGIL
Aeneid
1. 717–22: 181
2. 27–9: 189
3. 173–4: 182
3. 202: 184
3. 321–9: 113
4. 23: 181
4. 86–9: 180
4. 244: 181
4. 267: 181
4. 276–8: 181
4. 278: 185 n. 52
4. 323–4: 187 n. 55
4. 344: 177
4. 386: 177
4. 431: 177
4. 487–8: 181 n. 41

4. 549: 67 n. 25
5. 315–6: 210 n. 35
5. 842: 183
5. 846: 183
5. 854: 183
5. 871: 184
6. 714–5: 183
7. 322: 177
8. 42: 182
8. 112–3: 184
8. 630–4: 110–1
10. 58: 177
Eclogues
5. 10: 56
10. 6: 176
10. 10: 176
10. 29: 176
10. 60: 176
10. 61: 67 n. 25
10. 69: 159, 176
Georgics
1. 78: 182
1. 101: 134
2. 173–6: 237
3. 10: 219
3. 232–4: 168
3. 285: 168
3. 286: 93

XENOPHON
Oeconomicus
10. 7–8: 124

General Index

Alexandria 103–4
amor/ Amor 5–8, 143–7, 151, 158–63, 166, 172–3, 241–3, 259, 261–2, 269, 302, 304, 314
  (as) cultural (Roman) construct 84–5, 236–51, 258, 275
  Lethaeus Amor 178–86
  (art of) teaching, 193–4, 241–2, 261–2, 302
  (as) universal, 84–5, 243, 253–75
Andromache 11, 107–13, 116–20, 249–50, 295–6
anti-cosmetic tradition 123–7, 131–2
Ars Amatoria
  'anti-*exempla*' in 196–7, 208–9, 212–3, 247–8
  (verbal constellation of) *ars* in 197–8
  Ars 3 11–14, 37–9, 88–90, 121–42, 237–8, 244–51, 287–92, 328–33
  and Augustan / anti-Augustan readings 216–22
  (rhetoric of) civilization / *humanitas* in 198–203, 209, 212
  and comedy 98–100
  and (modern) courtship v–vi, 252–3
  dating of 2–3
  (reader's) dialogic experience of 302–3
  didactic affiliations of 4, 98–9, 173–4, 236–7, 262–3, 262 n. 41
  (concept of) family in 99–104
  fear of effect on reader of 298–300, 316–17
  (status of) female addressee in 11–14, 96–120, 133–5, 156–7, 237–8, 251, 293–4, 299–301, 327–9
  flattery in 7
  imperial family in 96–107, 222–34, 240 n. 9
  implied narrative in 23–39
  irrelevance (otherness) of 271–2, 314–16
  literary influences on 3–5
  love story in 23–39
  medieval commentaries on 307–15
  (rhetoric of) moderation in 96–7, 119–20, 121–42, 295
  (rhetoric of) modernization in 96–7, 198–201, 294–5
  (absence of) names in 98–9
  Naumachia (and Mars Ultor) in 9, 227–9, 231–34, 239–40
  Parthian expedition of Gaius Caesar in 32, 222–34
  pornographic reputation of 26 n. 7, 112–13, 116, 320–1, 320 n. 2
  (figure of) *praeceptor* in 238–9, 261, 333
  readers/ Readers of 18–19, 72–4, 217–8, 236–8, 285, 300–1, 321–3, 334–5

Ars Amatoria (cont.)
  reception of 19–20, 219–22, 235–6, 271–2, 279–97, 298–317, 318–37
  scholarship on 1–20
  serious messages in 5–11
  staged responses in 40–5
  structure of 2–3, 40–2, 71–95
  (used for) teaching Latin 305–17
  three book unit of 40–2, 77–95
  translations of 310–13, 320 n. 2
Ariadne/ Theseus 58–61
Atalanta (Atalante) 111–12
Augustus 8–11, 13–14, 48–9, 92 n. 34, 96–7, 101–4, 117–20, 136–42, 206–7, 219–22, 222–3, 230 *et passim*
  domus Augusta 101–4
  sexual legislation of 10–11, 13–14, 96–7, 119–20, 137–9, 237–8, 327–8

Catullus 43–5, 51, 53, 59–60, 175
componere 56–7
curse poems 60–1, 67–8

decorum 7, 10–11, 125, 127, 128–9, 134, 151 n. 23, 289–290
Demophoon, *see* Phyllis/ Demophoon
Dido 29, 177–8, 180–1
'digressions', mythological 16–18, 23–39, 194–215, 247–8
domus Augusta, see Augustus
St. Dunstan 304–5

(*Epistulae*) *Ex Ponto* 115, 189–90, 271, 279–80, 324–5, 336–7
erotodidaxis 54–74
excess, Ovid as poet of 121–3

Fasti 59, 172–3, 228–9, 270

Graves, Robert 92 n. 34, 318–37

Heroides 54–74

idem 169–70

Julius Caesar 44–5

Lethaeus Amor, see amor/ Amor
Livia 11, 104–7, 114–20, 138 n. 33, 226 n. 26
love, see *amor*
Lucretius 100–1, 236–7, 263
lupa 110–2

Martial 52–3, 109, 110, 279–97
Mens (Bona) 180
munditia 126, 130

narrative, *see* Ars Amatoria, implied narrative in

Phyllis/ Demophoon 62–72, 83 n. 12, 186–8
populus 98, 236
Propertius 112, 132–6, 170, 174–5, 180, 184–5, 200–1

recantare 150
Remedia Amoris
  and *Ars* 3, 79, 82–3, 90–1
  and didactic tradition 148
  as magical text 148–51
  readers of 171–3, 221–2
  reception of 299–300, 315, 328–31
  and reception of *Ars* 163–4, 219–20, 330
  as *renuntiatio amoris* 163–5, 173–6, 299 n. 8, 315–6, 331

General Index

scholarship on 14–16
staged responses in 45–52
(rhetoric of) unlearning
 in 147–8, 154–5, 157, 163–5,
 166–90
retexere 167
role-playing, love as 6–7, 54–6; see
 also *amor/ Amor*
Romulus 201–2, 206, 209–12

Sabine women 31–2, 62, 195–213, 267
 and *Consualia* 205–6, 212
 and *Seven Brides for Seven
 Brothers* 204–5

Thais 48–9, 108, 109
Theseus, *see* Ariadne/ Theseus
Tiberius 103, 106 n. 15, 115,
 225–6, 230
Tristia 48–9, 105, 117–19, 155,
 222, 279–80, 324–5,
 336–7

Vedius Pollio 106 n. 16, 116
Venus Erycina 180
Virgil
 Aeneid 110–11, 113, 177–8, 180–4
 Eclogues 176
 Georgics 168, 237